Images of America: The Painter's Eye, 1833-1925

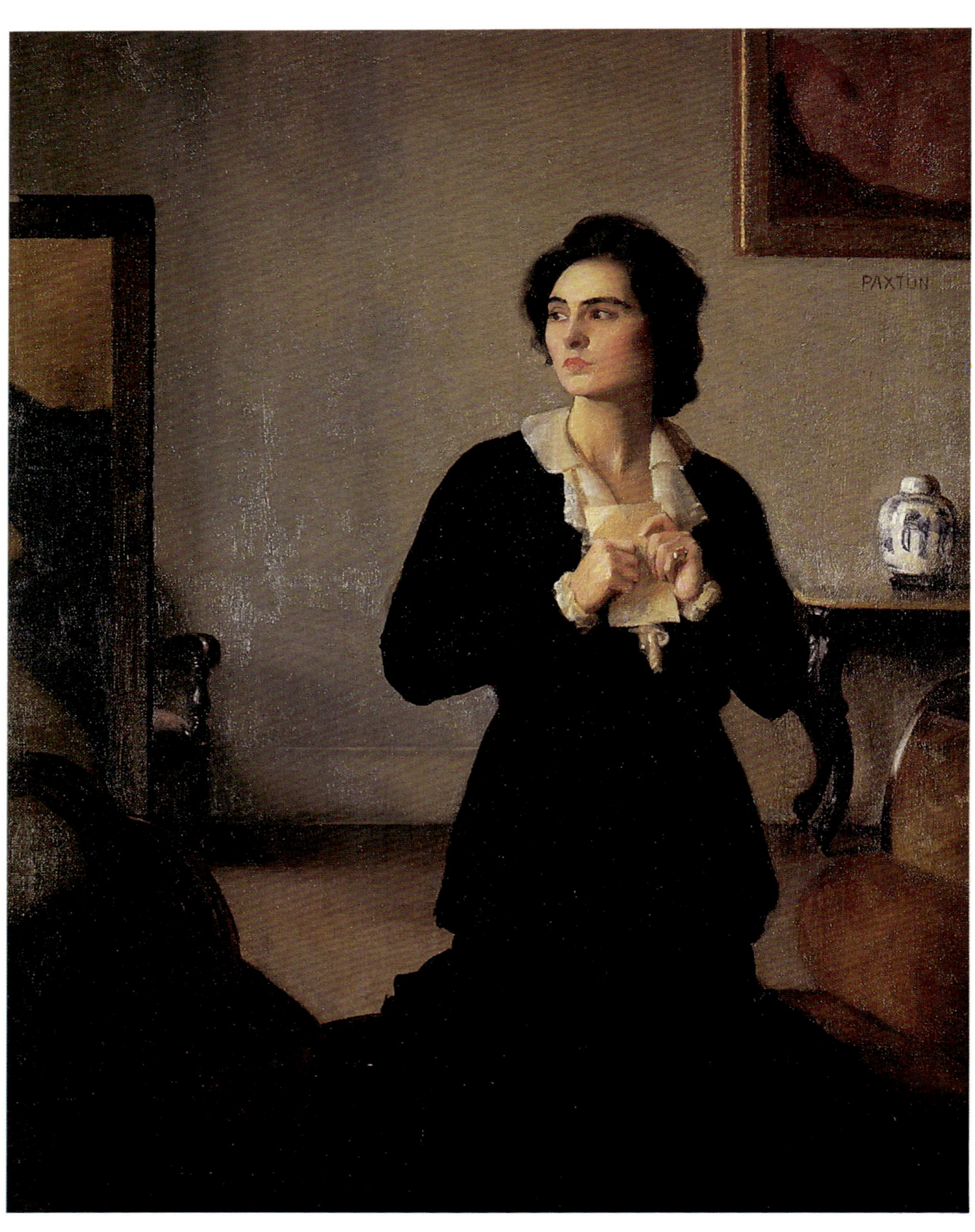
PAXTON

Images of America: The Painter's Eye, 1833-1925

by
Frederick Baekeland

Birmingham Museum of Art
Birmingham, Alabama

in association with the
University of Washington Press
Seattle and London

Images of America: The Painter's Eye, 1833-1925

Spencer Museum of Art
University of Kansas
Lawrence, Kansas
August 25 - October 13, 1991

Birmingham Museum of Art
Birmingham, Alabama
November 24, 1991 - January 5, 1992

The Art Gallery
University of Maryland at College Park
College Park, Maryland
January 29 - March 15, 1992

Herbert F. Johnson Museum of Art
Cornell University
Ithaca, New York
April 14 - May 24, 1992

This exhibition has been organized by the Birmingham Museum of Art. It has been funded in part by the Corporate Members of the BMA and the Alabama State Council on the Arts.

Library of Congress Cataloging-in-Publication Data

Baekeland, Frederick.
Images of America : the painter's eye, 1833-1925 / by Frederick Baekeland.
p. cm.
Exhibition held at the Spencer Museum of Art, University of Kansas, Lawrence, Kan., August 25-October 13, 1991 . . . [et al.].
Includes bibliographical references and index.
ISBN 0-931394-31-7 : $20.00
1. Painting, American--Exhibitions. 2. Painting, Modern--19th century--United States--Exhibitions. 3. Painting, Modern--20th century--United States--Exhibitions. 4. United States in art--Exhibitions. I. Birmingham Museum of Art (Birmingham, Ala.) II. Helen Foresman Spencer Museum of Art. III. Title.
ND1460.U54B34 1991
759.13'09'03407473--dc20 91-14798
CIP

ISBN - 0-931394-31-7

Printed in the U.S.A.
Distributed by the University of Washington Press, Seattle and London

Edited by Jeffrey H. Pettus

Designed by Joan Kennedy, this catalogue was typeset in Garth Graphic Condensed and Garth Graphic. It was printed by EBSCO Media, Inc., on Meade Signature dull text and Meade Mark V gloss cover. Separations by Color Unlimited.

(Cover) Paul Lacroix, *Vase of Flowers and a Shell*, 1867. Oil on artists' board, 14" x 10" (Cat. 50).

(Frontispiece) William McGregor Paxton, *The Telegram*, 1918. Oil on board, 18" x 15" (Cat. 43).

To Ferdinand H. Davis who showed me the door
and to Joan who held it open.

Table of Contents

Foreword

The Birmingham Museum of Art has collected and displayed fine American paintings since its inception in 1951. Motivated by the desire to stimulate an interest in American culture, the founders of the museum purposefully collected the landscapes, portraits, genre, and still life paintings of our leading artists. While the museum's collection was acquired primarily by gift, in recent years a substantial number of purchases have been made. The result is a very broad spectrum of taste that reflects the interests of various museum directors, curators, and over a hundred different donors. Until recent years, the late Dr. Harold Simon and Mrs. Regina Simon were the only major collectors of American art in Birmingham. Through their generosity, the museum acquired a significant collection of American genre paintings, bronzes by Frederic Remington, and other nineteenth- and twentieth-century sculptures. Over the last decade the Friends of American Art, a museum support group now consisting of thirty-two members, has further encouraged collecting and an appreciation of nineteenth- and early twentieth-century art. Another milestone for American art in Birmingham was the 1987 exhibition of selections from the superb collection of Jack Warner of the Gulf States Paper Corporation of Tuscaloosa, Alabama, followed by our 1990 exhibition of Thomas Moran's western landscapes.

It is with pleasure that the museum continues this tradition by organizing the national tour of the collection of Dr. Frederick and Joan Baekeland. These outstanding paintings, acquired over two decades of study and dedication, represent a very personal statement of the collecting philosophy of two astute connoisseurs. The American paintings of the Baekeland collection not only possess great aesthetic interest, but together illustrate the most important intellectual developments in the history of American art from 1833 to 1925. The devotion of both collectors to seeking out and finding examples of the highest quality is evident in each and every canvas, making it a pleasure for me to have observed the steady growth and refinement of their collection over the last decade. Now, I am delighted to be able to share this pleasure with the public. While canvases by prominent artists such as Albert Bierstadt and Worthington Whittredge have been loaned to major retrospectives in recent years, most of the Baekelands' paintings have never been exhibited and thus should offer welcome revelations to admirers of American art.

Over a twenty-one year period the Baekelands have traveled throughout the country tirelessly seeking examples of fine American art from a wide variety of sources. And without advisors, they have developed their own set of ground rules for collecting, including a mutual appreciation for whatever landscape, marine, still life, or genre painting may be acquired. Both must be satisfied that the work is of great distinction and on a par with earlier acquisitions. On many occasions we have discussed individual artists and how the collection was evolving, discussions that inevitably led to lengthy discourses on the individual merits and distinctions of many artists — both the familiar and the less widely known. One of the particular strengths of the collection is a reliance not on the known quantities, the acclaimed mainstays of American art, but on the actual appearance and substance of each painting, regardless of whether or not the painter may have already achieved widespread acclaim.

Dr. Baekeland's commitment to research, gained through a background in chemistry, medicine, psychology, and art history, is equally impressive and I am indebted to him not only for his illuminating essays on collecting and aspects of the social history of American painting but also for his thorough documentation of the artists and their works in the exhibition. In this instance, taste and scholarship have been combined and the result is a most impressive collection of American paintings.

Over the years I have developed distinct favorites, the Forster, Casilear, and Paxton, just to name a few, and have enjoyed becoming reacquainted with each example on subsequent visits to the Baekelands' home. They have a contagious passion for collecting, and enjoy looking and learning, visiting museums constantly. Individual exhibitions are for them pilgrimage sites on their journey to acquire more knowledge about American art and how it developed over the course of more than a century. I am grateful to them for their friendship and for their willingness to share their delight in the painter's eye.

Douglas K.S. Hyland
Director

Acknowledgments

This exhibition and its catalogue owe their existence to a suggestion of Douglas Hyland, who for years has followed the evolution of our collection with an informed and appreciative eye. At first the doleful prospect of a year spent with bare walls and picture hooks made us hesitate, but the learning opportunity writing this catalogue offered proved irresistible.

An enterprise as complicated as this exhibition depends on a network of helpers. They are too many to mention every one by name, but I thank them all.

By kindly reading a first draft of the manuscript Bruce Chambers saved me from committing a number of egregious errors in art history. John Wetenhall, who read first drafts of the essays, also made some excellent suggestions. My editor, Jeffrey Pettus, by dint of several impressively detailed perusals of the text rid it of many inconsistencies and stylistic errors, all the while patiently helping me to clarify the exposition of my ideas.

The following helped me solve special problems presented by certain artists: Linda S. Ferber (William Trost Richards), Gillian Gill (Russell Smith), Martin F. Krause, Jr. (William McGregor Paxton), Virginia Larribeau (Alice Brown Chittenden), Judith Ocker (Kate Bissell), Robert Poster (David Johnson), Samuel Robbins (Thomas Doughty), Bradley B. Williams of the Pasadena Historical Society (Colman landscape), and John Russell and Nancy Allyn Jarzombek about the roses in various paintings. Alfred C. Harrison, Jr. lent me his wide knowledge of California artists by critically reading the entries on Alice B. Chittenden, John Ross Key, and Raymond Dabb Yelland; Gwendolyn Owens helped correct several errors in my account of David Johnson; and Brucia Witthoft generously let me use the information in her exhaustive, unpublished study of George Henry Smillie.

My wife, Joan, the best organized person I have ever known, helped me with every conceivable aspect of this project and patiently word processed many versions of the text, each one of which she improved by her initial editing.

John Wetenhall, curator of painting and sculpture; Ann Friedman, the exhibition coordinator; Joan Kennedy, who designed the catalogue; and many others at the Birmingham Museum of Art helped bring this show to fruition.

Otto E. Nelson took all the photographs and with his wife Margaret helped in many ways. My search for depictions of the artists was facilitated by the staffs of the Archives of American Art, the Arden Collection, the Bancroft Library of the University of California at Berkeley, the Museum of Fine Arts, Boston, the Fall River Historical Society, the Free Library of Philadelphia, the Freer Gallery of Art, the Frick Research Library, the National Academy of Design, the Pennsylvania Academy of the Fine Arts, the UCLA Library, Vose Galleries of Boston, the Wood Art Gallery, the Yale University Art Gallery, and Larry Clark of the Brooklyn Museum, James P. Crain, Fred Keeler, and Virginia Larribeau.

Some of our most pleasant hours have been spent with dealers of American painting and much of what we know about the field we owe to them. Unfailingly patient, informative, and enthusiastic, over the years they have gotten to know our tastes. Twenty-one dealers supplied the sixty-three paintings in this exhibition. First and foremost are Kenneth Lux, with whom we started collecting twenty-one years ago, and Robert W. Vose III and Abbot W. Vose. Their galleries supplied over a third of the works in this show. We greatly enjoyed our visits with them as we did those with Eric Widing and Richard York, Deedee Wigmore, Martha Fleischman (Kennedy Galleries), Jeffrey Cooley, Jim Hill (Berry-Hill Galleries), John H. Garzoli, Bonnie Crane (The Crane Collection), Alfred C. Harrison, Jr. (Northpoint Gallery), Bruce Chambers and Nancy Condon Zander (Alexander Gallery), all of whom unstintingly lavished a great deal of time on us.
We also bought fine paintings from Ira Spanierman, Thomas Colville, Fred E. Keeler, Susan Powell, William Vareika, Jeffrey Altman and Russell Burke, Gerold Wunderlich, Ira Danikian (Arvest Galleries), and Judith Ocker (Childs Galleries). Our thanks to them all.

Frederick Baekeland

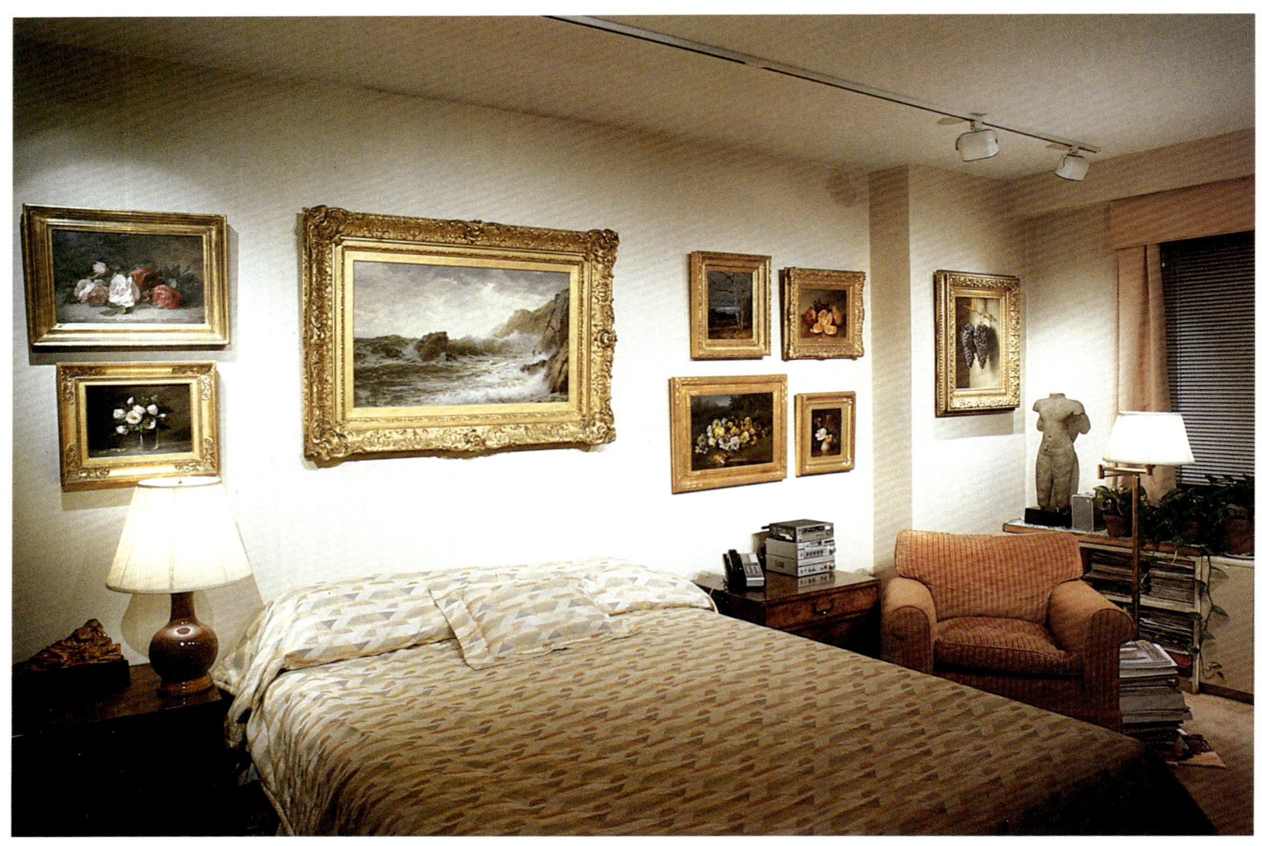

Dr. and Mrs. Baekeland's collection is a constant part of their lives, as seen here in a view of their bedroom. Photo by Howard Hensel, New York City.

Art Collecting: A Point of View

Art exhibition catalogues typically document and discuss the details of ephemeral events for a readership of specialists. Although they may reach a wider audience they are little read, purchased most often as souvenirs to leaf through cursorily, if at all. Not surprisingly, most people would rather look at art objects than illustrations of them, or else prefer to peruse them in reproduction rather than read about them. Consequently, without apology, I address this essay to all serious art collectors, seasoned or beginners, whoever and wherever you are and whatever you collect. If one were to accept at face value current media, auction house, and museum hyperbole about the so-called "art explosion," you are many. Yet, you know as well as I do that very few share your intense interest in art. Unless they are specialists, visitors rarely notice the paintings on your walls or the art objects on your tables and shelves. If you go, as I have done, to many smaller cities and stop to ask passersby for directions to the local museum, they usually haven't heard of it, or if they have, don't know where it is. If you visit on a weekday you may find yourself alone in its galleries. Valid, relevant hard data are not available, but I suspect that only a tiny fraction of those who visit special exhibitions ever set foot in their local museums at other times. You are probably among them. Why you and others like you collect art is still a moot question.

No experienced, serious collector is totally unmindful of the monetary value of his or her objects. Nevertheless, if investment were the primary motive, I doubt that any collector could ever sustain the long term commitment of time, attention, and energy needed to build a good collection expressing individual personality and taste. Unlike accumulating, collecting has a clear focus. It can enhance the collector's self-definition, especially if it becomes a serious enough preoccupation — in effect, a way of life — to compete with his or her vocation. Clearly, though poorly understood, it satisfies an aesthetic need often not nourished by one's career. On the other hand, it may simply cater to vanity and a desire for social advancement. Sometimes it helps fill an otherwise empty life. At others it may reflect acquisitiveness or a need for order and control (the psychoanalyst's orality and anality). Alternatively, it may satisfy the collector's need to compete, to be one up or even express a need for power. Others' interest in the collector's artworks can compensate for a current or childhood lack of love.[1]

Many other motives for art collecting have been proposed, but in my opinion, the most significant function of an artwork is to abstract from and restructure some aspect of life in a more ideal way. Similarly, an art collection is an ideal world, more perfect than the one in which the collector lives, and from which everything that does not conform to personal taste and psyche is excluded.

It can be argued that the particular form collecting takes is determined by the collector's personality. On the other hand, what kind of art an individual has been exposed to and where he or she has seen it seem just as important. In my own case, without a shred of artistic ability myself, I came from a family with a number of good amateur artists but no collectors. Thirty-two years ago when I started decorating the bare walls of an apartment, I found that I had a good eye and enjoyed exercising it. Soon discovering that I could not afford Western art of the quality I wanted, I started collecting Chinese art and went on to Japanese and Indian art. Ultimately, I became a specialist in Japanese art.

It was not, however, until I saw my father-in-law, Ferdinand H. Davis's, collection twenty-three years ago that I was exposed to nineteenth- and early twentieth-century American painting. A pioneer collector of Toulouse-Lautrec graphic work, in the 1940s before it became sought-after and too expensive for him, he turned in the early 1950s to American painting, where he was an astute, shoe-string collector in an area disdained by most of the art establishment. It was my good fortune that to justify his overwhelming interest in art collecting, he had taught his daughter since childhood both to enjoy it and that, as he put it, "buying art is not spending money but a transfer of capital." As she quickly learned to share my interests in Asian art, I realized that I knew more about the art, history, and culture of Japan than I did of my own country.

I found that American paintings were not only a delightful slice of American history but also a highly seductive — albeit selective and idealized — vision of much that had vanished from American life. Twenty-one years ago our first step together in American painting was a gentle little autumn landscape by an obscure immigrant Hudson River School artist,

J. Antonio Hekking (active 1840s-1880s). Although we later sold it to improve our collection, I still think it is the best, even if the smallest, of the few works by him that we have seen.

From there we went on without any particular agenda, simply buying what we both liked, could afford, and thought was of high quality. Fortunately, unlike some couples, we almost always agree about art objects. Consequently art collecting has never been a source of conflict between us. Sometimes we had to trade in paintings to buy others. This was never easy but we always considered it an opportunity to upgrade.[2] The limited wall space and low ceilings of a modern apartment led us to prefer small works to the point that our facetious motto is, "Big is bad, small is good." Limited finances have also determined the nature of our collection. Many of the works are by artists who were once popular, but are now obscure and unfashionable. Others are well known but represented by modest examples, most of which we bought long ago. Fortunately, because their best work is very expensive, the better trompe-l'oeil still life artists have never appealed to us, except for John F. Peto (1854-1907), whom we cannot afford. Nor do we have works of painters such as Frederic Remington (1861-1909) and Charles Marion Russell (1864-1926), who specialized in depictions of the West. Except for Henry F. Farny (1847-1916), who has always been too expensive for us, we consider them overrated and overpriced relative to other schools of American painting. Similarly, we think most American Impressionist painters are relatively overestimated and overvalued. Unfortunately, we cannot possibly afford good examples of the few we like, such as Theodore Robinson (1852-1896) and William Merritt Chase (1849-1916). Luckily, again, we neither hunt, fish, nor sail so are immune to the special charms of sporting paintings and portraits of boats. These works also cost more than they should because of the many art buyers who often let their interest in special subject matter outweigh aesthetic considerations. So many collectors share our interest in the Hudson River School that we can rarely afford first-rate examples. On the other hand, we have come to like American Barbizon and Tonalist painting which, except for the work of George Inness (1825-1895), is still reasonably priced. Regular trips to Boston and California have exposed us to their artists, most of whom we would otherwise probably never have seen, known about, or bought.

With few exceptions we have avoided buying published works. Once published, art objects become more expensive and, despite the strange magic of publication to which even experts are susceptible, they are no better aesthetically than they were before. Furthermore, contrary to popular belief in the art world, publication is not a guarantee of authenticity.

Our taste runs to figurative paintings with a still life flavor, moody, understated landscapes, and marine paintings. On the other hand, we prefer still lifes with clearly defined forms and strong compositions. We like the freshness and brilliance of watercolor and the softness of pastel but always worry about the conservation problems they pose. As a result, our collecting of them has been limited by the availability of inner spaces where we can protect them from daylight.

If we had started buying American paintings a generation earlier or later than we did, our collection would doubtless have taken a very different shape. Everything that has a history has a history of fashion. So, too, do art history and art collecting. Consequently it is naive to think that one's tastes are independent of the times. Like fish who swim in the ocean unaware of the existence of water, we swim, equally unaware, in a sea of fashion. If we had been born earlier — if we had collected American paintings at all — we would probably have collected history painting, narrative genre, and portraits. That we have not bought the first two probably reflects a modern bias in favor of so-called pure painting and abstract values in art. However, the absence of portraits in our collection is not due to lack of interest in them but rather because the art dealers we know do not stock them unless they are by famous artists, depict well-known persons, or capitalize on the beauty and charm of women and children, all features that make such portraits expensive.

I used to think that I was indifferent to subject matter and only responded to the more abstract qualities of paintings, such as their composition, color, and brushwork. However, even abstract art has roots in the unconscious. As should have been clear to me from the beginning because of my background in psychology and psychiatry, I gradually discovered that subject matter is important to me in many ways not at first apparent. From childhood, the Adirondacks played an important part in my life. Although we bought only one actual view of the mountains (cat. 3), we have accumulated a fair number of "pseudo-Adirondack" paintings that in a pinch could pass for some corner of them.[3]

I am firmly convinced that serious collectors of long standing, whatever their special interests, reach more or less the same practical conclusions about art objects and how best to acquire them. In my opinion, first and foremost is the "grab test." In other words, when we first consider a painting, we ask ourselves if it strongly attracts us. If it doesn't, we don't buy it. Despite their apparent cogency, all other reasons should be secondary. Collectors who ignore this cardinal rule are generally condemned to realise later, after their purchases have begun to pall, that they have put the artistic cart before the horse. We try not to consider an art object for purchase when we are very tired or distracted any more than we would order a superb and expensive meal with palates dulled by fatigue or worry. On the other hand, if we have given our full, rested attention to an object, it should remain fixed in our minds a few days later. In art as in everyday life, love at first sight can be misleading. If possible, we try to look at a work we like a second time before making a final decision about it. If on second viewing it doesn't seem as good or better than before, we let it go because it is surely weaker than we first thought.

Above all, we try to resist the blandishments of names. Individuals who want to be in the social swim and museums dominated by rich trustees feel compelled to buy them: we do not. Instead, our collecting strategy has emphasized quality rather than marquee value. A fine work by an obscure artist will always give more long-term pleasure than a mediocre one by a big name, even if a celebrity purchase might impress one's guests more. Other things being equal, paintings by little-known artists, or atypical works by well-known ones, give the most artistic value for the dollar. Daubs by famous artists (yes, they also painted them) sell dearly.

When considering paintings by unfamiliar artists, we try to acquaint ourselves with the range of their work. Otherwise, how can we know whether we are buying an inferior, average, or fine example? We try to settle for the best or near best. This means seeing as many museum, gallery, and auction house exhibitions as possible, familiarizing ourselves with public and private collections, making regular rounds of dealers to see their changing stock, and looking at good quality illustrations in art books and museum, dealers', and auction catalogues.

We have found that although a good personal library is helpful, the only way we have been able to develop connoisseurship and get to know an artist to the point where we can buy the work with confidence is to see many actual examples of it. Photographs and reproductions may supplement but can never take the place of art objects. Although interpreting photos of art works is a skill that can be learned through experience, the viewer is nonetheless always at the mercy of the photographer. Black and white photos obviously misrepresent paintings more than color transparencies and slides, but all tend to make mediocre works look stronger than they are because reduction in scale increases contrast. On the other hand, they often diminish fine paintings that rely on subtle tonal variations for much of their effectiveness. Consequently, museum curators, dealers, and collectors sometimes pass up the opportunity to see worthwhile objects that have been misrepresented by photographs. Art historians are often asked by collectors and dealers to authenticate works based on photos. Depending on the care and attention they devote to this task, the quality of the photos sent them, and how much they fear making a mistake, they may damn genuine objects as fakes or give fakes clean bills of health. No wonder, then, that more often than they like to admit, art historians and museum curators come to erroneous conclusions about objects, sometimes with serious practical consequences, when they make definitive judgments from photos or slides. This is like a doctor's making a diagnosis over the telephone. Much as in the case of *Penthouse* and *Playboy* center-folds, a good photographer can lend a deceptive glamor and romance to what may be altogether ordinary objects. When I started collecting, I was often enticed by auction catalogue photos of objects which in the flesh turned out to be disappointing. The most egregious — but, amazingly, fairly common — mistake collectors can make is to trust auction catalogue illustrations to the extent of actually bidding on objects they have never seen. Even if you have had someone look at a painting for sale at auction in your stead, you are still bidding on an artistic mail order bride. I learned this the hard way during my first or second year of collecting when, on the basis of a color illustration, I bid on and bought an eighteenth-century Turkish Kutahia ware lemon squeezer at a major auction house in London. It turned out to be a fine, beautiful piece, but there was a hairline crack on the side not shown in the catalogue illustration. There is nothing to lose except time, and potentially much to be gained, by looking at the object itself.

A reputable dealer may in good faith offer a customer a misattributed painting. Artists famous in their day or those curently popular are most likely to have their signatures added to stylistically similar works or to be forged outright. Certain artists often did not sign their paintings.[4] The attribution of unsigned works makes special demands on the collector's connoisseurship. The issue of what constitutes connoisseurship as opposed to expertise (outstanding academic knowledge) and what influences it is very complex. Yet, most students of the subject agree that the authentication of art objects includes the appraisal of their characteristic morphological features (brushwork, color, motifs, etc., in a word, style) and artistic or aesthetic value (quality), and examination of methods, materials, and documentary information. In any event, artistic judgments tend to be global and synthetic. Appraisals of art objects are structurally the same as diagnoses in clinical medicine. The obvious fake or diagnostic picture is not the problem, but rather the puzzling, borderline situation. Difficult artistic judgments have many elements, each of which in itself cannot guarantee certain identification but is only a probable indicator of authorship. Hence, sometimes the collector has to make a leap of faith across a chasm of marginal uncertainty to buy a painting. Here, the specialist's opinion is most useful, but one should remember that even Homer nods.

We try to buy only works in good condition. A painting that is overcleaned or otherwise damaged is an impaired, weakened version of what the artist painted. Similarly, one with extensive repairs represents the work of at least two hands and is not the original. In any case, damaged or repaired works are harder to sell or trade in later than those in fine condition. We learned this by trying to sell one of the first American paintings we bought. It had been significantly repainted and despite its famous authorship, several dealers were unable to sell it and we were forced to dispose of it at auction. Not without reason have auctions been called the graveyards of dealers' and collectors' mistakes and failures. It is heart wrenching when we find that a painting to which we are passionately drawn has extensive repairs and inpainting when examined under a black light — which only supplements careful examination — but we reject it and remind ourselves that there are many other appealing American paintings on the market and that there are more of them than we can possibly buy. Sooner or later we know we will find another painting in fine condition that attracts us as much or more. Fond of maxims to rationalize my conduct, I remind myself that since life is imperfect, one has a right to demand perfection of art.

The foregoing remarks are an implicit argument in favor of eclecticism. My tastes in the arts have always been very eclectic. In my opinion Mozart and Wagner do not contradict or exclude each other any more than Durand (cat. 3) and Hoeber (cat. 28) do; they are merely different and complementary. Eclecticism can serve collectors well. Above all, it keeps them from developing rigid collecting programs. Museums must have them, but collectors are under no pressure to fill in gaps. Attempts to do so often lead collectors to lower their standards, by putting artists, schools, periods, styles, or subject matter ahead of quality and the "grab test."

Ideally, collectors should continue to upgrade the quality of their collections. We have done so in two ways. One is to try never to buy another example of an artist's work unless it is as good or better than the one we already own, and the other is to trade in lesser paintings to help buy better ones.

For every valid primary reason to buy an artwork there are many invalid secondary ones. Filling in gaps is dangerous, but the worst is bargain hunting, which puts price and the transitory feeling of triumph at having gotten a wonderful buy ahead of quality. The bargain hunter's finds are usually mediocre. We expect to pay a fair market price for the paintings we buy, but have never bought from certain famous dealers because their high overheads and markups put their stock out of our reach. Over the years we have visited many dealers but have gravitated toward a few with similar tastes, sympathetic personalities, low-pressure sales approaches, and affordable prices. Good dealers are honest, knowledgeable, pleasant to deal with, and will unswervingly stand behind what they sell. We invite them to visit. If they see our collection, they can understand our taste better and offer us what we like.

Auctions are also an important source of material for many collectors. Oddly enough, we have never bid successfully at one. Every time we failed, however, we later found something else we liked as well or better at a dealer's. Often it was a better buy because American painting auctions have become a top retail market.

The setting in which a painting is first seen is

important. Art works look more glamorous and their apparent merit tends to be greater in luxurious surroundings. On the other hand, they look worse in crowded settings or where they are cheek by jowl with inferior works. It is astonishing how many collectors fail to display and light their art objects properly. To discover the importance of good lighting and display, one has only to lend a painting to a museum, where it suddenly takes on a previously missing allure and brilliance. It is pennywise and pound foolish not to install good lighting. Similarly, good period or period-style frames enhance nineteenth- and early twentieth-century American paintings, even if they are sometimes expensive. The smaller a painting is, the more its appearance is damaged by a cheap, ugly, or inappropriate frame.

Should collectors have advisors? In my opinion, only if they must. If they have the time and inclination to do their own homework, they should proceed alone because they will learn much more that way. An expert advisor is a comfortable cushion. Not having one forces the collector to develop connoisseurship and expertise. On the other hand, those who cannot or are not inclined to spend a lot of time on collecting should probably get the help of an expert or buy only from the best and most reliable dealers.

In theory, experienced scholarly dealers should make the best advisors provided they can resist giving self-serving advice, but few dealers can be consistently objective about competitors' wares or advise a collector to buy a cheaper rather than a more expensive painting from their own stock. Museum curators are more likely to be objective and can also be very helpful, but only if they regularly visit dealers and auction houses. Unfortunately, many of them do not either because they are based in provincial museums without adequate funds for travel and purchase, or they patronize only a couple of dealers, or are simply too lazy to seek out paintings that are not brought to their attention. Art historians are unlikely to give very useful practical advice unless they also collect themselves. An experienced fellow collector can also be helpful.

If you use an advisor, there always remains the nagging question of whose taste and eye has been exercised in forming your collection — your own or someone else's? In a sense, advisors to collectors are the interior decorators of the art world. Independently formed collections always have an inner unity and personal flavor, while those put together with the help of advisors almost always reflect current official taste.

Although serious collectors usually do not buy art just for investment, it is widely believed that they do. The media, in particular, subscribe to the idea of investment as a primary motive for collecting. They do so because what really fuels their interest in art objects is not the objects themselves but the high prices some of them sell for and the promise that others will fetch even higher sums. Knowing little about art and less about its history, journalists seem unaware that art works pass in and out of fashion and that as they do so their prices go up and down. Equally obsessed with the prices of art objects, but for very different, self-serving reasons, are the auction houses, which in their advertising implicitly promise the buyer future appreciation on all purchases. At times, journalists and auction houses seem perilously close to knowing the price of everything and the value of nothing. In their overwhelming fascination with the prices of art objects, they subscribe to a reductionistic bedrock of modern industrial culture, the engineer's fallacy, which says that if X is good, 2X is twice as good. This formula makes museums all-too-frequent victims of both the tyranny of the turnstile and the rich trustee syndrome. Because of the former, their success and that of their exhibitions are solely measured by attendance figures. The latter often makes them reject worthwhile objects for acquisition because they are not "important" (i.e., expensive) enough. It is easier to count than it is to make complex value judgments.

The art collector lives in a kind of cultural minefield that exalts the quantitative over the qualitative. Even before the "art explosion," this manifested itself in popular ideas about physicists. Unknown to the public before World War II, they achieved recognition only after they had perfected a device that killed several hundred thousand people. Similarly, the vast majority of our population subscribes to and idealizes only the easily measurable bottom line of money, whether it is achieved in business, professions like law or medicine, or as a sports or media star. Art can be subsumed in this scheme of things only if it is expensive or it is thought that it will become expensive. American society brands as "elitist" other kinds of accomplishment that cannot be measured simply in terms of money and views them with envy, suspicion, and disdain. Hence serious interest in art collecting, as opposed to investing in art, must remain the province of a few, as it has always been.

Notes

1. See Frederick Baekeland, "Psychological Aspects of Art Collecting," *The Journal of Psychiatry* 44.1 (1981): 45-59.

2. Over the years we have deaccessioned about 20% of what we bought.

3. These paintings are: Ward, cat. 2; Bierstadt, cat. 6; Martin, cat. 7; Cropsey, cat. 9; Jones, cat.10; Bellows, cat. 13; Hart, cat. 14; Enneking, cat. 21; Palmer, cat. 24; and Smillie, cat. 29.

4. This was true of Thomas Birch (cat. 30), Jacob Caleb Ward (cat. 2), Samuel Colman (cat. 22), John La Farge (cat. 37), and John F. Francis (cat. 47).

The Artist in Context

The ninety-two years between Thomas Doughty's *A Lake in the White Mountains*, 1833 (cat. 1) and Frederick Bosley's *The Pageant*, 1925 (cat. 44) saw a United States transformed. At first largely rural and agricultural, it became wealthier, larger, and more populous, urban, and industrial. Towns grew into cities, railroads crisscrossed the countryside, and huge numbers of immigrants poured in. Communication and education advanced apace, and more and more Americans traveled abroad. Yet, the American paintings in this exhibition, like those in other collections shown in the last twenty years, hardly reflect these changes. Railroads, factories, and telegraph wires are absent from rural landscapes, and middle- or upper-class life, well-fed farmers, or painless urban poverty are the rule in genre paintings. This is only natural since most modern collectors like us share the artists' patrons' wish to buy undisturbing beauty rather than renewed encounters with the problems of everyday life.

With the exception of a few who were famous or the subjects of idolatrous biographies by admirers and two who wrote autobiographies, we know little about the personalities and private lives of the fifty-eight painters in this exhibition. The broad outlines of their lives and backgrounds nonetheless reflect some of the changes that took place in American society. In Doughty's time, the artist's biggest problems were a paucity of patrons, teachers, and good painting collections to study. Outside of the Pennsylvania Academy of the Fine Arts in Philadelphia and the National Academy of Design in New York City, there was nowhere else an artist could get institutional training. For seven painters in this exhibition this was a serious problem. All born by 1832, they were entirely self-taught or learned to paint through work in associated industries, such as architecture, engraving, coach painting, and drafting.[1]

Fortunately for American art and artists, standards of living rose and their patrons increasingly considered painters professionals rather than craftspeople. The occupations, and presumably the attitudes toward art, of the artists' fathers reflect this. Of those born by 1835, the majority came from families of artisans and farmers, while most of those born after 1835 were brought up in the homes of artists, businessmen, and professionals. As might be expected in an age of immigration, a quarter of the fathers and a fifth of the painters were immigrants.[2] Only about a quarter of those born in the United States grew up in large cities. The rest came from rural or small town backgrounds, but most of them later sought the comforts and cultural and business advantages of the large urban centers where they settled. Not surprisingly, almost 90 per cent came from the more populous, wealthy, educated, and culturally developed East. The rest hailed from the Middle West, mostly from farming communities around Cincinnati, which until the Civil War was one of a small number of cultural centers outside of the East Coast.

By 1860 Philadelphia and Boston had ceded the commercial and artistic palm to New York City, which had become a magnet for ambitious painters for two reasons. It had more of both art collectors of modest means and wealthy patrons than other art centers and, until 1869, the National Academy of Design excluded those living outside the city from membership. Through the 1870s, National Academy of Design exhibitions remained the most important annual exhibitions in America. An official hanging committee, which tended to display members' works at eye level while those by outsiders were frequently "skied," chose paintings accepted for display. Accordingly, more than half of our artists had studios in the New York area, followed by Boston, Philadelphia, San Francisco, and Chicago. Those working outside of New York found it very hard to establish national reputations without close ties to its art organizations and galleries. Not surprisingly, the least-known artists in this exhibition lived in small towns or provincial cities.[3]

In a country relatively poor in art institutions and patronage, European study and travel was the goal of most painters. It promised up-to-date foreign training and exposure to great public collections. Moreover, it offered immersion in artistic circles in countries where painters were both more numerous and more highly regarded than in the United States. Finally, it gave the artists and their work an added cachet when they returned home.

Fortunately, life in Europe was cheap. Painters got there any way they could manage. They saved up for trips, sold the contents of their studios, borrowed money, or received grants from patrons or family. They stayed abroad by selling to wealthy American tourists who might not have bought from them at home, copying old masters for their domestic patrons, or sending back original works for sale or exhibition at home. Some learned by studying and copying old master paintings. Others underwent some kind of formal instruction in an art academy, in outside classes given by academy faculty members or other well known artists, or by apprenticeship. After the Civil War foreign travel became less expensive. Formal study in Europe was more common but foreign sojourns became shorter, perhaps because artists so often supplemented training in increasingly numerous and well-developed American art academies. Of the artists in this exhibition, only about one in five did not go abroad. Most of these were immigrants, the majority of whom had arrived in America fully trained and well aware of its greater social and political freedom and potential opportunities.[4]

American artists typically preferred to visit or live in England, by virtue of language and descent, Italy, because of its antiquities and old master paintings, and France and Germany, because of their superiority as training centers. England was popular until 1850 while Rome was the obligatory destination for Hudson River School painters in particular between 1830 and 1880.[5] Russell Smith's views of Wales (cats. 4 and 5) typify this early phase of foreign study and travel. By the 1870s, Rome's charms had begun to pall for most artists compared to those of Venice.[6] In the 1840s and 1850s Düsseldorf was in vogue with American painters for a number of reasons: the Düsseldorf style of painting had been popularized through exhibitions in New York; the German-American Emmanuel Leutze (1816-1868) taught there; its Academy offered thorough training that included landscape; and it welcomed foreign students.[7] After Leutze left in 1859 and the outbreak of the Civil War discouraged northerners' travel to Europe, the Royal Academy in Munich subsequently replaced the Düsseldorf Academy as the most popular German destination for American painters, many of whom were Middle Westerners of German descent.[8] By the mid-1870s, however, France and especially Paris had overtaken Munich as the goal of art students. There, in addition to the official training opportunities at the Ecole des Beaux-Arts, famous painters offered instruction at their own schools.[9] James Wells Champney's depiction of two little French children (cat. 40) is typical of the kind of Salon figurative style and subject matter American artists acquired during periods of study in France.

Formal, academic study in Europe had the disadvantage of stressing figurative painting at the expense of landscape. A number of artists such as Arthur Hoeber (cat. 28) and Walter Launt Palmer (cat. 24) studied figure painting abroad for years, but after their return to the United States soon abandoned it for landscape, which had been their main interest all along. Even though new art schools sprang up in both the East and West after the Civil War, America's persistent cultural inferiority complex continued to drive painters to Europe for instruction until the First World War.

Study was not the only reason for artists' foreign travel. Even first trips abroad were partly motivated by simple curiosity, the lure of the exotic, and an interest in new subject matter. As continental Europe and its sights became better known to American collectors, the need for novelty took painters even farther afield.[10] Some such as Samuel Colman (cat. 22) and George Henry Hall (cat. 52) enlarged their repertoires by visits to Spain, North Africa, and Egypt, while William Trost Richards (cat. 35) combed remote coastal areas of England, Scotland, Ireland, and Norway in search of the exotic marine views for which he was known. Others such as John La Farge (cat. 37) made artistic capital of visits to Japan and the South Seas, while Walter Launt Palmer (cat. 24) visited Spain, Morocco, and the Far East simply as a well-to-do tourist. Typically, those who kept going back to Europe initially had made relatively long stays there, felt comfortable with foreign languages, and were highly successful artists. Hall and James Wells Champney (cat. 40) even maintained studios both in New York and abroad. Life in Europe was undoubtedly more civilized than in the United States. No wonder then that John O'Brien Inman (cat. 39) at age thirty-eight went there already fully trained and well established to live and work for twelve years. Others not in this exhibition even made successful careers as permanent expatriates.[11]

Most artists who studied in Europe contented themselves with one limited foray abroad, concentrating thereafter on local scenery. As settlement increasingly began to alter the American countryside, landscape painters rapidly began to realize the prophetic truth of the words of Thomas Cole (1800-1848) who, as early as 1835, lamented that "the ravages of the axe are daily increasing — the most noble scenes are made desolate, and oftentimes with a wantonness and barbarism scarcely credible in a civilized nation."[12]

As early as 1825 Hudson River School painters were drawn to the unspoiled mountains, forests, and numerous lakes and ponds of the Catskills (cat. 2),[13] Adirondacks (cat. 3),[14] and White Mountains (cats. 1 and 6).[15] Artists were pioneers in visiting these wild, sparsely settled areas, their paintings educating a subsequent wave of upper-class tourists to their sublime and picturesque beauty. With Albert Bierstadt (cat. 6) leading the way in 1859, a number of other artists were drawn to the vast, unsettled, and uncharted spaces of the West. By the 1880s, however, the spell of the Barbizon aesthetic lured most landscapists away from vistas of mountains, forests, and plains to more intimate views of settled, semirural, or even suburban areas such as Arthur Parton's depiction of the Navesink Valley (cat. 17). Most of our Barbizon and Tonalist landscapes, however, express our fondness for depictions of more isolated spots.

Well into the twentieth century, it was much more difficult for women than men to make careers in art. Training and travel were harder for them because such pursuits interfered with their traditional roles as wife and mother and they usually did not have independent sources of income. As a result, many women with successful artistic careers had independent means and did not marry or did so only briefly. Although they could exhibit at venues such as the National Academy of Design, outside of Boston they were denied access to the exhibitions and artistic social life of the men's clubs where artists met patrons and critics. Partly because it was easier to paint at home and partly because of sex role stereotypes, they tended to specialize in portraiture, genre, and still life.[16] The five women artists in this exhibition reflect these cultural determinants. Active after the Civil War, four were still life specialists and one was a figurative painter. The three with full professional careers either never married or did so only briefly; one was an artist's daughter and the other two had wealthy parents.

Although some of the hurdles the woman painter had to overcome were peculiar to her sex, others were the same for artists of both sexes. How best to sell their work was always the biggest problem. Before 1850 there were almost no art galleries and few wealthy patrons. Only portraitists were able to move outside the restrictive sales environment available to artists before mid-century, which limited opportunities to sales made from their studios or the few exhibitions open to them.

From 1839 to 1851, however, the Apollo Association (later the American Art-Union) provided another sales route for artists. Subscribers paid a yearly fee to defray expenses, buy paintings, and produce engravings, which were distributed to all members. Paintings were obtained by lottery. Yearly attendance at the American Art-Union was 250,000 — more than half the population of New York City — and 2,841 paintings by over 200 artists were distributed. These included forty-six autumn landscapes by Cropsey (cat. 9), forty-nine landscapes by Durand (cat. 3), and ten by Casilear (cat. 11). Unfortunately for the artists, the National Academy of Design, which resented the American Art-Union's competition with its own exhibitions, sued successfully to have it discontinued on the grounds that it promoted a form of gambling.

Even with the rise of art galleries after the Civil War, an important way for artists to meet and woo potential customers was to join prominent men's clubs such as the Century Association and the Lotos and Salmagundi Clubs, which had wealthy members and often sponsored art exhibitions. Even as late as 1893, the well-established painter George H. Smillie's (cat. 29) business was so badly affected by a major economic depression that he spent three summers in Bar Harbor more in search of new patrons than of subject matter. Not surprisingly, the most successful American painters such as Albert Bierstadt (cat. 6)[17] were also good self-publicists and businessmen.

Serious collectors of American painting did not appear until the 1830s. Up to the Second World War, with very few exceptions, they always also collected European works. Mostly merchants, they were primarily self-made men rather than professionals and lived in Baltimore, Cincinnati, Hartford, Boston, Philadelphia, and, especially, New York. From 1840 to 1860 their generous patronage of Hudson River School artists, who had similar social origins and depicted the familiar landscapes of their youth, produced the heyday of the American artist. After the Civil War, increased foreign travel and the widespread importation of European Salon and French Barbizon paintings affected the market for American art adversely, causing many artists to change their style. Their efforts to do so were successful for a while. However, the rapid decline of the once flourishing Hudson River School in the 1880s proved to be only a prelude to the precipitous fall from grace of American Barbizon, Tonalist, and Impressionist painting after the Armory Show in 1913.[18] As modernism took hold, most realist nineteenth-century art was damned as "academic" and serious collectors of nineteenth- and early twentieth-century American works vanished from the scene.

As late as 1960, the standard truth revealed by museum curators and art historians about pre-World War I American painting emphasized figurative artists. It excluded from serious consideration all but a select group of painters: Colonial and earlier nineteenth-century portraitists, such as John Singleton Copley (1738-1815) in Boston and the Peales in Philadelphia; Winslow Homer (1836-1910) and Thomas Eakins (1844-1916); the expatriate artists James Abbott McNeill Whistler (1834-1903), John Singer Sargent (1856-1925), and Mary Cassatt (1855-1926); and Albert Pinkham Ryder (1847-1917) as a precursor of modernism. Then, nineteenth- and early twentieth-century American painting began to profit from a revival of scholarly and collecting interest in more academic realist styles of painting. Ignored previously because they did not fit into the accepted, orthodox line of descent of abstract modern art starting with Eugène Delacroix (1798-1863) and Gustave Courbet (1819-1877) and proceeding through Impressionism, Post-Impressionism, the School of Paris, and Abstract Expressionism, their merit became apparent. By 1970 a surprised art establishment discovered that excellence in nineteenth-century art was widespread in countries other than France, "academic" styles were no longer beyond the pale, and American nineteenth-century painting again found itself in respectable company. Retrospective exhibitions of major nineteenth-century artists made it fashionable. Typically, these early exhibitions recapitulated its historical development by starting with the Hudson River School but skipped Barbizon-influenced styles, jumping instead to American Impressionism, which made fewer demands on a new class of nouveau riche collectors with little background in nonabstract art beyond a passing exposure to French Impressionism. Now, exhibitions of nineteenth- and early twentieth-century American painting have become so frequent that it is difficult even for the specialist to keep up with them.

A survey of thirteen exhibitions of private collections of nineteenth-century American painting since 1967 reveals that about three-fifths of them were strongest in landscape while the rest emphasized figurative painting. Six of these exhibitions had strengths in both areas. Unlike us, none of the collectors had a significant interest in still life or marine painting, and the Hudson River School and American Impressionist, rather than Barbizon and Tonalist, artists were the most popular. Generally, the collectors had advisors. It goes without saying that the highest quality collections belonged to those who spent the most money, which is not to say that they got the most for their dollars. Such collections have tended to be more encyclopedic and "textbook" in composition, as befits those formed under extensive advice.[19] As prices continue to rise, I suspect that interest will shift to less popular schools such as American Barbizon and Tonalism, and that more attention will be paid to little-known regional artists[20] and to the "lesser media" of watercolors and drawings.

Notes

1. Artists who learned to paint in these ways include Doughty (cat. 1), Durand (cat. 3), Whittredge (cat. 19), Cropsey (cat 9), Hart (cat 14), Hall (cat 52), and Key (cat 12).

2. England, Scotland, Germany, and France figure in that order.

3. Of a sample of nineteen painters born by 1835, three of their fathers were artists, thirteen were artisans or farmers, and three were businessmen or professionals; of seventeen born later, six of their fathers were artists, five were artisans or farmers, and six were businessmen or professionals. Fifteen of fifty-eight (25.9%) fathers of artists and twelve (20.7%) of the artists were immigrants. Fourteen of fifty-six artists (25%) about whom data are available were born in large cities (eight in New York City), while forty out of forty-six (87%) who were native-born came from the East (fifteen from New York State). Thirty-three of fifty-eight (56.9%) had studios in or near New York City.

4. Of the fifty-four artists about whom information is available, ten (18.5%) did not go to Europe. Of these, seven were immigrants, five of whom (Birch, cat. 30; Forster, cat. 49; Lacroix, cat. 50; de Longpré, cat. 55; and Partington, cat. 25) came to the United States as trained artists. Of the thirty-five painters whose exact lengths of stay abroad are known, eighteen born by 1835 averaged four years of foreign study, while seventeen born later averaged only 3.2 years.

5. See Charles C. Eldredge and Barbara Novak, *The Arcadian Landscape: Nineteenth-century American Painters in Italy* (Lawrence: University of Kansas Museum of Art, 1972) and John W. Coffey, *Twilight of Arcadia: American Landscape Painters in Rome, 1830-1880* (Brunswick, ME: Bowdoin College Museum of Art, 1986).

6. See Margaretta M. Lovell, *Venice: The American View 1860-1920* (San Francisco: The Fine Arts Museums of San Francisco, 1985).

7. See Donelson F. Hoopes and Wend von Kalnein, *The Düsseldorf Academy and the Americans* (Atlanta: The High Museum of Art, 1972) and Anneliese Harding and Brucia Witthoft, *American Artists in Düsseldorf: 1840-1865* (Framingham, MA: Danforth Museum, 1982).

8. See Michael Quick, Eberhard Ruhmer, and Richard V. West, *Munich & American Realism in the 19th Century* (Sacramento: E.B. Crocker Art Gallery, 1978).

9. See H. Barbara Weinberg, "Nineteenth-Century American Painters at the Ecole des Beaux Arts," *American Art Journal* 13 (Autumn 1981): 66-71; John Milner, *The Studios of Paris: The Capital of Art in the Late Nineteenth Century* (New Haven: Yale University Press, 1988); and Sellin.

10. See, for example, Katherine Emma Manthorne, *Tropical Renaissance: North American Artists Exploring Latin America, 1839-1879* (Washington, D.C.: Smithsonian Institution Press, 1989).

11. See Michael Quick, *American Expatriate Painters of the Late Nineteenth Century* (Dayton: The Dayton Art Institute, 1976).

12. Quoted in John W. McCoubrey, ed., *American Art 1700-1960: Sources and Documents* (Englewood Cliffs, NJ: Prentice-Hall, 1965), 108.

13. See Myers.

14. See Maria Naylor, "The Wilderness Arcadia: Views of the Adirondack Forests, Lakes and Mountains in 19th Century American Paintings", *The Kennedy Quarterly* 7.3 (1967) and Patricia C.F. Mandel, *Fair Wilderness: American Paintings in the Collection of the Adirondacks Museum* (Blue Mountain Lake, NY: The Adirondacks Museum, 1990).

15. See Campbell and Blaine; Donald D. Keyes, et al.; and McGrath and MacAdam.

16. See Nancy Mowll Matthews, "American Women Artists at the Turn of the Century: Opportunities and Choices," in Meredith Martindale, Pamela Moffet, and Nancy Mowll Matthews, *Lilla Cabot Perry: An American Impressionist* (Washington, D.C.: The National Museum of Women in the Arts, 1990), 105-13.

17. For a good account of Bierstadt's energetic self-promotion and grand life style see Linda S. Ferber, "Albert Bierstadt: The History of a Reputation" in Ferber and Anderson, 21-68.

18. For discussions of various aspects of patronage and the role of the artist see Maybelle Mann, *The American Art-Union* (Otisville, NY: ALM Associates, 1977); Neil Harris, *The Artist in American Society: The Formative Years 1790-1860* (New York: George Braziller, 1966); Lillian B. Miller, *Patrons and Patriotism: The Encouragement of the Fine Arts in the United States 1790-1860* (Chicago: The University of Chicago Press, 1966); John K. Howat, "A Climate for Landscape Painters;" Kevin J. Avery, "A Historiography of the Hudson River School;" and Doreen Bolger Burke and Catherine Hoover Vorsanger, "The Hudson River School in Eclipse" in Avery et al., 49-70, 94-95; 3-20, 91-93; and 71-90, 95-98; Wayne Craven, "Introduction: Patronage and Collecting in America, 1800-1835" in Ella M. Foshay, Wayne Craven, and Timothy Anglin Burgard, *Mr. Luman Reed's Picture Gallery: A Pioneer Collection of American Art* (New York: Harry N. Abrams, 1990), 11-18; and Baekeland.

19. See Stuart P. Feld, *American Paintings and Historical Prints from the Middendorf Collection* (New York: The Metropolitan Museum of Art, 1967); William H. Gerdts, Jr., *Nineteenth Century American Painting from the Collection of Henry Melville Fuller* (Manchester, NH: The Currier Gallery of Art, 1971); Dianne H. Pilgrim, *American Impressionist and Realist Paintings and Drawings from the Collection of Mr. and Mrs. Raymond J. Horowitz* (New York: The Metropolitan Museum of Art, 1973); John A. Mahey, *American Paintings from the Collection of Mr. and Mrs. Fred D. Bentley, Sr. and Mr. and Mrs. J. Alan Sellars* (Jacksonville, FL: The Cummer Gallery of Art, 1975); E.P. Richardson, *American Art: An Exhibition from the Collection of Mr. and Mrs. John D. Rockefeller 3rd* (San Francisco: The Fine Arts Museums of San Francisco, 1976); Bruce Chambers, *Selections from the Robert P. Coggins Collection of American Painting* (Rochester, NY: Memorial Art Gallery of the University of Rochester, 1977); Gerald M. Ackerman, et al., *The Preston Morton Collection of American Art* (Santa Barbara: Santa Barbara Museum of Art, 1981); John Paul Driscoll, *All That Is Glorious Around Us: Paintings from the Hudson River School on Loan from a Friend of the Museum of Art* (University Park: Museum of Art, The Pennsylvania State University, 1981); John Wilmerding, et al. (1981); Howard E. Wooden, *The John W. and Mildred L. Graves Collection* (Wichita, KS: Wichita Art Museum, 1984); John I.H. Baur and Christine Murray, *American Masters: The Thyssen-Bornemisza Collection* (Lugano: Thyssen-Bornemisza Collection, 1984); D. Scott Atkinson, et al., *A Proud Heritage: Two Centuries of American Art* (Chicago: Terra Museum of American Art, 1987); and Henry Adams, et al., *American Paintings from the Manoogian Collection* (Washington, D.C.: National Gallery of Art, 1989).

20. The interested reader can decide how much merit there is in little-known regional artists by perusing Gerdts (1990).

Landscape Painting

The seventy-five years from 1833 to 1908 spanned by the twenty-nine landscapes in this exhibition witnessed a major shift in artistic emphasis from portraiture and classical history painting to landscape, marine painting, genre, and still life. The first popular native landscape style became known as the Hudson River School, which remained the dominant approach to American landscape painting until well after the Civil War. It was so called because of its members' liking for precisely rendered and often panoramic views of both wild and domesticated areas of the Hudson Valley, the Catskills, and the Adirondack Mountains. Heavily influenced from the first by notions of the beautiful, the picturesque, and the sublime derived from English landscape painting and theory, which in practice took the work of Claude Lorrain (1600-1682) and Salvatore Rosa (1615-1673) as its models, Hudson River School compositions reflected the thematic and formal goals of its sources. The beautiful was often represented by compositions with well-defined series of spatial planes, which emphasized the orderly progression from foreground darkness through a middle-ground body of water to a luminous, light-filled background crowning distant mountains (cat. 1). Representations of the picturesque stressed irregularity and variety of form as well as strong contrasts of light and shadow (cat. 2). The sublime capitalized on spectacular scenes which were taken as spiritually and emotionally exciting (cat. 11). The beautiful was most clearly expressed in settled, pastoral landscapes with Elysian and Arcadian overtones, while the picturesque and the sublime were both exemplified by the wild scenery of primeval forests and mountains. Under the influence of Emersonian transcendentalism, nature was seen as an expression of God, so that the sublime became part of a religious, moral concept of nature. In the 1860s and 1870s, this idea was given form in spectacular, exotic landscapes or in grandiose views of the West that were imbued with the idea of Manifest Destiny. Starting with Thomas Doughty (cat. 1) and ending with David Johnson (cat. 15) in this exhibition, Hudson River School artists strove to effect a compromise between idealism and realism in which the latter increasingly triumphed.

After 1875, the French Barbizon school of painting and its offshoots began to dominate American landscapes. An outgrowth of both seventeenth-century Dutch painting and the work of John Constable (1776-1837) in England, it offered a fashionable, foreign alternative to the Hudson River School. Rather than elaborately composed, detailed views, it stressed more intimate glimpses of nature that tried to capture transitory effects of weather and light. American artists enthusiastically took up its brighter palette, plein-air execution, simpler, more open compositions, freer, more vigorous, and unblended brush strokes, and greater use of impasto. However, they could not translate its preoccupation with rural peasant life into American terms as the American farmer could not easily be equated with the French peasant. Under Barbizon influence American landscapists used less specific titles and, for the most part, stopped dating their paintings, which now referred to the season, time of day, or weather conditions rather than to the locales they were depicting.

Some of the Hudson River School artists in this exhibition such as William McDougal Hart (cat. 14) and David Johnson (cat. 15) made slight adaptations to the Barbizon approach without giving up their basic style. Others, however, abandoned the Hudson River School manner completely. In the hands of several this eventually took the form of a tonal impressionism quite different from the style employed in France. It emphasized instead divided, scumbled brush strokes and, often, a rather somber, muted palette as in the later works of Arthur Parton (cat. 18) and Homer Dodge Martin (cat. 20). A third group started as American Barbizon painters but became practitioners of Tonalism. This approach emphasized variations within a narrow range of color in open, simplified compositions suggesting mood and atmosphere as in Samuel Colman's circa 1888 view of the Pasadena Valley (cat. 22). Yet a fourth group of artists such as Walter Launt Palmer (cat. 24) and Henry Farrer (cat. 27) evolved related styles in watercolor.

In 1913 the Armory Show ushered in modernism, which soon made American Barbizon, Tonalist, and Impressionist painting all seem old fashioned. Impressionism persisted as a new kind of academic style until its recent resurgence of popularity, but the first two have not yet regained their former standing in the art world.

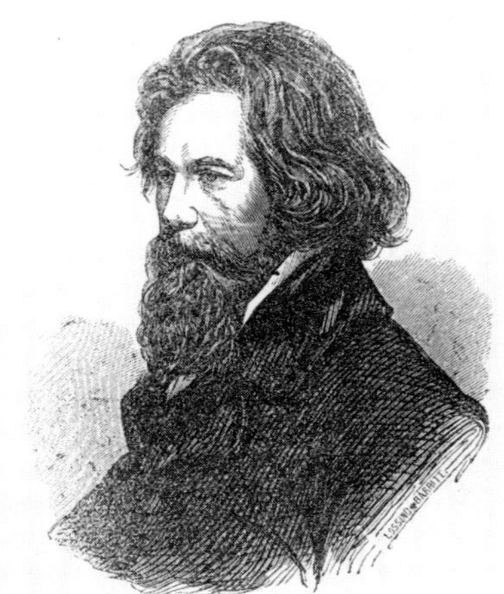

Thomas Doughty, 1854. Photo courtesy of the Free Library of Philadelphia.

1. Thomas Doughty

(born 1793, Philadelphia; died 1856, New York)
A Lake in the White Mountains, 1833
Oil on canvas
16 3/4" x 20 7/8"
Signed lower center: T. Doughty 1833

Thomas Doughty was both America's first native-born landscape specialist and one of the earliest artists of the Hudson River School. Although his work is uneven, at its best it is of high quality. Even in his own day, critics disagreed about it. In 1840 one wrote: "His forte lies in scenery of a softer and inland character – the lonely forest-brook, the misty wood-lake, the still river, the heart of the quiet wilderness. . . . In painting those features of Nature, he has (in his peculiar style) no rival among American painters."[1] In 1854, however, another said, "He has painted too much, too hastily."[2] American art specialists tend to give his landscapes a passing nod on historical grounds, but ignore their great aesthetic merits. As an example of current official opinion, his work was not included in the Metropolitan Museum of Art's recent blockbuster exhibition devoted to the Hudson River School.[3]

Doughty's painting has been underestimated for two reasons. One is its unevenness. The other is that it does not fare well in black and white reproductions, where it loses most of its subtlety and refined charm. Unfortunately, reproductions rather than art objects are the staple diet of most art historians and museum curators during their training periods when their tastes and opinions are formed.

Born in Philadelphia, Doughty was one of five sons of a ship's carpenter. His interest in art was encouraged by his successful oldest brother, who eventually owned many of his paintings. He was mostly self-taught, and his only documented training consisted of studying drawing for part of a term at a night school, copying landscapes in a patron's collection, and informal advice from the figurative painters Rembrandt Peale (1778-1860) and Thomas Sully (1783-1872). He did not become a full-time artist until 1820, when his friends were astounded that he dared give up a successful leather business to embark exclusively on the novel and uncertain specialty of landscape painting. In 1824, however, he became an Academician at the Pennsylvania Academy of the Fine Arts, where he had first exhibited in 1816, and progressed, during the 1820s, from topographical landscapes to true nature paintings of scenes in Pennsylvania, Delaware, Connecticut, Massachusetts, and upstate New York. As his work grew in finesse in the late 1820s, his palette broadened and lightened to his advantage. During two stays in Boston (1829 to 1830 and 1832 to 1837), he made trips to the Adirondacks and Catskills as well as on the coasts of Massachusetts, Maine, and New Hampshire. Besides executing many fanciful, romantic landscapes he painted multiple versions of successful works in order to support his wife and five children. During two trips to London, from 1837 to 1838 and from 1845 to 1847, he was significantly influenced by nineteenth-century English picturesque landscapes but executed many American views. Despite his increasing production of replicas of previous work, his popularity continued into the 1840s, as evidenced by the American Art-Union's purchase of more than fifty of his paintings for distribution through its periodic members lottery. After 1848, when he moved to New York, there was a marked drop in the quality of most of his paintings. Relatively inactive in his later years, he died in poverty in 1856.

Unlike Cole's sublime, heroic view of nature, Doughty's vision was one of peaceful harmony. His work abounds in lyrical, pastoral landscapes which sometimes combine features of several locales. It includes a variety of topographical landscapes, ideal, Italianized views, settings inspired by American literature and English travel books, fanciful, romantic scenes with classical references, winter scenes, and landscapes featuring moonlight or rainbows. In the 1830s and the late 1840s, he also executed a number

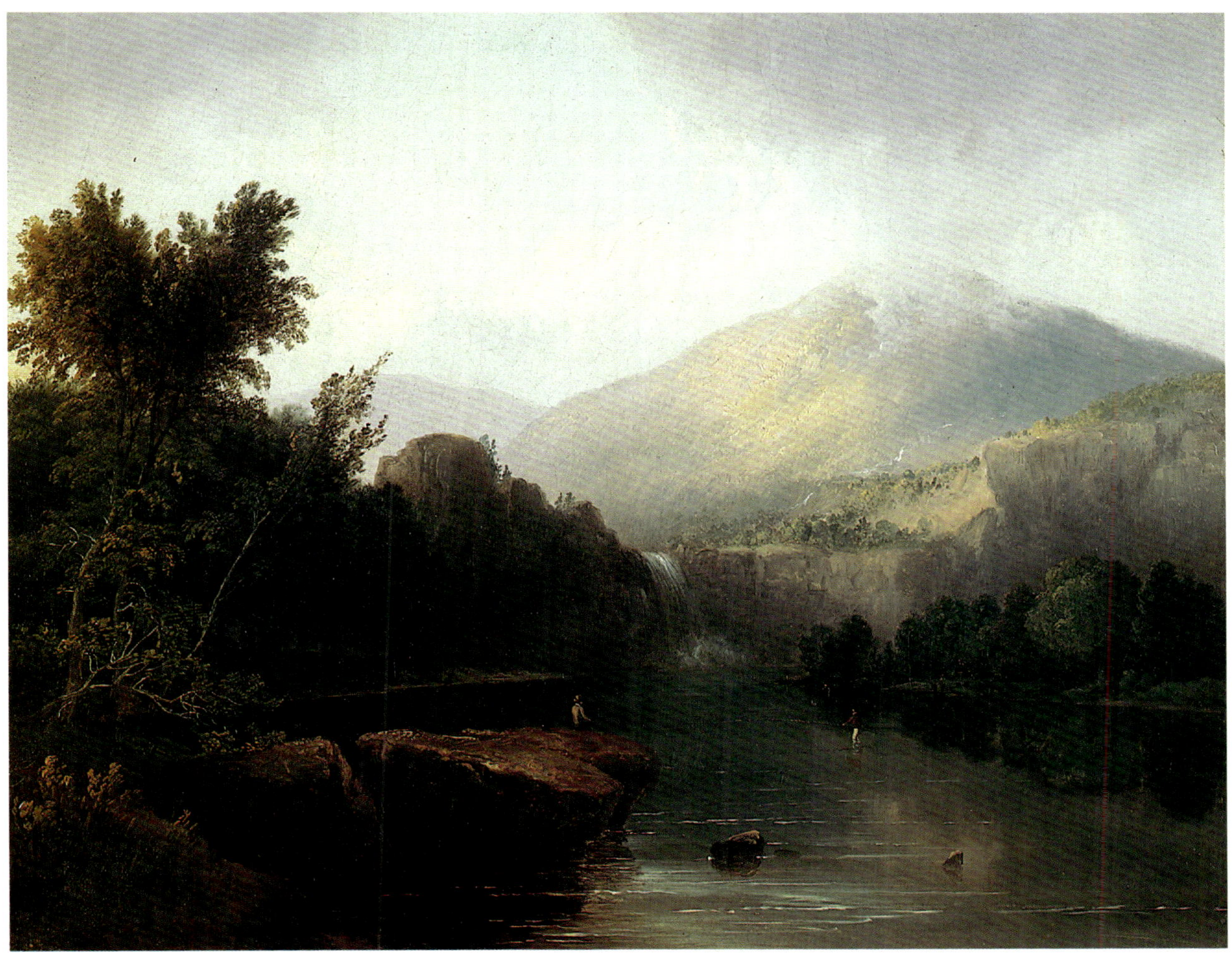

Thomas Doughty, *A Lake in the White Mountains*, 1833. Oil on canvas, 16 3/4" x 20 7/8".

of coastal scenes, some of which are peaceful, others violent and stormy. His eclectic but personal style draws on a number of sources. These include seventeenth-century Dutch and eighteenth-century English landscape paintings and engravings, and the work of English-trained or influenced American artists such as Joshua Shaw (1776-1860) and Thomas Birch (1779-1851) (cat. 30). Doughty's greatest strengths are his delicate, feathery brushwork, soft, warm, and subtly modulated colors, and sensitive concern for light and atmosphere. His landscapes almost always contain rivers, lakes, or waterfalls and at least one or two figures, sometimes as observers, but often sharing his strong interest in hunting or fishing.

A Lake in the White Mountains, like the bulk of Doughty's dated, published work,[4] was painted when he lived in Boston. It shows a placid lake and two fishermen[5] with a waterfall, rocky cliffs, and a mountain as a backdrop. With each receding spatial plane there is a characteristic progression from darker to lighter tones. The solid composition with framing trees and rocks at the left corner is organized in a stepwise progression of large, contrasting masses. The foliage is rendered with a soft, light brush and the background in warm pinkish tan shaded with blue. Although indebted to English and continental notions of the picturesque in its simple contrasts of light and dark, land and water, and foreground and distance, this landscape is indelibly stamped with Doughty's poetic personal touch. As the critic John Neal wrote in 1869, "His range was narrow, but within that range he had no rival."[6]

The accuracy of this painting's title cannot be verified because around the time Doughty painted it he not only visited New Hampshire but also the Catskills and Adirondacks. There are a number of documented views of New Hampshire lakes by the artist, including Echo, Squam, and Winnipesaukee.[7] According to a specialist collector of depictions of New Hampshire who has driven, hiked, or boated through much of the region, however, this lake does not resemble any he knows. Moreover, he does not recall seeing any with a prominent waterfall like this one. It is likely, then, that this is a compositional pastiche in which the artist combined elements drawn from several locations, a frequent practice of his.[8]

1. Nathaniel P. Willis, *American Scenery*, vol. 2 (London: George Virtue, 1840), 37. Doughty did an illustration for this work.

2. E. Anna Lewis, "Art and Artists of America," *Graham's Magazine* 45 (1854): 484.

3. See Avery et al.

4. Twenty-eight (40.6%) of a sample of sixty-nine are dated. Of these, eighteen (64.3%) come from the 1830s.

5. For his figures Doughty, like Birch, probably used William H. Pyne's *Etchings of Rustic Figures for the Embellishment of Landscape*, published in London in 1815.

6. Harold Edward Dickson, ed., *Observations on American Art: Selections From the Writings of John Neal (1793-1876)* (State College: Pennsylvania State College, 1943), 82-83.

7. For examples see Campbell and Blaine, 48-49.

8. Thus, see *Sportsman by a Lake*, 1835, in Robert L. McGrath and Barbara J. MacAdam, *"A Sweet Foretaste of Heaven": Artists in the White Mountains* (Hanover: Hood Museum of Art, Dartmouth College, 1988), no. 1, ill p. 41, which is a pastiche in which Echo Lake is embellished with a waterfall and set against a background that includes Mt. Chocorua in the distance.

Bibliography

Goodyear, Frank H., Jr. *Thomas Doughty 1793-1856: An American Pioneer in Landscape Painting.* Philadelphia: The Pennsylvania Academy of the Fine Arts, 1973.

2. Jacob Caleb Ward

(born 1819, Bloomfield, New Jersey; died 1891, Bloomfield, New Jersey)
South Lake, ca. 1840
Oil on panel
23" x 31"
Unsigned

The landscape and portrait artist Jacob Caleb Ward had a long but poorly recorded life and only a few of his works have come to light. Born in Bloomfield, New Jersey, he presumably studied with his father, the painter Caleb Ward. He first exhibited at the National Academy of Design in 1829 and in the 1830s and 1840s also exhibited at the American Academy of Fine Arts, the Apollo Association, and the American Art-Union. It is known that in 1830 he painted the Hamilton-Burr duel at Weehauken, New Jersey, and for the next ten years drew illustrations for medical texts.

Ward traveled widely. The titles of the landscapes he exhibited show that he visited scenic locales in New Jersey, New York, Pennsylvania, and Virginia and later journeyed to the West and South America. In 1836 he traveled to Iowa with a friend, where he saw the Mississippi and made portrait studies of Indians. In 1845 Ward, who was a pioneer photographer, went to Santiago, Chile, to set up a daguerreotype business with his brother, the landscape and daguerreotype artist Charles V. Ward. After staying there for two years, he crossed the Andes into Peru, Bolivia, Colombia, and Panama, from which he returned home by boat. In 1852, when he last exhibited at the National Academy, he had a London address. He spent the rest of his life in his hometown of Bloomfield, perhaps working as a photographer rather than as a painter.

Stylistically, Ward's landscapes resemble both those of the Maine artist Charles Codman (1800-1842) and Thomas Cole (1801-1848). In fact, from the mid-nineteenth century until recently, his 1833 *Wolf in the Glen* (Catskill Falls) was misattributed to Cole, partly because of common stylistic features and partly because of a general resemblance to Cole's 1827 *Falls of the Kaaterskill.*[1] Similarly, Ward's *South Lake* in this exhibition is a different view of a spot in the Catskills that the older artist painted in 1825.[2]

Looking southwest toward its outlet, the view depicts an autumn sunrise on a small wilderness lake in the shadow of High Peak. This carefully framed, well balanced composition is full of romantic,

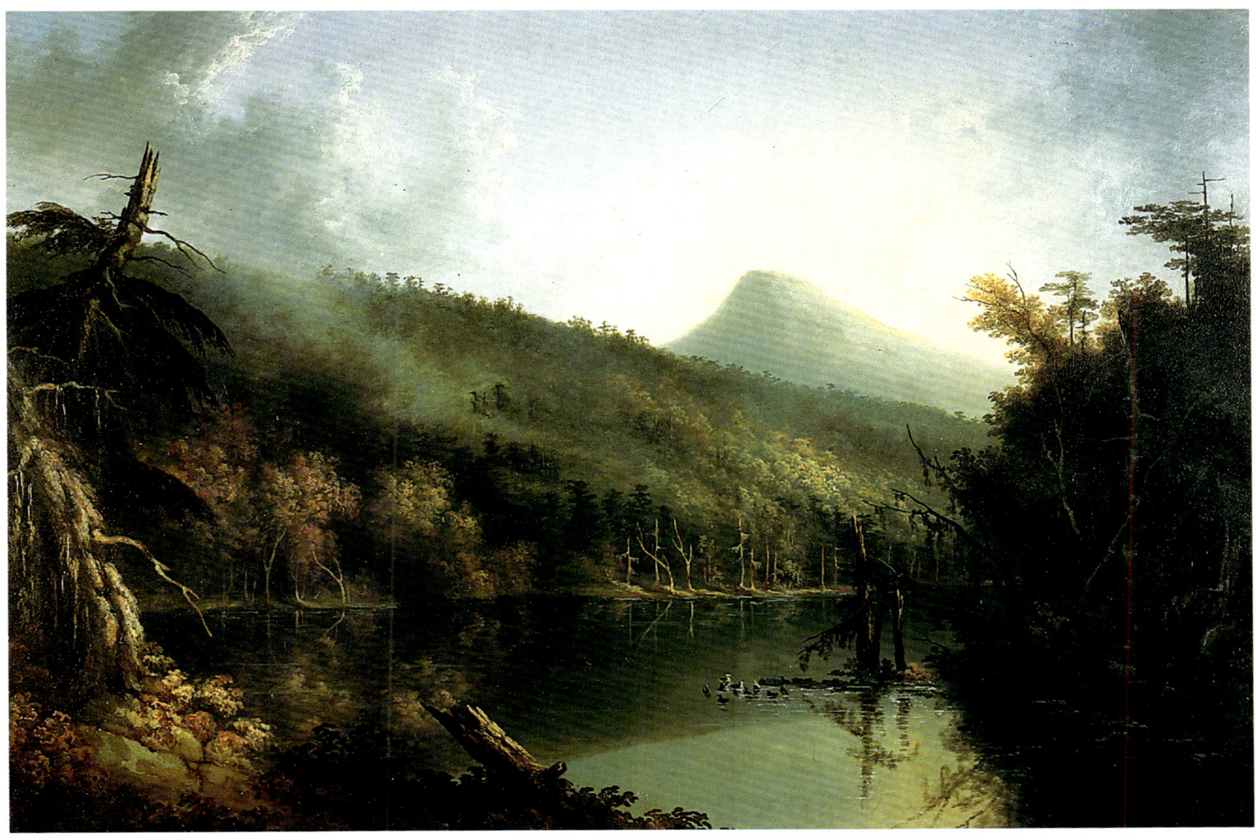

Jacob Caleb Ward, *South Lake*, ca. 1840. Oil on panel, 23" x 31"

picturesque details. These include dead trees, many of them standing in the water, a blasted, topless pine, and rising mist dissipating in the rays of the early morning sun which is still dramatically concealed behind the asymmetrical form of High Peak. The scale and loneliness of this scene are emphasized by the small forms of a group of swimming ducks. Ward's treatment differs in many ways from Cole's, which shows a foreground deer and many more dead trees. The trees had died as a result of the damming of Lake Creek, which feeds Kaaterskill Falls. The sawmill Silas Scribner built there provided the lumber for the Catskill Mountain House, which became a favorite haunt of artists and tourists.

Until recently this painting was one of a pair. Like all of Ward's known landscapes, it is unsigned. Several other of his works, clearly by the same hand, were the subject of contemporary engravings which allow them to be dated, and confirm Ward's authorship of the unsigned landscapes.

1. See Myers, pl. 18, fig. 9.
2. Myers, pl. 12.

Bibliography

Cowdrey, vol. 2. 379-80.

Folsom, Joseph F. "Jacob C. Ward — One of the Old-time Landscape Painters." Proceedings of the New Jersey Historical Society (1918): 83-93.

Manthorne, Katherine Emma. *Tropical Renaissance: North American Artists Exploring Latin America, 1839-1879.* Washington, D.C.: Smithsonian Institution Press, 1989. 40-42, 190.

Myers, Kenneth. *The Catskills: Painters, Writers and Tourists in the Mountains 1820-1895.* Yonkers, NY: The Hudson River Museum of Westchester, 1988. 48, 190.

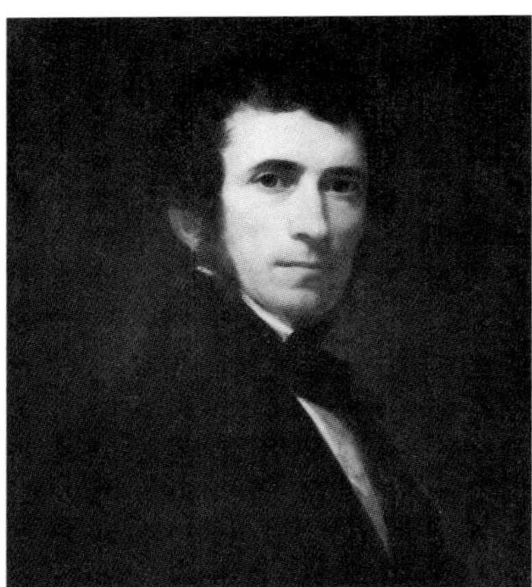

Asher B. Durand, *Self-portrait*, ca. 1835. Collection of the National Academy of Design, New York.

3. Asher Brown Durand

(born 1796, Jefferson Village [now Maplewood], New Jersey; died 1886, Maplewood, New Jersey)
Hurricane Mountain, 1848
Oil on canvas
18" x 24"
Signed lower right: A.B.D. Adirondacks 1848

Next to Thomas Cole (1801-1848), Asher Durand was the major figure in the Hudson River School. Tempering Cole's romanticism with a strong dose of realism, after the older man's death he became this school's leader for over a generation. Born in 1796, he was the eighth child of a New Jersey farmer, watchmaker, and silversmith. Starting in 1812 as an apprentice to the Newark engraver Peter Maverick (1780-1831), he was made a partner in 1817 and settled in New York. Over the next eighteen years he was one of America's best engravers, famous for his imposing masterpiece *Ariadne*, which he engraved in 1835 after the John Vanderlyn (1775-1852) painting he owned.

His heart, however, lay in painting rather than engraving. After trying a few landscapes in the 1820s and early 1830s, in 1833 he began to exhibit portraits. Fortunately, they attracted the attention of the perceptive collector Luman Reed (1785-1836),[1] whose patronage and encouragement enabled him to give up engraving for painting. Starting in 1837 Durand devoted himself exclusively to landscapes, establishing his reputation with the nine he exhibited at the National Academy of Design in 1839. After Reed's death, his partner Jonathan Sturges (1802-1874) became an important patron of Durand, lending him money for a trip to England and the Continent in 1840-1841 where he sketched and painted with John F. Kensett (1816-1872) and John W. Casilear (cat.11), among others.

Durand was an important figure in the art politics and organizations of his day. Elected president of the National Academy of Design in 1845, an organization he had helped establish nineteen years earlier, he was also a founder of the Century Association in 1847. By his retirement in 1861 he had become one of the grand old men of American painting whose landscapes were eagerly sought by collectors. In 1869 he moved to his birthplace in New Jersey where he painted his last picture in 1878, eight years before his death.

At first Durand flavored his American views with Arcadian, Elysian, or Utopian features that gave them a classicizing, European flavor. From as early as 1832, however, he had experimented with plein-air oil studies. Influenced by Ruskin, Constable, and modern German painting, after 1848 he turned increasingly to painstaking, direct observation of nature. His plein-air, close-up, landscape studies took two basic forms; one was the pencil or oil sketch, the other the more detailed oil study. Both provided a stock of detail he could later draw on to compose larger, more finished, but basically true-to-life works. In his nine "Letters on Landscape Painting" (1855), he not only spelled out his philosophy of art but also in effect advocated his own working procedures.[2] Among other things, they stressed the importance of painting directly out-of-doors,[3] choosing simple foreground objects emphasized by strong light and shade,[4] and doing "portraits" of rocks, trees, tree trunks, plants, and the like.[5]

Durand was the first native American landscape artist to become a great technician able to achieve total realism through complete mastery of detail. Moreover, he was the first Hudson River School painter to adhere closely to those details of landscape, atmosphere, and light that he had actually observed. This is not to say that he totally abandoned idealism and Claudian devices. He often did not. Even in the 1850s, and increasingly thereafter, many of his paintings have repoussoir framing elements and recede in successive, carefully spelled-out spatial planes into a bright, hazy, and glowing distance. In subject matter these works take two forms. The first, more idealized and essentially pastoral, ignores industrialization by selecting views of settled areas with their fields, domestic animals, and

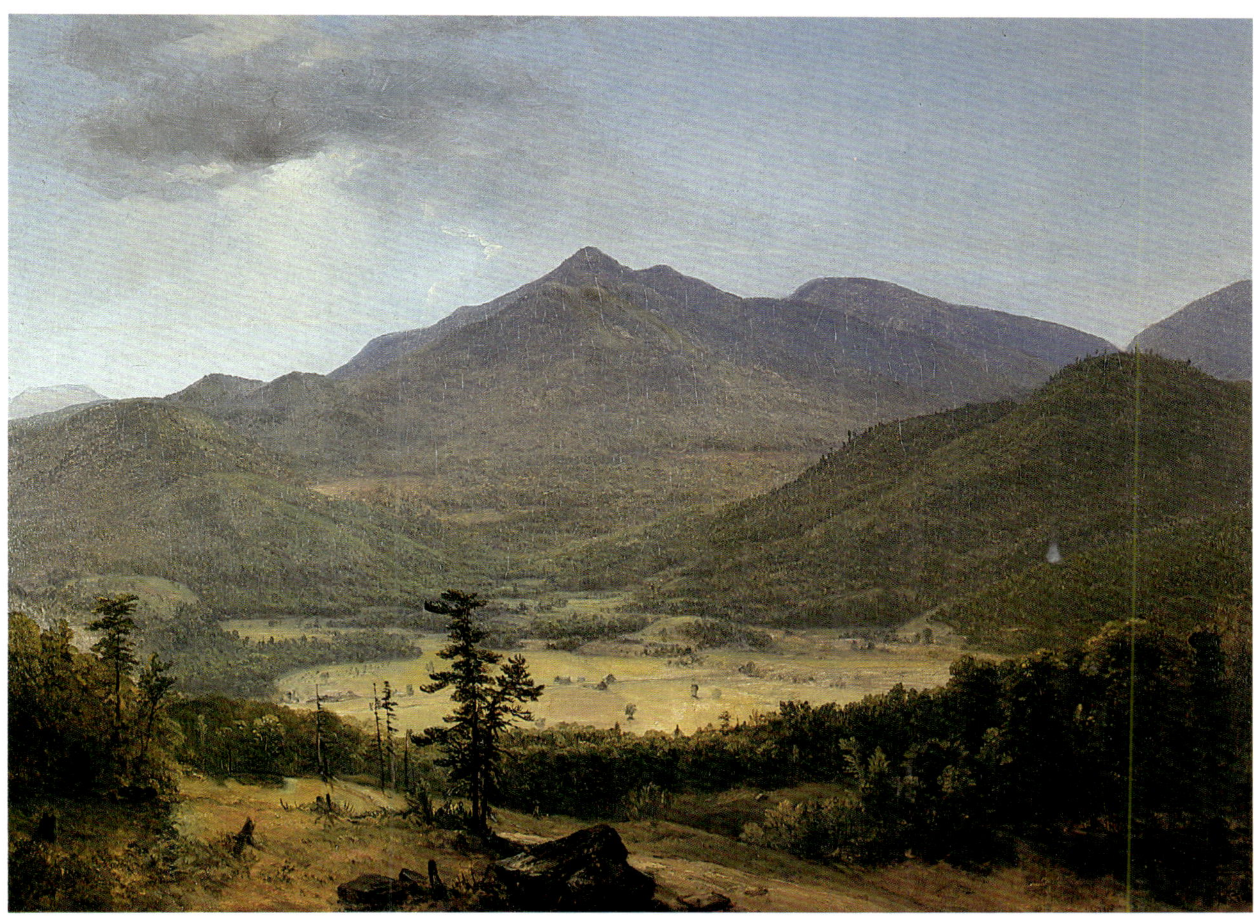

Asher Brown Durand, *Hurricane Mountain*, 1848. Oil on canvas, 18" x 24".

houses. The other, more factual, depicts the unsettled wilderness of the Catskills or Adirondacks, often without human or animal life. Even here, he prefers a tranquil mood very different from the grandiose sublimity favored by Church and Bierstadt (cat. 6). Influenced by transcendentalism he strove in all his work to express the spiritual essence of nature.

Durand made ten visits to the Adirondacks between 1837 and 1877. *Hurricane Mountain* was painted on the second of these trips in the summer of 1848, when he and Casilear (cat. 11) used nearby Elizabethtown as a base. This straightforward, objective view shows Hurricane Mountain on the Elizabethtown side as seen from a vantage point part way up the opposite hill. Unlike most Hudson River School landscapes, this painting forgoes framing details to give an open view down the partially cleared hillside dotted with stumps, just as Durand must have seen it. The viewer looks over a middle ground group of rocks and pines and a band of trees farther down to a partially cleared valley. Beyond, heavily wooded hills rise sharply at either side to frame the dominating, irregular contours of Hurricane Mountain. At the upper left a patch of grayish clouds hovering in the blue sky obscures the midmorning sun. Both the deftly handled atmospheric perspective and a rhythmic alternation of light and dark areas help establish a convincing sense of space. This painting's slightly painterly brushwork and its inscription telling where it was painted suggest that it is a finished plein-air study.[6] It surfaced only recently, before which it was known as a lost work that had been engraved in 1852, 1854, and 1868.[7] Currently the hillside shown in it is overgrown with trees but the valley below has been kept cleared. Now, as in 1848, not a house is visible.

1. Reed also recognized the talents of Cole and William Sidney Mount early in their careers and was their first patron. See Ella M. Foshay, "Luman Reed: New York Patron

and his Picture Gallery" in Ella M. Foshay, Wayne Craven, and Timothy Anglin Burgard, *Luman Reed's Picture Gallery* (New York: Harry N. Abrams, 1990), 19-71.

2. Asher B. Durand, "Letters on Landscape Painting," *The Crayon* III, 1 (1855): 1-2, 34-35, 66-67, 97-98, 145-46, 209-11, 273-75, 354-55; III, 2 (1855): 16-17.

3. Durand, I: 2

4. Durand, III: 66.

5. Durand, V: 145.

6. Other examples are *New England Hills* (inscribed: August 3, 1850), Christie's, no. 29, 12/6/85 and *Study of a Tree* (inscribed: Aug 14, 1859) in *For the Collector: Selected American Paintings of the 19th and 20th Centuries* (New York: Wunderlich and Co., 1986), no. 4, ill. p. 7. The former is about the same size (15 1/8" x 24") as the present work.

7. See Lawall (1978), p. 75 re cat. no. 128A, ill. in fig 64A.

Bibliography

Durand, John. *The Life and Times of A.B. Durand.* New York: Charles Scribner's Sons, 1894.

Lawall, David B. *A.B. Durand 1796-1886.* Montclair, NJ: Montclair Art Museum, 1971.

_____. *Asher Brown Durand: His Art and Art Theory in Relation to His Times.* New York: Garland Publishing, 1977.

_____. *Asher B. Durand: A Documentary Catalogue of the Narrative and Landscape Paintings.* New York: Garland Publishing, 1978.

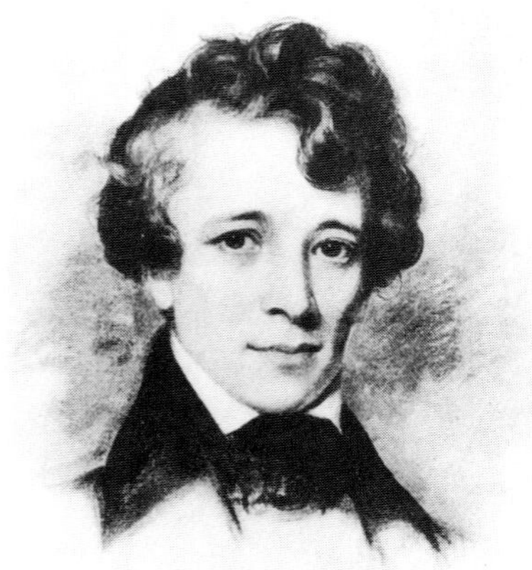

James R. Lambdin (1807-1889), *Portrait of Russell Smith,* 1838.

4. [William Thompson] Russell Smith

(born 1812, Glasgow, Scotland; died 1896, Weldon, Pennsylvania)
Llyn Bochlwyd, Wales,[1] 1851
Oil on paper
7 7/8" x 11 7/8"
Inscribed on back: Llyn Bachllyd, Russell Smith May 1851

5.

Llyn Dinas, Wales, 1851
Oil on paper
7 3/4" x 11 3/4"
Inscribed on back: Llyn Dinas with fine weather and East wind, Russell Smith July 1851

The Pennsylvania scenic designer and landscape painter Russell Smith had a long, successful career. Yet, like other Philadelphia-based artists who were affiliated only with the Pennsylvania Academy of the Fine Arts and did not exhibit at the National Academy of Design, he has been overshadowed by many of his New York-based contemporaries.

The third of seven siblings, he was born in Scotland to a maker of mathematical instruments, artists' tools, and general cutlery and a mother who had studied medicine. In 1819 his family emigrated to a farm outside of Pittsburgh, where three years later his father established a cutlery business and his mother was active as a midwife.

In 1827 Smith did his first scenery painting for a local thespian society and the following year began studying with Thomas Sully's pupil, the portrait and

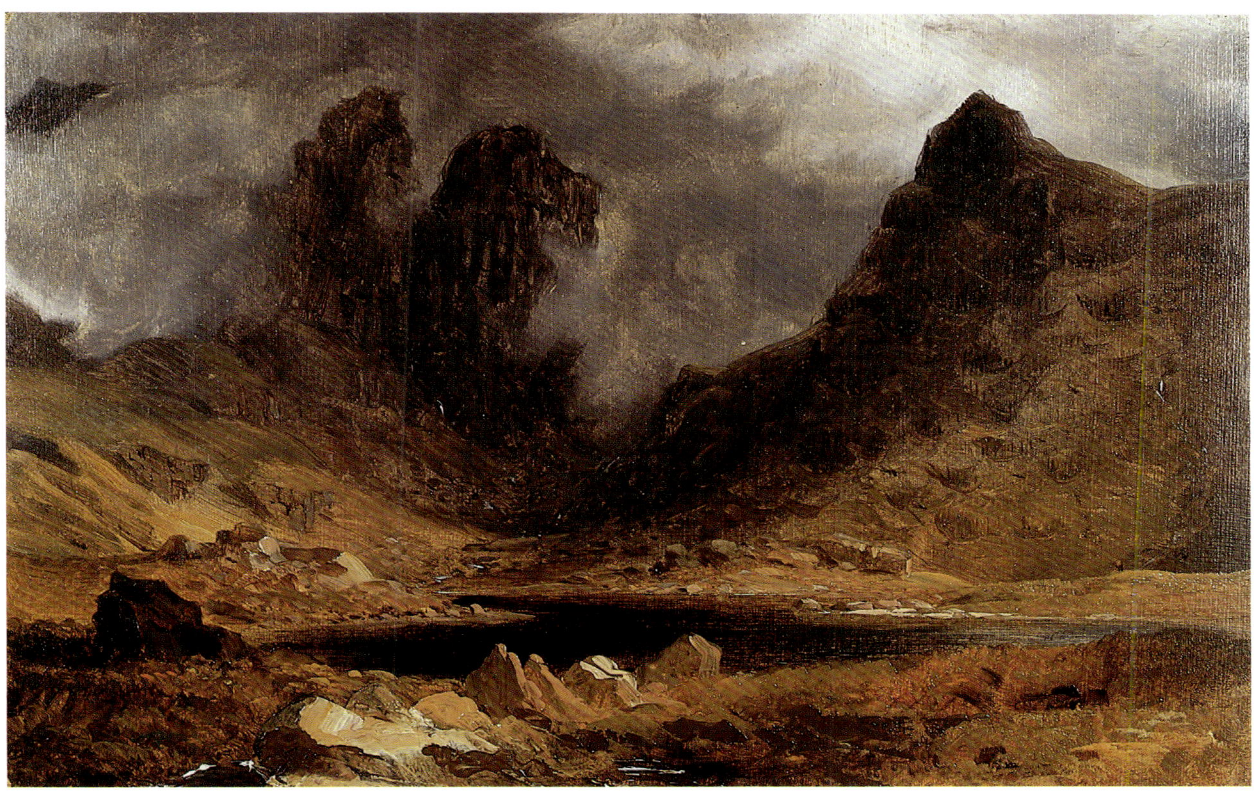

Russell Smith, *Llyn Bochlwyd, Wales*, 1851. Oil on paper, 7 7/8" x 11 7/8".

miniature artist James Reid Lambdin (1807-1889). He was painting portraits and landscapes on his own by 1831, but he continued to design and execute stage scenery and drop curtains for major theaters along the East Coast throughout his life. Unlike most scenic artists, he worked without assistants but still managed major commissions in Boston, Baltimore, Washington, D.C., and Philadelphia where he settled in 1835. In 1838 he married Mary Priscilla Wilson, who, along with their two children, was also an accomplished artist.[2]

By 1836 Smith began to concentrate on landscape painting. The Juniata and Susquehanna Rivers and the valleys of western Pennsylvania became his special province. He spent five summers during the 1840s in the White Mountains, and also painted in upper New York State and Virginia. During this period, he supplemented his income by doing illustrations for a number of eminent geologists, who used them to illustrate their lectures and record their expeditions.

By 1840 he was successful enough to design and build Rockhill, a country house constructed in classical revival style, in Branchtown outside of Philadelphia. From 1851 to 1852 he traveled with his wife and two children in Britain and on the Continent, summering in Wales, the Scottish highlands, Italy, Switzerland, and the Netherlands and wintering in London and Paris. While abroad, he received many commissions from friends and patrons for paintings to be executed later, and over the years the small oil sketches he painted then became the basis for many larger works.

In 1854, Smith sold Rockhill and built a Romanesque revival-style castle near Weldon, north of Philadelphia, where he spent the rest of his life, and which has been a local landmark ever since. Although he exhibited at several New York venues during his career, he was never lured into the circle of the National Academy of Design. His paintings were displayed at the Artists' Fund Society, the Apollo Association, and the American Art-Union, but his primary focus remained in Philadelphia. From 1834 to 1890, he exhibited regularly at the Pennsylvania Academy of the Fine Arts where he was an Academician, as well as at the 1876 Philadelphia Centennial Exposition.

Smith's palette lightened somewhat over the years. Yet he remained a conservative romantic realist who was concerned with mood and atmosphere in his

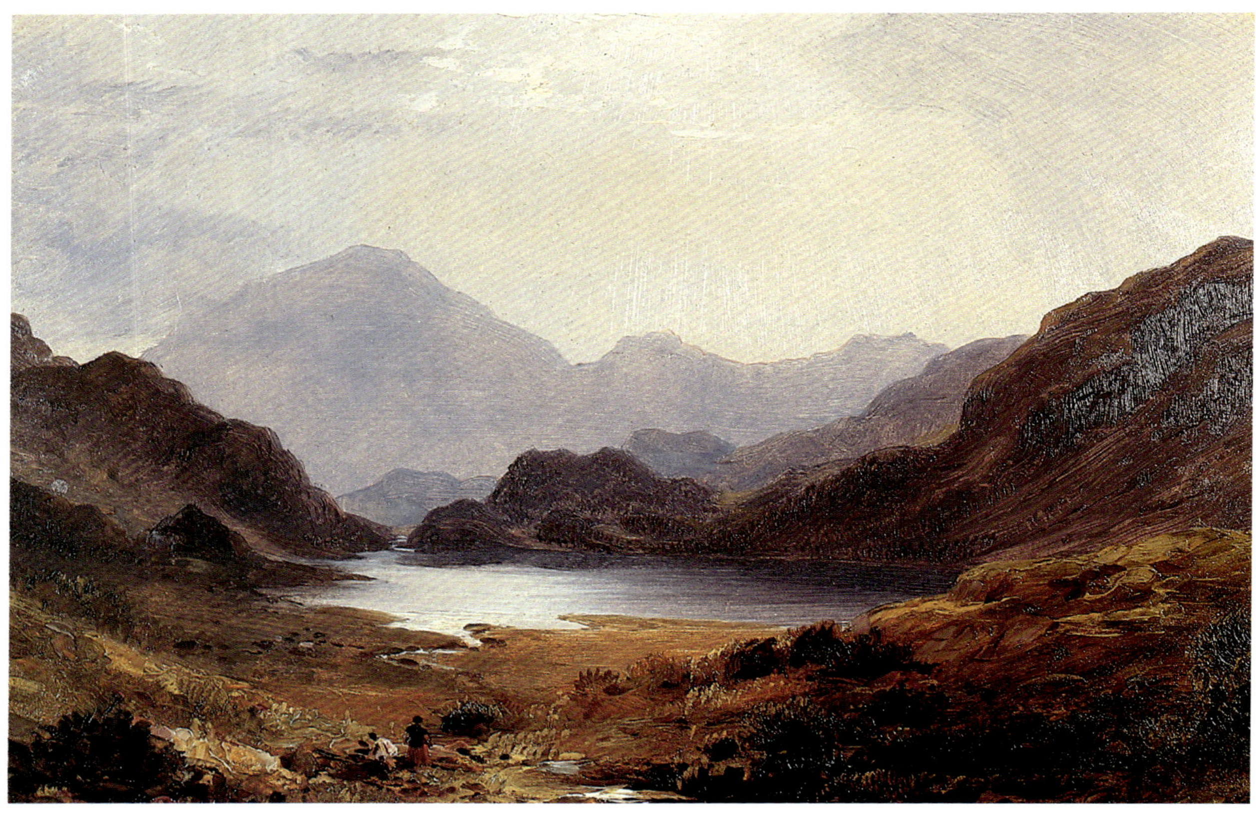

Russell Smith, *Llyn Dinas, Wales*, 1851. Oil on paper, 7 3/4" x 11 3/4".

generally intimate landscapes. Although most of his works are small, each is the product of numerous careful plein-air studies from nature. Of his small works he said: "The small landscapes were not painted for sale but because I felt in the mood for the particular subject taken up at the time; and they represent some arrangement of color, of light and shade or tone which something I had recently seen in nature suggested; they are therefore likely to be the best representations of my mind or character as a painter, and to be more original than subjects selected by and painted for another."[3]

The sources of his style are not clear, but in a number of ways his landscapes recall features found in works by English painters like the London-based John Constable and John Robert Cozens (1752-1799) and the Norwich School artists John Crome the Elder (1768-1821) and the Younger (1793-1842) and Joseph John Cotman (1814-1878), whose work Smith must have seen.

Llyn Dinas and *Llyn Bochlwyd* were painted in Wales, Smith's first painting stop abroad and one which probably reminded him of the Pennsylvania hills. Like all his pictures done in Britain and the Continent, they are small, finished oil sketches painted on paper. Often, they feature expansive vistas and wild, isolated, or picturesque spots, usually with a body of water. Cupped between steep hills on either side and mountains in the background in a panoramic composition that recedes in parallel planes, Llyn Dinas shines in the sun. In the foreground two small figures share the vista with the viewer. The dark water of Llyn Bochlwyd, on the other hand, is seen from ground level across grass and rocks. With cloud-shrouded peaks rising abruptly behind it, it seems like a stage setting waiting for an actor's entrance. Unlike his later work, these pictures are dominated by muted colors, mostly shades of brown, as they follow a European tradition as yet untouched by the lighter, brighter palette that ultimately grew out of plein-air painting. As befits sketches, their brushwork is freer here than in his large works. Both of these views draw on an established tradition of the sublime and the picturesque. Smith was delighted with the wild, rugged scenery of Wales, of which he wrote: "I saw some of the best scenery of Wales and got a much higher idea of its picturesqueness, beauty and grandeur than I had entertained before. . . . I was agreeably surprised and charmed with wonderful variety of form — so infinitely varied as we always see it in Nature."[4]

1. The artist correctly noted the place name Llyn Dinas (Lake Town) but his unfamiliarity with Welsh led him to understand Llyn Bochlwyd as "Llyn Bachllyd." Llyn Dinas is in northeast Wales, six miles south of Snowdon, the highest peak in Wales, and three miles east of Beddgelert. Llyn Bochlwyd, also in north Wales, is near Nant Ffancom Pass.

2. Mary Wilson Smith (active 1839-1852) was a flower and landscape painter who exhibited at the Pennsylvania Academy of the Fine Arts and the Apollo Association. Their son Xanthus Russell Smith (1839-1929) became a well-known marine, landscape, portrait, and historical painter, and their daughter Mary Smith (1842-1878) was a flower, animal, and landscape artist who exhibited at the Pennsylvania Academy of the Fine Arts between 1859 and 1869.

3. Lewis, 135.

4. Lewis, 157.

Bibliography

The First Exhibition of Fifty Years of Oil Paintings by Russell Smith 1812-1896 and His Son Xanthus Smith 1839-1929. Boston: Vose Galleries of Boston, 1979.

Russell Smith (1812-1896) Xanthus Smith (1839-1929): Pennsylvania Landscapes 1834-1892. Boston: Vose Galleries of Boston, n.d.

Russell Smith (1812-1896): Views of Europe 1851-1852 and Later. Boston: Vose Galleries of Boston, 1981.

Lewis, Virginia E. *Russell Smith: Romantic Realist.* Pittsburgh: University of Pittsburgh Press, 1956.

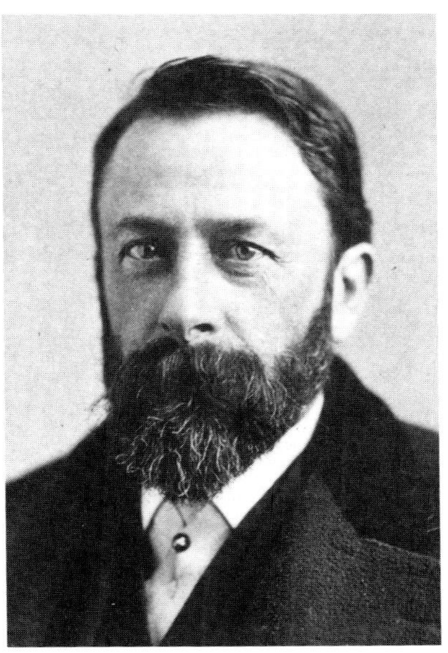

Napoleon Sarony, New York, *Albert Bierstadt.* Carte de visite. Collection of James P. Crain; photo courtesy of the Brooklyn Museum.

6. Albert Bierstadt

(born 1830, Solingen, Germany; died 1902, New York)
Ferns and Rocks on an Embankment, 1869
Oil on board
19 1/4" x 13 1/2"
Signed lower left: Bierstadt
Publication: Ferber, Linda and William H. Gerdts, *The New Path: Ruskin and the American Pre-Raphaelites* (Brooklyn: The Brooklyn Museum, 1985), no. 83, ill. p. 234.

Albert Bierstadt is the most dramatic example of the Hudson River School's fall from grace as a growing taste for figurative painting and Barbizon style landscape eclipsed it both in the eyes of the public and art critics. Between 1863 and 1895 he saw himself transformed from one of the most celebrated artists in the world to a bankrupt practitioner of a rejected, outmoded style of painting.

Born in 1830 in Solingen near Düsseldorf, Germany, he was the youngest of six children of a cooper who emigrated to the prosperous whaling town of New Bedford, Massachusetts, in 1832. Already a self-taught painter by 1850, he went to Düsseldorf to study three years later, thanks to the sponsorship of a local ship's captain. However, instead of registering at the Academy of Fine Arts, he became friends with the history, portrait, and landscape painter Emanuel

Gottlieb Leutze (1816-1868) and worked in landscapist Worthington Whittredge's studio (cat. 19), possibly receiving some instruction from both artists. After traveling and sketching in Germany, Switzerland, and Italy, he returned home in 1857 and the next year successfully exhibited at the National Academy of Design for the first of many times.

Initially, Bierstadt painted several excellent views of Europe and a number of New England, mostly the White Mountains of New Hampshire, based on trips made in 1857 and 1860 and largely executed between 1859 and 1870. It was his depictions of the then-exotic Wild West, however, that made him a celebrity. Between 1859 and 1881 he undertook six trips to the uncharted and unsettled wilds of Kansas, Nebraska, Wyoming, Colorado, Utah, California, Washington, Alaska, and Canada. His paintings of the West, especially large-scale works such as his 1863 *The Rocky Mountains — Lander's Peak,*[1] which sold for a record $25,000, were a great popular success, as were his many picturesque views of Yosemite in California. Some dissenting critics nonetheless found fault with his monumental landscapes' excessive size, sensationalism, and artificial, stagelike quality. Others carped at the artist's limited modulation of tone and color. All, however, had to concede his obviously fine draftsmanship and sense of composition and frequent mastery of light effects. In any case, his paintings romanticized and idealized an often dangerous and inhospitable West for Eastern drawing-room walls. Full of expansive grandeur, they became beckoning symbols for a young nation imbued with the idea of Manifest Destiny.

Ever sensitive to the importance of knowing the right people, Bierstadt was the first American artist to become an international social lion. In 1865 he built Malkasten, an enormous studio-house in Irvington-on-Hudson; the following year he married a beauty who proved to be a great social asset; and, traveling in grand style, he made a number of trips to Europe, where he was presented to Queen Victoria and awarded the Legion of Honor by Napoleon III.

Immensely energetic, he indefatigably promoted the sale of his work with an openness that alienated many artists and critics. Their hostility and a growing preference for French influenced styles led to a change in his fortunes. First, he had to rent Malkasten, which ultimately burned down in 1882. Next, in 1889, when he submitted his *The Last of the Buffalo*[2] to the Paris Exposition Universelle, the American selection committee, which included other Hudson River School artists, arbitrarily rejected it as too large and old-fashioned. On similar grounds, the selection committee of the 1893 Chicago World Columbian Exposition turned down his *The Landing of Columbus,*[3] for which he had made special trips to Spain, Italy, Portugal, and the West Indies in 1891. His wife, who had contracted tuberculosis in 1877, died in 1893. The next year he married Mary Hicks Stewart, daughter of a wealthy Brooklyn family and the widow of the millionaire banker David Stewart. Nonetheless, in 1895 he had to declare bankruptcy and sell his paintings to cover his debts. Until his death in 1902, he busied himself with a number of inventions and continued to paint sporadically.

In a sense, there are three Bierstadts. One is the painter of vast Western views, where lack of variation in surface textures, inconsistent handling of light, and problems with the integration of forms with their surroundings are sometimes a problem. Here both the influence of certain Düsseldorf artists and contemporary photography are most apparent.[4] The second is the painter of smaller, more intimate works. The third Bierstadt is a painter of quick, small oil sketches that served as studies for his larger paintings. In the 1960s a number of these were exhibited by a New York gallery, contributing to the "rediscovery" of Bierstadt by the public. His name again became respectable, probably because the simpler, more abstract works could be superficially related to twentieth-century modern art.[5]

Some of them, such as *Ferns and Rocks on an Embankment*, are quite finished and detailed. Although only a study, it is strongly composed and stands by itself. The brush strokes, even if small, are visible so that this is not highly precise, photographic realism. It is a closeup view of a rocky embankment with a variety of green vegetation, including Christmas ferns and Queen Anne's lace. The water below is accented with lily pads, rocks, and dead branches. It has been suggested[6] that this is one of several hundred preparatory studies Bierstadt did for his most important Eastern work, *The Emerald Pool,* 1869,[7] executed during his stay at Glen House in Pinkham Notch in the White Mountains.[8] Although it is consistent with certain passages in that painting, there is not a one-to-one correspondence between the two works.[9]

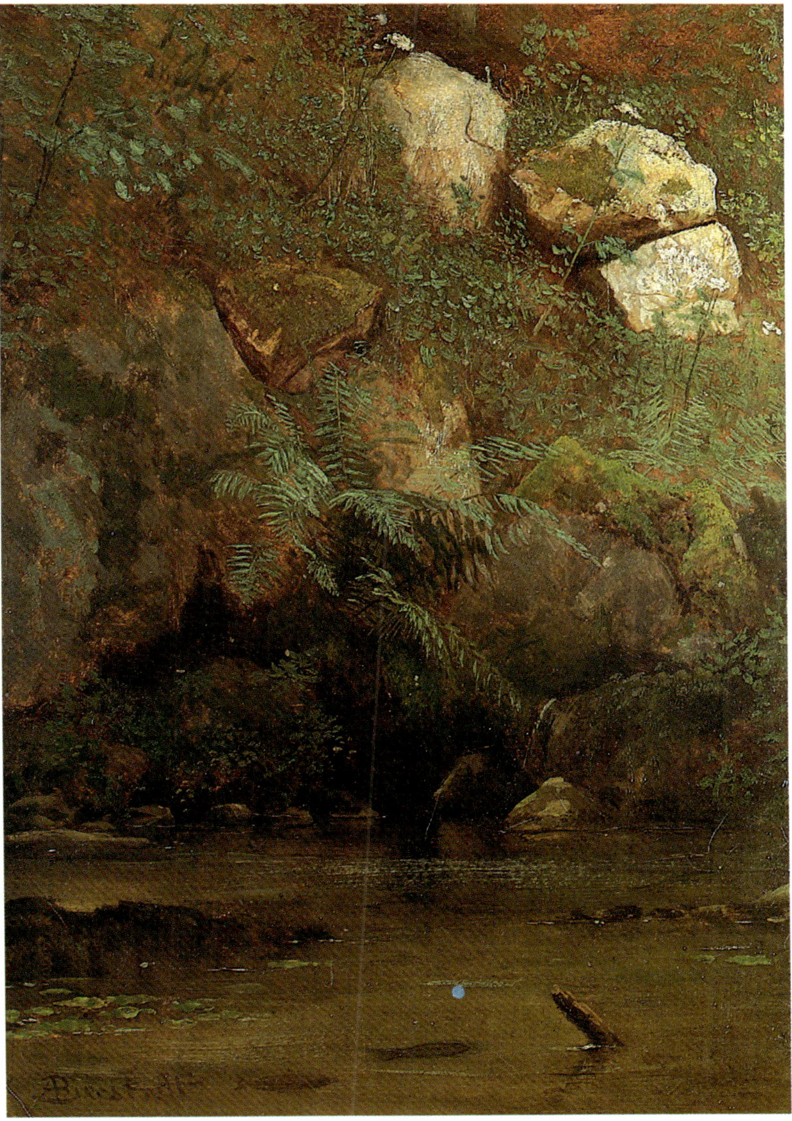

Albert Bierstadt, *Ferns and Rocks on an Embankment*, 1869. Oil on board, 19 1/4" x 13 1/2".

1. See Avery et al., 285-87 for a color illustration and discussion of this important work.

2. See Baigell, 64, pl. 25. Exercising his privilege as a previous medalist of the French Academy, Bierstadt sent the picture anyway. He sold it for $50,000 to Col. J.T. North, the nitrate king. The immediate stimulus for this painting, which also exists in several other versions, was the first official census of America's remaining buffalo, which had dwindled from an estimated twenty million in 1850 to 551 in 1889.

3. See Baigell, 68, pl. 27 for a color illustration of another version and a discussion of this work.

4. See Baigell, 28, and Lindquist-Cock.

5. See Florence Lewison, "The Uniqueness of Albert Bierstadt," *American Artist* 28 (September 1964): 28-33; *The Creative Core of Bierstadt: The Abstract Basis of His Art* (New York: Florence Lewison Gallery, 1963); and *Bierstadt, His Small Paintings* (New York: Florence Lewison Gallery, 1968).

6. See Ferber and Gerdts, 234-35.

7. See Hendricks, fig. 147. Currently this painting is owned by the Chrysler Museum, Norfolk, Virginia.

8. See Keyes, Campbell, et al., 80.

9. According to Nicholas Clark, curator of American Art at the Chrysler Museum, July 1990.

Bibliography

Anderson, Nancy K., and Linda S. Ferber. *Albert Bierstadt: Art & Enterprise*. New York: Hudson Hills Press, 1990.

Baigell, Matthew. *Albert Bierstadt*. New York: Watson-Guptill Publications, 1981.

Hendricks, Gordon. *Albert Bierstadt. Painter of the American West*. New York: Harry N. Abrams, 1973.

Lindquist-Cock, Elizabeth. "Stereoscopic Photography and the Western Paintings of Albert Bierstadt." *The Art Quarterly* 23 (Winter 1970): 360-78.

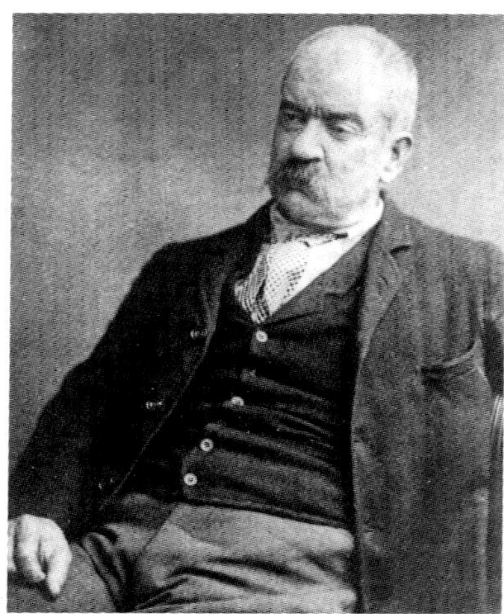

Homer Dodge Martin, 1890. Photographs of Artists I, Archives of American Art, Smithsonian Institution.

7. Homer Dodge Martin

(born 1836, Albany, New York; died 1897, St. Paul, Minnesota)
Waterfall, 1869
Oil on canvas
11 1/2" x 19 3/8"
Signed lower right: Homer Martin 69

In his day Homer Dodge Martin had a small, devoted following and was highly respected by critics, many of whom compared him with George Inness (1825-1894) and Alexander Helwig Wyant (cat. 8). Later, like Wyant, he gradually slipped into obscurity from which he is just beginning to emerge.

Born in Albany, New York, in 1836, he was the youngest of four children of a mild-mannered carpenter and a strong-willed, witty, but devoutly Methodist mother who loved literature and art. He started to draw as soon as he could hold a pencil and always preferred art to school, which he left at the age of thirteen. He failed successively as a carpenter's helper, a shopkeeper's clerk, and an architect's assistant, before the sculptor Erastus Dow Palmer (1817-1904) persuaded Martin's father to let the boy take up art as a career in 1852. His formal study of painting consisted of a two-week stint with the Hudson River School artist James McDougal Hart (1828-1901), whose approach he did not like. Thereafter essentially self-taught, he doggedly made himself into a significant artist although he never became an outstanding technician.

In 1861 he married Elizabeth Gilbert Davis. Later a literary critic and novelist, she was better educated than Martin and came from a wealthier background. This was not a surprising match, however, since Martin, who always loved poetry and music, was drawn to literary people rather than painters. Indeed, John La Farge (cat. 37), Winslow Homer (1836-1910), and James McNeill Whistler (1834-1903) were the only artists whom he found congenial.

Martin did not fit the stereotype of the sensitive and sophisticated artist. Whistler said about him: "Gentlemen, this is Homer Martin. He doesn't look as if he were, but he is."[1] Not only was he a very sloppy dresser whose face was ravaged by chronic eczema, but he also put others off by his behavior. A heavy drinker, a woman once asked him if he didn't drink too much beer. He replied succinctly, "Madame, there is not too much beer."[2] He was a good but unconventional talker whose biting wit polarized people and isolated him from most of his fellow artists. A moody individual, he was subject to long fallow periods. About one of these he said: "I cannot paint. I do not know where the impulse comes from, nor why it stays away. All I know is that when it comes I can do nothing but paint, and when it goes I can do nothing but dawdle."[3] Moreover, Martin had a congenital eye defect which made it difficult for him to draw vertical lines.

Nonetheless, between 1857 and 1874 he exhibited an impressive series of landscapes of the Catskills, White Mountains, Adirondacks, and Lake Ontario at the National Academy of Design. In 1862 he moved to New York City where he first painted in James David Smillie's (1833-1909) studio and thereafter in the Tenth Street Studio Building. He was elected as an Associate of the National Academy in 1860 and as a member of the Century Club six years later. He was made an Academician somewhat later, in 1874.

His thinly painted earlier work consisted of somewhat detailed and often panoramic views of wilderness mountains and lakes. By the 1870s, however, he began to abandon his strict Hudson River School style for a softer, looser Barbizon-style brushwork and more impasto. In 1876 he spent nine months in London, where he saw much of Whistler, and also visited France, in particular Barbizon, as well as Holland and Belgium. Thereafter, his brushwork loosened even more, developing into a unique brand of tonalist impressionism which was very different from the brighter, higher-keyed French Impressionism. In 1877, he was one of the few Academicians asked to join the more progressive Society of American Artists. In 1881 Martin again traveled to England, this time on com-

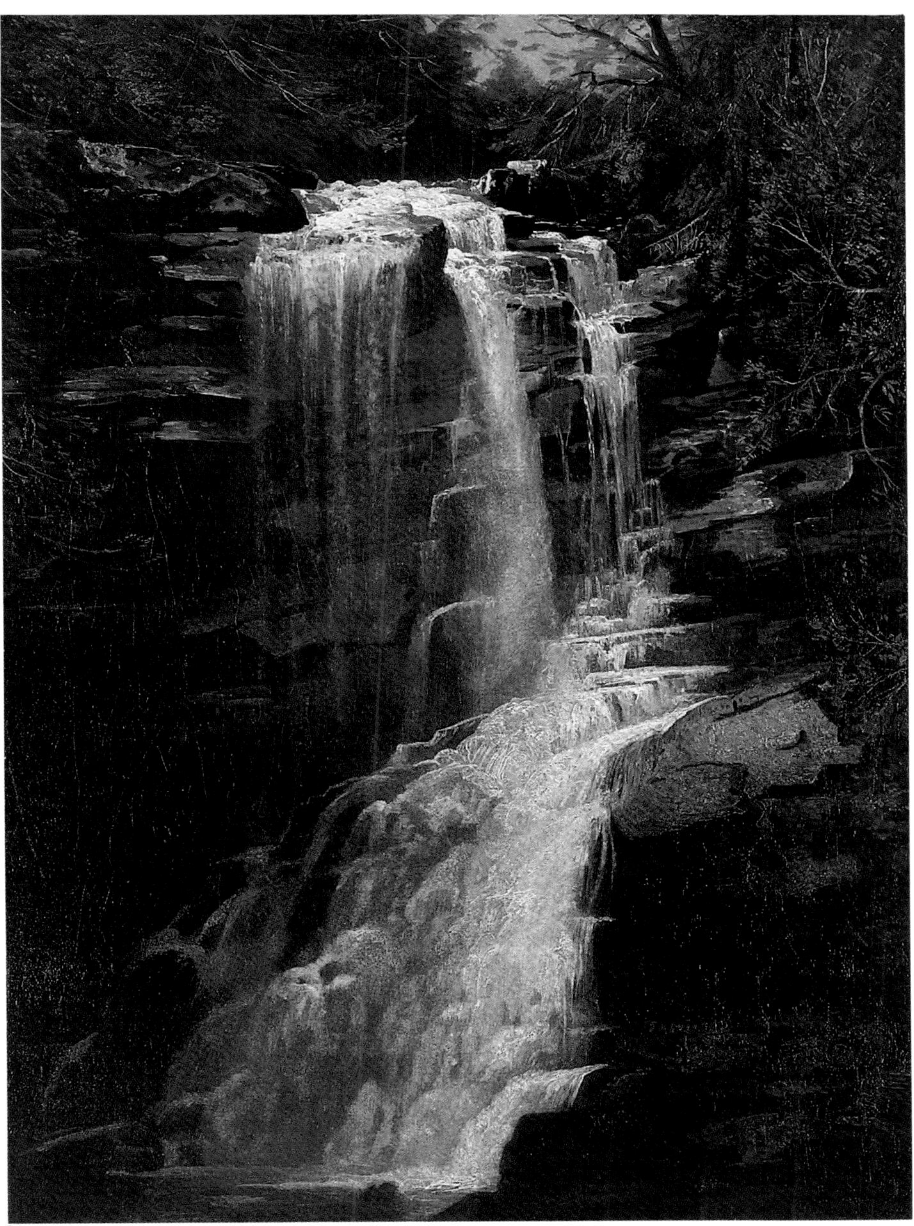

Homer Dodge Martin, *Waterfall*, 1869. Oil on canvas, 11 1/2" x 19 3/8".

mission for *Century Magazine*, and from 1882 to 1886 lived in Normandy. In 1893 he joined his wife, now in bad health, and his eldest son in St. Paul, Minnesota. His own health and vision had begun to fail three years earlier (he became blind in one eye and had a cataract in the other), but he resolutely continued to paint at a high level until 1895. Two years later he died of cancer.

Martin always endorsed the traditional scenic ideal of a landscape view and, unlike Inness and Wyant, never attempted isolated vignettes of nature. His subdued, often somber paintings, which tend to have simple, well balanced compositions devoid of people, usually convey a mood of calm isolation and loneliness. Although he avoided strong bright colors, he was a fine colorist with a sensitive control of tonal variations. The simplicity and unity of effect he strove for were the result of his working habits. He usually executed his paintings long after the rough sketches on which they were based. Made in the field, they became the basis of his studio paintings, to which he would add detail and color from memory.

Woodland waterfalls were a popular subject

among Hudson River School artists, and Martin was no exception. *Waterfall*, painted in his earlier style, is a head-on view of three streams of water. Starting near the top of the picture, they cascade down to join in a broad sheet that falls into a pool at the bottom. On both sides the yellowish green foliage stands out against the gray and brown rocks. This subdued work is in effect both a large finished study and an exercise in contrasts, juxtaposing the skillfully painted translucent white water and the dark rocks visible through it, and the diagonals of wet stone against the vertical and diagonal course of the waterfall.

It is not certain where Martin painted this scene since he often took several years to develop his summer sketches into finished oils and often continued to rework them even after they had been exhibited. However, since he spent every summer from 1864 to 1869 in the Adirondacks, it was probably painted there. He painted at least two other views of waterfalls. Both are also early efforts but they are more distant views.[4]

1. Mather, 7.
2. Mather, 9.
3. Mather, 21.
4. *Bash Bish Falls*, ill. p. 171 of Agnes Halsey Jones, *The Hudson River School* (Geneseo: Fine Arts Center of the State University College of New York at Geneseo, 1968) and *The Waterfalls*, ca. 1861, ill. p. 76 of Gwendolyn Owens and John Peters-Campbell, *Golden Day Silver Night: Perceptions of Nature in American Art 1850-1910* (Ithaca, NY: The Herbert F. Johnson Museum of Art, Cornell University, 1982).

Bibliography

Carroll, Dana H. *Fifty-eight Paintings by Homer D. Martin*. New York: Frederic Fairchild Sherman, 1913.

Martin, Elizabeth Gilbert. *Homer Martin: A Reminiscence*. New York: William Macbeth, 1904.

Mather, Frank Jewett, Jr. *Homer Martin: Poet in Landscape*. New York: Frederic Fairchild Sherman, 1912.

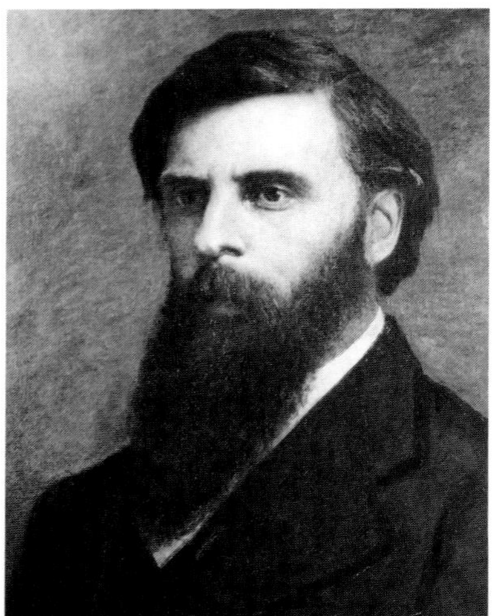

Alexander Helwig Wyant, *Self-portrait*, 1868. Collection of the National Academy of Design, New York; photo courtesy of the Frick Art Reference Library.

8. Alexander Helwig Wyant

(born 1836, Evans Creek, Ohio; died 1892, New York)
Sunset in Kentucky, ca. 1869
Oil on canvas
17" x 28"
Signed lower left: A.H. Wyant
Exhibition: *Recognizing the Painterly Tradition in American Art 1850-1920* (Buffalo, NY: Burchfield Center, Buffalo State University College, 1980), no. 71.

Alexander Helwig Wyant was gloomy, introspective, taciturn, and unsociable. In his landscapes, his dour personality took two very different but equally effective forms. Eschewing the human figure, both emphasized quiet views painted with a restricted, subtly varied palette dominated by somber greens and grays. The first was an expansive, detailed Hudson River School style. The second was a softer and more intimate tonalist impressionism, for many years the more popular of the two. Now, however, tides of critical fashion have shifted to let us enjoy both.

The son of an itinerant farmer and carpenter, Wyant grew up in rural Ohio outside of Cincinnati. An early interest in art had by 1857 led him from apprenticeship to a harness and saddle maker to sign painting. Paintings by George Inness (1825-1894) he had seen spurred him to visit the artist in New York. He was able to spend a year there in 1860 with the aid of Inness's patron, the Cincinnati collector Nicholas Longworth. After Longworth's death, he returned to New York in 1863 to study at the

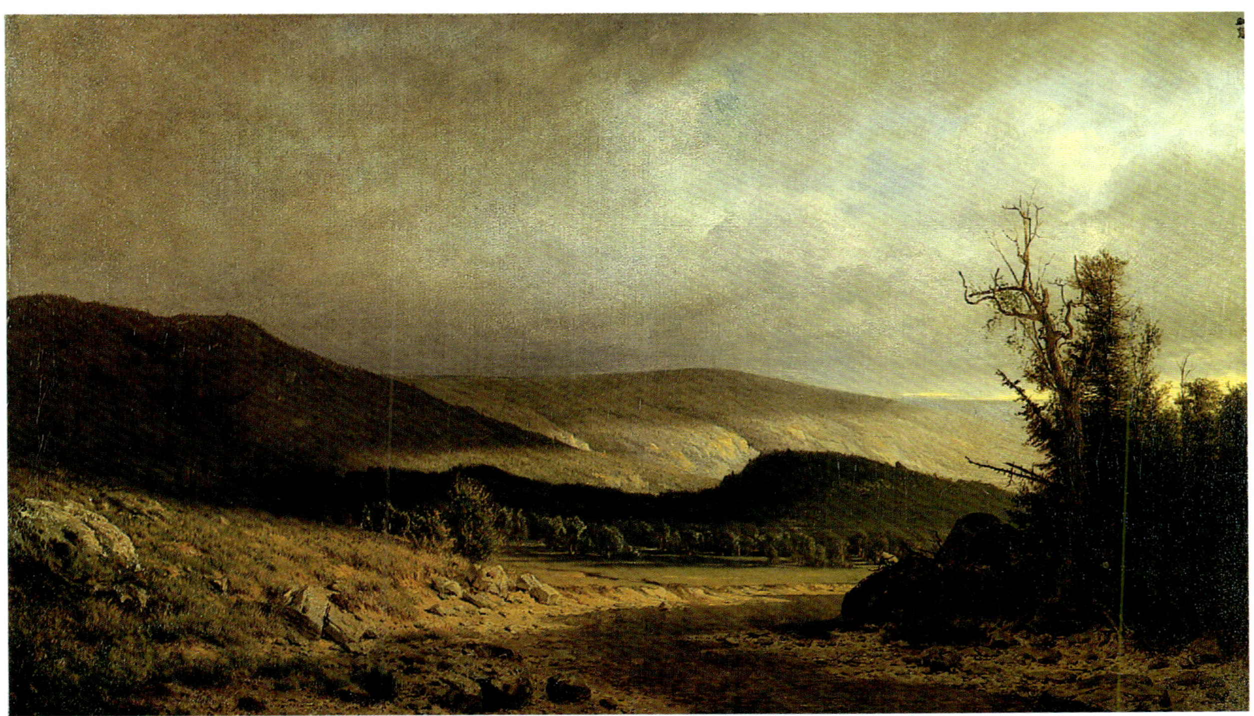

Alexander Helwig Wyant, *Sunset in Kentucky*, ca. 1869. Oil on canvas, 17" x 28".

National Academy of Design. Exposure to paintings by the Norwegian landscapist Hans Fredrik Gude (1825-1903) in an exhibition of work of contemporary Düsseldorf artists inspired him to study with Gude in Karlsruhe in 1865. Lonely and dissatisfied with his training, he left in 1866 for Paris and later, London, where he was exposed to J.M.W. Turner's (1775-1851) and John Constable's (1776-1857) free brushwork and treatment of atmospheric effects.

After settling again in New York in 1867, he rapidly became a major figure in the Hudson River School. Joining the American Society of Painters in Water Color, he advanced from Associate of the National Academy of Design in 1868 to Academician the following year and participated widely in major exhibitions. In typical Hudson River School fashion, he traveled extensively in search of subject matter as he sketched in upstate New York, New Jersey, Connecticut, West Virginia, Ohio, Pennsylvania, Tennessee, and Kentucky. From the mid-1870s he spent his summers in the small, picturesque Adirondack community of Keene Valley that later became an artists' colony.

From 1869 to 1872 Wyant was plagued by poor health, and in 1873 fate dealt him a blow that would have destroyed most other painters' careers. Accompanying a government expedition to Arizona and New Mexico, he suffered a stroke that partially paralyzed his right side. Undeterred, he learned to paint with his left hand under the portrait, genre, and landscape painter Joseph Oriel Eaton (1829-1875). In 1874 he began to take on some students, the best known of whom was Bruce Crane (cat. 26), in 1878 joined the progressive Society of American Artists, and in 1880 married his pupil, the watercolorist Arabella Locke (d. 1919). By 1886, however, he suffered from increasing pain. The creeping paralysis that had affected his entire right side now made him move with an awkward, crablike sideways shuffle. He died in his New York studio in 1892.

It is harder than it should be to get a complete picture of Wyant's Hudson River School style because his widow destroyed many of his earlier pictures in the belief that they were inferior to his later works. It is clear, however, that after 1865 they began to soften slightly and show a more sensitive appreciation of light. After his stroke in 1873 he painted on a smaller scale and, starting in the late 1870s, his work increasingly fell under the influence of Inness and Barbizon painters such as Théodore Rousseau (1813-1867), Charles Daubigny (1817-1878), and Camille Corot (1796-1875). As his brushwork began to loosen, he used more impasto and relied less on detail, his forms becoming less distinct. This was not a result of painting with his left hand. Rather, it reflected a conscious stylistic choice because, even as late as 1881, he was able to paint landscapes with considerable detail.[1]

Wyant's abandonment of his previously successful style surprised collectors and critics. In 1879 G.W. Sheldon wrote concerning his recent work: "It [is] almost incredible that their maker ever studied at Düsseldorf. The works of no painter in this country are farther away from the aims and results of the Düsseldorf school."[2] His landscapes became progressively more intimate, indistinct, and simplified; like Inness and Martin (cats. 7 and 20), he forged an individualized tonal impressionism very different from French Impressionism. Characteristically, he emphasized the sky in his later works, the titles of which tend to refer to weather and atmospheric conditions rather than the locales they ostensibly depict. His increasing dependence on memory rather than studies produced more and more pictures executed according to formula. As a result, Wyant is more often successful in his early style than as a tonal impressionist.

Like most of his early works, *Sunset in Kentucky* is a slightly dry, meticulously and thinly painted open panorama. It is less somber than usual, however, as it captures the tranquil poetry of a deserted valley flooded with the light of the late afternoon sun. Standing at the edge of a stream the viewer looks across a bare, sunlit green valley that effectively contrasts with the rhythmic alternation of the distant sloping hills covered with horizontal bands of light and shadow. It is not dated. Assuming that it bears its original title, it is known that Wyant spent a good deal of time in Frankfort, Kentucky, in the 1850s or 1860s[3] and painted views of Kentucky in 1863 and 1866.[4] However, the sensitive treatment of light and atmosphere suggest a date in the late 1860s.

1. See *An Old Clearing*, 1881, ill. p. 417 of Spassky et al., and *A Summer Haunt*, 1881, Sotheby's, 5/31/84, no. 105.

2. Sheldon, 165.

3. See Olpin (1971), 79, 85.

4. He painted *Falls of the Ohio at Louisville* in 1863, no. 55, ill. on p. 87 of Louis Hawes, *The American Scene 1820-1900* (Bloomington: Indiana University Art Museum, 1970), and *Tennessee* in 1866, ill. pp. 320-21 of Avery et al.

Bibliography

Clark, Eliot. *Alexander Wyant*. New York: Privately published, 1916.

_____. *Sixty Paintings by Alexander Helwig Wyant*. New York: Privately published, 1920.

Olpin, Robert S. *Alexander Helwig Wyant, 1836-1892*. Salt Lake City: Utah University Museum of Fine Arts, University of Utah, 1968.

_____. *Alexander Helwig Wyant (1836-1892), American Landscape Painter: An Investigation of His Life and Fame and a Critical Analysis of His Work with a Catalogue Raisonné of Wyant Paintings*. Ph.D. Dissertation. Boston University, 1971. Ann Arbor, MI: University Microfilms, 1978.

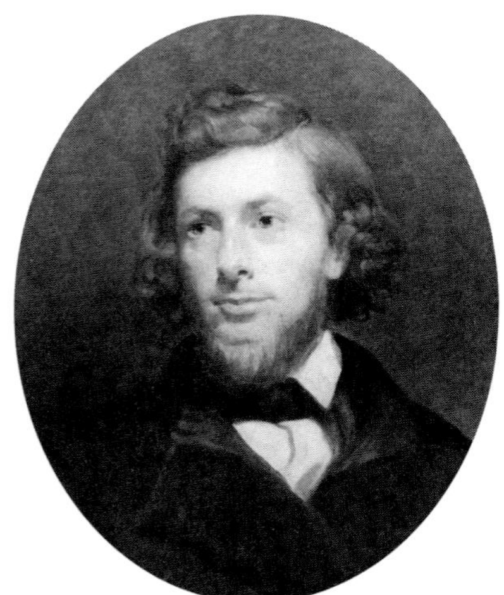

Charles Loring Elliott (1812-1868), *Portrait of Jasper Francis Cropsey*, 1845. Collection of the National Academy of Design, New York.

9. Jasper Francis Cropsey

(born 1823, Rossville, Staten Island, New York; died 1900, Hastings-on-Hudson, New York)
Adam and Eve Mountains, 1874
Oil on canvas
12" x 20"
Signed lower center: J.F. Cropsey 1874

Jasper Francis Cropsey became a virtual specialist in autumn landscapes. These colorful, often garish works were very popular until the decline of the Hudson River School, but his repetitious approach ultimately led him in the direction of banality and cliché.[1]

The son of a Staten Island farmer, he was artistically precocious and virtually self-taught. As a child he liked to sketch and became interested in architecture. A prize-winning model house he submitted to the fair of the Mechanics Institute of the City of New York in 1837, at the age of fourteen, led to a five-year apprenticeship with a New York architect, who encouraged him to paint watercolors. The figurative artists William Tylee Ranney (1813-1857), William Sidney Mount (1807-1869), and Henry Inman (1802-1846) supported his interest in oil painting, and by 1843 Cropsey had exhibited for the first of many times at the National Academy of Design, where he became an Associate at the age of twenty-one and an Academician seven years later. From 1847 to 1849 he went abroad to paint well-received views of England, Scotland, Wales, Italy, and France. After establishing a studio in New York, he consolidated his reputation with landscapes based on summer trips to scenic spots in New York, Vermont,

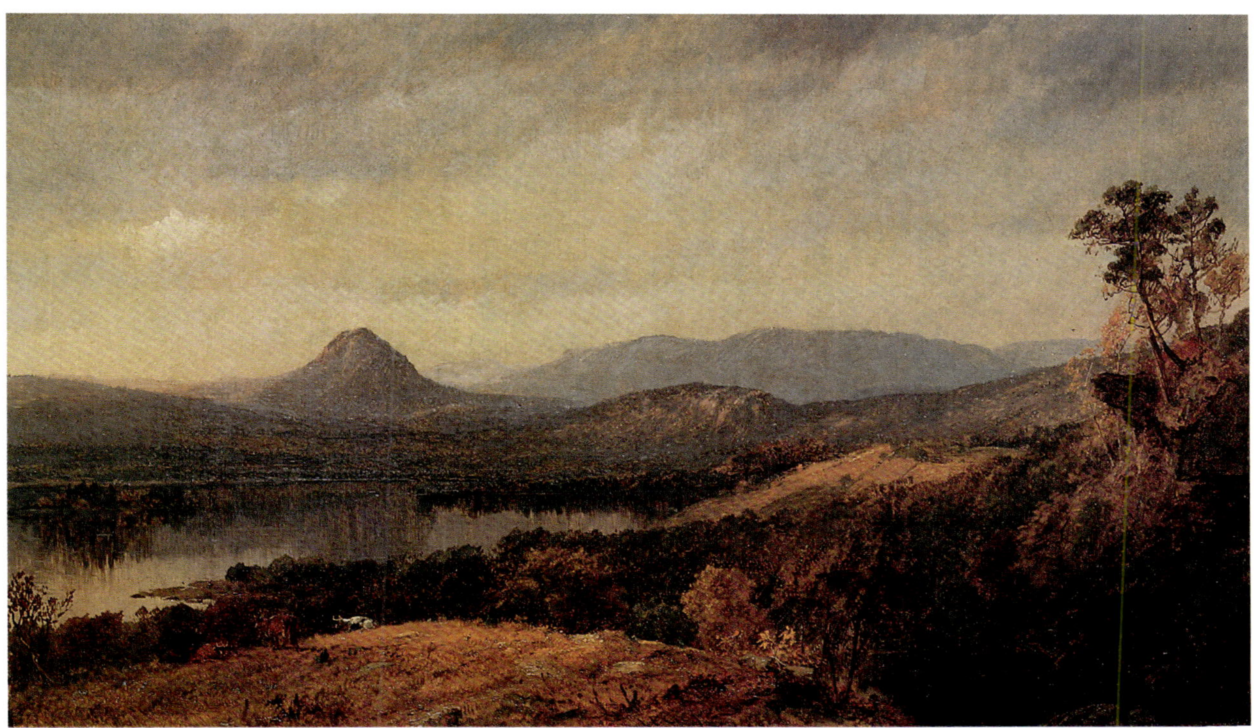

Jasper Francis Cropsey, *Adam and Eve Mountains*, 1874. Oil on canvas, 12" x 20".

and New Hampshire.

From 1856 to 1863 he lived in England, where he successfully exhibited American views. Because of its riotous autumn colors, his monumental *Autumn On the Hudson*, 1860, occasioned criticism and disbelief among some of its viewers who were unfamiliar with American autumns.[2] After solidly establishing himself with a number of large-scale, dramatic panoramas, he turned increasingly in the mid-1860s to smaller, often more lyrical works. By 1866 he was so successful that he was able to design and start building Aladdin,[3] a twenty-nine room Victorian mansion and studio near Greenwood and Wickham Lakes in Warwick, New York. He used it as his summer residence beginning in 1869.

His last great success was at the 1876 Philadelphia Centennial Exposition. By 1884, his detailed, somewhat romantic Hudson River School paintings had become so unfashionable that he had to sell Aladdin at auction and move into a much smaller house at Hastings-on-Hudson. Afterwards, Hudson Valley views dominated his work, and from 1885 watercolors became the most important part of his oeuvre. His always variable health began to deteriorate in 1890, but he continued to paint until not long before his death in 1900.

Most of Cropsey's best work was done between 1850 and 1875. Although his earlier paintings, especially those of the 1840s and 1850s, draw on the drama, active brushwork, and brilliant colors of Cole, Cropsey is the more realistic of the two. In his large landscapes he tended to follow the models set by Cole, Durand (cat. 3), and Church, but often made them less grandiose by using a lower, more intimate point of view. By the mid-1860s, his paintings grew more placid and bucolic and he became increasingly concerned with sunrise, sunset, and atmospheric effects. During the 1870s, he tried to adapt his style to that of John F. Kensett (1816-1872) and Sanford R. Gifford (1823-1880) in a number of works that come close to Luminism.

Throughout his career, he tried with varying success to reconcile conflicting desires for topographical accuracy and idealization of his subject matter. Not only did he never modify the Hudson River School compositional schemes he inherited, but eventually he made them into personal clichés that became vehicles for increasingly harsh and mechanical repetitions of previously used motifs. The unevenness of his work in his last twenty-five years has been attributed to chronic ill health. Even then, however, he occasionally managed to execute superior paintings.

Adam and Eve Mountains was painted while Cropsey was living at Aladdin, which served as a base for many of his sketching excursions. The twin peaks rising from the valley below were visible from his studio-mansion, the front lawn of which looked west across the valley to the southern Catskills.[4] This panoramic autumn view is unusual in his oeuvre as it is not the kind of garish, hotly colored autumn scene, often embellished with a brilliant, colorful sunset, that collectors past and present have preferred. Instead, understated and subdued, it shows an overcast late autumn afternoon. Despite occasional foreground accents of yellow and red with touches of light green, the overall tonality is dark brown and green. The purplish blue haze that slightly obscures the contours of the background hills and mountains and soft, thick, gray and white clouds suggests impending rain. On a gentle, grassy foreground elevation, a group of cows adds a characteristic bucolic touch to this prospect of apparently undefiled wilderness.

1. It is not hard to trace Cropsey's development since most of his paintings are dated. In a sample of 106, 101 (95.3%) were dated. Eighty-two (77.4%) were autumn scenes.

2. See Talbot (1970), 33-34.

3. From 1863 on Cropsey executed occasional architectural commissions. Most notably, beginning in 1876 he designed the passenger stations of the Gilbert Elevated Railway, which ran over 6th Avenue in New York City. It was torn down in 1939.

4. See *Mt. Adam and Eve*, 1872, Talbot (1970), no. 58, ill. p. 98. For other views of these two peaks see *Mounts Adam and Eve, Warwick, New York*, no. 10 and ill. in *American Painting* (New York: Davis and Long, 1976) and *Mounts Adam and Eve – Haymaking*, 1883, ill. p. 24 of Bruce W. Chambers, *American Paintings* III (New York: Berry-Hill Galleries, 1985). Cropsey painted at least two other autumn views of Wickham Lake. See *Wickham Lake*, 1876, ill. p. 13 of *A Century of American Painting 1850-1950* (New York: Gerold Wunderlich, 1988) and *Sugarloaf from Wickham Lake*, 1876, no. 4 and ill. in William H. Gerdts and Penelope L. Schmidt, *The Civilization of a Landscape – American Paintings, 1848-1930* (New York: David Findlay, Jr., 1983).

Bibliography

Bermingham, Peter. *Jasper F. Cropsey: A Retrospective View of America's Painter of Autumn*. College Park: University of Maryland Art Gallery, 1968.

Foshay, Ella M., Barbara Finney, and Mishoe Brennecke. *Jasper F. Cropsey: Artist and Architect*. New York: The New York Historical Society, 1987.

Rebora, Carrie and Annette Blaugrund. *Jasper Cropsey Watercolors*. New York: National Academy of Design, n.d.

Talbot, William S. *Jasper F. Cropsey 1823-1900*. Washington, D.C.: Smithsonian Institution Press, 1970.

_____. *Jasper F. Cropsey, 1823-1900*. New York: Garland Publishing, 1977.

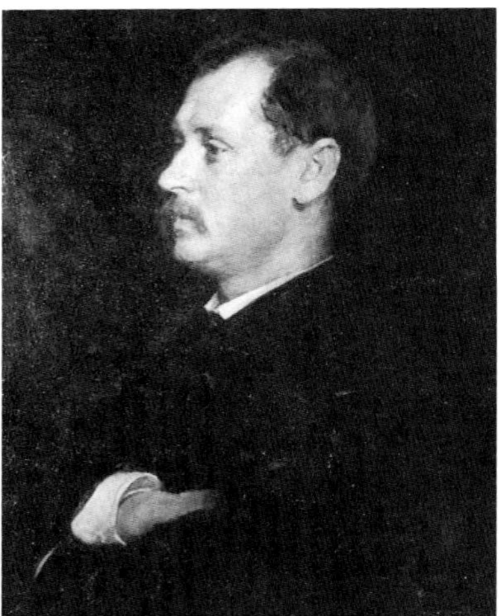

Irwin Benoni, *Hugh Bolton Jones*, 1881. Collection of the National Academy of Design, New York.

10. Hugh Bolton Jones

(born 1848, Baltimore; died 1927, New York)
Evening on the Severn, 1874
Oil on canvas
13 1/2" x 21 1/2"
Signed lower left: H. Bolton Jones 1874
Inscribed on back: Evening on the Severn, H. Bolton Jones, N.Y., Feb. 20-30, 1874

The landscape painter Hugh Bolton Jones has yet to regain his former popularity. Like Wyant (cat. 8), he started as a Hudson River School artist only to surrender to the siren song of Barbizon, which did not serve him as well.

He was born in Baltimore, where he grew up and first attended the Maryland Institute of Design. In 1865 he studied briefly in New York City with the Baltimore-born landscape painter Horace Wolcott Robbins (1842-1904), a pupil of the Hudson River School landscapist James McDougal Hart (1828-1901), and in 1867 started exhibiting at the National Academy of Design. From 1866 to 1867 he painted well-received Hudson River School-style views of spots in Maryland, West Virginia, and north to the Berkshires. Despite his success, in 1876 with his younger brother, the painter Francis Coates Jones (1857-1932), he decided to go to France to the artists' colony of Pont-Aven,[1] perhaps under the influence of his Baltimore friend Thomas Hovenden (1840-1895), who had preceded him there. It was doubtless at Pont-Aven that he received his first concentrated taste of the Barbizon aesthetic.

After painting in France, North Africa, and Spain

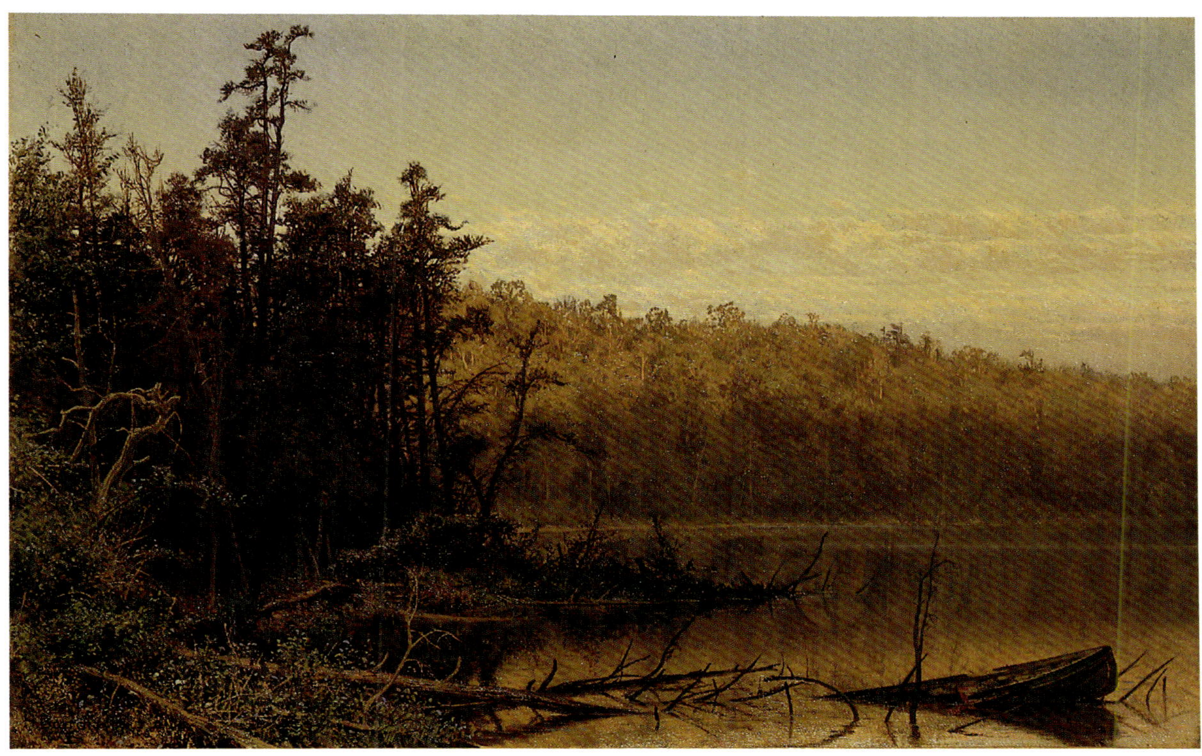

Hugh Bolton Jones, *Evening on the Severn*, 1874. Oil on canvas, 13 1/2" x 21 1/2".

and exhibiting at the Royal Academy in London in 1880, he returned to New York in 1881 to share a studio with his brother and very rapidly established himself. He joined the Society of American Artists and the American Watercolor Society and, in 1883, became an Academician at the National Academy of Design. Working in an increasingly Barbizon-influenced style, he had a long, successful career painting landscapes of Maryland, New Jersey, New York, Connecticut, and Massachusetts, for which he won many prizes and medals.[2]

Throughout his career there were two constants in Jones's treatment of landscapes. They are usually spring or summer views, and three-quarters of them contain a body of water, most often a stream winding its way through meadows and bordered by bushes and small trees.[3] Before he left for France, he painted in a detailed but soft and subdued Hudson River School manner used to greatest advantage in Luminist scenes of dawn or twilight. During his stay in Pont-Aven his palette lightened, and he started using impasto and strong contrasts of light and shadow. Although he did landscapes with genre and architectural features there, after his return to the United States he painted only pure landscapes. During the 1880s and 1890s he adopted a cooler, brighter palette and continued to reduce detail and simplify forms, returning to his earlier interest in light and color as a function of season and time of day. By the turn of the century, he had arrived at what amounted to a formula — a simply composed, very green view of a stream meandering through fields — and the quality of his work began to drop.[4]

In the 1860s and early 1870s, Jones often painted woodland views of the Maryland countryside with titles indicating not only the location but also the season or time of day. *Evening on the Severn* is one of these.[5] It is a variation on the favorite Hudson River School theme of twilight in the wilderness. Here, however, the artist declines to exploit obvious vivid aerial color to study the unspectacular effects of the setting sun in early twilight. In this subdued, sensitive, and meticulously rendered scene, the viewer looks across the Severn as if standing on the near shore, which is already in shadow. Four dead trees, one erect and grotesquely twisted, the others lying in the water along with a half-sunken rowboat, provide a note of solitude and abandonment. Across the river, which serves as a mirror for sky and trees, the bluish haze of mist beginning to form over the water softens the dense woods of the far shore as the sun baths them with its soft, warm, but attenuated light. Above them, seen against a pale blue sky, a modest band of cumulus clouds takes on a slightly pinkish tinge. Within the compositional framework of three planes, there is a rhythmic progression to larger and larger masses and from light to dark to light again. Additional variety and balance accrue from the repeated opposition of vertical and horizontal elements. Although the artist has restricted his palette to a relatively narrow range of green and brown, it is rich in subtle variations.

1. For a discussion of Pont-Aven, see Sellin.

2. At the Paris Expositions Universelles of 1889 and 1900; Chicago Columbian Exposition, 1893; Society of American Artists, 1902; St. Louis Louisiana Purchase Exposition, 1904; and San Francisco Panama-Pacific Exposition, 1915.

3. In a sample of forty-two paintings, thirty-one (73.8%) contain water, and of these, twenty-eight (90.3%) feature a stream, river, or brook. Thirty-seven (88.1%) are spring and summer scenes.

4. It is hard to be precise about this phase of Jones's career since, in the sample studied, less than a third (twelve, or 28.6%) were dated and these fall between 1868 and 1894.

5. The year before Jones painted a morning view of the Severn River. See Sona Johnston, *American Masterpieces from the Peabody Art Collection* (Baltimore: The Peabody Institute of the John Hopkins University, 1983), no. 17, and illustrated. The Severn is a tidal river that empties into the Chesapeake Bay at Annapolis.

Bibliography

Johnson, Sona K. *American Paintings 1850-1900 from the Collection of the Baltimore Museum of Art.* Baltimore: The Baltimore Museum of Art, 1983. 95-97.

Zeizel, Joan Hanson. "Hugh Bolton Jones. American Landscape Painter." Master's Thesis. The George Washington University, 1972.

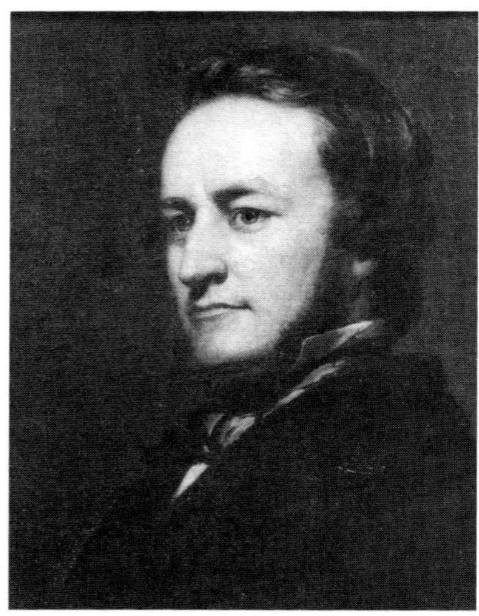

Thomas P. Rossiter (1818-1871), *John William Casilear,* 1843. Collection of the National Academy of Design, New York; photo courtesy of the Frick Art Reference Library.

11. John William Casilear

(born 1811, New York; died 1893, Saratoga Springs, New York)
Rocky Mountain Landscape, ca. 1875
Oil on canvas
18" x 30"
Signed lower left: JWC

It is easy to overlook the understated landscapes of John William Casilear. Yet, in his Luminist paintings of mountain lakes, where his calm, refined and lyrical art is at its best, he is the equal of his better known friends Asher B. Durand (cat. 3) and John F. Kensett (1816-1872).

Born in New York City in 1811, he was first apprenticed to the engraver Peter Maverick (1780-1831). After the engraver's death in 1831 he continued his training under Maverick's pupil Durand, who encouraged and taught him to paint. Durand was so impressed with Casilear's ability that he bought one of his first efforts in 1831. The next year Casilear and his brother started a successful banknote engraving business which was part of a chain of companies that became the American Bank Note Company, still an important firm today. In 1833 he submitted his first engravings for exhibition at the National Academy of Design, but with each year thereafter gradually included more and more paintings among his entries. After 1836, when he was made an Associate, he submitted only paintings.

Along with Durand, Kensett, a friend from his

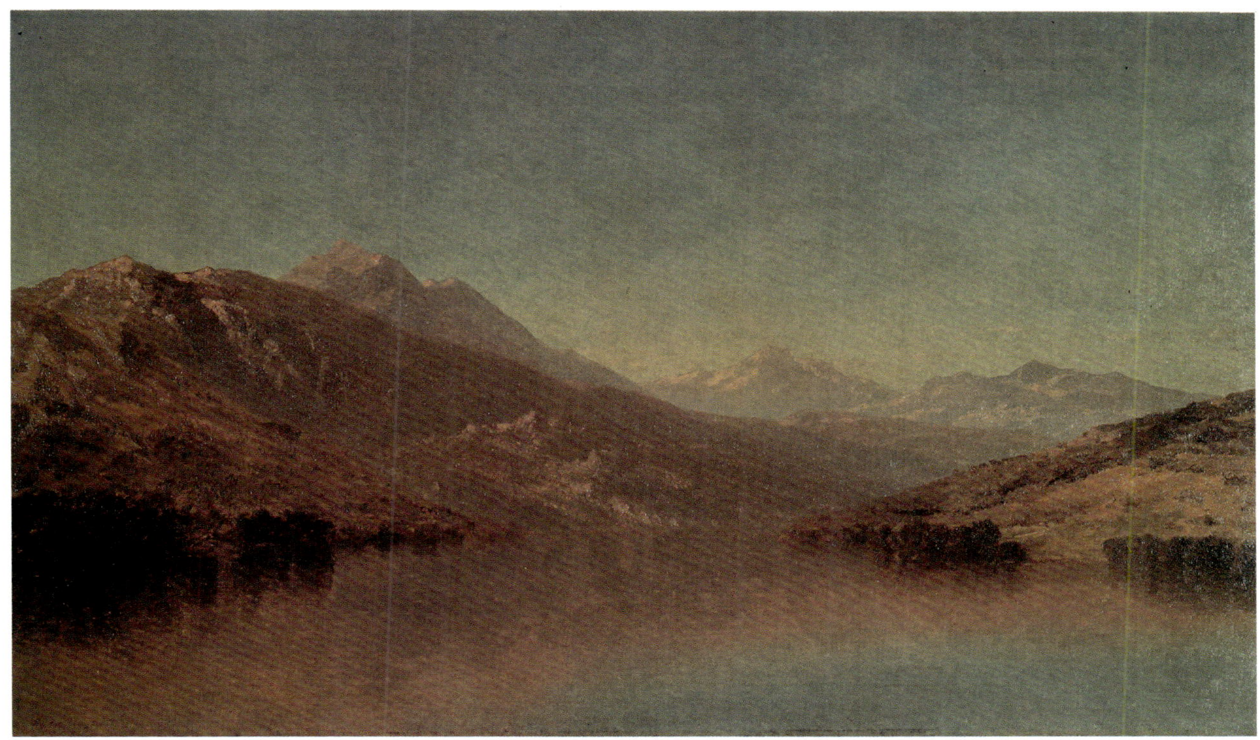

John William Casilear, *Rocky Mountain Landscape*, ca. 1875. Oil on canvas, 18" x 30".

apprenticeship days, and Thomas P. Rossiter (1818-1871) he embarked on his first trip abroad in 1840, which took him to London, Italy, France, Switzerland, and through the Rhineland. While in Europe, Durand introduced him to the work of Claude Lorrain (1600-1682) and he and Kensett made many trips together to sketch the countryside and study paintings. He returned to New York in 1843 to paint the landscapes that made him an Academician in 1852. The sole support of a widowed mother and a number of siblings, he had to continue engraving longer than either Durand or Kensett, but was finally able to paint full-time in 1854, when he opened a studio with Kensett and the portrait and genre painter Louis Lang (1814-1893). Three years later, he made a second and last trip to Europe that took him to Paris, the Savoy, Switzerland, and England. On his return in 1858 he took a studio in the Tenth Street Studio Building, which he occupied for the rest of his life. Thereafter, he continued his established pattern of sketching scenes in rural areas of New York and New Hampshire which he would transform into paintings during the winter. During his long career Casilear exhibited at the Apollo Association (1838-1843), the American Art-Union (1845-1852), the Pennsylvania Academy of the Fine Arts (1855-1865), and the National Academy of Design (1833-1893). He continuted to paint until not long before his death in 1893.[1]

Casilear's work, like that of Durand and Kensett, bears the imprint of his training as an engraver in its mastery of detail and gradation of tone. Claudian influences, which were widespread among Hudson River School artists, include framing devices such as rocks and groups of trees, a progression from darker to lighter tones, a well-defined development of spatial planes, and luminous, light-filled backgrounds. Contemporary critics were impressed with his paintings. Henry Tuckerman referred to their careful finish, fastidious choice of subject matter, correctness of detail, delicacy, elegance, and grace.[2] Casilear's fellow artist and friend Benjamin Champney (cat. 58) wrote even more perceptively: "His pictures are more delicate and refined than either Cole's or Durand's but not so vigorous. There is not a lack of sweetness of tone and pervading color, for his skies are luminous, and his distances tender and melting. . . . In fact, there is a poetic pastoral charm in all his work, pleasing to the eye, and possessing beautiful qualities. He can only be reproached with a want of vigorous treatment."[3] For subject matter he went to Long Island, the Hudson and

Genesee valleys, and the Catskills, Adirondacks, and White Mountains. His two trips to Switzerland provided material for an 1850 painting and a series of works from 1850 to 1877. Wherever he painted, lake scenes were his forte.

Rocky Mountain Landscape is both an exception and a puzzle. Instead of framing this view with his usually elaborate and exquisitely rendered foreground detail, he shows the morning mist rising over the calm, hazy surface of a lake which stretches back between sloping hills to rugged mountains in the distance. The nearer hills are covered with grass and dotted with trees, but the treeless peaks in the distance indicate the high altitude of this primeval lake. Casilear's handling of this scene is reminiscent of Sanford R. Gifford, especially in the thinly applied but painterly brush strokes, the warm, soft colors, and the treatment of the mist glowing in the sun.[4] Casilear usually favored a less dense and luminous but more silvery aerial haze in his lake scenes. It is not certain where this view was painted. Its topography does not resemble any of his depictions of Eastern United States or Swiss lakes. However, he sketched in Colorado between late June and mid-September of 1873[5] and exhibited a painting entitled *Rocky Mountains, from Greely* (sic) at the National Academy of Design in 1881.[6] Consequently, it may be a Rocky Mountain lake. Dating is complicated by Casilear's habit of painting views long after he had sketched them.[7]

1. See Cowdrey, vol. 2, 58-59; Falk (1988), 45; and Naylor, 146-48.
2. Tuckerman, 521-22.
3. Champney, 144.
4. See Ila Weiss, *Poetic Landscape: The Art and Experience of Sanford R. Gifford* (Newark: University of Delaware Press, 1987), pls. 14, 26, 32.
5. See Patricia Trenton and Peter H. Hassrick, *The Rocky Montains: A Vision for Artists in the Nineteenth Century* (Norman: University of Oklahoma Press, 1983), 221, 225, pls. 81, 82.
6. See Naylor, 147.
7. Thus, he painted an 1850 view of Switzerland eight years after his first trip there (see Cowdrey, vol. 2, 59) and an 1866 view of Lake Leman also at least eight years after his second trip to Switzerland.

Bibliography

Ball, Barbara Buff. "John W. Casilear (1811-1893)." In Avery et al. 141-44.

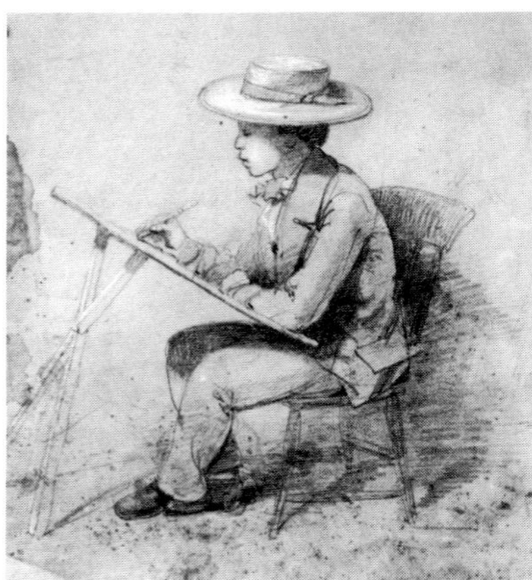

James McNeill Whistler (1834-1903), *Portrait of John Ross Key*, 1854. Crayon and white chalk on brown paper. Photo courtesy of the Freer Gallery of Art, Smithsonian Institution, Washington, D.C., 08.200.

12. John Ross Key

(born 1832, Hagerstown, Maryland; died 1920, Baltimore)
Cherry Mountain, New Hampshire, ca. 1875
Oil on canvas
16" x 30"
Signed lower right: John R. Key

The landscapist John Ross Key was all but forgotten until a few years ago, when it turned out that a large panoramic view of the bombardment of Fort Sumter in the Civil War long attributed to Albert Bierstadt (cat. 6) was actually by Key.[1] Born shortly after his father's death in 1837, he was brought up in Georgetown in the District of Columbia until the age of seven by his grandfather, Francis Scott Key, author of "The Star-Spangled Banner." When he was fourteen, he had to go to work to help support his mother and in the 1850s became a draftsman and mapmaker for the U.S. Coastal Survey, where he worked alongside James McNeill Whistler (1834-1903). In 1859 he traveled to California in this capacity for the advance party of the Lander Expedition, which Bierstadt also accompanied. While serving as a mapmaker and topographical engineer for the Confederacy during the Civil War, he began painting in his spare time and by 1865 had become competent enough with landscapes to devote himself full-time to art.

After the war he painted in western Maryland and Cincinnati and rented a New York studio for a short time. Partly because of family connections he went West in 1869, painting extensively in California and exhibiting in San Francisco before returning to the East

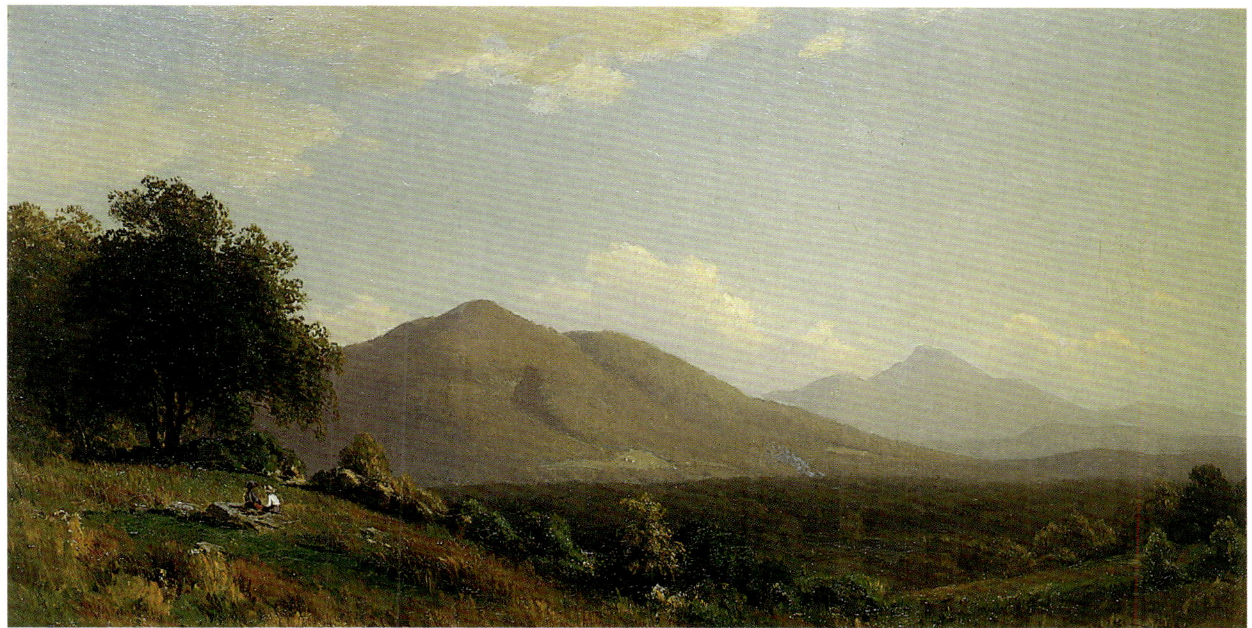

John Ross Key, *Cherry Mountain, New Hampshire,* ca. 1875. Oil on canvas, 16" x 30".

the next year. Except for a study trip abroad from 1873 to 1874, spent mostly in Munich and Paris, he mainly painted views of Massachusetts and New Hampshire while based in Boston in the 1870s. In 1876 his painting of the Golden Gate won a prize at the Philadelphia Centennial Exposition. In 1881 he opened an interior decorating business in Chicago, which significantly limited the time he could devote to painting. In 1893, however, he was awarded a commission to paint views of the buildings and grounds of the Chicago Columbian Exposition, which encouraged him to undertake exposition paintings in Omaha, Buffalo (1901), and St. Louis (1904). After he moved to Washington about 1903, he often painted views of patriotic monuments until his death in Baltimore in 1920.

Like many other artists of the period, Key's early work reflects the traditional Hudson River School style, but his brushwork loosened considerably by the turn of the century under the influence of Barbizon painting. Many of his best earlier works are open horizontal panoramas with relatively low horizons. Many show a strong Luminist preoccupation with light and atmosphere. Some use a very precise linear style while others, such as the present example, which shows the influence of his sojourn in France, rely on softer brushwork. From the vantage point of a grassy, wooded knoll, this sunny late summer or early autumn view of Cherry Mountain[2] gives a panorama of a forested valley and mountain range surmounted by a blue sky and soft white cumulus clouds. Alternating light and dark masses anchor a foreground characterized by strong forms and accents of color. The small figures of two little boys establish the grand scale of the vista that opens out before them. Key achieves a sensitive atmospheric perspective through the use of warm colors and the skillful manipulation of purple, blue, and green tones which infuse the haze enveloping the valley and mountains.

1. Alfred C. Harrison, Jr., "Bierstadt's Bombardment of Fort Sumter Reattributed," *Antiques* 129.2 (1986): 416-22.

2. Cherry Mountain is in the White Mountains of northern New Hampshire. For a more expansive version of this view from farther back on the hill with the same two boys and grazing cows, see John I. H. Baur, *Regions of the Land: American Landscape Painting of the 19th and 20th Centuries* (New York: Kennedy Galleries, 1985), no. 13. Key painted at least four other views of Cherry Mountain. See Campbell and Blaine, 106.

Bibliography

Gerdts (1990), vol. 2. 55-56; vol. 3. 243.

Glassie, Henry H. and Andrew J. Cosentino. *The Capital Image: Painters in Washington, 1800-1915.* Washington, D.C.: Smithsonian Institution Press, 1983. 112, 113-115, 264.

Harrison, Alfred C., Jr. "John Ross Key." *Art of California* 2.2. (1988): 21-27.

_____."Bierstadt's Bombardment of Fort Sumter Reattributed." *Antiques* 129. 2 (1986): 416-22.

Hughes. 306-07.

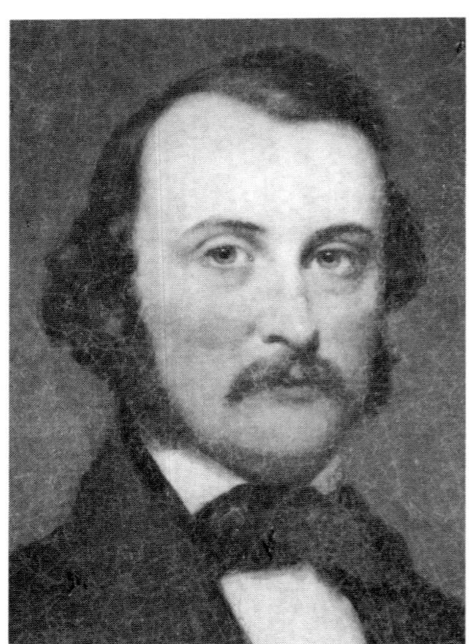

G. A. Baker, Jr. (1821-1880), *Albert Fitch Bellows*, 1859. Collection of the National Academy of Design, New York; photo courtesy of the Frick Art Reference Library.

13. Albert Fitch Bellows

(born 1829, Milford, Massachusetts; died 1883, Auburndale, Massachusetts)
Picnic in a Summer Landscape, 1879
Oil on canvas
10 1/4" x 16 1/8"
Signed lower right: A.F.B. '79

In his day Alfred Fitch Bellows was a well-known, successful artist. Now he is a relatively obscure figure, familiar mainly to specialists and for the most part relegated to smaller museums and private collections. Yet, his deftly painted genre paintings and unassuming, poetic landscapes merit more attention.

Born in 1829 in Massachusetts, he came from an old New England family. Bellows showed an early interest in art, but it is not clear how he got his first training. At age sixteen he moved to Boston, where he presumably learned the rudiments of painting while working for several architects. From 1850 to 1856 he served as principal of the New England School of Design. He then studied oil painting for three years in Paris and at the Royal Academy in Antwerp in order to become a specialist in genre painting. On his return to the United States in 1859, he established himself as a genre painter in New York, where he was made an Associate of the National Academy of Design and became an Academician in 1861.

His involvement in watercolor, which started in 1865, coincided with an interest in landscape that came to dominate his work. This new interest led him two years later to spend sixteen months in England where he became acquainted with the leading watercolor artists. During that time, he was elected as an honorary member of the Royal Belgian Society of Painters in Water Colors. Bellows was also an early member of the American Society of Painters in Water Color, which published his *Water Color Painting: Some Facts and Authorities in Relation to Its Durability* in 1868.

In 1872 a fire destroyed his studio in Boston, where he had moved after his return to the United States, along with much of his work. This loss gave him the opportunity to move to New York, where he devoted himself to watercolor and etching during the remaining years of his life.

From the mid-1860s, Bellows concentrated on landscapes rather than the genre paintings with children that had previously dominated his output. His landscapes, however, typically contain figures and often have genre features. Like all of his work, they show high finish, concern for detail, and a sound instinct for composition. They are generally quiet, harmonious scenes of rural life and often portray picturesque old houses and mills. In his watercolors, he could make loose landscape studies but was better known for his highly finished, detailed exhibition pieces.

Picnic in a Summer Landscape shows several women and children picnicking or berry picking at the edge of the woods on a bright, sunny day. Although the mother and child in the right foreground and another pair at the back have colorful garments, they are small and incidental. The real subject of this painting is the depiction of light and shade played out in the dramatic contrast of intensely sunlit open areas and deep shade under the trees peppered by light filtering through the leaves. The interplay of light and shade can also be appreciated more subtly in meticulously rendered details such as leaves, tree trunks, logs, and moss-covered rocks.

Bibliography

Benjamin. Ch. 2.

Clement and Hutton, vol 1. 52.

D.A.B. 167.

Sheldon. 158-59.

Tuckerman. 486, 566.

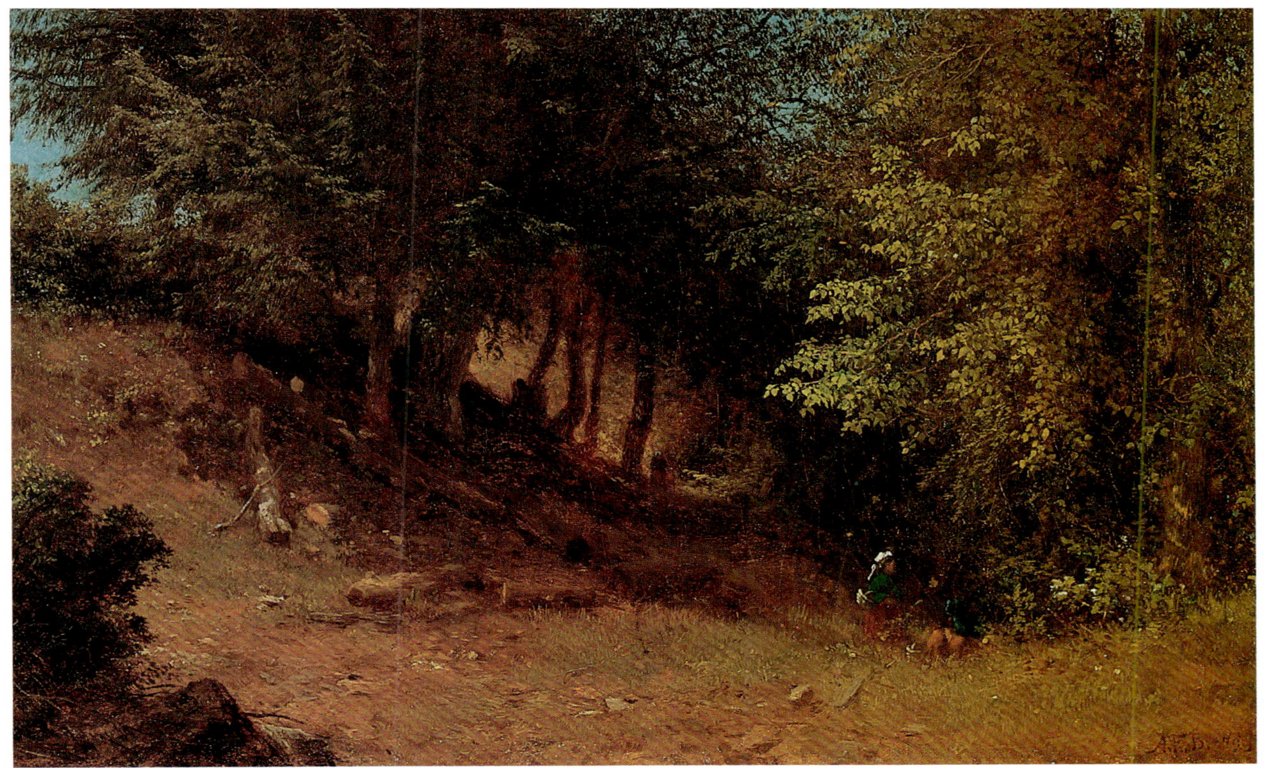

Albert Fitch Bellows, *Picnic in a Summer Landscape*, 1879. Oil on canvas, 10 1/4" x 16 1/8".

14. William McDougal Hart

(born 1823, Paisley, Scotland; died 1894, Mount Vernon, New York)
Hudson River Landscape, 1879
Oil on panel
8 3/4" x 14"
Signed lower left: W. Hart 1879

Like so many other American painters who grew up before the middle of the nineteenth century, William McDougal Hart was virtually self-taught. He was one of a number of successful second-generation Hudson River School artists who would not or could not adapt their styles to the growing taste for French Barbizon painting that sprang up in the late 1870s. Oddly enough, when he finally made a half-hearted attempt to incorporate the Barbizon aesthetic into his work in the 1880s, his popularity did not suffer and he was still bought by all the major collectors. Nonetheless, the subject matter and variable quality of much of his later work have tarnished his reputation with art historians and, consequently, he is not represented in major public or private collections.[1] His best paintings, however, achieve a sensitivity and refinement which justify a reevaluation of his oeuvre.

He and his brother, the Hudson River School landscape painter James McDougal Hart (1828-1901), were born in Scotland but emigrated with their parents to Albany, New York, in 1831. In the 1830s he apprenticed to a carriage maker, for whom he decorated coach panels and window shades, and on his own he also sketched from nature. In 1841 he started doing portraits in Troy, New York, and over the next four years, worked as an itinerant portrait painter in Virginia and Michigan. When poor health forced him to return to Albany in 1845, he limited himself to landscape painting. By 1848 he had already made his debut at the National Academy of Design, where he continued to exhibit over the next forty-five years. The following year, with the assistance of a local physician, he went to Scotland to regain his health. Once he had recovered, he sent back paintings to local patrons, studied works at the Royal Scottish Academy in Edinburgh, and painted in Scotland and other parts of Great Britain. In 1852 he returned to Albany to open a studio, but two years later established himself in New York, where his career rapidly blossomed. He became an Associate of the National Academy of Design and an Academician in 1858, and in 1865 was one of the founders of the Brooklyn Academy of Design, serving as its first president. In 1866 he was a cofounder of the American Society of Painters in Water Color, of which he was a president from 1870 to 1873. A frequent and popular contributor to major exhibitions in all the largest Eastern cities, he died in 1894 in Mount Vernon, New York.

Most of Hart's paintings, especially those of the 1880s, are set in the Hudson Valley, but he also worked in the Adirondacks and White Mountains and painted views along the New England coast. His pictures of the 1850s are precise and tight in style, but in the 1860s and 1870s his brushwork loosened a little as he began to emphasize effects of light and weather in paintings which have quasi-Luminist features. During the 1870s, his most productive period, autumn scenes were especially common. Starting in the 1870s but especially in the 1880s and 1890s, he tried to adapt to the Barbizon style with open compositions of fields, trees, water, and cows. Although cows had occasionally appeared before as incidental, distant staffage, now this stubbornly prosaic animal became the focus of his paintings.[2]

In 1867 Tuckerman praised Hart.[3] In 1879, however, the repetitiousness of his later works provoked the ire of Sheldon, who wrote: "Mr. Hart was never a copyist of anybody but himself. His recent works, for the most part, closely resemble one another." Sheldon praised him, however, for his fine draftsmanship, and went on to note approvingly the cheerfulness, brightness, warmth, and quietness of Hart's landscapes of settled areas.[4] Sheldon's jibe about Hart as a copyist was doubtless a reference to a talk entitled "The Field and the Easel" that the artist had given at the Brooklyn Academy of Design. After recommending the careful study and sketching of objects, landscape, and sky, he had advised against the choice of hackneyed scenes and the habit of following a favorite artist too closely.[5]

Like at least half of Hart's paintings, *Hudson River Landscape* is quite small.[6] Although it shows two cows on a bushy bit of land by the water, the main focus of this autumn scene is a narrow sandy beach and a clump of varicolored trees with a bluish purple hill as a backdrop. The basic mood of this brightly accented but richly subdued work is set by the late afternoon sky, its broken gray and white clouds and patches of blue suggesting clearing skies after a recent rain. The small but visible brush strokes of this painting, its moodiness, and open but snapshot-like composition

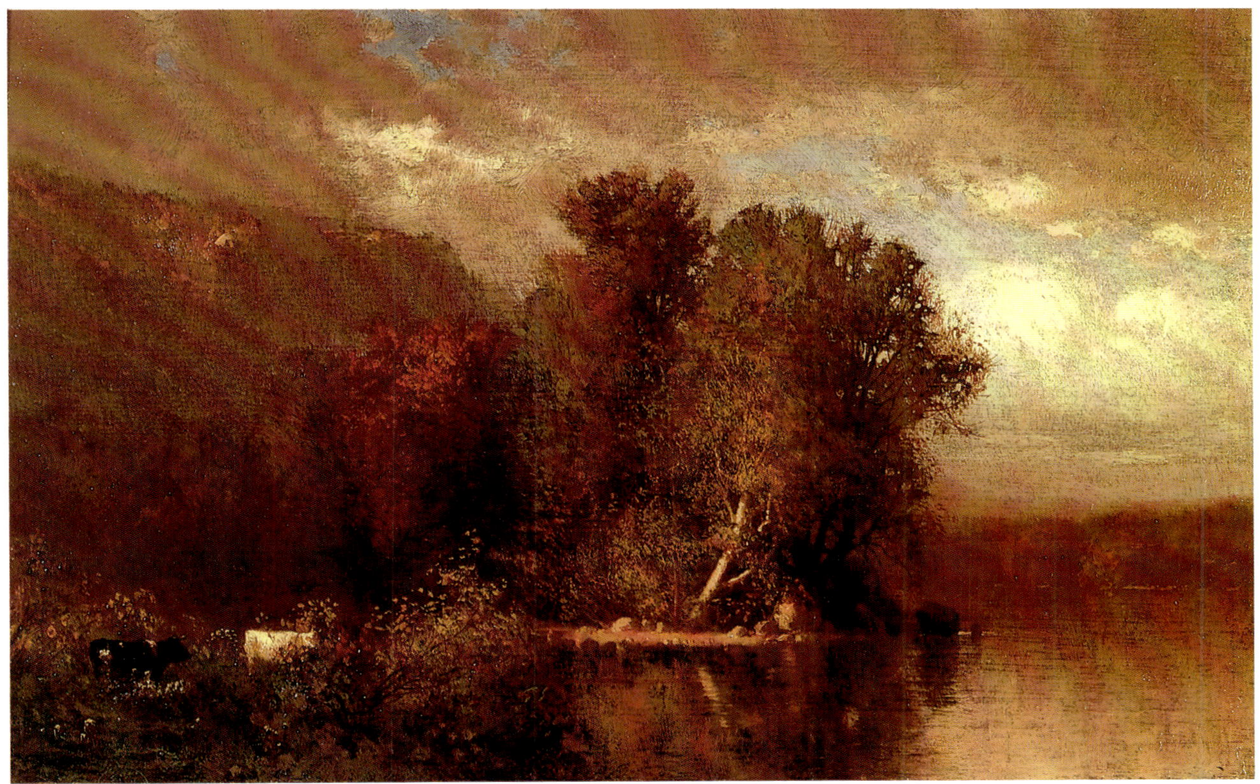

William McDougal Hart, *Hudson River Landscape*, 1879. Oil on panel, 8 3/4" x 14".

all point to the influence of Barbizon painting.[7]

1. An exception is the Metropolitan Museum of Art, which owns two large Harts, *Seashore, Morning*, 1866, and *Scene at Napanoch*, 1883. How the museum felt about these paintings in 1985 is indicated by their having been on deposit at the Federal Reserve Bank of New York since 1972. See Spassky et al., 183-84.

2. Hart's oeuvre is easy to trace because out of a sample of seventy-eight paintings forty-four (56.4%) are dated. Of these only nine (11.5%) are coastal scenes. He produced most of his autumn views - nine of sixteen (56.2%) - in the 1870s and most of his paintings with cows - five of six (83.3%) - in the 1880s. No dated paintings from the 1890s were included in this sample. Analysis of National Academy of Design exhibition records from 1861 to 1894 show similar trends with cow paintings on the increase from the mid-1870s and becoming most prevalent in the 1890s. See Naylor, 403-06. In focusing on the cow, Hart probably was taking the lead of the popular Barbizon artist Constant Troyon (1810-1865) and his followers. See Bouret, 110-14. Troyon's works were exhibited outside of France more often than those of any other Barbizon artist. See Weisberg, 311.

3. See Tuckerman, 547.

4. Sheldon, 85-87.

5. See Tuckerman, 549-51.

6. Thirty-nine of seventy-eight (50%) are twelve inches or less in one dimension and twenty inches or less in the other.

7. See, for example, *Morning in the Mountains*, ca. 1865, no. 31 and ill. in John K. Simon, *Recognizing the Painterly Tradition in American Art* (Buffalo: State University College at Buffalo, 1980); *The Prairie*, no. 62, ill. p. 94 of Louis Hawes, *The American Scene 1820-1900* (Bloomington: Indiana University Art Museum, 1970); and *Upland Meadow*, 1872, in Wilmerding et al., 203, pl. 27.

Bibliography

Spassky et al. 181-84.

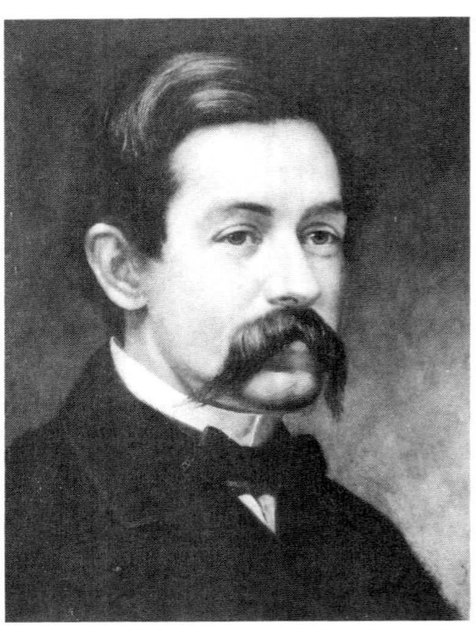

David Johnson, *Self-portrait*, 1860. Oil on canvas, 17 5/8" x 13 5/8". The Arden Collection.

15. David Johnson

(born 1827, New York; died 1908, Walden, New York)
Safely Anchored, ca. 1880
Oil on canvas
13" x 19"
Signed lower right: D.J.
Inscribed on back: 'Safely Anchored' David Johnson. New York

In 1956, just before the revival of interest in the Hudson River School, the influential E.P. Richardson, then the pope of American painting, opined, "David Johnson (1827-1903) in his early years produced a few lucid, hard, exact paintings that impress one by a certain power of statement; but later he fell into dull routine work."[1] However, later reappraisals of the artist's contributions, such as John I.H. Baur's 1980 article and his inclusion in a major exhibition devoted to Luminism, made it safe to take his work seriously, and Gwendolyn Owens's 1988 Johnson retrospective made it mandatory.

The artist, whose father was a New York City coach maker, was born in 1827 and educated in public schools. It is not known how he learned to paint well enough to exhibit for the first time in 1849 at the National Academy of Design. It was previously believed that Johnson was self-taught, except for a few sessions with Jasper Cropsey (cat. 9) in 1850. The idea of the self-taught artist appeals both to the common wish for something for nothing and the notion of native genius, but with sufficient research a significant artist usually turns out to have had some formal training. It was recently discovered that Johnson was registered at the Antique School of the National Academy of Design from 1845 to 1847, although relatively little else is known at present about his life. He was named an Associate of the National Academy of Design in 1859, made an Academician in 1861, married in 1869, and exhibited at the Paris Salon in 1877. At some point, he must have visited Europe and been exposed to Barbizon paintings because his widow owned many works he purchased abroad.

His rise and fall in popularity paralleled that of other Hudson River School artists. Following a period of increasing success with maximum production in the 1870s, his output and fortunes rapidly declined after 1880.[2] In 1890 he had to have a two-day auction sale to dispose of unsold works; in 1893 he gave up his studio; and he last showed at the National Academy in 1899. In 1904 he moved to Walden, New York where, already forgotten, he died four years later.

Johnson had a passion for accuracy. Fortunately, it went beyond the confining strictures of American Pre-Raphaelitism into a desire for order that gave him an excellent, selective sense of balanced composition. He wedded this precision, order, and balance to an impressive mastery of subtle variations of tone and atmosphere. Though his pictures are usually small, many could have been successfully painted in much larger formats. Never dramatic or colorful, they are restrained, harmonious, and subtle. His primary concern was always for botanical and topographical accuracy, which he achieved through drawings so accurate that different species of trees can be easily identified in them and his finished paintings. His mild obsessiveness also led him to paint series of finished paintings at the same locale from different viewpoints in successive years.

Fortunately, he dated over half of his works and most of the time he indicated where he had painted them.[3] As a result, it is relatively easy to summarize his oeuvre. Since he was neither in search of the exotic nor the spectacular, he was not a frequent traveler but contented himself with sketching trips in New York, New Jersey, Connecticut, and New Hampshire with a couple of forays into Maine and Virginia. He often painted in New York State, in particular central New York, an area neglected by his prominent contemporaries, but in the 1850s and 1860s he worked fairly extensively in New Hampshire.[4]

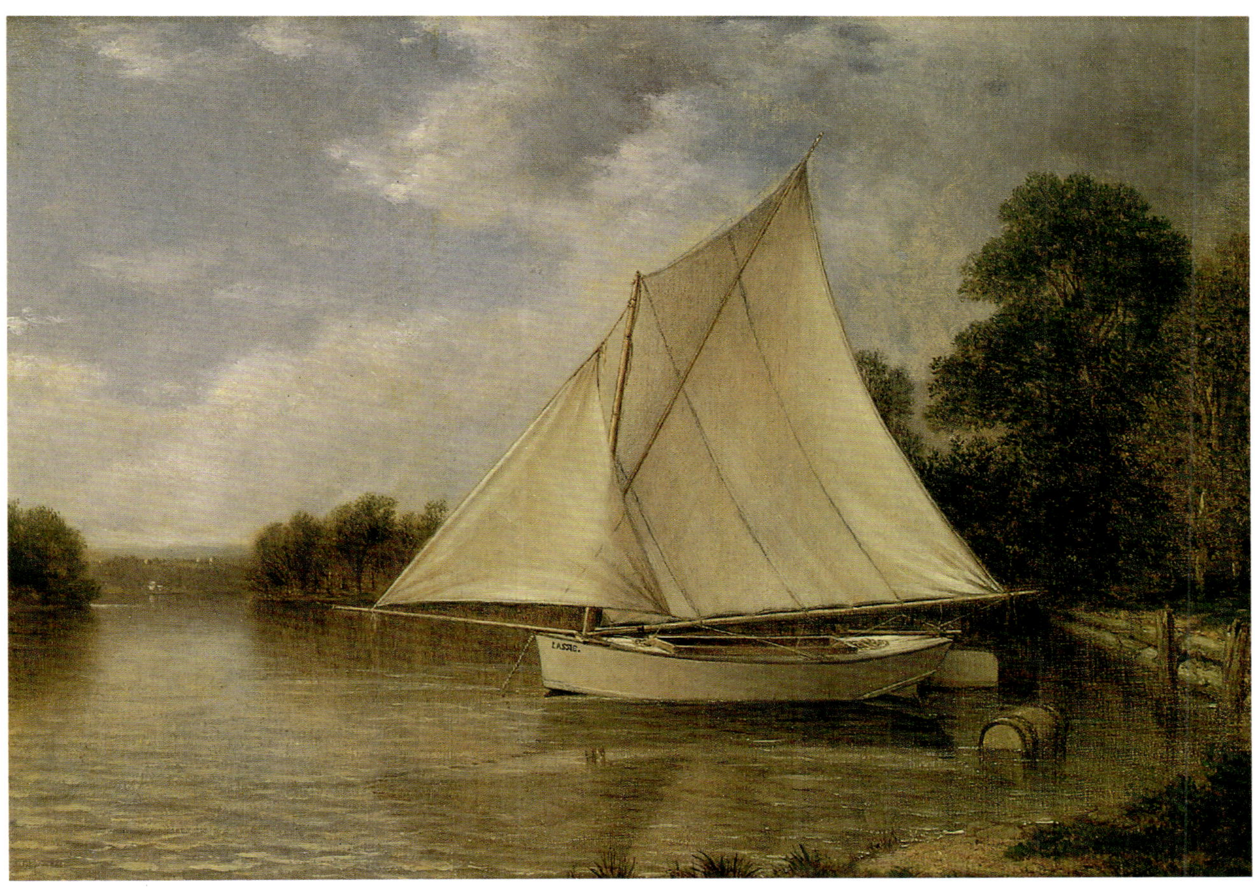

David Johnson, *Safely Anchored*, ca. 1880. Oil on canvas, 13" x 19".

During his first, early period (1849-1864), he concentrated on careful studies of rocky forest interiors and landscapes with framing trees at either side and a distant view opening up in the middle, compositions derived from the work of Cropsey (cat. 9). His second, middle period (1864-1878) often featured open views of gently rolling valleys or placid mountain lakes in which he developed his own cool but stunning version of Luminism. The former frequently emphasize the sky with relatively low horizons while the latter often follow a compositional format in which the lake occupies the fore- and middle ground and a hill or mountain abruptly rises in the background. In his third, late period (1878-1899), Johnson made his peace with Barbizon painting without neglecting precision and accuracy of detail. Concentrating more on river landscapes, he often focused on a large tree or group of large trees, used cattle and figures more frequently and prominently, stressed contrasts between light and dark, and filled his skies with extensive fluffy white clouds. His late paintings were reminiscent enough of Théodore Rousseau (1812-1867) for him to be known as the "American Rousseau." Although his output dropped off near the end of his life, the quality of his work did not. Along with his successful adaptation of the Barbizon aesthetic, this consistency helped him escape the criticism allotted to so many other Hudson River School artists. In 1894 he was still called "the best painter of trees in America." Still, although an established artist in his day, he received little critical attention, and only now for the first time, is he being taken seriously.

Safely Anchored is unique in Johnson's oeuvre. In effect, the portrait of a spritted sloop on a bright sunny day, it may have been painted on commission. Asymmetrically moored in the calm, reflecting water at right angles to the viewer, its fore- and mainsails are still unfurled as if on display for inspection. A nearby floating barrel provides a homely touch. The water funnels back to two points through which a channel opens out to a distant view of water, hills, and houses set against a sky filled with soft, grayish white cumulus clouds. Throughout, the artist makes the most of slight variations in the play of light and shade in the water and the sails of the boat with thinly painted, seamless brush strokes. The strong contrasts between the darker trees and the light clouds and sails in this bright, high-keyed painting suggest a date around 1880 when Johnson had begun to absorb Barbizon influences. Although he specifies the name of the boat, *Lassy,* but not the locale, it was probably set on a lake or river in New York, New Jersey, or Connecticut.

1. E.P. Richardson, *Painting in America From 1502 to the Present* (New York: Thomas Y. Crowell, 1956), 228-29.

2. Owens's (1988) working list of Johnson paintings supplemented by a few others yields the following number of dated or datable paintings for each decade: 1850s, forty-four; 1860s, sixty-nine; 1870s, one hundred; 1880s, twenty-three; and 1890s, one.

3. Out of a sample of 414 paintings, 237 (57.2%) were dated or datable. Contrary to Owens's assertion, the proportion of dated and datable paintings where the artist indicates a location remains about the same for each decade: 1850s, 72.7%; 1860s, 82.6%; 1870s, 85%; and 1880s, 78.3%. See Owens (1988), 52.

4. Works painted there amount to 23.5% in the 1850s; 35.1% in the1860s; 7% in the 1870s; and none in the 1880s.

Bibliography

Baur, John I.H. "'. . . the exact brushwork of Mr. David Johnson,' An American Landscape Painter, 1827-1908." *American Art Journal* 12 (Autumn 1980): 32-65.

Owens, Gwendolyn. "David Johnson (1827-1908)." In Avery et al. 169-276

_____. *Nature Transcribed: The Landscapes and Still Lifes of David Johnson (1827-1908).* Ithaca, NY: Herbert F. Johnson Museum of Art, 1988.

Wilmerding et al. 99, 108, 214, 216, 237, figs. 110, 274.

16. [John] Leon Moran

(born 1864, Philadelphia; died 1941, Watchung, New Jersey)
Cabbage Pickers, 1883
Oil on canvas
18" x 26"
Signed lower left: Léon Moran - - - 3
Publication: Michael David Zellman, ed., *American Art Analog*, vol. II (New York: Chelsea House, 1986), 605.

Scholars have largely neglected the work of John Leon Moran. In fact, of the seven artists in his family, only two, his uncle Thomas (1837-1926) and his father Edward (cat. 34), are familiar to nonspecialists.[1]

Born in 1864 in Philadelphia, he studied with his father and at the National Academy of Design. From 1877 to 1879 he traveled in France with his family but it is not known whether he received additional instruction there. After his return to New York, he made his debut at the National Academy of Design in 1881, where he exhibited for many years. He had a studio in New York from 1883 until sometime after 1901 when he moved to Plainfield, New Jersey, where he was still living in 1929. A member of the American Watercolor Society and the Plainfield Art Association, he also exhibited at the Art Club of Philadelphia (gold medal, 1893) and the American Art Society in Philadelphia (gold medal, 1902).

It is hard to say much about Moran's work beyond his having been primarily a genre painter whose brushwork became increasingly painterly. It is rarely dated, appears not to be owned by museums, and in recent years has figured in only one museum exhibition.[2]

Cabbage Pickers is a puzzle. The date, which is effaced but clearly ends in 3, could only correspond to 1883 or 1893. Since it is set in France, it was probably painted during or not too long after his stay there.[3] It is signed with the accented French spelling of his middle name, Leon, which he used rather than his given name, John, presumably in order to avoid confusion with his painter uncle John (1831-1903). It may have been intended for a French exhibition or might be a youthful affectation, emphasizing the artist's links to fashionable French painting.

In this vignette of rural peasant life, a woman picks cabbages with the help of her kneeling daughter. Up the slope from them is a second mother and child. At the top of the hill, two clumps of trees stand out against

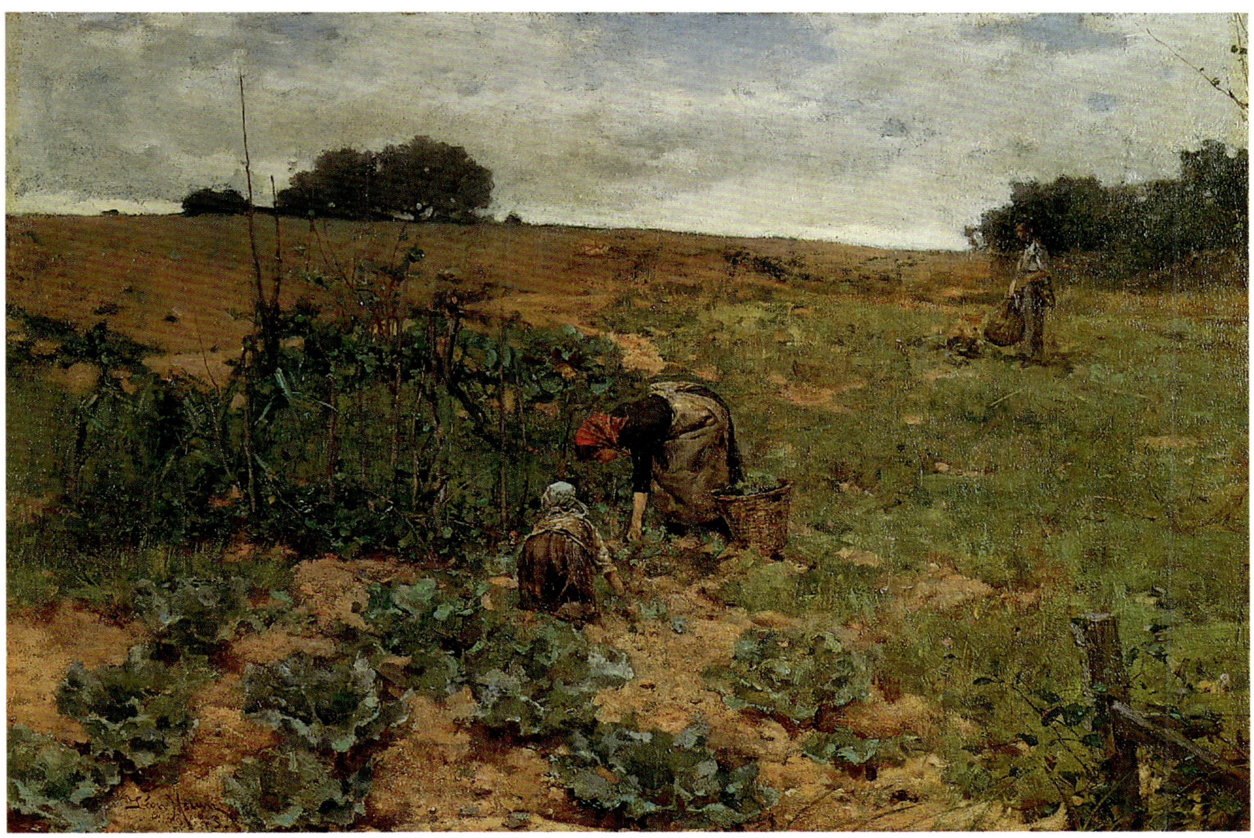

Leon Moran, *Cabbage Pickers*, 1883. Oil on canvas, 18" x 26".

fleecy white clouds that fill most of the bright blue sky. This painting's complete command of composition and brush technique belies its author's youth. The figures' distance from the viewer and their averted faces give them the anonymity of still life. Their detached treatment, the high horizon, and the painterly, scumbled brushwork all suggest the influence of Léon Lhermitte (1844-1925), who was well known for his depictions of peasant life.

1. Also poorly studied are his other uncles, the animal and landscape painter and etcher Peter (1841-1914), and the landscapist and photographer John (1831-1903), Thomas's wife, Mary Nimmo Moran (1842-1899), and his younger brother, [Edward] Percy Moran (1862-1935), a specialist in colonial and historical genre.

2. Out of a sample of twenty paintings gathered from books, exhibition and auction catalogues, and a 1984 National Museum of American Art Inventory of American Paintings, sixteen (80%) were genre and only four (20%) were dated (1881, 1882, 1884, 1896).

3. From 1883, the titles of Moran's submissions to the National Academy of Design no longer specifically suggest European subjects. See Naylor, 650. For a related 1881 watercolor of a French peasant girl sitting on a grassy slope, see Christie's, 9/30/88, no. 115.

Bibliography

Mantle Fielding. 654.

Zellman, Michael David, ed. *American Art Analog*. Vol. II. New York: Chelsea House, 1986. 605.

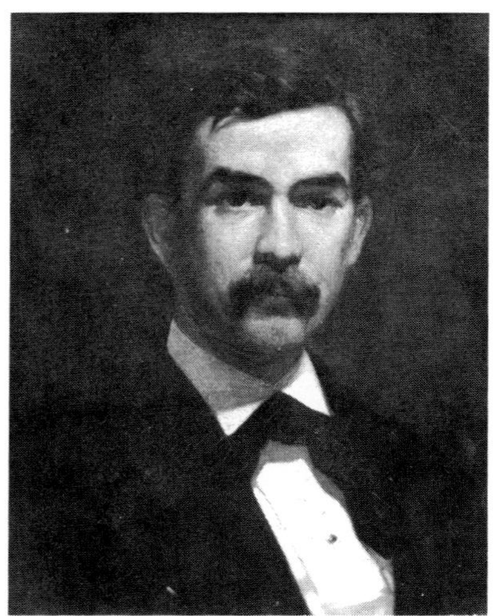

William Magrath (1838-1918), *Arthur Parton*, 1871. Collection of the National Academy of Design, New York; photo courtesy of the Frick Art Reference Library.

17. Arthur Parton

(born 1842, Hudson, New York; died 1914, Yonkers, New York)
In the Neversink Valley, 1883
Oil on canvas
24" x 40"
Signed lower right: Arthur Parton

18.

Evening in the Forest, ca. 1890
Oil on canvas
18" x 24"
Signed lower left: Arthur Parton

During a long and successful career that spanned over half a century, Arthur Parton first won his spurs as a Hudson River School painter only to achieve greatest recognition as an American Barbizon artist. Currently, however, scholars ignore his work.

He was born in Hudson, New York in 1842 and at the age of seventeen went to Philadelphia to study with William Trost Richards (cat. 35). In 1861 he began exhibiting Hudson River School-style paintings at the Pennsylvania Academy of the Fine Arts and the next year became a regular exhibitor at the National Academy of Design. By 1864 he had settled in New York City. From 1869 to 1870 he briefly visited Paris but spent most of his time abroad in England and Scotland. He became an Associate of the National Academy of Design in 1874 and an Academician ten years later. In 1876 he exhibited successfully at the

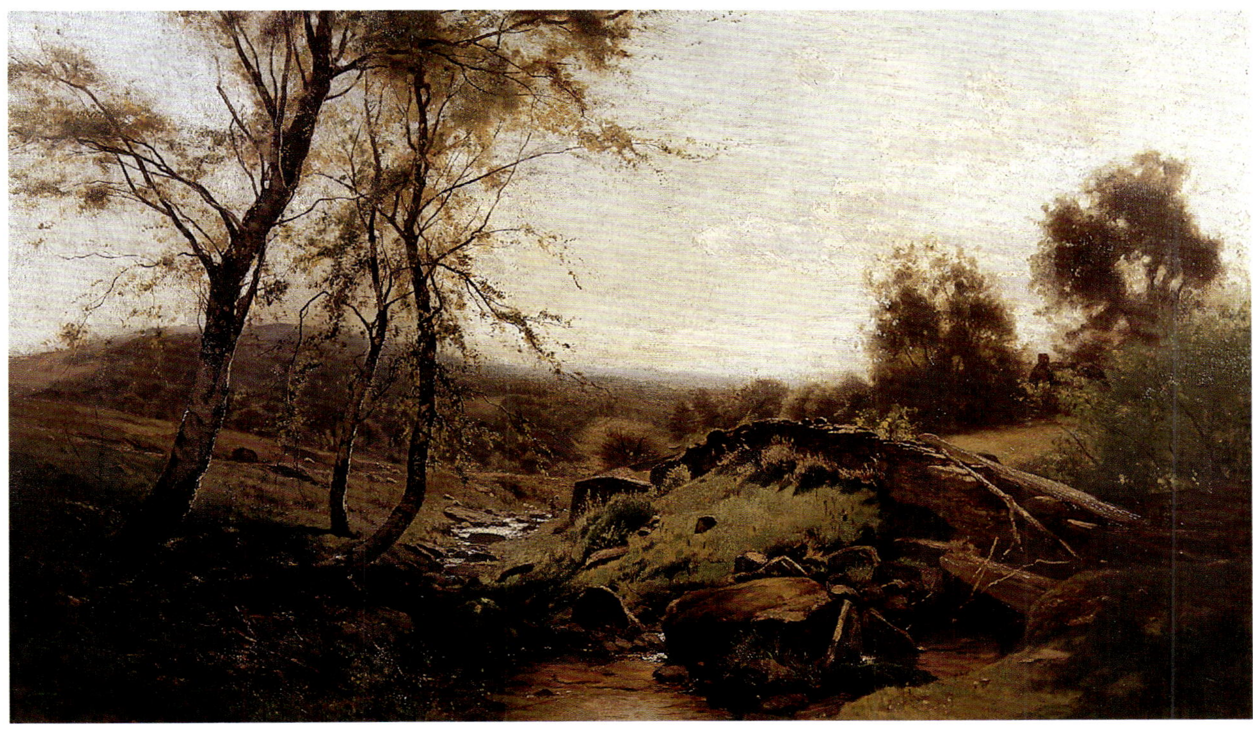

Arthur Parton, *In the Neversink Valley*, 1883. Oil on canvas, 24" x 40".

Philadelphia Centennial Exposition, and in 1877 was able to marry and move to Yonkers. During the 1870s he summered in the Adirondacks but in 1880 bought a cottage in Arkville in the Catskills near his friends Alexander Wyant (cat. 8), J. Francis Murphy (1853-1921), and Charles Warren Eaton (1857-1937). However, he continued to make occasional visits to Keene Valley in the Adirondacks. Starting in the 1880s, he successfully converted from his Hudson River School style to a Barbizon approach, garnering him a number of prizes and medals.[1] When he died in 1914, the year after the Armory Show, his soft, fluent style was already out of fashion.

As befits a student of Richards in his Pre-Raphaelite phase, Parton painted highly detailed landscapes through the 1870s. By the early 1880s, however, they began to soften under Barbizon influence as he gradually developed a warm, soft, atmospheric, and slightly blurry tonal style. Obviously indebted to Jean-Baptiste-Camille Corot (1797-1875), it was well suited to the more intimate, pastoral Catskill scenes that replaced the wilds of the Adirondacks in his earlier work. Throughout the 1870s and 1880s, he also painted some views of Scotland and occasional ones of Pennsylvania. It is hard to chart his development after 1886, when he virtually stopped dating his paintings. One constant, however, was his penchant for water, be it a mountain stream, forest pool, waterfall, river, pond, or lake. He painted a number of spring landscapes with blossoming trees but summer was his favorite season, and he preferred early to late autumn and totally avoided winter.[2]

In his New Jersey landscape *In the Neversink Valley*, Parton is beginning to break away from the clarity and crispness of the Hudson River School with softer brushwork while still adhering to some of its compositional conventions. It shows a narrow, rocky stream winding its way down between a sloping, rock-strewn field at the left and a gentle grassy hill with a stone wall, culvert, and trees at the right. Hills in the background keep this from becoming a panorama, but a clump of three carefully delineated trees on a left foreground hillock recall Asher B. Durand (cat. 3). A fisherman where the stream disappears around the hill and a house nestled between trees add a domestic touch. Chiaroscuro and back lighting soften this sunny scene dominated by subdued, well modulated browns and greens. Both the colors and soft, hazy vegetation are reminiscent of early Barbizon Corot, but the complex composition with many carefully modeled

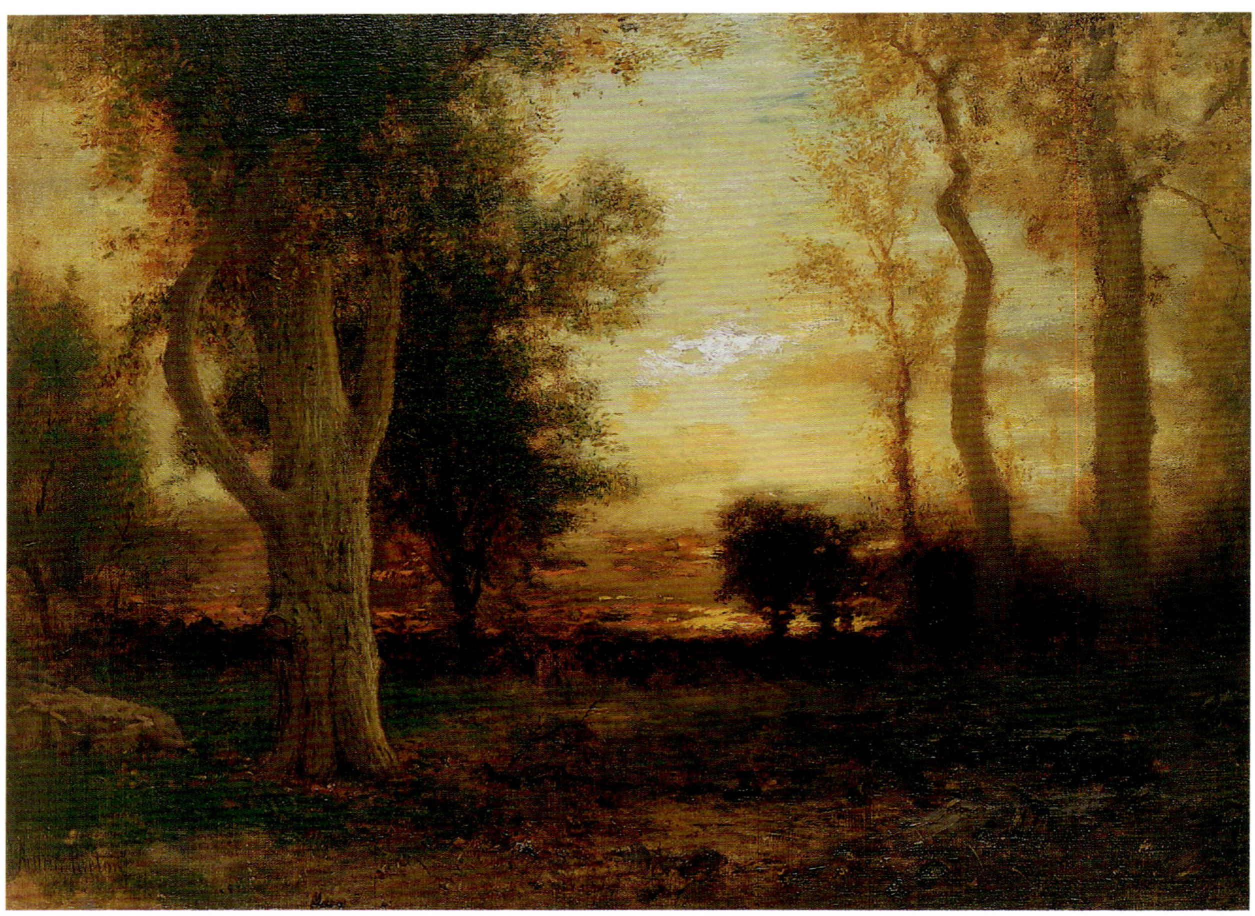

Arthur Parton, *Evening in the Forest*, ca. 1890. Oil on canvas, 18" x 24".

details is a legacy of the Hudson River School. This landscape is not dated, but it is probably a work exhibited at the National Academy of Design in 1883.[3]

Evening in the Forest is clearly painted later than *In the Neversink Valley* because of the large step it takes in the direction of Barbizon moodiness, reduction in the number of visual elements, and blurring and abstraction of forms. This late twilight view makes the most of a succession of trees silhouetted against each other and a somber yet colorful sky. Seen through their gray trunks and dark green foliage, the cloudy sky is accented with rich but muted patches of orange and yellow at the bottom while the rest is suffused with much paler shades of the same colors. The broken, patchy brushwork, softened forms, and carefully spaced progression of trees in some ways recall Théodore Rousseau (1812-1867), but the strongest influence is clearly that of George Inness (1825-1894).

1. The American Art Association medal and Temple gold medal of the Pennsylvania Academy of the Fine Arts, 1886; honorable mention, Paris Exposition Universelle, 1889; and a prize, Paris Exposition Universelle, 1900.

2. In a sample of one hundred thirty-four paintings culled from books, catalogues, and a National Museum of American Art Inventory of American Paintings, only forty-one (30.6%) are dated (1858-1886, with one example in 1890), twelve (8.9%) are spring landscapes with flowering trees, and eighty-one (80.4%) feature a body of water.

3. See Naylor, 723. National Academy records give the same dimensions as the present work, which in the course of reframing and relabeling acquired the title *The Valley of the Neversink*. The name "Neversink" was probably the artist's misunderstanding of "Navesink." The Navesink River in Monmouth County, New Jersey, starts at Red Bank and runs out to sea beyond Rumson. The Navesink highlands, the Navesink Valley, and the town of Navesink are on the upper two-thirds of the river. *In the Month of June*, 1886, ill. in Nancy Grinnell, *American Paintings From the Collection of the Art Complex Museum* (Duxbury, MA: Art Complex Museum, 1985), 31, is closely related stylistically to the present work.

Bibliography

Steinberg, David. "Arthur Parton (1842-1914)." In Avery et al., 326-29.

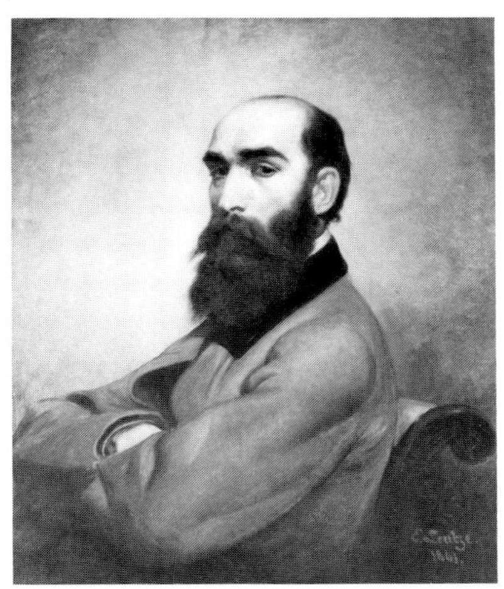

Emanuel Leutze (1816-1868), *Worthington Whittredge*, 1861.
Collection of the National Academy of Design, New York.

19. [Thomas] Worthington Whittredge

(born 1820, Springfield, Ohio; died 1910, Summit, New Jersey)
No Water in the Well, ca. 1885
Oil on canvas
14 1/2" x 18 1/2"
Signed lower right: W. Whittredge
Publication: Anthony F. Janson, *Worthington Whittredge* (New York: Cambridge University Press, 1989), 189, fig. 149.

During their training, artists often learn formulas that serve them well for a while, only to become shackles they cannot outgrow. Similarly, a painter's addiction to a successful manner and subject matter developed during his maturity may eventually lessen the quality of his work. Until he was an old man, Worthington Whittredge avoided both traps through diversity of subject matter and evolution of style. Unlike Bierstadt, he learned how to escape the confines of his Düsseldorf training. Later, he was the oldest and most successful of the few Hudson River School artists who adapted to French Barbizon painting after the Civil War.

This descendant of seventeenth-century English immigrants was born in a log cabin on the Little Miami River near Springfield, Ohio. He was the youngest of five step-siblings and two brothers. Nothing in his background or circumstances prepared him to be an artist, nor did either parent encourage his interest in the arts. His father, a transplanted Massachusetts sea captain turned farmer, would not let him attend high school and abhorred even the word "artist." Whittredge loved nature but showed no particular early interest or ability in art. Nonetheless, in 1837 at the age of seventeen, he was allowed to live with a half-sister in Cincinnati in order to learn house and sign painting from her husband, who also did occasional portraits and landscapes. After starting an abortive daguerreotype business in Indianapolis in 1838, he tried portraiture in Charleston, West Virginia, but was dissatisfied with his attempts. By 1839 he had turned exclusively to landscape painting, which earned him a good local reputation through works exhibited at the Cincinnati Academy of Fine Arts. Like other provincial artists, he suffered from a paucity of good examples, but the few Doughtys and Coles he saw helped him improve so much that in 1847 the National Academy of Design accepted one of his landscapes which Asher B. Durand (cat. 3) admired enough to send Whittredge a personal letter of praise.

By 1849, he was an experienced, respected, but mostly self-taught professional artist. Keenly aware of his limitations, he embarked on what became a ten-year sojourn in Europe. After brief stays in Belgium and Paris he settled in Düsseldorf, which he used for seven years as a base for travel in Germany. He became close friends with Eastman Johnson (1824-1906) and Emanuel Leutze (1816-1868), for whose monumental *Washington Crossing the Delaware*, 1851, he posed both as George Washington and the steersman. Without becoming anyone's formal student, he successively absorbed the influence of the landscapists Andreas Achenbach (1815-1910), Carl Friedrich Lessing (1808-1880), and Johann Wilhelm Schirmer (1807-1863). By 1856 he had mastered the accurate, somewhat dry Düsseldorf approach to landscape which was predicated on reinterpreting nature in large studio works full of precise detail.

He made his way to Switzerland, where he found the grandeur of the scenery impressive but overpowering. Florence was a disappointment because he discovered that the great paintings of the past were not landscapes. Finally he settled in Rome, a repository of old master paintings which made him uneasy. Their superior technique exacerbated his self-consciousness, but again he felt guilty at his indifference to their figurative subject matter. He used Rome as a base, both for painting in the Campagna and nearby mountains and trips to the north Italian lakes and Switzerland, until his return to New York City in August 1859.

Dropping his first name, he took a studio in the Tenth Street Studio Building which he used until 1900. The next year he successfully exhibited previously executed Swiss and Italian views at the National Academy of Design, which made him an Associate in 1861 and an Academician the following year. Nevertheless, he found his ten years of foreign study less an asset than a liability. He described the problems that beset an American landscape artist trained in Europe as follows: "It was the most crucial period of my life. It was impossible for me to shut out from my eyes the works of the great landscape painters I had so recently seen in Europe. . . . Sure, however, that if I turned to nature, I should find a friend . . . I hid myself for months in the Catskills. But how different was the scene before me from anything I had been looking at for many years! The forest was a mass of decaying logs and tangled brushwood, no peasants to pick up every vestige of fallen sticks to burn in their miserable huts, no well-ordered forest, nothing but the primitive woods with their solemn silence reigning everywhere."[1]

Fortunately, he was able to develop a looser style more suitable to the mostly unspectacular corners of American landscape that appealed to him. From 1859 to 1866 and again from 1872 to 1876, with the example of Durand (cat. 3) before him, he executed freely painted Catskill woodland interiors which earned him a strong following. One of them was even shown abroad at the 1867 Paris Exposition Universelle.[2] Subtly dappled with light and shade, they often featured a reflecting stream or pool of water. During this period, Whittredge also experimented with more romantic treatments of landscape. From 1863 to 1865 under the influence of his friend Sanford Gifford (1823-1880), he also painted a number of subtle and richly luminous landscapes culminating in his highly praised *Twilight on the Shawangunk*, 1865,[3] which was later reexhibited at the 1876 Philadelphia Centennial Exposition.

He next availed himself of a totally different kind of scenery in three trips to the Western plains.[4] Rather than the spectacular, rugged verticality of the mountains found in Bierstadt's work, he concentrated on the tranquil expansiveness of the plains.[5] The result was a series of outstanding depictions of the air and light of the West.

In 1872 Whittredge bought a summerhouse in Newport, Rhode Island. From 1872 to 1885, some of the paintings he did in the area were quasi-Luminist Newport beach scenes. Most, however, were pastoral

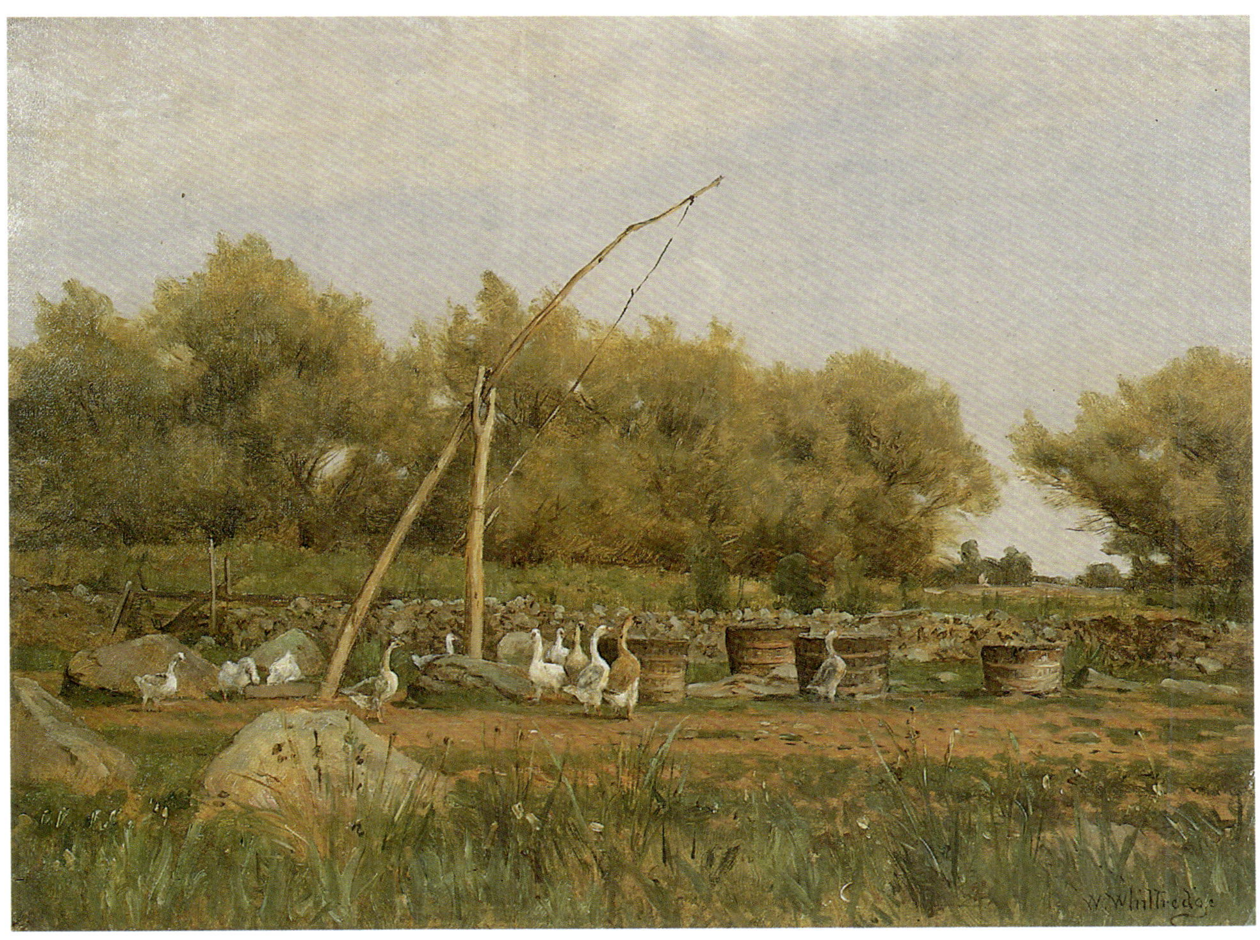

[Thomas] Worthington Whittredge, *No Water in the Well*, ca. 1885. Oil on canvas, 14 1/2" x 18 1/2".

landscapes in nearby Tiverton and Little Compton showing weather-beaten farmhouses with the flat coast and sea as a distant backdrop. One was exhibited at the 1889 Paris Exposition Universelle.[6]

From 1870 to 1876 Whittredge was at the peak of his powers and success. He belonged to all the men's clubs of most benefit to an artist and, from 1874 to 1875, successfully shepherded the National Academy of Design through a financial crisis as its president. Yet, beginning in 1876 at the age of fifty-six, with Charles-François Daubigny (1817-1878) as his example, he started to move toward Barbizon naturalism. This contrasted oddly with his and his Hudson River School friends' exclusion of American Barbizon works from exhibitions at the National Academy and at the 1876 Philadelphia Centennial Exposition. Yet, as early as 1874 he must have realized that the battle against Barbizon influences was a losing one. He wrote to the collector James Pinchot, "Immense numbers of pictures however are imported and seem to find sale, some at enormous prices, while the Bierstadts, the Churches, the Giffords and Johnsons, are not sold or even wanted."[7] Whittredge's gradual acceptance of the Barbizon style is underscored by his selection as president of the New York jury for submissions by American residents to the 1889 Paris Exposition Universelle.

After he moved to Summit, New Jersey, in 1880, views of its pastoral environs increasingly permeated his work, although he did some paintings based on trips to Mexico made in 1893 and 1896. His gradual retirement starting after 1885 was signaled by the 1887 sale at Ortgies' Art Galleries in New York of seventy-two of his paintings, which kept bringing lower and lower prices. The year 1883 marked the start of an inconsistent decline with reversions to earlier prototypes. It accelerated in the 1890s and had become marked by 1900, when he made his last National

Academy of Design submission. He executed his last painting in 1902 and finished his memoirs in 1905. Once famous but now forgotten, he died in 1910.

No Water in the Well is a smallish plein-air study. Across an open foreground of grass and earth we see eleven brown and white geese gathered around the rocky environs of a well with four low, broad wooden water barrels on its right. A stone wall, shrubs, and grass lead to a backdrop of trees against a hazy blue sky with soft white clouds. This airy, cheerful picture with its mundane agricultural subject matter, well-balanced, open composition, palette of contrasting shades of green, gray, and tan, and painterly brushwork is an unequivocally Barbizon-style painting. Although it looks as if it could have been painted in France, it was probably executed near Whitehall, Bishop Berkeley's farm, which was the subject of a number of other works by Whittredge in the 1880s.[8]

1. See Whittredge, 42.

2. See *The Old Hunting Grounds*, ca. 1864, in Avery et al., 80-82, ill. p. 181.

3. See Avery et al., 182-83.

4. To Missouri, Kansas, Nebraska, and Colorado in 1866; Colorado and Wyoming, with Gifford and Kensett in 1870; and Colorado in 1871.

5. His antipathy to Swiss alpine landscapes is consistent with such a choice: "My thoughts ran more upon simple scenes and simple subjects, or it may be I never got into the way of measuring all grandeur in a perpendicular line." Whittredge, 32.

6. *The Old Road to the Sea*, ca. 1884, painted at Little Compton, Rhode Island. See Annette Blaugrund, et al., *Paris 1889: American Artists at the Universal Exposition* (Philadelphia: The Pennsylvania Academy of the Fine Arts, 1989), 229-32, fig. 328, and Janson (1989), 184-85, 188, 190, pl. XVI.

7. See Janson (1989), 156.

8. See Janson (1989), 184 for a discussion. *No Water in the Well* seems to be a different view of the same well that figures in *Old Homestead by the Sea*, 1883, fig. 137 and *A Home by the Sea*, Christie's, 12/1/89, no. 40. The latter even appears to include the same geese.

Bibliography

Cibulka, Cheryl A. *Quiet Places: The American Landscapes of Worthington Whittredge*. Washington, D.C.: Adams Davidson Galleries, 1982.

Dwight, Edward. *Worthington Whittredge: A Retrospective Exhibition of an American Artist*. Utica, NY: Munson-Williams-Proctor Institute, 1965.

Janson, Anthony F. "The Western Landscapes of Worthington Whittredge." *American Art Review* 3. 6 (November/December 1979): 58-69.

_____."Worthington Whittredge: The Development of a Hudson River Painter, 1860-1868." *The American Art Journal* (April 1979): 71-84.

_____. *Worthington Whittredge*. New York: Cambridge University Press, 1989.

Mitnick, Barbara J. *Worthington Whittredge: Artist of the Hudson River School*. Morristown, NJ: Morris Museum of Arts and Sciences, 1982.

Whittredge, Worthington. "The Autobiography of Worthington Whittredge, 1820-1910." Ed. John I.H. Baur. *Brooklyn Museum Journal* 1 (1942): 5-68.

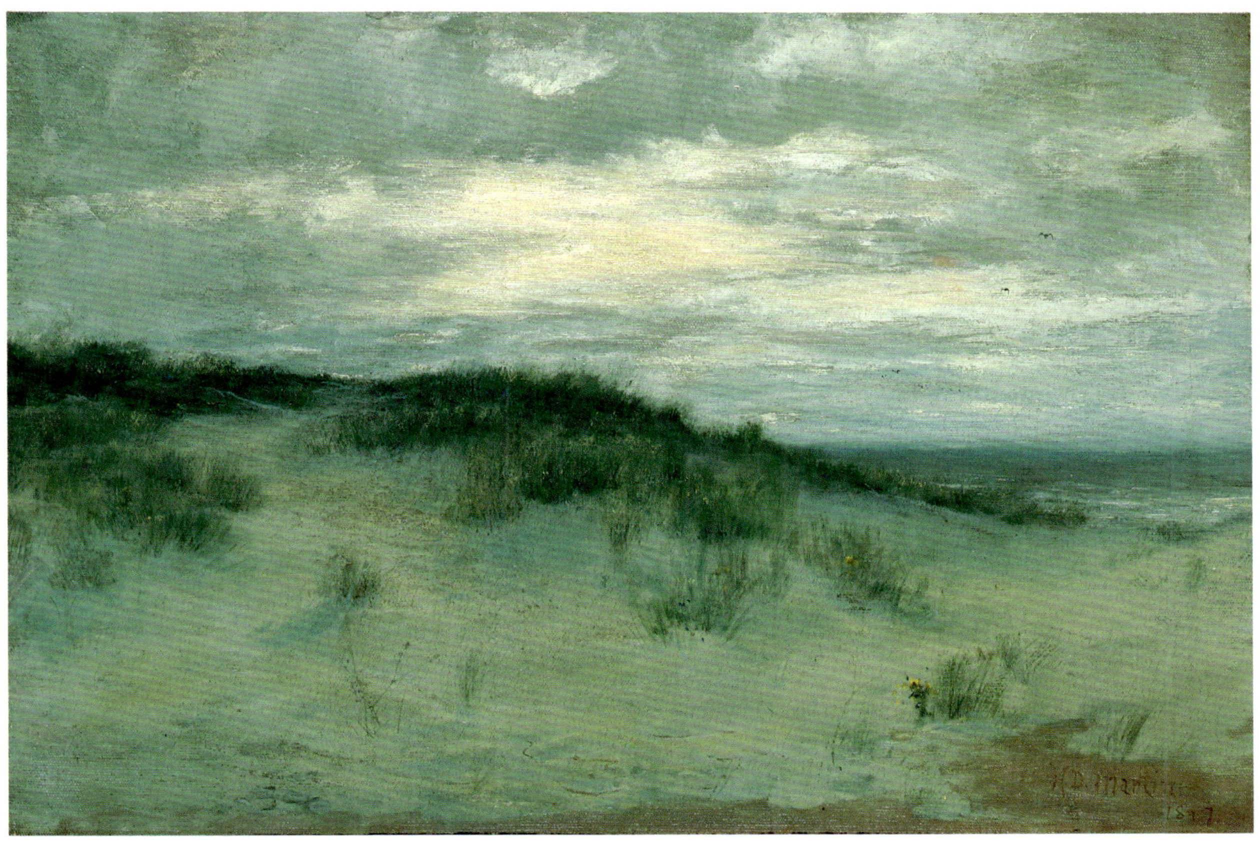

Homer Dodge Martin, *The Sand Dunes*, 1887. Oil on canvas, 17 3/4" x 25 1/2".

20. Homer Dodge Martin

(born 1836, Albany, New York; died 1897, St. Paul, Minnesota)
The Sand Dunes, 1887
Oil on canvas
17 3/4" x 25 1/2"
Signed lower right: H.D. Martin 1887

(See cat. 7 for a discussion of Martin's life and oeuvre.)

The Sand Dunes, executed in Martin's later tonal impressionist style, is the simplest of his four treatments of the sand dunes on Lake Ontario,[1] painted between his initial visit to the site in 1874 and 1887. In the foreground this moody work shows a couple of gently undulating dunes crowned with beach grass and a few yellow wild flowers, and in the distance a glimpse of water and a cloudy, streaked sky. The tiny, barely visible forms of a few gulls emphasize the loneliness of the scene. Martin uses scumbled, smudgy brushwork and a complex mixture of subdued colors to achieve a compelling mood of isolation.

1. *Sand Dunes, Lake Ontario*, 1874, in Carroll, no. 32; *Ontario Sand Dunes*, 1887, in Carroll, no. 13; and *Behind Dunes, Lake Ontario*, 1887, ill. p. 429 of Spassky et al.

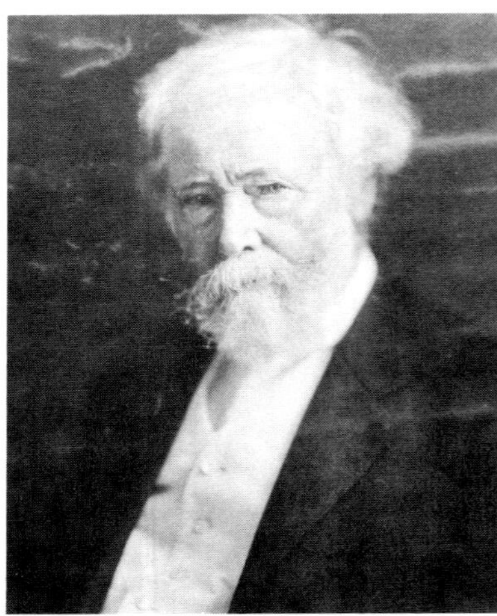

John J. Enneking, ca. 1910. Photo courtesy of Vose Galleries of Boston.

21. John Joseph Enneking

(born 1841, Minster, Ohio; died 1916, Hyde Park, Massachusetts)
Brook in Spring, 1888
Oil on canvas
18" x 24"
Signed lower right: Enneking 88
Publications: R.C. Vose, *Paintings by John J. Enneking: The First Comprehensive Exhibition of His Work in 35 Years* (Boston: Vose Galleries of Boston, 1962), ill.; *Exhibition of Paintings by John J. Enneking 1840-1916* (Brockton, MA: Brockton Public Library, 1962), cat. no. 8, ill. on title page; and *Exhibition of Paintings by John J. Enneking 1840-1916* (Hyde Park, MA: Boston Public Library, Hyde Park Branch, 1962), cat. no. 5, ill. on title page.

In his prime John Joseph Enneking counted as a major landscape painter, but after his death in 1916 he vanished into the limbo of forgotten reputations. Despite some currency in the Boston area since 1962, when the contents of his studio were found stored in a warehouse scheduled for demolition, he is still a neglected artist.

Enneking became a painter by fits and starts. An only child, he was born in a small town outside of Cincinnati. Although his farmer father threw his drawings into the fire and opposed his interest in art as unmasculine his mother encouraged it. He was fifteen when both parents died, forcing him to move to Cincinnati to live with an aunt. From 1858 to 1861 he attended Mount St. Mary's College and studied drawing, but left to join the Union Army during the Civil War. After recuperating from war wounds, he went to Boston in 1864, where he studied lithography and industrial drawing for a year, married, and built a home in the suburb of Hyde Park. In 1865 he started a tinware manufacturing business. When it failed he began painting full-time.

Although able to support his family, he was dissatisfied with his technique and by 1872 he had saved $13,000, which enabled him to leave with his family for four years of intensive and varied academic and informal study in Europe. This included six months at the Munich Royal Academy with the figure painter Eduard Schleich (1813-1879) and the landscapist Adolphe-Heinrich Lehr (1826-1882), sojourns in Venice and Switzerland and, starting in late 1873, a three-year stint in Paris with the academic portraitist Joseph-Florentine-Léon Bonnat (1833-1924). While there Enneking also was exposed to Barbizon and Impressionist painting. He made friends with the Barbizon painters Camille Corot (1796-1875) and Jean-François Millet (1814-1875), and studied informally with Charles-François Daubigny (1817-1878). In 1874 he also studied for three months with Eugène Boudin (1824-1898), a painter of beach and harbor scenes and the teacher of Claude Monet (1840-1926), with whom Enneking also painted. He returned home in 1876 only to revisit Paris in 1878 and spend six months in Holland, where he sketched and studied Dutch painting.

Finally satisfied with his training he returned to Boston that year to open a studio. Starting in 1878 he exhibited frequently there and in other major cities, winning a number of prizes and medals in official exhibitions and at international expositions. His success and prestige are indicated by a testimonial dinner held in his honor in Boston in 1915, which was attended by over 1,000 people.

Although Enneking painted some precisely rendered still lifes from 1869 to 1879 and is known to have done genre and portraits in the 1880s,[1] he was primarily a landscape artist. The style that he brought back from Europe softened the heavy impasto of the Munich Academy and combined it with a lighter palette and plein-air realism derived from the Barbizon school. By the mid-1880s, his brushwork became looser and more broken and his impasto thickened again as he developed a densely painted impressionism using rich, deep colors reminiscent of Adolphe Monticelli (1824-1886).[2] Drawing on the woods and fields of Massachusetts and Maine, where he bought a summer home in

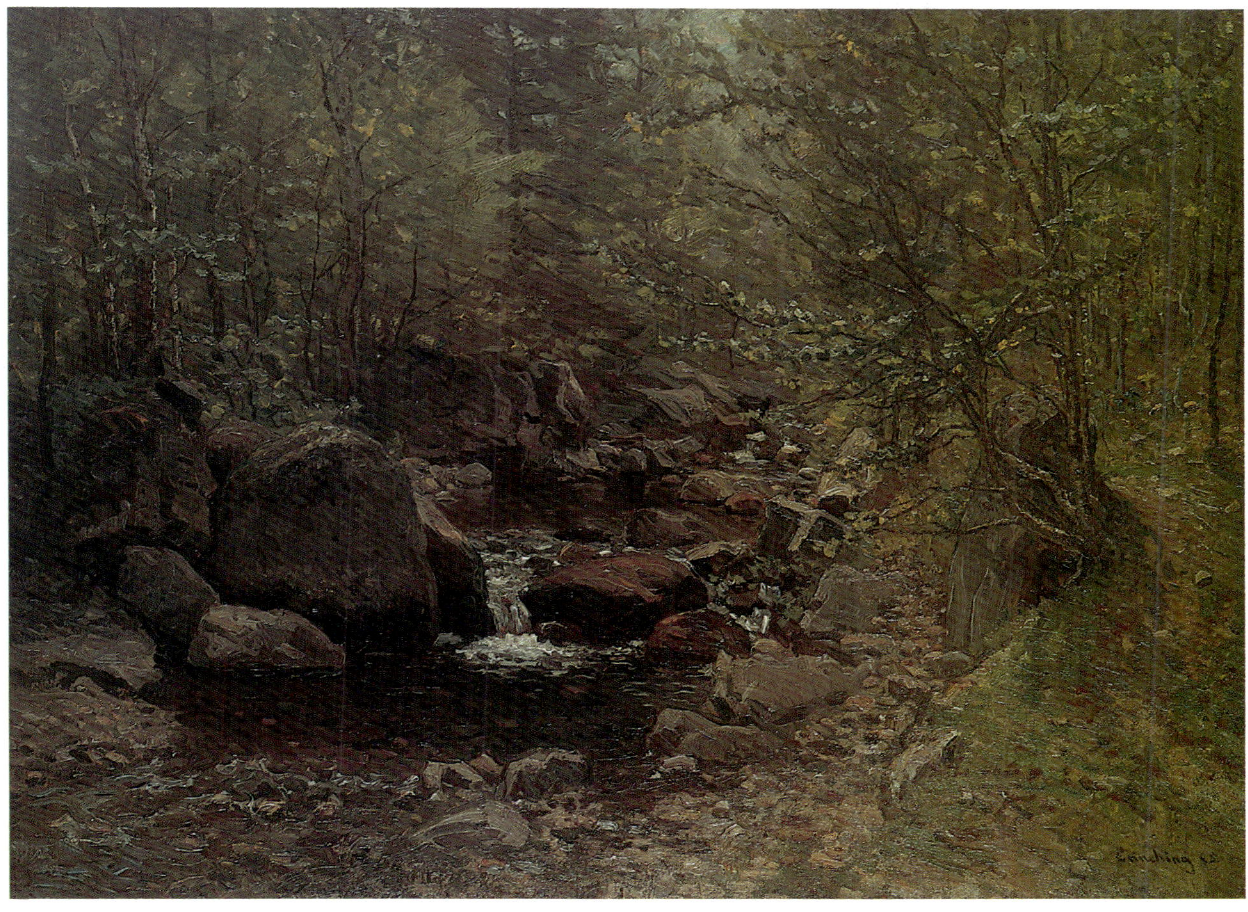

John Joseph Enneking, *Brook in Spring*, 1888. Oil on canvas, 18" x 24".

the 1880s, in simply composed, well balanced compositions, he concentrated on four kinds of subject matter: November twilights; woodland brooks; mist-wreathed, wooded hills seen through a screen of foreground trees; and spring landscapes with flowering trees. Scenes of autumn, especially November, were common in his paintings after 1890.[3] An indefatigable worker, he painted quickly and may have been America's most prolific, and variable, artist. Throughout his career, the titles of his paintings reflect a concern with season, time of day, and mood which was typical of Barbizon and Tonalist painters.

Brook in Spring strikes an even balance between free brushwork and strong, solidly modeled forms. An intense, even midday light illuminates this carefully developed composition which shows a rocky woodland stream that whitens twice as it makes its way toward the viewer between massive boulders, and small, leafy, truncated trees. The darker gray and brown tree trunks and rocks contrast strongly with the warm, yellowish green sunlit leaves and a grassy bank at the right. This kind of subject was used to good effect by Hudson River School artists, but here the painterly brushwork and light colors fall somewhere between a Barbizon style and Impressionism, with a variety of forms and a strength of definition rarely found in either.

1. Out of a sample of seventy-nine works, forty-four (55.7%) were dated and eight (10.1%), executed between 1869 and 1879, were still lifes. There were no genre or figurative paintings in this sample.

2. Gerdts (1980) seems uncertain whether he should label Enneking as an Impressionist, Barbizon, or Tonalist painter.

3. Out of twenty dated works from 1891 to 1913, thirteen (65%) were autumn scenes. Spring landscapes with flowering trees account for seven of seventy-one (9.9%) landscapes that included dated and undated works.

Bibliography

Dunn, Roger T., et al. *John J. Enneking: American Impressionist*. Brockton, MA: The Brockton Art Center, Fuller Memorial, 1975.

Pierce, Patricia Jobe, and Rolf H. Kristianson. *John Joseph Enneking; American Impressionist Painter*. North Abington, MA: Pierce Galleries, 1972.

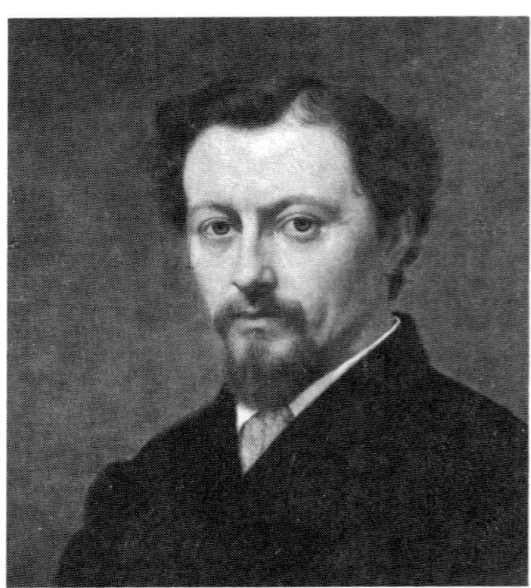

George H. Yewell (1830-1923), *Portrait of Samuel Colman*, 1855. Collection of the National Academy of Design, New York.

22. Samuel Colman

(born 1832, Portland, Maine; died 1920, New York)
View from the Raymond Hotel, Pasadena, ca. 1888
Oil on academy board
9 1/4" x 25 3/4"
Unsigned

Versatility was the one constant in Samuel Colman's long life. Not content to paint oils in two very different styles, he also became a watercolorist, etcher, pastelist, interior designer, collector of Japanese art, and art theorist.

Colman had an early exposure to art through his father, a successful Portland, Maine bookseller and publisher who later moved to New York City, where he opened a publishing house and operated a bookstore that also sold contemporary prints and engravings and was a popular haunt of writers and artists. In 1851 the nineteen-year-old Colman exhibited for the first time at the National Academy of Design, where he became an Associate in 1854. He may have studied with Asher B. Durand (cat. 3). Whatever his specific training, during the 1850s he painted views of New York and New Hampshire in a Hudson River School style and, by 1856, shared a summer studio at Jackson near North Conway with a number of like-minded National Academy colleagues. In 1860 Colman left on a two-year trip abroad, where he studied old master painting and lived in Paris and Madrid, which served as bases for trips to Italy, Switzerland, southern Spain, and Tangier. During the 1860s, he painted a very successful series of exotic Spanish scenes and also Hudson River and New York harbor views, all of which were praised by Tuckerman for their delicacy and refinement of detail and color and fluid, sensitive handling of atmospheric effects.[1]

After 1862, when he became an Academician, Colman's broad interests took him in many directions. In 1866 he was a founder of the American Society of Painters in Water Color and was its first president until 1870. One of the founders of the progressive Society of American Artists, he bought a painting by twenty-one-year-old John Singer Sargent (1856-1925) at the organization's inaugural exhibition.[2] In 1878 he joined the New York Etching Club and exhibited prints in many New England shows. With Louis Comfort Tiffany (1848-1933), Lockwood de Forest (1850-1932), and Candace Wheeler, he founded the design and decorating firm Associated Artists, in 1879, for which he served as consultant. Of the many important commissions executed by the firm, the best known was the decoration of the Rembrandt Room, the library of the Henry O. Havemeyer house in New York City (1890-91).[3] In 1883 he designed the interiors of a house McKim, Mead, and White built for him in Newport. His interest in the decorative arts also led him to become an early collector of Japanese art.[4] His penchant for the exotic made him an inveterate traveler including four trips to the West, and one for four years to Europe and North Africa. From the mid-1860s watercolors were a more important part of his output than oils, and after the turn of the century pastel became a major interest (see cat. 38). In his later years his interest in art theory led him to write *Nature's Harmonic Unity, A Treatise on Its Relation to Proportion and Form* (1912) and *Proportional Form* (1920), which was published five days before his death.

Under the influence of French Barbizon painting, Colman moved from precision of detail in the 1850s and 1860s to looser brushwork and the gradual elimination of nonessential detail in the 1880s and 1890s, arriving at his own rather abstract version of Tonalism after the turn of the century. Throughout his career he maintained a harmonious, subtle use of color and concern for the depiction of atmospheric effects and changes in light, where the influence of J.M.W. Turner (1775-1851) and Sanford R. Gifford (1823-1880) are apparent.

In *View from the Raymond Hotel, Pasadena* Colman has already arrived at his mature style, which features open compositions emphasizing mood and atmosphere and focuses on tonal variations within a narrow range of colors. The viewer looks across the

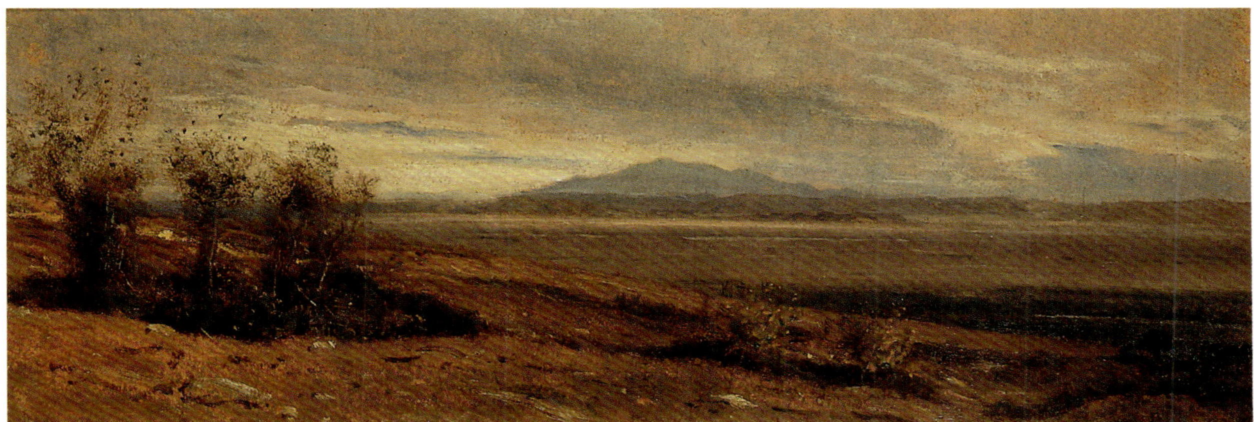

Samuel Colman, *View from the Raymond Hotel, Pasedena*, ca. 1888. Oil on academy board, 9 1/4" x 25 3/4".

gentle slope of Raymond Hill over the deserted expanse of the Pasadena Valley with distant foothills and mountains at the horizon. The artist has reduced details to a somewhat summarily indicated clump of trees at the left and a few bushes and scattered rocks. The colors are rich but muted throughout. Colman painted this somber, overcast late afternoon scene on the grounds of a famous and popular resort hotel which opened in 1886, burned down in 1895, and reopened in 1901. At this time, Pasadena was a small town of less than two thousand people that had been founded a decade before by a group of moderately well-to-do Hoosiers trying to escape the cold winters of Indianapolis.[5] Needless to say, the empty valley in the picture is now filled with houses.

1. Tuckerman, 559-60.

2. Sheldon, 72. Colman answered a friend's question as to why he had bought this unknown artist's painting: "Because I wanted to have it near me to key myself up with. I am afraid that I may fall below just such a standard, and I wish to have it hanging in my studio to reproach me whenever I do."

3. For Colman's activities as a decorator, see Alastair Duncan, Martin Eidelberg, and Neil Harris, *Masterworks of Louis Comfort Tiffany* (New York: Harry N. Abrams, 1990); Richard Guy Wilson, Dianne H. Pilgrim, and Richard N. Murray, *The American Renaissance 1876-1917* (Brooklyn: The Brooklyn Museum, 1979); and Doreen Bolger Burke, et al., *In Pursuit of Beauty: Americans and the Aesthetic Movement* (New York: The Metropolitan Museum of Art, 1986).

4. See Julia Meech-Pekarik, "Early Collectors of Japanese Prints and the Metropolitan Museum of Art," *Metropolitan Museum Journal* 17 (1982): 93-118.

5. See Arthur E. Raymond, *A Gentleman of the Old School: Walter Raymond and the Raymond Hotel* (Pasadena: Pasadena Historical Society, 1982), 2-3, and *Our Town: Pasadena 1886, Honoring Pasadena's Centennial 1887-1986* (Pasadena: Pasadena Historical Society, 1986).

Bibliography

Benjamin. Ch 9.

Craven, Wayne. "Samuel Colman (1832-1920): Rediscovered Painter of Far-Away Places." *American Art Journal* 8. 1 (May 1976): 16-37.

Moure, Nancy Dustin Wall. "Five Eastern Artists Out West." *American Art Journal* 5.2 (November 1973): 15-31.

Sheldon. 72-76.

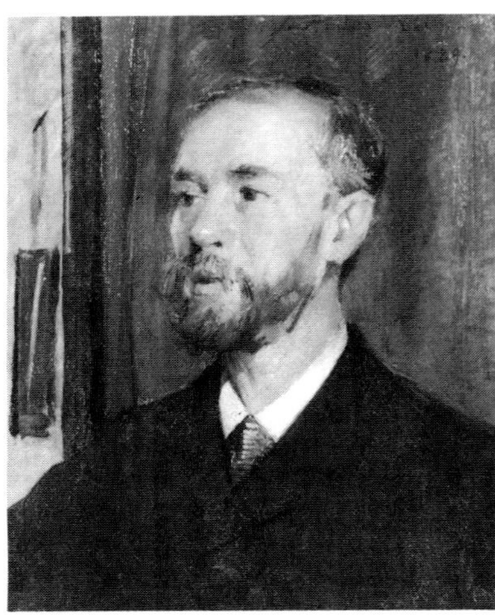

J. Alden Weir (1852-1919), *Robert Minor*, 1888. Collection of the National Academy of Design, New York.

23. Robert Crannell Minor

(born 1839, New York; died 1904, Waterford, Connecticut)
On the Heights, Mt. Hotskind, 1889
Oil on board
17 3/4" x 22 1/2"
Signed lower right: Minor
Inscribed on back: Mt. Hotskind. R.C. Minor

Like so many other once well known American Barbizon artists, Robert Crannell Minor has slipped into obscurity. Born in New York City in 1839, he began painting at the age of twelve, but his wealthy coal dealer father persuaded him to abandon a risky career in art for the safety of the family business. The business failed, however, in 1870 when Minor was thirty-one, granting him a second opportunity to pursue painting as a career. After studying in New York with the landscape and genre painter Alfred C. Howland (1838-1909) and Arthur Parton (cats. 17 and 18), he went to Paris, where he briefly studied with the figure painter Gustave Boulanger (1824-1876). His longest and most important period of training came at Barbizon with the landscapist Narcisse Virgilio Diaz de la Peña (1807-1875), who encouraged him to adopt a less detailed approach. Minor next studied with Joseph van Luppen at the Royal Academy in Antwerp, and traveled in Germany, Italy, and England where he did a number of paintings. He exhibited at the Royal Academy and Grosvenor Gallery in London and at the Paris Salon in 1872 before returning to New York the following year.

He set up a studio in the city and made his debut at the National Academy of Design, where he became a regular contributor, was made an Associate in 1888, and an Academician in 1897. After his return from Europe, he first exhibited views of Holland, Belgium, and England which were soon supplanted by scenes of the Adirondacks and Connecticut. He spent his summers near his friend Alexander Wyant (cat. 8) in Keene Valley in the Adirondacks until 1894, when he bought a house in Waterford on the coast of Connecticut. He suffered from a painful, crippling disease that decreased his productivity and the quality of his work after 1890. He died in 1904 in Waterford.

Minor belonged to a number of important art organizations including the National Academy of Design, the Artists' Fund Society, the American Watercolor Society, and the Salmagundi Club, of which he was president in 1898. He won awards at several international expositions as well, winning a bronze medal at the 1889 Paris Exposition Universelle and a silver medal at the Buffalo Pan-American Exposition in 1901.

Because he rarely dated his work, it is difficult to trace the development of his style, which consistently showed a Barbizon influence. His repertoire ranges from early forest interiors influenced by Diaz to more open landscapes. In typical Barbizon fashion he often emphasizes the season, usually either autumn or summer, time of day, and weather.[1] His palette varies from the dark glazes of his forest interiors to light, delicate shades of green, brown, and blue in his open views.

On the Heights, Mt. Hotskind is an airy, sunlit landscape set at midday in early autumn. Looking across this Connecticut mountain's grassy brow with a cloudy, blue sky as a backdrop, the view reveals a stand of trees, a few rocks, a rough fence, an indistinct hilltop below, and a valley beyond. Smudgy brush strokes overlay each other to soften every form. The delicate, high-keyed palette with admixtures of white runs a gamut of soft greens, while the ageing leaves of the underbrush are suggested by patches of reddish brown. *On the Heights* is probably the painting of the same name that Minor exhibited at the National Academy of Design in 1889.[2]

1. In a sample of paintings, all but one of which were landscapes, drawn from exhibition and auction catalogues and a National Museum of American Art Inventory of American Paintings, only seven of seventy-nine (8.9%)

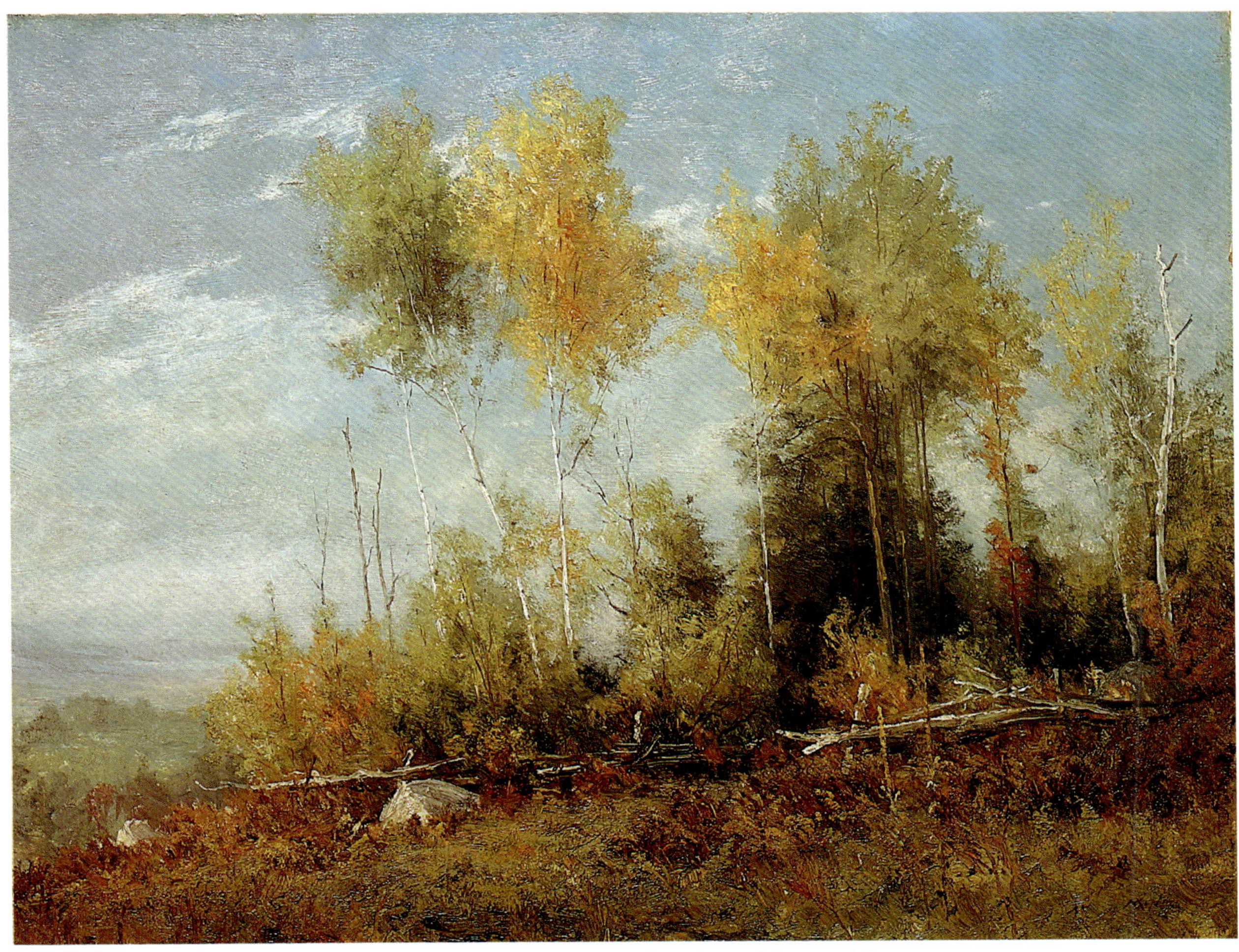

Robert Crannell Minor, *On the Heights, Mt. Hotskind*, 1889. Oil on board, 17 3/4" x 22 1/2".

were dated. Twenty of seventy-nine (25.3%) depict evening and the remaining seven (8.9%) are nighttime scenes. Examination of the titles of seventy-four landscapes exhibited at the National Academy of Design yields twenty-three (31.1%) twilight scenes, seventeen (22.3%) designated by season or month, and ten (13.5%) set in autumn. See Naylor, 646-39.

2. See Naylor, 638.

Bibliography

Andersen, Jeffrey, W., and Barbara J. MacAdam. *Old Lyme: The American Barbizon*. Old Lyme, CT: The Lyme Historical Society, Florence Griswold Museum, 1982. 42-43.

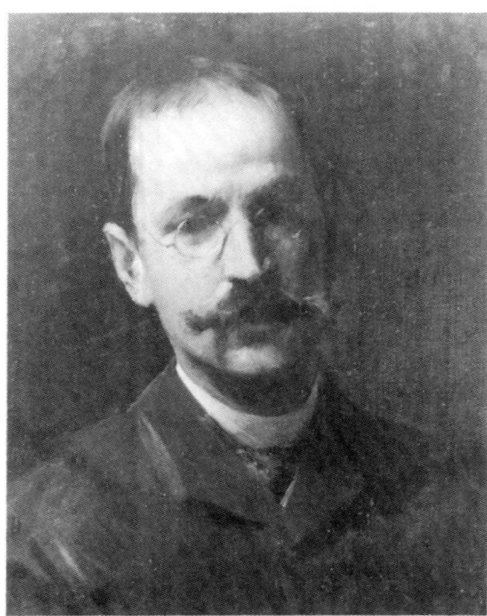

William Merritt Chase (1849-1916), *Walter L. Palmer*, 1887. Courtesy of the National Academy of Design, New York.

24. Walter Launt Palmer

(born 1854, Albany, New York; died 1932, Albany, New York)
Snow Laden, 1890
Watercolor on board
13" x 17"
Signed lower left: W. L. Palmer 1890
Publication: Maybell Mann and Alvin Lloyd Mann, *Walter Launt Palmer: Poetic Reality* (Exton, PA: Schiffer Publishing Co., 1984), 116, no. 176.

In his day Walter Launt Palmer was *the* painter of snow scenes. His popular and easily accessible style and subject matter, which he had adopted by 1890, ensured his lifelong success. After his death in 1932, his somewhat impressionistic decorative realism fell out of favor in the modernist market and his work was deaccessioned as old-fashioned by many museums after World War II. A recent monograph on Palmer has, however, begun to rekindle interest in his paintings.

He was the son of the famous Albany sculptor Erastus Dow Palmer (1817-1904) who, along with his distinguished artist friends, encouraged the artistic interests of his sickly son.[1] Palmer started drawing at the age of six and was given his first set of paints and brushes at age twelve by the portraitist Charles Loring Eliott (1812-1868). Four years later he began studying with the landscapist Frederic E. Church (1826-1900) during the summers, and first exhibited at the National Academy of Design when he was eighteen. He went to Paris twice, in 1874 and again from 1876 to 1877, to study with the figurative painter Emile-Auguste Carolus-Duran (1838-1917). On his return, he opened a studio in New York and enjoyed some success from a series of interior views, most of which contained figures that were a transient legacy of his study with Carolus-Duran. In 1881 he went to Venice, which became a continuing source of subject matter.

After returning to the United States, he became a member of the Society of American Artists and opened a studio in Albany, an odd choice for a sophisticated man who was an avid reader, good linguist, serious amateur musician, theatre lover, and very active socially. In the 1880s watercolors became an important part of his work. By the 1890s snow scenes dominated his subject matter to the extent that, by 1910, he had become a virtual specialist in winter landscapes. He traveled to Japan and Hong Kong in 1899, and in 1902 to Spain and Spanish Morocco, but thereafter stayed home to produce the snowy views of central New York with which he became synonymous. Popular alike with public and official taste,[2] they were widely shown at important New York and Boston dealers and at various institutions[3] and won a number of prizes at international expositions.[4] He was active as a painter until just before his death.

Palmer was a sensitive colorist who used rich, subtle colors to good advantage in his picturesque Venetian views, which are datable primarily to the 1880s and 1890s. It is somewhat puzzling that he became a specialist in winter scenes, where so little color is possible. Not surprisingly, he excelled in the depiction of delicate shades of colored light reflected on snow. It is hard to appreciate now, but his use of blue shadows was considered radical at the time. Many of his winter landscapes, which he painted from sketches and photos, have the same titles and are variations on the same scene.

They fall into three categories: extensive open views, partially blocked scenes, and completely blocked ones in which background development is either limited or absent. The first includes streams or roads winding back through the woods, fields seen from an unobstructed view or through a light screen of trees, and views from the bottom or top of rolling hills. The second and third kinds feature progressively shallower foregrounds and truncated trees. These are intimate woodland views, often supplemented with streams, where cedars, pines, and hemlocks predominate, perhaps because of the green color accents they

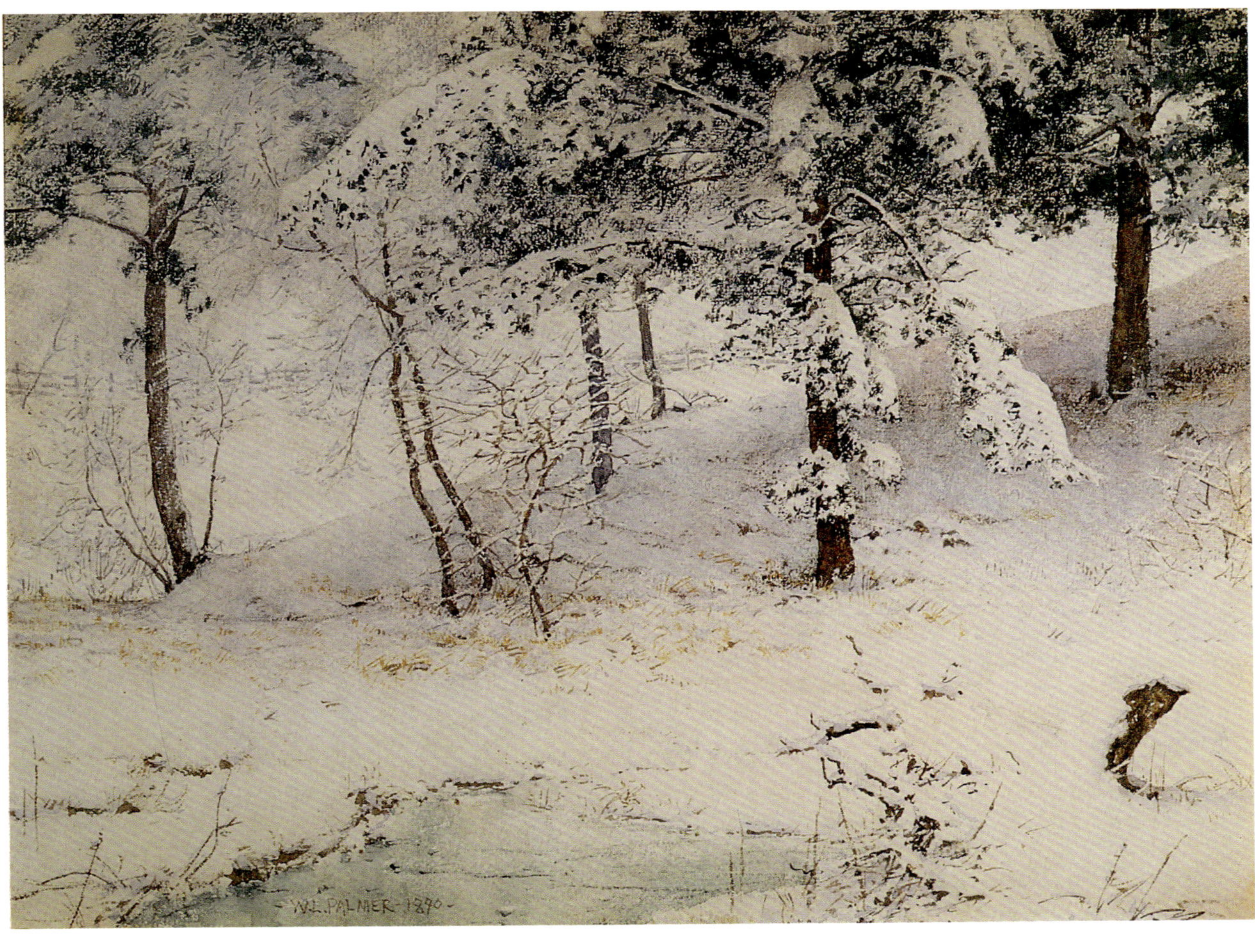

Walter Launt Palmer, *Snow Laden*, 1890. Watercolor on board, 13" x 17".

make possible. His watercolors, especially the earlier ones, tend to be painted in more detail than his oils, which are quite painterly and often have a pastel-like quality. On balance, they are more sensitive and memorable.[5]

At his best, he adroitly captures the stillness of winter and subtle alterations in the color of snow and the light and shadow of the woods. As the art historian Samuel Isham noted in 1905, Palmer successfully captures American winter, "crisp and dry in the keen cold and shining dazzling white against the blue horizon," reproduces "the exact tone of the shadows," and pushes details "to the ultimate point of elaboration," so that his pictures have "the sharpness and completeness of nature."[6]

In *Snow Laden*, the artist successfully renders the coldness and purity of freshly fallen snow on a clear winter day. His snapshot-like vignette encompasses a patch of water in the foreground, the truncated, snow-laden forms of six evergreens, and a couple of spindly bushes arranged in a careful rhythmic zigzag that ascends a gentle slope. In the background a split rail fence is just visible. The color of the evergreen needles, the pale blue of the water, and the deeper blue shadows pooled beneath the trees contrast with the white of the snow, which is produced by blank paper. Here Palmer uses only watercolor, but in some other paintings he approximates some of the qualities of oil by using a thick base of opaque white and adds other media, including gouache, to give depth and texture. From 1893 to 1929 he painted five other works with the same title as this watercolor, which was exhibited at the American Watercolor Society in 1891.[7]

1. Palmer had a severely crossed eye which was only partially corrected by surgery and he was subject to attacks of conjunctivitis throughout his life.

2. In 1901 a critic wrote about his snow scenes and views of Venice, "These pictures are equally popular with the Philistine, the art patron, and the critical fellow artist." See Theodore Purdy, "Walter Palmer's Landscapes," *Town and Country,* 28 September 1901, reproduced in its entirety on p. 82 of Mann and Mann.

3. Society of American Artists, National Academy of Design, American Watercolor Society, Pennsylvania Academy of the Fine Arts, and the Corcoran Gallery of Art.

4. Honorable mention, 1900 Paris Exposition Universelle; silver medal for watercolor, 1901 Buffalo Pan-American Exposition; silver medal for watercolor and bronze for oil, 1904 St. Louis-Louisiana Purchase Exposition; and bronze medal, 1910 Buenos Aires Exposition.

5. Analysis of 936 oils, watercolors, and pastels listed in Mann and Mann show that 20.1% of his production in the 1880s was devoted to pastels, which he seldom used thereafter. Watercolor predominated in the 1890s (58.3%) and gradually fell to 38% by the 1920s, while conversely the proportion of oils gradually rose. He was most productive from 1900 to 1909. Views of Venice amounted to 22.2% and 26.5% of his work in the 1880s and 1890s respectively, but dropped off after 1900. Palmer's first winter scene was painted in 1875. By the 1890s they amounted to 48.8% and by 1910 comprised virtually all of his paintings. Extensive open views comprise 46.4% of the 151 works reproduced in Mann and Mann. Bodies of water occur in 55.6% of them.

6. Samuel Isham, *History of American Painting* (New York: Macmillan, 1905), 440-43.

7. See Mann and Mann, nos. 317 (1898), 546 (1909), 824 (1923), 899 (1927), and 940 (1929). It is closest to a watercolor in Mann and Mann, no. 298, entitled *After the Snow*, 1898.

Bibliography

Palmer, Walter Launt. "On Painting of Snow." *Palette and Bench* 2 (February 1910): 90-91.

Mann, Maybelle and Alvin Lloyd Mann. *Walter Launt Palmer: Poetic Reality*. Exton, PA: Schiffer Publishing Co., 1984.

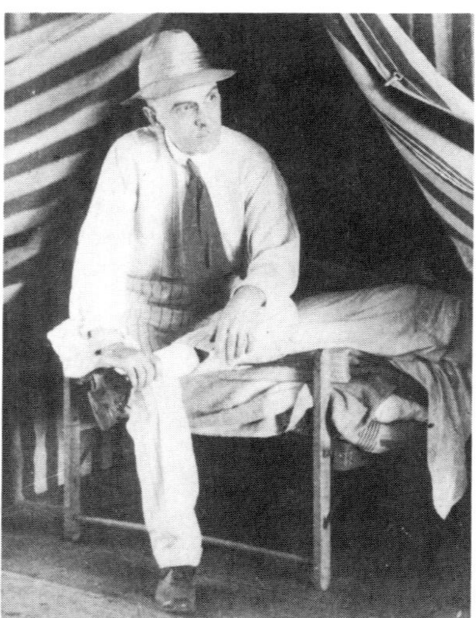

Richard Langtry Partington. Photo courtesy of The Bancroft Library, University of California, Berkeley, California.

25. Richard Langtry Partington

(born 1868, Stockport, England; died 1929, Philadelphia)
Lake Merritt, Oakland, California, 1891
Watercolor on paper
9 1/2" x 16"
Signed lower right: R. Langtry Partington, Oakland, Cal. 19/9/91

The California portrait and landscape painter Richard Langtry Partington is hardly known in the East. Doubly typical of nineteenth-century America, he was an immigrant and his family sought opportunity in the rapidly expanding West rather than the more settled East.

Born in England, he was a fully trained artist when he came to Oakland, California, with his family in 1889 at the age of twenty-one. His father, the portrait painter John Herbert Evelyn Partington (1844-1899), educated his children himself. Besides reading, writing, poetry, and music, they all learned to draw and paint; his sister, Gertrude Partington Albright (1883-1959), also became an artist. In 1891, together with his father, Partington started the Partington Art School in San Francisco, which he ran after his father's death until it burned down in the great fire of 1906. He then became curator of the Piedmont Art Gallery in Oakland but in 1916 moved to Philadelphia, where he stayed until his death in 1929. Although Partington painted many landscapes, he was best known for his portraiture.

Urban development has transformed Lake Merritt

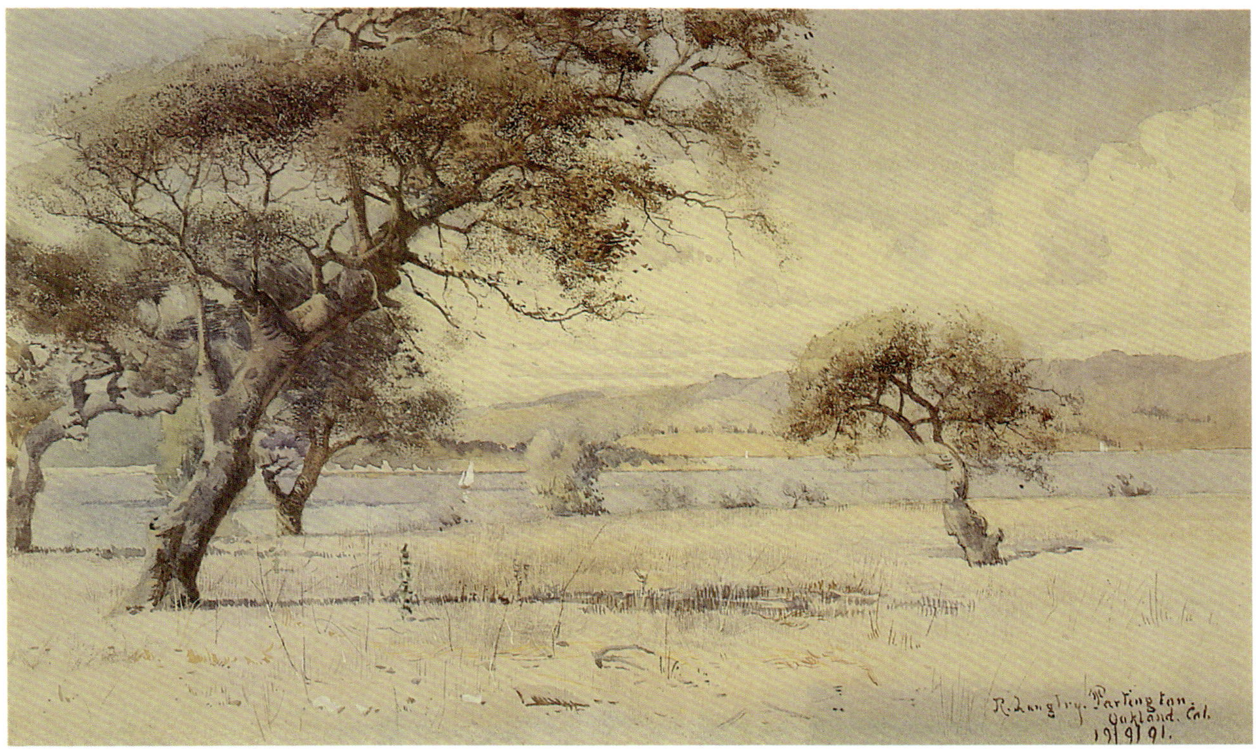

Richard Langtry Partington, *Lake Merritt, Oakland, California*, 1891. Watercolor on paper, 9 1/2" x 16".

and its environs since Partington painted this rather desolate, untended countryside scene in 1891. Now this small lake is surrounded by a fringe of lawn and ringed by roads and high rise buildings, but in his sensitive watercolor painted on a hot September day a century ago there is only a suggestion of one house in the distance. In the foreground, the intense sunlight beats down on grass already parched by a summer without rain. Beyond, the pale blue of Lake Merritt leads to a backdrop of tan and blue hills set against a pale blue sky dominated by white cumulus clouds. All this is a foil for the picturesque twisted shapes of live oaks that lead the eye to the pale sliver of a lake punctuated by a few white sails. Except for the detailed, carefully modeled forms of the larger trees and the billowing clouds in the background, this deft watercolor charms the eye with subtle tonal gradations effected by washes of diluted colors. Here, man has yet to overwhelm nature.

Bibliography

Hughes. 424-25.

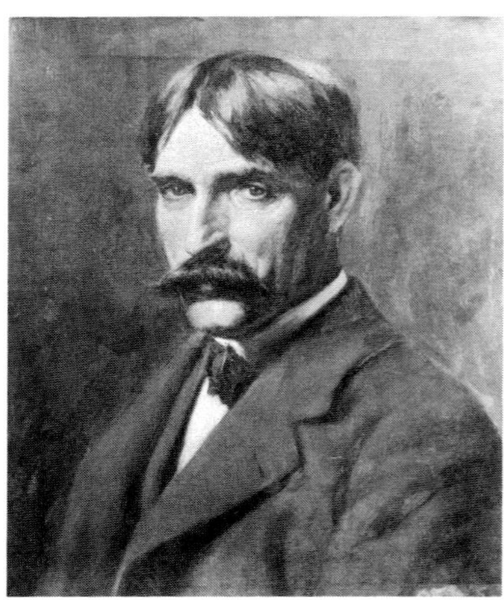

Bruce Crane, *Self-portrait*, 1897. Collection of the National Academy of Design, New York; photo courtesy of the Frick Art Reference Library.

26. [Robert] Bruce Crane

(born 1857, New York; died 1937, Bronxville, New York)
Long Island Landscape, ca. 1890-1895
Oil on canvas
16" x 22"
Signed lower left: Bruce Crane

By 1910, Bruce Crane's mastery of atmosphere and mood had made him one of America's best known Tonalist landscape painters, his name synonymous with the portrayal of rural autumn and winter scenes.[1] He was one of a number of New York area painters such as Colman (cat. 22), Martin (cats. 7 and 20), Smillie (cat. 29), and Wyant (cat. 8) who gave up the precision of the Hudson River School for the greater expressiveness and freedom of the Barbizon and Tonalist styles.

Crane came to art naturally. His father, an amateur artist, encouraged his interest. In 1874, when the seventeen-year-old Crane and his family moved from New York City to Elizabeth, New Jersey, he honed his skills as a draftsman for an architect and builder. The business failure of his employer spurred the young artist to concentrate on painting. By 1876 he had had a painting accepted by the National Academy of Design. From 1877 to 1878 he studied both with Alexander Helwig Wyant (cat. 8), whose subdued, introspective art exerted an important influence on him, and at the Art Students League.

During visits to London and Paris museums and galleries in 1878 and 1880, he must have been exposed to the new French Barbizon style, which he preferred to that of the Hudson River School. It is not surprising that after first painting in the Catskills and Adirondacks, he began to focus in 1879 on the more intimate farmland meadows and estuaries of Long Island. In the summer of 1882, he deepened his exposure to modern French landscape painting by spending the summer in the artists' colony of Grez-sur-Loing southeast of Paris near Barbizon. There he studied with the landscapist Stanislas-Jean-Charles Cazin (1841-1901), whose Tonalist approach affected his style and palette. Subsequently, Crane continued to paint views of Long Island, New Jersey, and Connecticut with increasing success.

In 1902 he was the center of a scandal in which his wife, who had been hospitalized for alcoholism, unsuccessfully sued him for adultery with his twenty-one-year-old artist step-daughter, whom he married two years later. He then started spending his summers in Old Lyme, Connecticut, and its environs dominated his subsequent work. In 1914 Crane moved his studio to the New York suburb of Bronxville, an area popular with many other artists.[2] In 1919 he started exhibiting with the Lyme Art Association, whose members included a number of American Barbizon, Impressionist, and Tonalist artists with whom he had become friends.[3]

Crane's career was typical of many successful post-Civil War artists who disavowed the Hudson River School in favor of Barbizon and Tonalist modes of painting. He first exhibited at the progressive Society of American Artists in 1881, although he continued to show paintings at the more conservative National Academy of Design where he became an Associate in 1897 and an Academician in 1901. Between 1897 and 1919, when he was at the height of his powers, he won prizes and medals at nine important exhibitions, five of them international expositions. However, by 1937 when he died in Bronxville, his paintings were considered old-fashioned.

Crane produced excellent works in every phase of his career. At first he tended to paint high-keyed sunlit scenes, but by 1884 a natural penchant for restricted, subdued palettes became evident. His first major success was *The Waning Year*, 1884, a late afternoon November landscape painted mainly in browns but with a little green. About it he later said, exaggerating somewhat, "The production of this November landscape put an end to green pictures."[4] Green did indeed become only an accent in his later paintings, which are

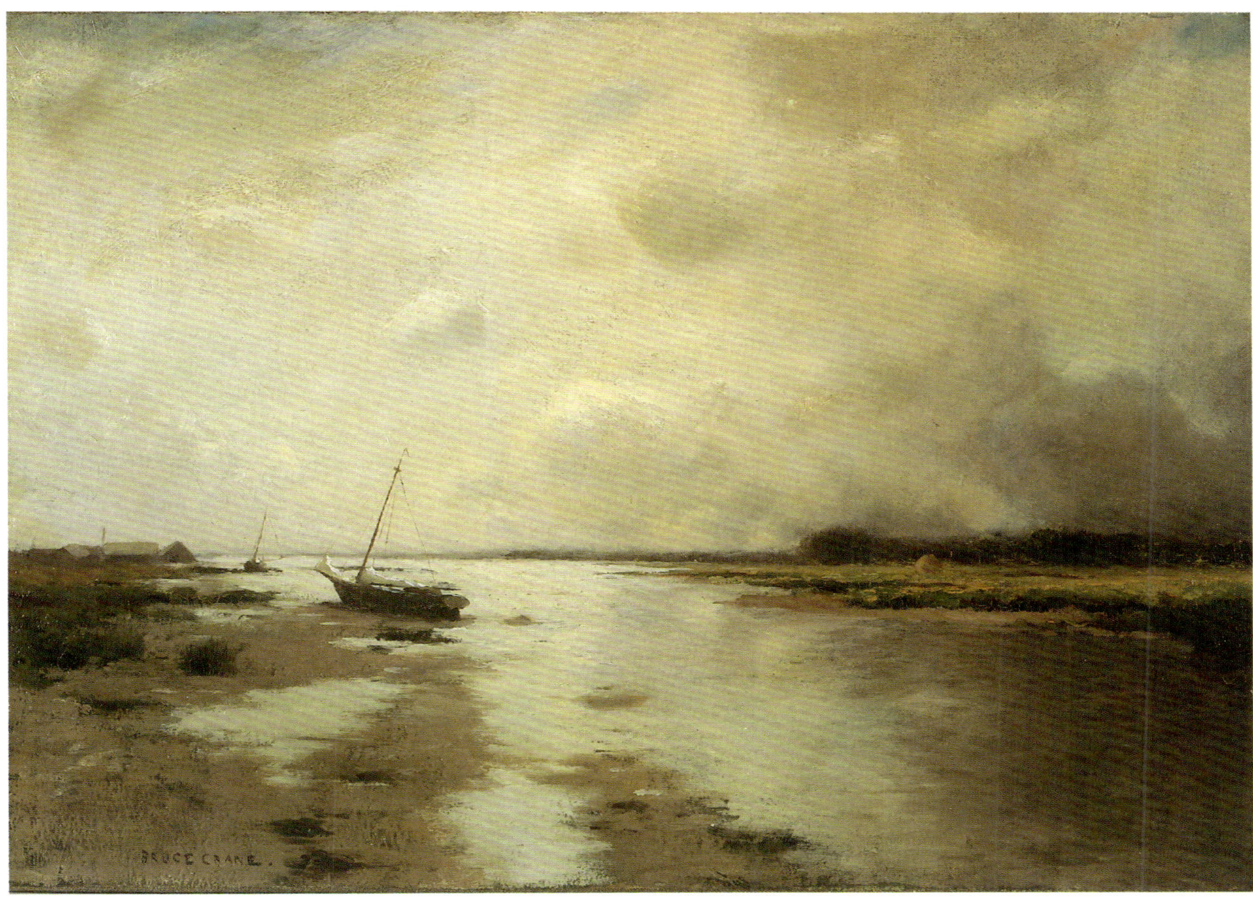

Bruce Crane, *Long Island Landscape*, ca. 1890-95. Oil on canvas, 16" x 22".

dominated by shades of brown.

Whatever their subject matter, his paintings always depict a domesticated but unpeopled landscape. They were invariably well composed, but as time passed used less and less detail. After 1910 his brushwork became rougher and looser, the surfaces of his canvases more scumbled and full of impasto, his colors less saturated, and his forms fewer and less distinct. Restricting his subject matter to depictions of late autumn and winter, he repeatedly reworked a few motifs, such as Connecticut woodlots, until they descended into predictable formulas. After 1920, such repetition and reductionism led to a decline in the quality of his work. His method of painting, which he shared with Wyant, may also have been responsible because he relied on memory, which fades with time. He described his method as follows: "For my part, I seldom look at a sketch when about to paint a picture. I do not need to do so except rarely, when I am in doubt about some particular point."[5]

Long Island Landscape typically focuses on season, time of day, and conditions of light and atmosphere. This moody work capitalizes on the subdued drama of a storm brewing over a Long Island estuary on a late summer afternoon. It is dominated by sky and water. A complex mixture of gray and white clouds looms menacingly at the right, presaging a squall. Lighter on the left, they thin to transmit and diffuse sunlight that shines onto the reflective surface of the water. Retreating, it interlaces with the tan mud of the narrowing shore that stretches back to include a couple of moored sailboats and a few buildings in the distance. In the background, a thin strip of green and tan meadow fringed with dark trees is the only color accent. This expansive, open Tonalist composition with its strong sense of spatial recession belongs to a tradition of river and estuary scenes that starts in seventeenth-century Dutch painting. It seems to relate most directly, however, to the subdued Tonalist paintings of his teacher Cazin.[6]

1. Out of a sample of eighty-nine landscapes, sixty-seven (75.3%) are autumn or winter views. Crane tended not to date his paintings (twenty-two of one hundred and three, or 21.4% of a larger sample, including coastal and night scenes, are dated) but all his dated landscapes from 1900 on depict either autumn or winter.

2. See Barbara Ball Buff, *The Artists of Bronxville: 1890-1930* (Yonkers, NY: The Hudson River Museum of Westchester, 1989).

3. See Jeffrey W. Anderson and Barbara J. MacAdam, and William H. Gerdts, Jeffrey W. Andersen, and Helen A. Harrison, *En Plein Air: The Art Colonies at East Hampton and Old Lyme 1880-1930* (Old Lyme, CT: Florence Griswold Museum and East Hampton, NY: Guild Hall Museum, 1989).

4. See *Quarterly Illustrator* (November 1893): 302.

5. Harold T. Lawrence, "A Painter of Idylls--Bruce Crane," *Brush and Pencil* 11. 1 (October 1902): 7.

6. See Weisberg, 227-28, 281-82, pls. 134, 199, 200.

Bibliography

Clark, Charles Teaze. "Bruce Crane, Tonalist Painter." *Antiques* (November 1982): 1061-63.

Clark, Charles Teaze and Mary Muir. *Bruce Crane: American Tonalist*. Old Lyme, CT: The Lyme Historical Society, Florence Griswold Museum, 1984.

27. Henry Farrer

(born 1843, London, England; died 1903, Brooklyn, New York)
On the River, 1896
Watercolor on paper
10 1/4" x 15 1/2"
Signed lower left: H. Farrer 1896

Watercolor has always languished in the shadow of oil and watercolorists generally become well known only if they also establish themselves as oil painters. As a result, Henry Farrer's highly accomplished works with their superb technique and soft, understated poetry remain the province of specialists.

Farrer, the younger brother of the artist Thomas Charles Farrer (1839-1891), was born in London in 1843. He is thought to have been self-taught. After coming to America in 1863, he opened a studio in New York City and became a landscapist specializing in watercolor and etching. A founding member of the American Society of Painters in Water Color in 1866, he was its secretary for many years and often exhibited there. He also showed his works at the National Academy of Design from 1876 to 1881 and the Brooklyn Art Association from 1867 to 1884, contributed works to the 1876 Philadelphia Centennial Exposition and the 1878 Paris Exposition Universelle, and was a member of the Artists Fund Society. A founder of the New York Etching Club, he became its president, and was also a member of the Royal Society of Painter-Etchers in London. He lived and worked in Brooklyn from 1887 until his death in 1903.

At first, Farrer painted under the spell of his Pre-Raphaelite brother, who was a member of the Association for the Advancement of Truth in Art. Both it and its official organ, *The New Path* (1863-1865), preached the doctrine of John Ruskin (1819-1900), which insisted on carefully reproducing objects in their natural, out-of-doors settings.[1] Farrer's watercolors first obeyed Pre-Raphaelite strictures using a tight, detailed, stippled approach.

Like most early adherents to Ruskin's precepts, by 1875 he found such detail so impractical and aesthetically limiting that he started to execute the more freely painted watercolors for which he is best known.[2] Mostly set in New York, New Jersey, or Long Island, they range from harbor, coastal, river, and estuary scenes to inland views. Although he painted without gouache, his transparent watercolors spread

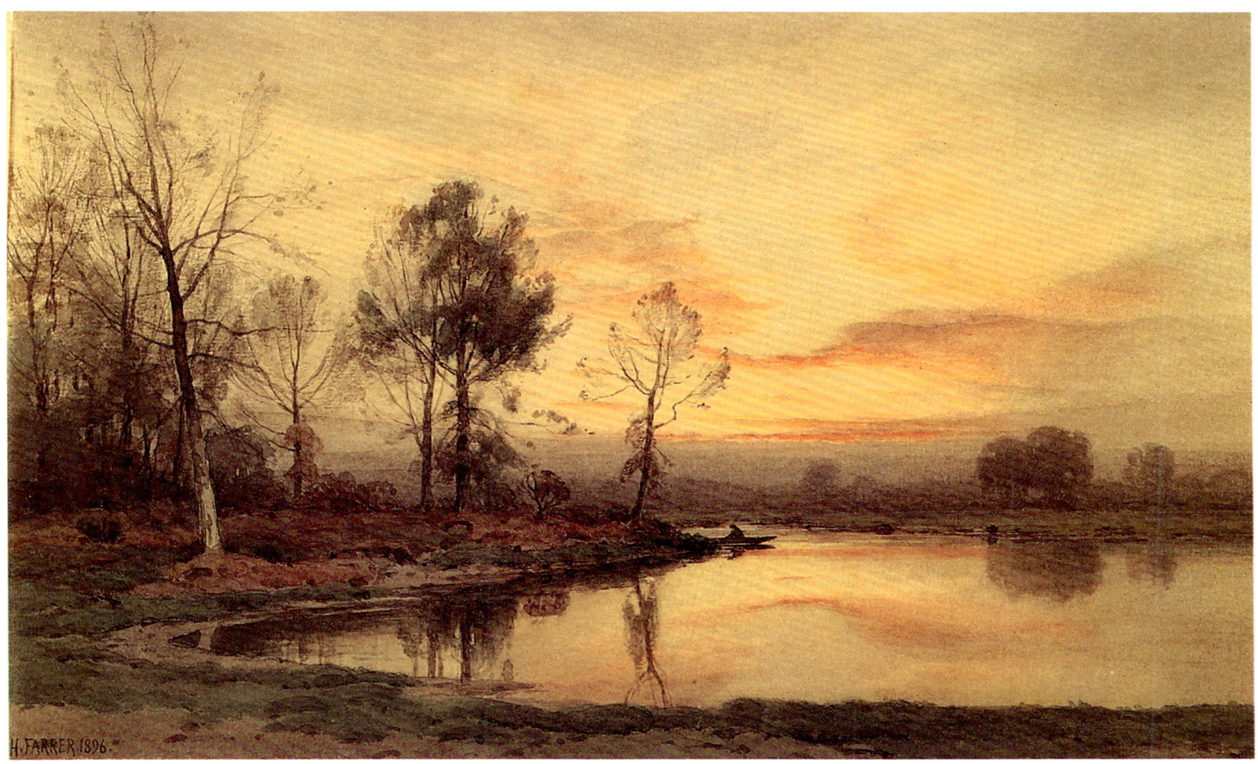

Henry Farrer, *On the River*, 1896. Watercolor on paper, 10 1/4" x 15 1/2".

over the whole sheet in overlapping, soft, thin washes become almost opaque at times. His simple, open compositions are restricted to a narrow range of muted colors executed in subtly varied and carefully controlled washes. More often than not, these depictions of lonely, unpeopled marshes or meadows with winding estuaries or streams seen in the subdued light of dawn or sunset exude a compelling mood of slightly melancholy tranquillity.[3] At times, especially in his harbor scenes, Farrer arrives at true Luminism. In the great attention he pays to variation in light, color, and cloud formations, he seems to have profited from direct study of J.M.W. Turner (1775-1851), as did Thomas Moran (1837-1926), William Trost Richards (cat. 35), and Samuel Colman (cat. 22).[4]

On the River is one of Farrer's many variations on the theme of a body of water seen at twilight. It is probably set in Long Island. At the left corner the narrow foreground strip of shore broadens and angles back toward a wooded point of land with a silhouetted rowboat and figure at its end. Across the water on the far shore, above blurred, indistinct trees and a band of dark clouds, the sky glows with the light of the hidden sun. Alternating areas of blue sky and subtly melded orange and gray clouds create a complex aerial pattern. Although muted, this fading sunset still makes a strong statement against the dull greens of the grass and trees and the gray of the earth. Farrer manipulates a limited tonal range in the service of elegiac visual poetry without reducing the composition to near abstraction or stripping it of detail, a familiar pitfall of so many Tonalist artists.

1. See Linda S. Ferber, "Determined Realists: The American Pre-Raphaelites and the Association for the Advancement of Truth in Art," in Ferber and Gerdts, 11-37.

2. Compare, for example, *A Pair of Birds*, 1867, Christie's, 6/25/89, no. 144 and *Coastal Highlands*, 1875, Ferber and Gerdts, no. 106, color pl. 7, ill. p. 135 with *Sunrise, East River*, 1875, Ferber and Gerdts, no. 107, ill. p. 262.

3. Of a sample of twenty, all but one (95%) include water and twelve (60%) are sunrises or sunsets.

4. See Kathleen A. Foster, "The Pre-Raphaelite Medium: Ruskin, Turner and American Watercolors," in Ferber and Gerdts, 79-107.

Bibliography

Gallati, Barbara Dayer. "Henry Farrer (1843-1903)," Ferber and Gerdts. 256-62.

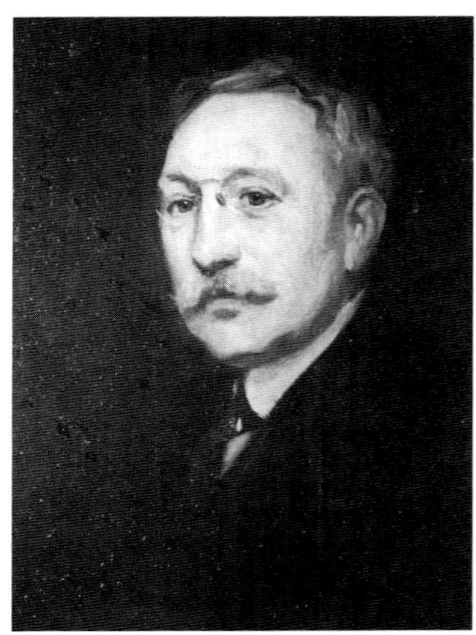

Augustus Vincent Tack (1870-1949), *Arthur Hoeber*, 1909. Collection of the National Academy of Design, New York.

28. Arthur Hoeber

(born 1854, Nutley, New Jersey; died 1915, New York)
Grainfield, ca. 1900
Oil on canvas
14" x 22"
Signed lower left: Arthur Hoeber

Before his death in 1915, Arthur Hoeber was well known for his spare, moody Tonalist landscapes, but now his name is familiar only to specialists and his oeuvre awaits reappraisal. Born in Nutley, New Jersey, in 1854, he first studied in New York City at the Cooper Union and the Art Students League with the landscape, genre, and portrait painter J. Carroll Beckwith (1852-1917). In 1881, he carried a letter of introduction to the London-based Pre-Raphaelite artist John Everett Millais (1829-1896), who sent him to Paris to study with the figurative painter Jean-Léon Gérôme (1824-1904) at the Ecole des Beaux-Arts. During his five years in France, he exhibited at the Paris Salon from 1882 to 1885 and spent his summers in Normandy and at Concarneau, where he shared a studio with American expatriate artist Thomas Alexander Harrison (1853-1930). Like many other Americans there he painted landscapes with peasants. After his return to New York City in 1886, figurative painting continued to dominate his work for a few years, but starting in 1888 he turned to pure landscapes. These either featured Cape Cod, where he later summered, Long Island, or the environs of Nutley, New Jersey, which had become an art colony by the time he moved back there in 1892.

Hoeber was active in the art world of New York, where he belonged to influential art clubs such as Lotos and Salmagundi, and often exhibited at the Brooklyn Art Association and the National Academy of Design, which made him an Associate in 1909. He also won a prize at the 1901 Buffalo Pan-American exposition. Between 1890 and 1915, he was a prolific and widely read art critic whose articles appeared in a variety of magazines such as *Harper's Weekly* and *The International Studio*, and newspapers such as the *New York Globe* and *The New York Times*.

After Hoeber became a landscapist, he turned more and more to views of flat meadows or marshlands with low horizons which he depicted in the fading light of late afternoon or early evening. Stripped of all but a few details, their real subject matter is the subtle alteration in the appearance of land and sky as light and color change in the transition from day to night. Depending on when they were done, they range among Barbizon, Impressionist, and Tonalist styles. Most of Hoeber's currently known works are landscapes which are rarely dated. Only a few of these are in museum collections.[1]

Grainfield focuses on a time of day when thirty seconds spell the difference between evening and night, when objects easily discernible one moment become indistinct the next. Above a little patch of water and two truncated trees, a sliver of a moon stands out in the pale but darkening sky. At the horizon is a faint reminiscence of what must have been a spectacular sunset. Except for the well-articulated trees, the soft smudgy brushwork suggests rather than explicitly defines. However, the anchoring rectangle defined by the water, trees, and moon, and the contrast between the vertical trees and successive horizontal bands of grass, grain, hills, and sky, give this composition enough structure to save it from diffuse banality.

1. Out of a sample of thirty-four culled from exhibition and auction catalogues, books, and a 1990 National Museum of American Art inventory of American paintings, twenty-five (73.5%) were landscapes and only four (11.8%) were dated.

Bibliography

Caffin, Charles H. "Arthur Hoeber—An Appreciation." *New England Magazine* 28. 2 (April 1903): 223-33.

Sweet, Diana Dimodica. "American Tonalism: An Explanation of the Ideas Through the Work and Literature of Four Major Artists." In Gerdts, Sweet, and Preato, 29-38.

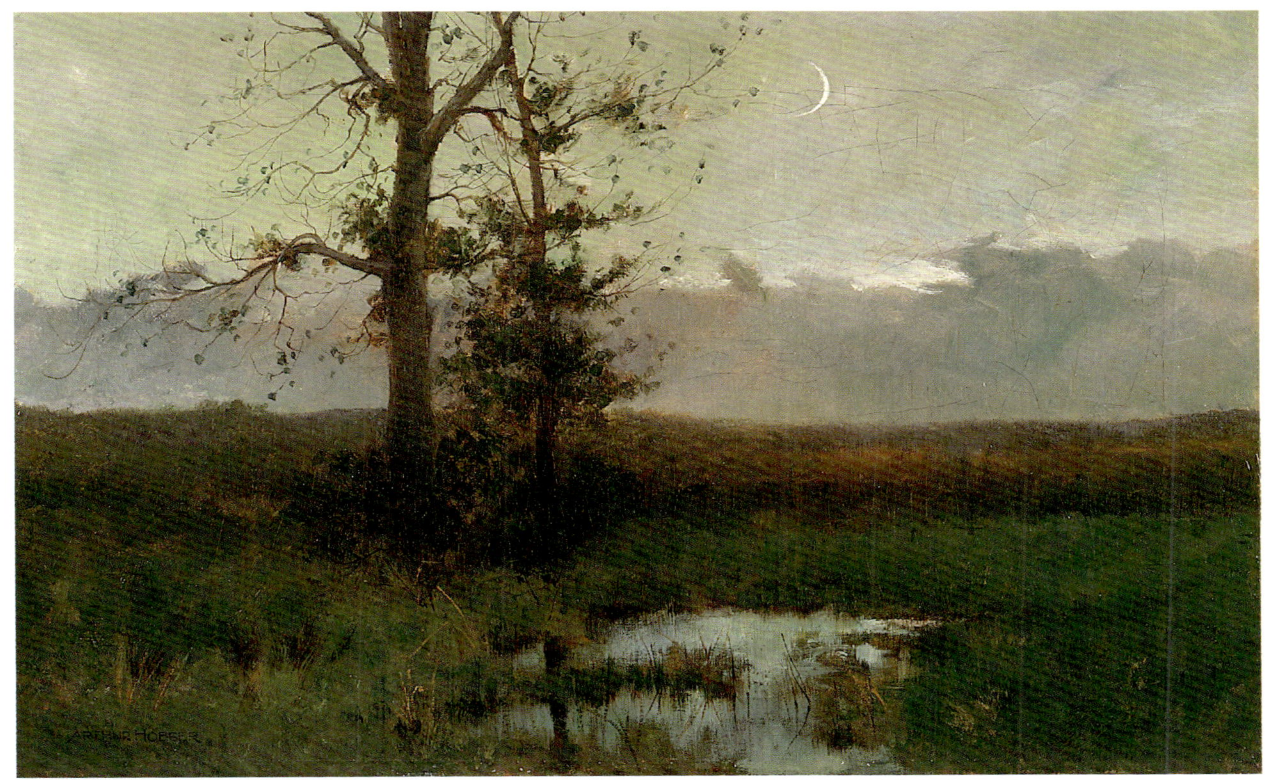

Arthur Hoeber, *Grainfield*, ca. 1900. Oil on canvas, 14" x 22".

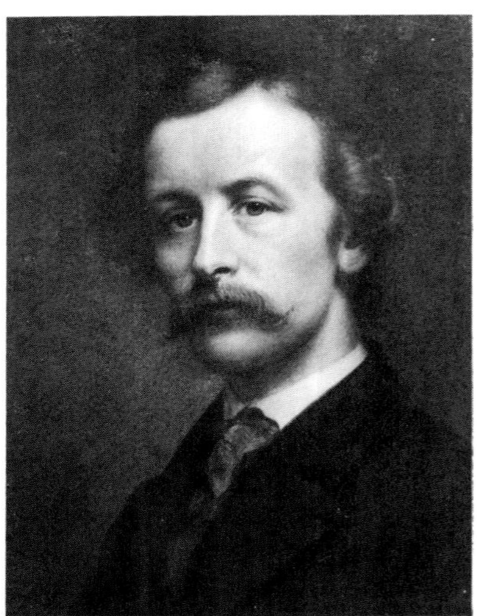

Robert M. Pratt (1811-1880), *George H. Smillie*, 1864. Collection of the National Academy of Design, New York; photo courtesy of the Frick Art Reference Library.

29. George Henry Smillie

(born 1840, New York; died 1921, Bronxville, New York)
Lake Mohonk, 1908
Oil on canvas
20" x 30"
Signed lower left: Geo H. Smillie N.A.

The once popular work of American Barbizon landscapist George Henry Smillie still awaits renewed attention and appreciation. He was the third of four sons and the fifth of seven children of the distinguished Scottish-born engraver James Smillie (1807-1885). His brothers were all artistically gifted, but it was his elder brother, the engraver and landscape painter James David Smillie (1833-1909), whom his father favored and trained. Smillie grew up in Poughkeepsie and New York City. His early training is undocumented, but in 1861 he studied with the Hudson River School landscapist James McDougal Hart (1828-1901).

In 1862, he opened a New York studio and exhibited for the first of many times at the National Academy of Design, where he became an Associate two years later and an Academician in 1884. He also exhibited at the Brooklyn Art Association from 1863 to 1885. During this period, his life and career were closely linked with those of James David. They often traveled together, shared adjacent studios for a time, accepted joint commissions, and if one were ill the other even taught his pupils. Only in the 1880s did George's career catch up with and outstrip his brother's.

He first painted in a detailed Hudson River School style, influenced both by Hart and James David, that typically combined topographic exactitude and dramatic color or atmospheric effects. His works of the 1860s and early 1870s not only depicted nearby Pennsylvania, the Hudson Valley, and the Catskills but also reflected trips farther afield to the Adirondacks, the White Mountains, and Colorado, Utah, and California. Those of the later 1870s continued to portray local areas and the Adirondacks as well as Florida, which he visited in 1874. During much of that decade he was intermittently inactive because of depression.

By the late 1870s, he was fully recovered and his style began to reflect the influence of Barbizon painting with freer, more vigorous brushwork, the use of impasto, and more open compositions. The next decade opened auspiciously. In 1881 he married Helen Sheldon Jacobs (1855-1926), a beautiful and talented artist who was the former pupil and girlfriend of James David. A trip to Europe in 1884 spent mostly in Etretat in France produced few paintings with foreign subjects but did lead him to use brighter, more broken color. It ushered in the most successful period of his career. He began to concentrate on coastal views of Maine, Massachusetts, and Long Island and inland scenes set in rural Connecticut, where he summered and finally bought a house in Ridgefield in 1890. In these paintings, simpler scenery replaced the picturesque subjects of his earlier work.

As an early member and later an officer of the American Watercolor Society, recording secretary of the National Academy of Design, and a member of the Century Association and the Lotos Club, he was a substantial figure in the New York art scene and his work was officially recognized by a number of prizes and medals.[1] At some point after 1900, he joined a number of other artists living in Lawrence Park in Bronxville, where he continued to paint until the end of his life.[2]

Unlike several other Hudson River School treatments of *Lake Mohonk*,[3] Smillie's opts only for a glimpse of the water rather than a panoramic view, much as a hiker might chance upon it.[4] A rocky cliff slopes down from the left to the elevated foreground vantage point of a flat ledge overlooking a mass of trees and a small triangle of water. Beyond, a sharply rising bluff looms under a cloudy sky. *Lake Mohonk* is typical of Smillie's mature work in three ways: the free, vigorous brushwork; the fresh color contrasts among the gray

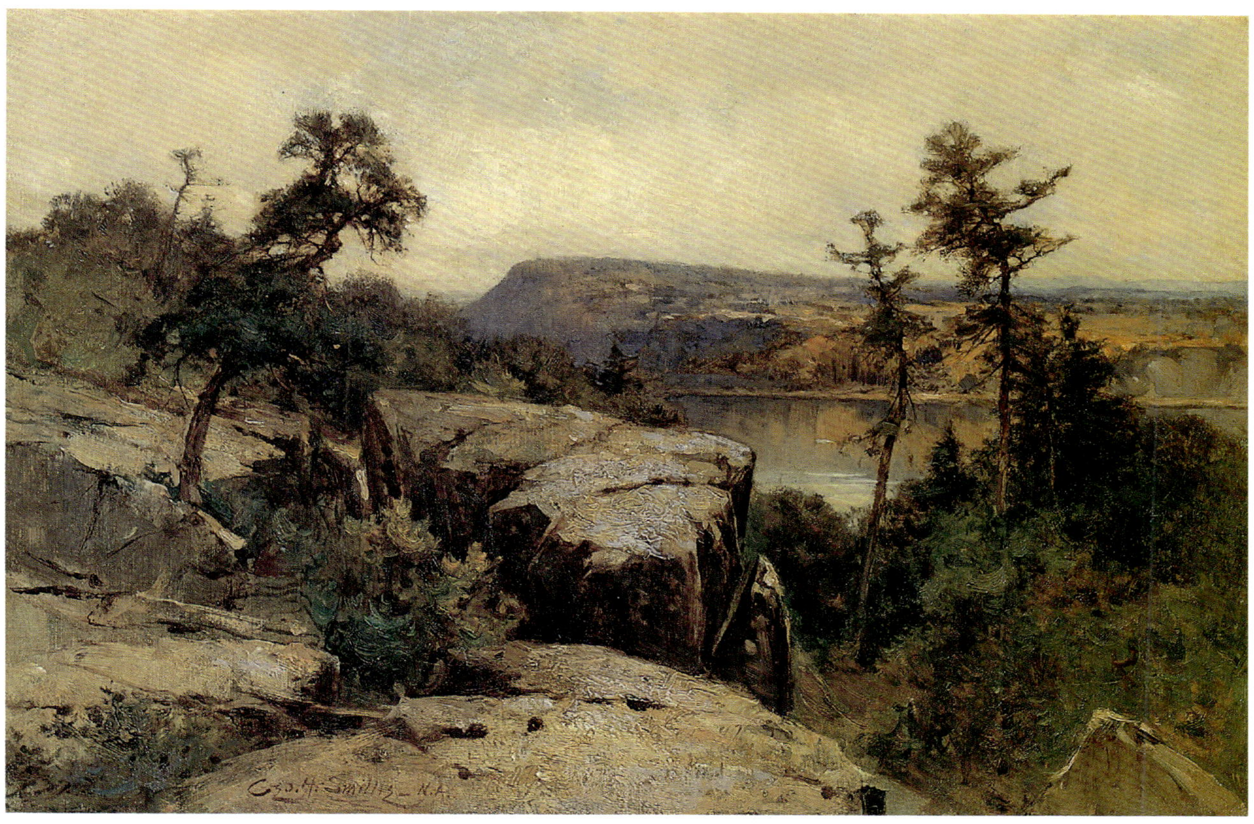

George Henry Smillie, *Lake Mohonk*, 1908. Oil on canvas, 20" x 30".

rocks, green vegetation, and light blue bluff; and the compact, highly structured composition reinforced by the strong, simply modeled forms of the massive cliffs and several asymmetrical pines. Like most of Smillie's later paintings it is not dated,[5] but National Academy records show that he exhibited a version of this subject in 1908.[6]

1. Society of American Artists, 1885; St. Louis-Louisiana Purchase Exposition, 1904; and Society of American Artists, 1907.

2. For this and other information about Smillie I am indebted to Brucia Witthoft, who kindly made available to me her extensive unpublished manuscript, "George Henry Smillie, 1840-1921: Painter-Brother."

3. Mohonk Lake is in the 24,000-acre Shawangunk Mountain nature preserve near New Paltz north of New York. It is the site of Mohonk Mountain House, a National Historic Landmark built in 1869.

4. See J. Antonio Hekking's (active 1840s-1880s) *Mohonk Lake*, Christie's, 5/30/86, no. 21 and Daniel Huntington's (1816-1906) *Lake Mohonk*, 1899, ill pp. 770-71 of *Antiques* 87. 4 (April): 1990.

5. Of seventeen dated, published works by Smillie located by the author, fourteen are dated before 1886 and the others bear dates of 1891, 1902, and 1913.

6. See Falk (1990), 478, where it is listed as *Lake Mohunk (sic), New York.*

Bibliography

Bermingham, Peter. *American Art in the Barbizon Mood.* Washington, D.C.: Smithsonian Institution Press, 1975. 166.

Myers, 180-81.

Marine Painting

Thomas Birch's *On the Shrewsbury River,* ca. 1840 (cat. 30) and Samuel Colman's *Barnegat Bay,* ca. 1914 (cat. 38) were painted at sites not very far from each other in New Jersey. Yet, the three-quarters of a century that separates them spells the difference between seventeenth- and eighteenth-century English and Dutch traditions of marine painting and near abstraction. The repertoire of nineteenth-century marine artists included harbor, river, and coastal scenes and views of the open sea. Before about 1860, portrayals of storms and shipwrecks that stressed the drama of man against the sea continued an earlier tradition derived from late eighteenth-century aesthetic theory, romantic poetry, and the works of seventeenth-century Dutch artists, the French painter Claude-Joseph Vernet (1712/14-1789), and the English artist J.M.W. Turner (1775-1851). A different, equally traditional but more documentary approach exemplified by Birch and Robert Salmon (1775-ca. 1844) concentrated on the details of battle scenes and calm views of ships and harbors. Salmon, in particular, painted clear, precise, light-filled compositions emphasizing well-defined atmospheric effects. In the hands of Fitz Hugh Lane (1804-1865), the depiction of transient changes in light and atmosphere reached a new level of subtlety that was mirrored in spacious, Luminist coastal views of a number of Hudson River School artists, including John F. Kensett (1816-1872) and Whittredge (cat. 19). In these works boats are either absent or depicted as small, distant details entirely incidental to the sea.

This nonanecdotal approach with its strong emphasis on the horizontal is reflected in the coastal scenes of Raymond Dabb Yellend (cat. 31) and Francis Augustus Silva (cats. 32 and 33). On the other hand, in *Homeward Bound* (cat. 34) Edward Moran capitalizes on both the play of light on water and clouds and anecdotal detail.

Starting in the 1870s, Eastern marine painters started going farther afield to the coasts of California, Alaska, Labrador, England, and Ireland. Two who continued this tradition beyond the turn of the century were William Trost Richards and Alfred Thompson Bricher. Richards often chose to represent the contest between waves and shore, as in his rendition of the wave battered, rocky cliffs of Cornwall or Ireland illustrated in catalogue 35. Bricher, on the other hand, consistently preferred more tranquil evocations of coastal water and sky like the view painted in Casco Bay in Maine (cat. 36). A freer, more painterly approach to the sea coexisted with such precise, linear painting. Before the Civil War, it was exemplified by the Turner follower and marine specialist James Hamilton (1819-1878). Later, however, it took a different, more modern turn in the hands of nonspecialists who had absorbed French influences. One of the first was John La Farge, whose subtle, moody marine watercolor is shown in catalogue 37. Ultimately, the rendition of detail in marine views became of even less interest to painters like Samuel Colman, whose true subject in the Tonalist sunset view of Barnegat Bay (cat. 38) is atmosphere and mood. Here details vanish in a way that is but a step from later, modernist marine painters such as John Marin (1870-1953) and Milton Avery (1893-1965).

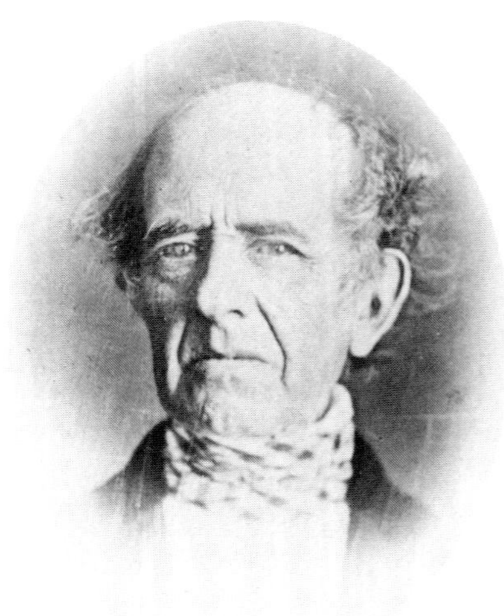

Thomas Birch, in *Pennsylvania Academicians and Philadelphia Artists - Photograph Album*. The Pennsylvania Academy of the Fine Arts, Philadelphia. Archives.

30. Thomas Birch

(born 1779, Warwickshire, England; died 1851, Philadelphia)
On the Shrewsbury River, Redbank, New Jersey, ca. 1840
Oil on panel
13 5/8" x 20"
Unsigned

Like his fellow Philadelphian Doughty (cat. 1) and many other artists who did not use New York as a base, Thomas Birch is considered historically important but is underestimated by collectors and general museums. Although best known as a pioneer American marine painter, he shares priority with Washington Allston (1779-1843) as one of America's earliest significant landscapists.

English born, he emigrated in 1794 at age fifteen with his family to live near Philadelphia. His father, William Russell Birch (1755-1834), an engraver, painter of miniatures on enamels, and landscape artist in the eighteenth-century English tradition, was his teacher. Thomas was clearly influenced by his father's collection of engravings of British landscapes and continental old masters and, later, by seventeenth- and eighteenth-century paintings owned by one of his early patrons, Joseph Bonaparte (1784-1844). He established a reputation first as a competent portraitist, leaving his father's studio after completing the drawings for their series of engravings, *The City of Philadelphia in the State of Pennsylvania As it Appeared in 1800.*

He may have done his first landscape in 1806. By 1811, however, when the Pennsylvania Academy of the Fine Arts held its first exhibition, all twelve of his entries were either landscapes or seascapes. He made his name with a series of paintings illustrating the War of 1812, later moving from such portrayals of naval battles to establish marine portraiture in the United States. He was the first to introduce drama into this previously static genre, which was later taken up in a more placid, less romantic vein by James Edward Buttersworth (1817-1894) and Antonio Jacobsen (1850-1921). Although his marine paintings often focus on the struggle between man and nature, they also depict the ordered calm and serenity of rivers and harbors. The influence of the eighteenth-century French artist Claude-Joseph Vernet (1712/14-1789) is apparent both in his dramatic, stormy scenes of shipwrecks and his idyllic harbor views. His battle paintings bear the imprint of seventeenth-century Dutch artists and their eighteenth-century English and continental followers. His other marine works' subject matter and compositional devices often recall those of Salomon van Ruysdael (1600/3?-1670) and Willem van de Velde the Younger (1633-1707). Oddly enough, although Birch showed meticulous care in his depictions of various kinds of boats, he was not a sailor and had little firsthand knowledge of them.

Since his harbor and river scenes often include landscape elements, it is not surprising that he painted many pure landscapes. Earlier, they were typically views of or from a particular estate but later became more general in their subject matter. He was known for his winter scenes. With a backdrop of fields, houses, and woods, they usually show a sleigh going down a road or crossing a bridge over a stream. Later, Régis-François Gignoux (1816-1882) and George Harvey Durrie (1820-1863) elaborated on this genre which Birch started in the United States. In the course of his career, he worked around Philadelphia, the Delaware River area, New York harbor, and the Massachusetts and Maine coasts.

Although his paintings underwent no major stylistic changes, his earlier works have a tighter, more linear quality while his mature style is marked by simpler compositions, looser brushwork, and lighter, brighter colors. At their best his clear, fresh, sensitive, and accurate depictions of sky, water, and land admirably express not only the romantic drama of the sea but also

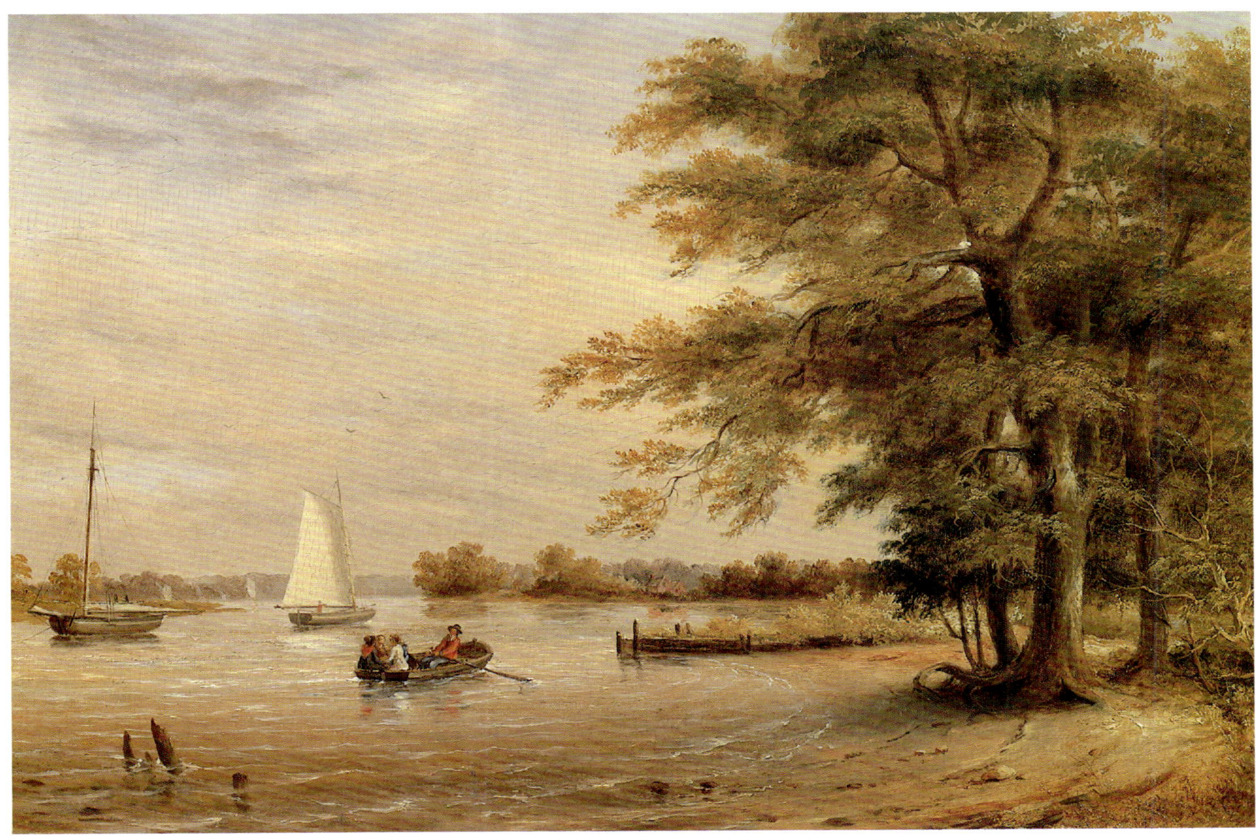

Thomas Birch, *On the Shrewsbury River, Redbank, New Jersey*, ca. 1840. Oil on panel, 13 5/8" x 20".

the placid poetry of harbors, waterways, and fields in an orderly vision of the civilizing hand of man.[1]

Like all of Birch's landscape, harbor, and river scenes, *On the Shrewsbury River, Redbank, New Jersey* portrays a specific place. Framed on the right by the doubly interrupted curve of a tree-lined shore, we see the river opening out at the left. In the foreground, a rowboat with four figures floats quietly along in front of two small sailboats, one of which proceeds slowly while the other, sails furled, rests at its mooring. Although this gentle, peaceful river scene draws on seventeenth-century Dutch prototypes, its palette is broader and warmer. The subtlety with which Birch depicts the soft, pinkish gray clouds perforated by traces of blue and the finesse with which he renders the reflections in the water and the wavelets gently moving toward the shore are hallmarks of his work. Typical, too, are its compositional scheme and mood. Arranged in parallel planes with vertical components silhouetted against horizontals, it effects an overall feeling of peace and order. Sometimes Birch incorporated his finely written signature into logs or tree trunks where it is hard to find. Here, however, as in some of his other paintings, none can be found.

1. Out of thirty-eight illustrated works, twenty-two (57.9%) are dated, twenty-two (57.9%) are of marine subjects, and sixteen (42.1%) are landscapes. All the estate views are early (1808-1818), while the winter scenes (six of sixteen or 37.5%) bear dates in the 1830s and 1840s.

Bibliography

Creer, Doris J. "Thomas Birch: A Study of the Condition of Painting and the Artist's Position in Federal America." Master's Thesis. University of Delaware, 1958.

Gerdts, William H. "Thomas Birch: America's First Marine Artist." *Antiques* 89 (April 1966): 518-34.

Wilmerding. 74-85.

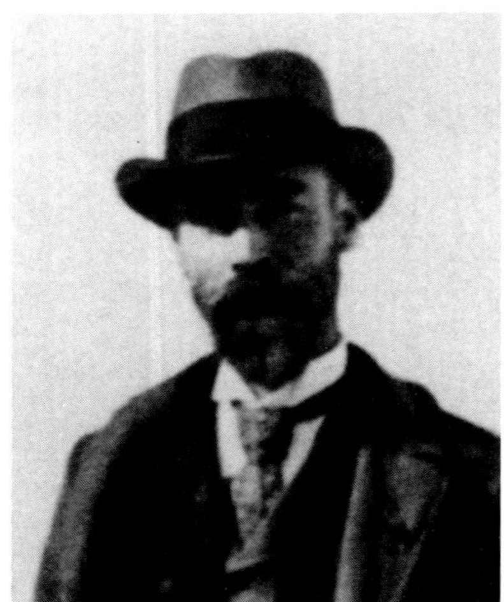

Raymond Dabb Yelland, ca. 1885-1890. Photo courtesy of Fred E. Keeler.

31. Raymond Dabb Yelland

(born 1848, London, England; died 1900, Oakland, California)
Point Lobos From Fort Point, 1880-1883
Oil on canvas
14" x 20"
Unsigned

The landscapist, marine artist, and teacher Raymond Dabb Yelland is one of a number of excellent nineteenth-century American painters who remain virtually unknown to East Coast collectors although highly regarded in the West.

The son of Nicholas Dabb and Mary Yelland, he was born in London, England, in 1848 and came to New York City with his family in 1851. After serving on the Union side in the Civil War, he briefly attended a seminary in New Jersey from 1866 to 1867 before deciding on a career in art. From 1868 to 1872, he studied at the National Academy of Design under the figurative artists Lemuel Everett Wilmarth (cat. 51) and William Page (1811-1885), and the landscape painter James Renwick Brevoort (1832-1918). He then became an instructor there until 1873, when he assumed his mother's name and moved to California to become professor of painting and drawing at Mills College in Oakland. In 1877 he was appointed assistant director of the California School of Design in San Francisco.

He painted in New York and Massachusetts from 1879-1882 and in 1886 left for London and Paris, where he studied with the history painter Luc-Olivier Merson (1846-1920) and exhibited at the Salon. After his return to California two years later, he succeeded Emil Carlsen (1853-1932) as director of the California School of Design, and also taught design, painting, and perspective. In 1893 he again returned East to work with Arthur Parton (cats. 17 and 18) among others. Yelland exhibited regularly at the National Academy of Design and the San Francisco Art Association, and notably at the 1893 Columbian Exposition[1] in Chicago and the 1894 California Midwinter International Exposition in San Francisco. He died in Oakland in 1900.

Although he painted excellent views of New England and Europe, his coastal scenes are best known. Some were done in Monterey, where he had a summer home, others around San Francisco, and yet others in Oregon. Especially effective are his moody sunset views of the marshes of Oakland, where he later lived and had his studio. In general, he was concerned with depicting the effects of changes in weather and the time of day. Throughout much of his career he used the clear, precise style of the Hudson River School in which he had been trained, but in his later years he softened his brushwork under the influence of Barbizon painting.

Point Lobos From Fort Point is probably a preliminary sketch for Yelland's major 1883 work of the same title, now in the collection of the California State Capitol in Sacramento. This moody, understated late afternoon view of the San Francisco Bay shows Point Lobos in the distance seen from Fort Point, which is now occupied by one end of the Golden Gate Bridge. The stage is set by a triangular strip of beach running into a massive cliff. The dark browns, grays, and reds of rock and sand contrast abruptly with the white of the gently breaking green waves. In the distance the lighter grayish green water merges with a horizontal sunstruck patch of white. The lighter streaks at the bottom of the cloudy sky contrast with the undulating grayish tan profile of Point Lobos. Just beyond the cliff, a few gulls wheel in the sky. The only other sign of life is the suggestion of a steam ship's smoke at the far right of the horizon. From 1880 to 1883 Yelland did a number of other views of San Francisco Bay.[2]

1. *Death Valley from Dead Water and Dante's View*, 1893. This huge 96" x 144" work was made for Yelland's friend, Borax Smith, who loaned it to the Columbian Exposition. A freight car was needed to transport it there. See Seavey.

2. See Naylor, 1070 and Seavey.

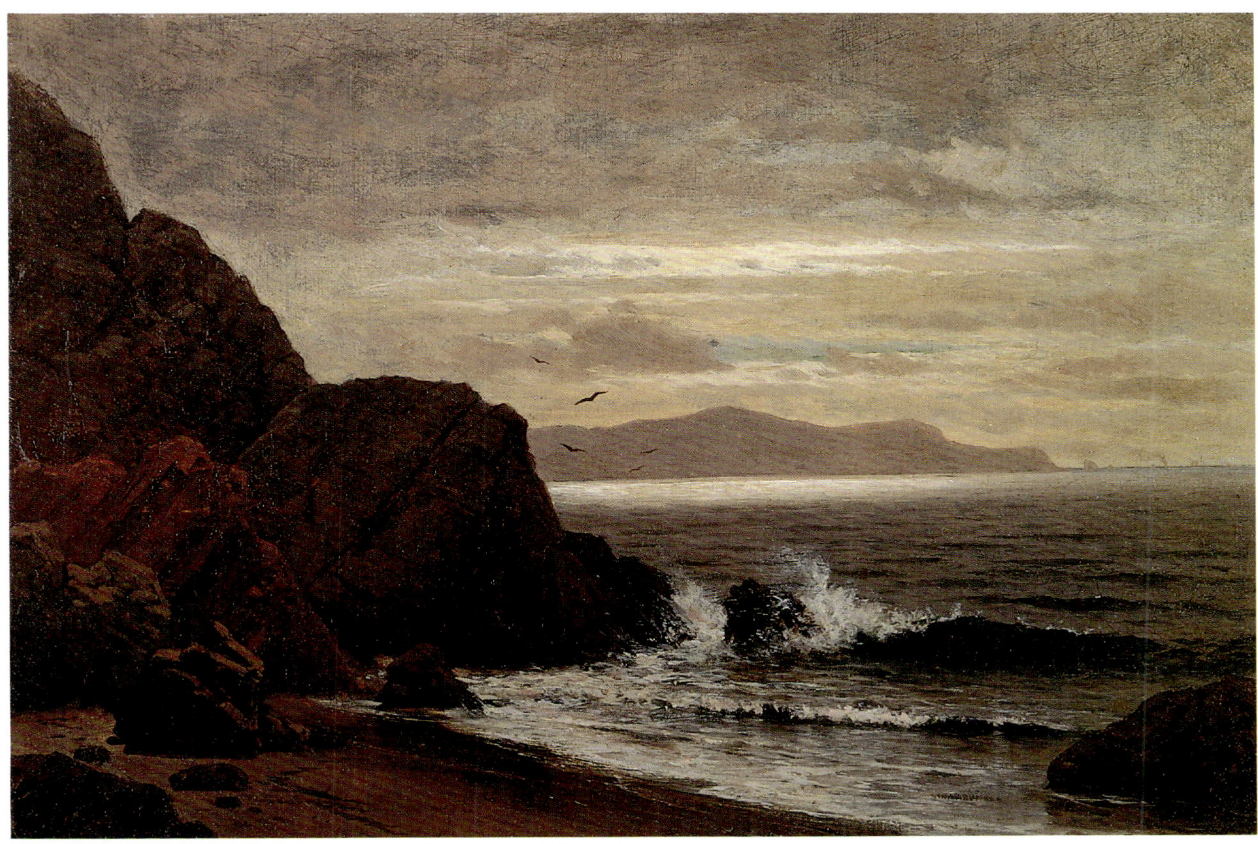

Raymond Dabb Yelland, *Point Lobos from Fort Point*, 1880-1883. Oil on canvas, 14" x 20".

Bibliography

Hughes. 624-25.

Orr-Cahall, Christina, et al. *The Art of California: Selected Works From the Collection of the Oakland Museum*. Oakland, CA: The Oakland Museum, 1984. 62.

Seavey, Kent L. *Raymond Dabb Yelland (1848-1900)*. San Francisco: California Historical Society, 1964.

Vincent, Stephen, Kevin Starr, and Paul Mills. *O California!: Nineteenth and Early Twentieth Century California Landscapes and Observations*. San Francisco: Bedford Arts, 1990. 8, 16, 52, 155.

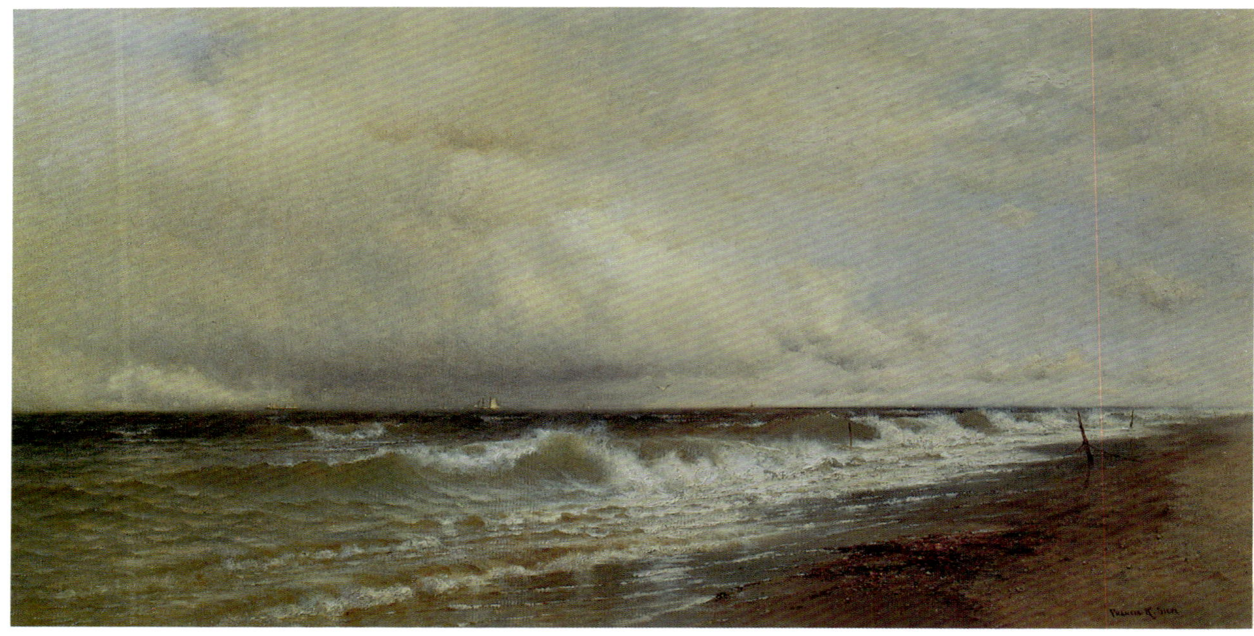
Francis Augustus Silva, *Clearing Off*, ca. 1883. Oil on canvas, 20" x 38".

32. Francis Augustus Silva

(born 1835, New York; died 1886, New York)
Clearing Off, ca. 1883
Oil on canvas
20" x 38"
Signed lower right: Francis A. Silva
Inscribed on back of frame: return to William M. Chase, 10th Street

33.

The Beach at Seabright, ca. 1883
Watercolor on paper
10 3/8" x 20"
Signed lower right: Francis A. Silva, Seabright Long Branch

When he died in 1886, the marine specialist Francis Augustus Silva was a well known figure in the art world of New York City, where he had been a regular exhibitor at both the National Academy of Design and the Brooklyn Art Association.[1] Thereafter, his work fell into almost complete obscurity until the distinguished art historian John I. H. Baur[2] brought it to light again in 1980. Silva's inclusion in a major exhibition devoted to Luminism at the National Gallery of Art in the same year also helped to make him popular with museums and collectors.[3]

The son of an immigrant Portuguese barber of French extraction, he was born in New York City in 1835. He tried several trades and disliked them all. Finally, his disappointed father let him apprentice to a sign painter. Otherwise apparently self-taught, he was first listed as an easel painter in 1858. After serving in the Union forces during the Civil War, he subsequently kept studios in Manhattan but lived in Brooklyn. He began exhibiting at the National Academy of Design as early as 1868, but his first extant painting is dated 1870. In 1872 he was elected to the American Society of Painters in Water Color and to the Artists' Fund Society the following year. During the 1870s he often painted the Hudson River, Cape Ann, and Narragansett Bay. In 1880 he moved to Long Branch, New Jersey, where he had painted as early as 1869. In his final years, he devoted himself largely to the New Jersey coastline. Active to the end, he died of pneumonia in New York City in 1886.

Although Silva's style during the last eighteen years of his life was remarkably consistent, he grew in his ability to render form, texture, and special conditions of light and atmosphere. Indeed, he is preoccupied with dawn, dusk, and night in almost a third of his works, where he often heightens color and haze in the service of emotion. It is no accident, then, that they have been compared with the Luminist marine

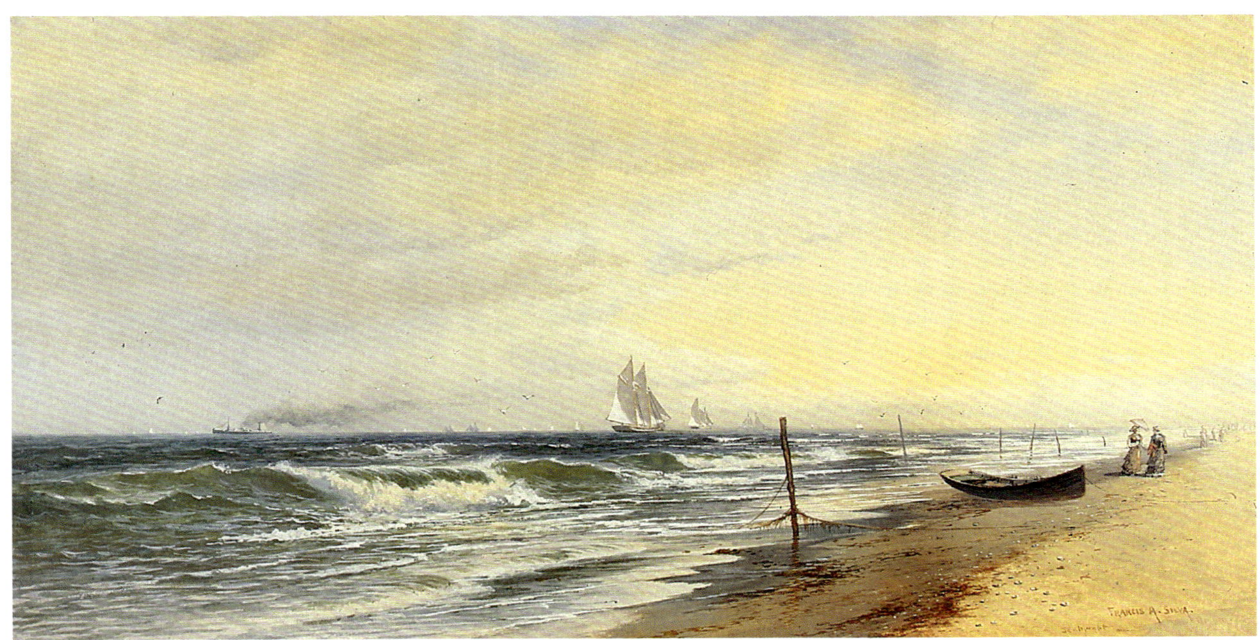

Francis Augustus Silva, *The Beach at Seabright*, ca. 1883. Watercolor on paper, 10 3/8" x 20".

paintings of artists such as Fitz Hugh Lane (1804-1865), Martin Johnson Heade (1819-1904), and John F. Kensett (1816-1872). Most of his views convey a sense of solitude and distance, whether of expanses of water along the coast, in a harbor, or on the open sea. He de-emphasizes anecdote by keeping boats small and omitting people most of the time. When figures do appear, they are always small and distant. Like Lane, a simple geometry usually underlies his compositions, which often favor a regular progression of objects into the distance.[4] In an 1884 article he summarized his working methods and aims as follows: "Some men can never paint from memory or feeling — they give us only cold facts in the most mannered way. I hold it impossible to paint a large and important work entirely out-of-doors, for light and effect change so rapidly that the mind becomes confused and involved in difficulty from which there is no escape except to take the picture into the studio to finish it. . . . A picture must be more than a skillfully painted canvas — it must tell something. People do not read books simply because they are well printed and handsomely bound."[5]

Silva was an accomplished oil and watercolor painter. In *Clearing Off* and *The Beach at Seabright*, he shows slightly different sections of the same beach in both media under different conditions of weather and light. The first, an oil painting, is a moody, somber depiction of a lonely stretch of beach on a windy, overcast day. A desolate triangle of sand strewn with wrack or seaweed stretches back, measured off by a row of stakes, until it vanishes in the distance. The dull green water near the shore breaks into a line of foaming surf. Beyond, it becomes dark blue and extends back to a horizon punctuated by a few tiny sails. Several small, inconspicuous gulls are the only other sign of life. Soft dark storm clouds move toward the left giving way to patches of blue sky.[6]

Even more precisely executed, but in the more transparent and brilliant medium of watercolor, *The Beach at Seabright*[7] revisits the same locale in better weather. The wind has abated somewhat and the water now sparkles with clear, bright blues and greens under sun-drenched clouds. The artist has enlivened beach and water with anecdotal detail. Beyond a beached rowboat a procession of strollers dwindles into the distance, and gulls and ships have multiplied. A steamer trailing smoke and a three-master whose sails make a pattern of light and shadow are closer and more prominent. The first post on the beach, much nearer now, functions as a triangulation point for the steamer, sailing ship, and passersby, emphasizing the apparent distances among them. The simple, strong compositions, clarity and subtlety of detail, and the specificity of time and weather conditions in these two paintings are typical of Silva's work, which always implies the presence of a detached observer.

1. See Naylor, vol. 2, 858-59, and Marlor, 332-33.

2. Baur (1980), 1018-031.

3. See Wilmerding et al.

4. Out of a sample of fifty-three published works, twenty-seven (50.9%) are dated, and figures occur in only twelve (20.6%). Sunrise, sunset, and moonlight are a feature of sixteen (30.2%). Examination of National Academy of Design and Brooklyn Art Association exhibition records yields similar figures of seven of twenty-four (29.2%) and twenty-three of seventy-one (32.4%), respectively.

5. Silva, 130.

6. Silva sometimes painted variants of the same scene. For another version, see *Passing Shower*, Sotheby's, 4/23/81, no. 66; Christie's, 12/7/84, no. 62; and *American Ship Portraits and Marine Exhibition* (Boston: Vose Galleries of Boston, 1990), reproduced in color.

7. For another, smaller watercolor of the same beach stretching to the left entitled *Seabright, N.J.*, 1883, see Baur, (1980), fig. 20. Seabright is an oceanside resort community north of Long Branch.

Bibliography

Baur, John I.H. "Francis A. Silva: Beyond Luminism." *Antiques* 188 (November 1980): 1018-031.

Silva, F.A. "American vs. Foreign-American Art." *The Art Union* (June-July 1880): 130.

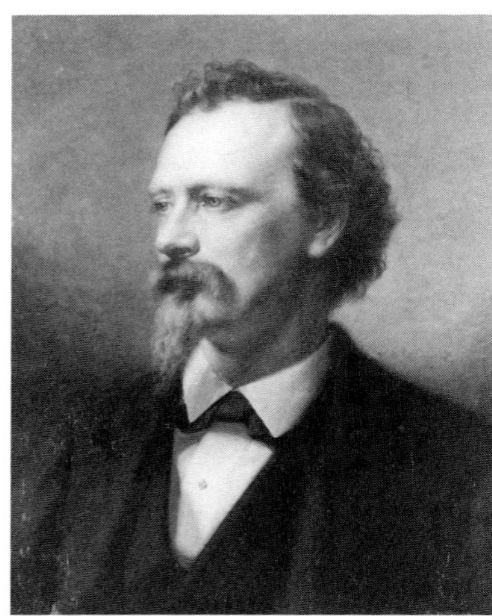

Benjamin F. Reinhart (1829-1885), *Edward Moran*, 1872. Collection of the National Academy of Design, New York.

34. Edward Moran

(born 1829, Bolton-le-Moor, England; died 1901, New York)
Homeward Bound, ca. 1880
Oil on canvas
11 1/2" x 19 3/8"
Signed lower left: Edward Moran

Today, although collectors are familiar with the marine artist Edward Moran, general histories of American painting do not mention him and histories and exhibitions of American marine painting still fail to feature him. At his death in 1901, however, he was almost as well known as his younger brother Thomas (1837-1926), who has since overshadowed him.

Moran was born in 1829 to a family of English weavers in Bolton-le-Moor, a cotton mill center in Lancashire where Thomas Cole also spent his early years. At the age of fifteen, he emigrated to Baltimore with his family but in 1845 moved to Philadelphia, where he became a power loom foreman by 1852. In 1853 he met the German-born-and-trained landscape and portrait painter Paul Weber (1823-1916) and became an assistant of the marine specialist James Hamilton (1819-1878). While supporting himself as a lithographer, he began exhibiting in 1854 at the Pennsylvania Academy of the Fine Arts, where he became an Academician six years later. During this period he also exhibited at the Boston Athenaeum and, increasingly, at the National Academy of Design. By 1866 he had become a regular exhibitor and six years later was elected an Associate member, completing the

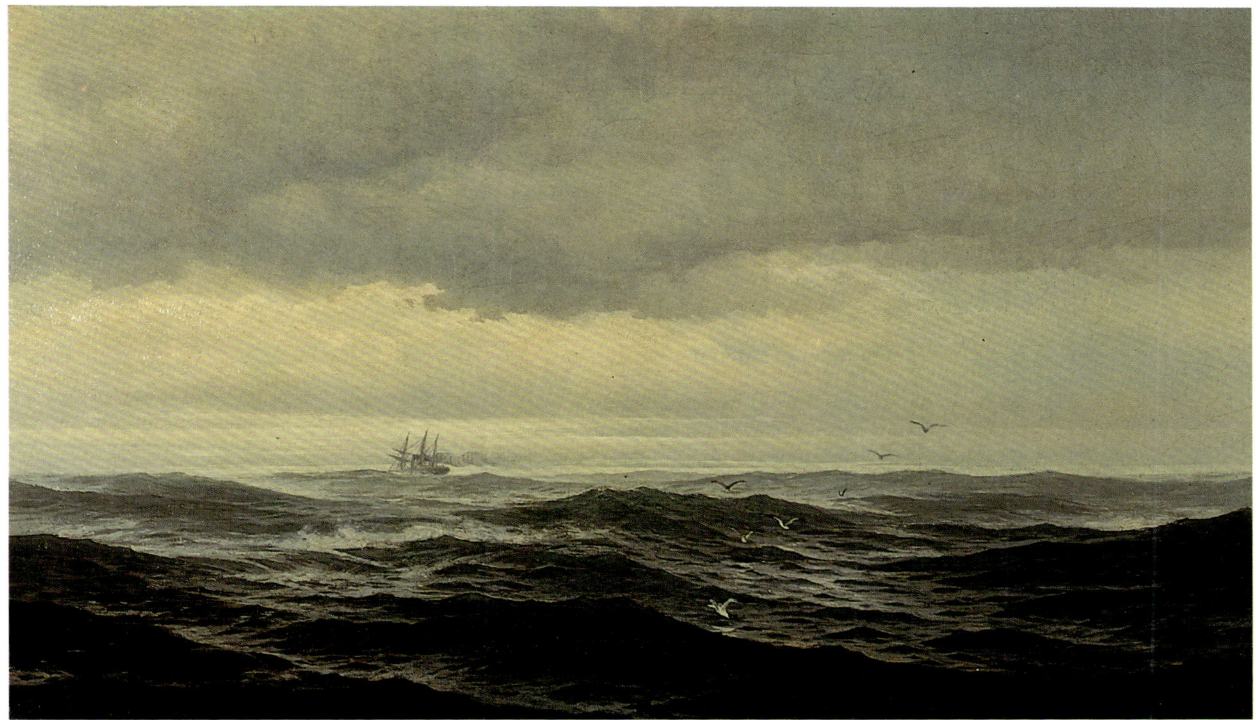

Edward Moran, *Homeward Bound*, ca. 1880. Oil on canvas, 11 1/2" x 19 3/8".

transition which shifted his artistic focus from Philadelphia to New York. He had severed his ties with the Pennsylvania Academy of the Fine Arts in 1869, after a dispute over the poor hanging of his pictures, and two years later had moved permanently to New York City, becoming active in its art life and exhibiting in several international expositions.

In 1877 he auctioned off the contents of his studio to go to France, where he stayed with his wife and two sons until 1879. It is not known with whom, if anyone, he studied, but in any case his figure style became bolder and more monumental and his handling of paint broader. Between 1892 and 1899, he devoted himself to a series of thirteen large paintings now in the United States Naval Academy in Annapolis, Maryland, which represent the maritime history of America from the landing of Leif Ericson to the Spanish-American War. He died in New York City in 1901.

Although Moran painted both landscapes and genre pieces he is primarily known as a marine artist. J.M.W. Turner's (1775-1851) early work is the major influence, at first indirectly through his teacher Hamilton, known as the "American Turner," and later through first-hand study of the English painter's work. The first ten years of his career were largely devoted to depictions of storms, shipwrecks, and rescues, but later he increasingly eschewed such romantic visions of the sea for a less dramatic but at times poetic approach.

Although he painted occasional coastal genre scenes with children as well as specific boat races and other historical subjects, the bulk of his work consists of portrayals of fishermen at work, coastal views, depictions of the open sea, and harbor scenes. He was particularly known for the latter, especially those of New York harbor. Many are set at sunrise or sunset and have a rich, Luminist quality. In fact, almost two-fifths of his oeuvre deals with the special light effects of dawn, dusk, and moonlight.[2] Always accurate in rendering the details of ships, Moran's paintings are quite variable in quality. At their best they show a good eye for the transitory effects of light on sky and water[3] and a strong sense of composition. Frequently, however, they are overloaded with anecdotal details made into clichés. Gulls skimming the water and floating barrels and buoys are inescapable in his harbor scenes, which are often needlessly overcrowded with boats.

Its relative lack of anecdotal detail and the simplicity and concentration of its imagery make *Homeward Bound* unusual in Moran's oeuvre.[4] Almost at the horizon, a three-masted boat steams off to the left, while in the foreground a group of six seagulls rises up from the water in a graceful arc to the right. In a few minutes both will have abandoned the viewer to water and clouds. The leaden bluish gray of the heavy swells is enlivened by the white of occasional foam and patches of light shimmering on the surface. The sky is entirely covered with clouds, lighter and streaky below, fluffier and gray above. All in all, this is a superbly controlled study of tonal variations within a narrow range of color.

1. Besides the National Academy of Design, he also exhibited at the Brooklyn Art Association (1873-84), became director and vice-president of the Lotos Club, and exhibited in the 1876 Philadelphia Centennial Exposition and the 1889 Paris Exposition Universelle.

2. Out of a sample of one hundred and two published paintings, four (3.9%) are genre pieces, fourteen (13.7%) are landscapes, and seventy-four (72.5%) are marine paintings. Of the latter, thirty-four (45.9%) are dated and twenty (39.2%) are devoted to dawn, dusk, or moonlight. Views of the open sea (eighteen of seventy-four, or 24.3%), coastal scenes (fourteen of seventy-four, or 18.9%), and harbor views (seventeen of seventy-four, or 23%) form the largest categories.

3. To record the effects of light on water, he recommended the use of a portable camera. See "Marine Painting: Mr. Edward Moran Continues His Hints for Practical Study," *Art Amateur* 19 (November 1888): 127.

4. The only other comparable examples are *Breaking Away After a Gale*, 1877, no. 12 and illustrated in *New Acquisitions in American Paintings* (New York: Kenneth Lux Gallery, 1982); *Casco Bay, Coast of Maine*, ca. 1889, in Schweizer, fig. 33, ill. p. 48; and *The Sea*, ca. 1870, in Schweizer, fig. 19, ill. p. 32.

Bibliography

"Marine Painting: Mr. Moran Gives Some Preliminary Hints for Practical Study." *Art Amateur* 19 (September 1888): 101-03. (November 1888): 127-28.

Schweizer, Paul D. *Edward Moran (1829-1901): American Marine and Landscape Painting*. Wilmington: Delaware Art Museum, 1979.

Sutro, Theodore. *Thirteen Chapters in American History*. New York: n.p., 1905.

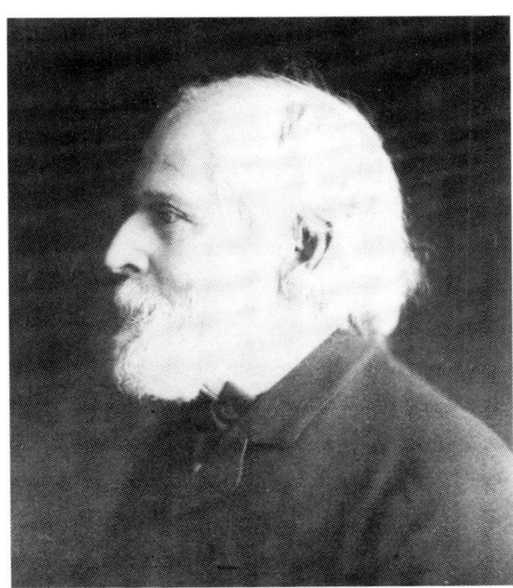

William Trost Richards, ca. 1900. Photographs of Artists I, Archives of American Art, Smithsonian Institution.

35. William Trost Richards

(born 1833, Philadelphia; died 1905, Newport, Rhode Island)
Breaking Waves, 1898
Oil on canvas
19 1/2" x 31 1/2"
Signed lower left: Wm T. Richards 98
Publication: Brucia Witthoft and Annalise Harding, *American Artists in Düsseldorf: 1840-1865* (Framingham, MA: Danforth Museum of Art, 1982), cat. 36, ill. p. 37.

Although he was an old-fashioned artist catering to a conservative audience, William Trost Richards was still America's most popular marine painter both in oils and watercolors when he died in 1905.[1] Born in Philadelphia in 1833, he was the eldest of four children of an immigrant tailor from Wales. His father died when Richards was only fourteen, forcing him to drop out of high school to help support his family. Both a job and his art training encouraged what eventually became an outstanding mastery of draftsmanship and detail. From 1850 to 1853 he worked full-time as a designer and illustrator of ornamental iron work and studied painting and drawing with the immigrant German landscape artist Paul Weber (1823-1916). From 1855 to 1856 he sketched widely in Europe, where he was exposed to the Düsseldorf School's detailed, realistic approach for several months.

By 1858 he had established himself sufficiently as a landscapist to marry and to make a living as a painter. From 1856 to 1866 he made his name with views of Pennsylvania, the Catskills, Adirondacks, and White Mountains. His landscapes were subject to a number of influences ranging from Thomas Cole (1801-1848), Durand (cat. 3), and Frederic E. Church (1826-1900), to John Ruskin (1819-1900). Ruskin's influence is particularly evident after 1858 in Richards' interest in increasingly minute detail. He became the best-known American Pre-Raphaelite artist and was a founding member of the Association for the Advancement of Truth in Art in 1863. The same year he was made an Academician by the Pennsylvania Academy of the Fine Arts, where he had exhibited since 1852. In 1870, however, he resigned only to be elected to that status at the National Academy of Design the following year.

From 1866 to 1867 he again traveled in Europe. According to tradition, his stormy return across the Atlantic so impressed him with the power of the sea that he resolved to concentrate on marine paintings. In any case, after 1868 while summering at various seaside locations on the East Coast he started concentrating on coastal scenes. Although he had occasionally executed marine paintings before, they became an increasingly important part of his oeuvre, finally displacing landscapes completely in the late 1880s. As a marine artist he became as well known for his watercolors as for his oils. Although his interest in watercolor, which started in 1860, reached a peak in the 1870s, it remained a lifelong preoccupation, earning him a reputation for his adept renditions in that medium of the special light effects of sunset, moonlight, and reflections on water.

When the progressive Society of American Artists, finding his detailed approach to landscape old-fashioned, failed to invite him to exhibit in 1878, his work came under severe attack. In reaction, and in search of new subjects and new customers, he traveled and exhibited on the Continent and in England from 1878 to 1880, where he was entranced by the wild, rugged coast of Cornwall. This trip marks the end of his concentration on native subject matter. From 1885 until his death he traveled to Europe almost every year, and from 1891 to 1906 he made trips that included Italy, Norway, and remote areas in England, Scotland, and Ireland. Very active as a painter right up to the end, Richards won his last award, a gold medal, at the Pennsylvania Academy of the Fine Arts in 1905.[2]

Like Silva (cats. 32 and 33), Richards was not a painter of ships or shipwrecks per se, and the human figure rarely appears in his marine paintings, which were generally executed in his studio during the

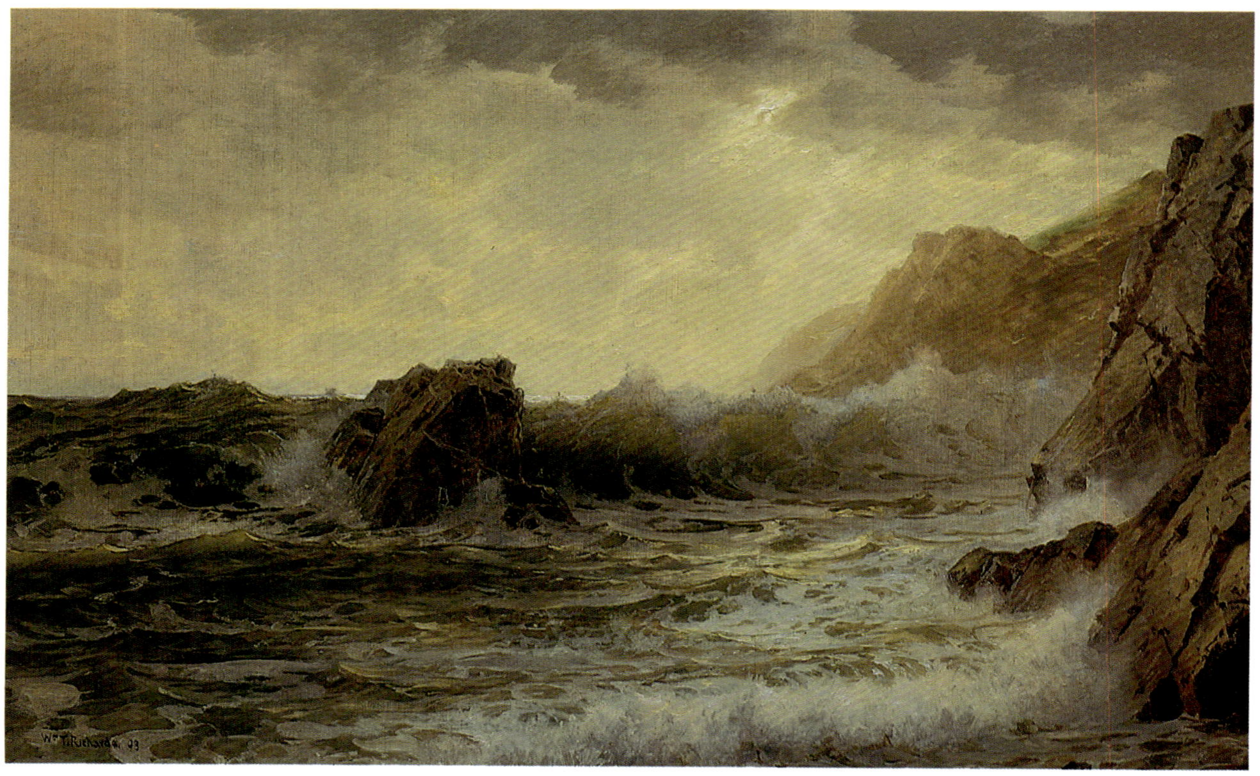

William Trost Richards, *Breaking Waves*, 1898. Oil on canvas, 19 1/2" x 31 1/2".

winter, based on sketches made the previous summer. Although occasionally of the open sea, they usually depict either a flat stretch of beach as a foil for the motion of the waves and effects of light in the sky and water, or the eternal conflict between sea and rocks, as he witnessed it on the coasts of Cornwall and Ireland.

Richards was a lifelong student of the sea. Sheldon wrote in 1879: "He makes now the best drawings of waves that this country can produce. The sea-shore has been his home."[3] Richards' biographer wrote: "He stood for hours in the early days of Atlantic City or Cape May, with folded arms, studying the motion of the sea, until people thought him insane. After days of gazing, he made pencil notes of the action of the water. He even stood for hours in a bathing suit among the waves, trying to analyse the motion."[4] From the 1870s on he worked mainly from quick pencil sketches made on the spot and he may also have used photographs, but for his marine paintings of the late 1880s and 1890s he relied on oil sketches.

His stress on exactness in both his landscapes and marine paintings may have derived in part from his experience as a commercial draftsman and his teacher Paul Weber's great emphasis on precision of drawing, but it must also have reflected a deep-rooted sense of caution. In connection with impressions he said, "There is such a sense of strangeness and unreality in everything one sees for the first time, that as a painter I somehow lose hold of the facts that help to produce the impressions, and I have dared to try to paint only those things which I have seen long enough to study in some way."[5]

During his later years Richards, who worked rapidly, turned out a great many works. He painted many of them virtually according to formula and, as a result, their quality varies a great deal. However, *Breaking Waves* shows him in good form. It portrays the sea and a stretch of desolate rocky coast which rises up sharply in the right foreground and continues into the distance.[6] A large breaker unfolds across the middle ground about to engulf a projecting rock at the center left. The stormy sky is capped with gray but shot through below with the light of the afternoon sun, which penetrates the background mist in places to strike the water surface. Although Richards carefully delineates all the facets of the nearer rocks, overall he has painted this scene more loosely than in his works before 1887, when his style became slightly more painterly.

1. Typical of later official attitudes toward his work until recently is the Metropolitan Museum of Art's handling of his large *New Jersey Beach*, 1901, which it put on deposit at Barnard College in the 1950s and at Borough Hall, Queens, in the 1970s. See Spassky et al., 359.

2. He previously had been awarded a bronze medal at the 1876 Philadelphia Centennial Exposition, a silver medal at the Pennsylvania Academy of the Fine Arts in 1885, and a bronze medal at the 1889 Paris Exposition Universelle.

3. Sheldon, 62.

4. Morris, 10.

5. Quoted in Ferber, (1973), 34.

6. According to Linda S. Ferber (personal communication), it portrays too narrow a section of coast to decide whether it was painted in Cornwall, Guernsey or Ireland.

Bibliography

Ferber, Linda S. *"Never at Fault": The Drawings of William Trost Richards*. Yonkers, NY: The Hudson River Museum, 1986.

_____. *Tokens of Friendship: Miniature Watercolors by William T. Richards from the Richard and Gloria Manney Collection*. New York: The Metropolitan Museum of Art, 1982.

_____. *William Trost Richards: American Landscape and Marine Painter 1833-1905*. Brooklyn: Garland Publishing, 1980.

Ferber and Gerdts. 214-28.

Ferguson, Charles B. *"He Knew the Sea": William Trost Richards, N.A.* (1833-1952). New Britain, CT: The New Britain Museum of American Art, 1973.

Morris, Harrison S. *Masterpieces of the Sea: William T. Richards, A Brief Outline of His Life and Art*. Philadelphia: J.B. Lippincott Co., 1912.

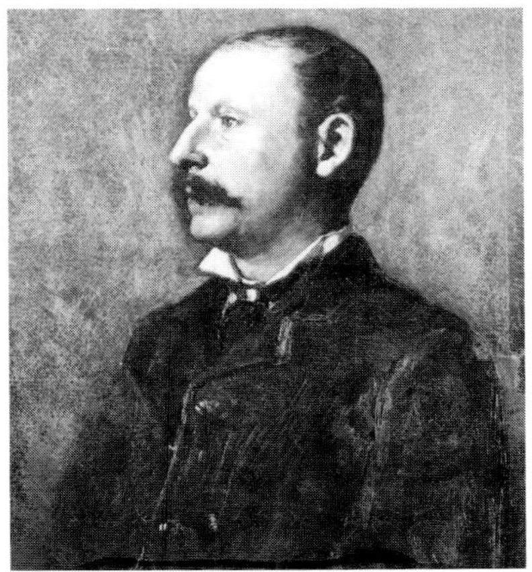

Percival De Luce (1847-1914), *Alfred Thompson Bricher*, 1879. Collection of the National Academy of Design, New York; photo courtesy of the Frick Art Reference Library.

36. Alfred Thompson Bricher

(born 1837, Portsmouth, New Hampshire; died 1908, New Dorp, New York)
Sunset, Bailey Island, ca. 1907
Oil on canvas
15" x 32"
Signed lower left: A.T. Bricher

Like William Trost Richards (cat. 35), Alfred Thompson Bricher first achieved distinction as a landscape artist only later to become a successful specialist in marine painting. After a long period of obscurity following his death in 1908, the first retrospective exhibition of his work in 1973 signalled his readmission to the official fold.[1] He has since regained the popularity he enjoyed during his lifetime and his paintings are now both widely sold to serious collectors and museums and included in their exhibitions.

He was born in 1837 in Portsmouth, New Hampshire, to an immigrant English father but grew up in Newburyport, Massachusetts. At the age of fourteen he started working as a clerk in Boston. It is not clear how he learned to paint, but he may have studied art at the Lowell Institute. At any rate, he painted his first known work in 1856, two years before he opened a studio in Newburyport. In 1859 he moved to Boston, where he may have studied with William H. Titcomb (1824-1888). Beginning in 1864 he exhibited a number of times at the Boston Athenaeum and the Boston firm of Lewis Prang and Company, who published and/or owned twenty-three of his paintings and published the first chromolithograph of his work.

After moving to New York in 1868, he established himself as a virtual marine specialist, exhibiting regularly there[2] and often in domestic and international expositions.[3] He made quite a comfortable living from painting. Despite his apparent success, however, he only became an Associate of the National Academy of Design in 1879, and never rose to the rank of Academician, perhaps the price he paid for neither frequenting artists' social clubs nor participating in their usual leisure activities. He had only one known patron, George Walter Vincent Smith (1832-1903), whose collection became the basis of the George Walter Vincent Smith Art Museum in Springfield, Massachusetts.[4]

Although twice a husband and also a father, Bricher led a largely solitary life consumed by travel to remote locations or nearby vacation spots. Over seventy percent of his landscapes, which amount to less than a third of his oeuvre, were painted by 1873. Until this time, he had painted widely in Massachusetts, New York, New Hampshire, and Maine as well as the upper Mississippi. More often than not his landscapes are small, usually of autumn scenes. They are precisely and at times even tightly painted with great finish in an individual style that draws on the romanticism of Thomas Cole (1801-1848), Durand's (cat. 3) plein-air naturalism, and the Luminism of John F. Kensett (1816-1872) and Sanford R. Gifford (1823-1880). At their best, they render light and atmospheric effects with great sensitivity and subtlety.

After 1874 Bricher mostly confined his sketching to the New England coast ranging from New York to Rhode Island, Massachusetts, Maine, and the great cliffs of Grand Manan Island in New Brunswick.[5] As a result, marine paintings dominated his output.[6] His works of the early 1870s often have a strikingly pellucid, still, and luminous clarity. Except for the period from 1878 to 1884 when charming, elegantly dressed young women frequently adorn them, the human figure plays a negligible role in his beach and coastal scenes. By the 1880s he tended to use a generalized color scheme in which each element is carefully related and subordinated to a dominant tone. His marine paintings are apt to be larger and use more impasto and slightly freer brushwork than his landscapes. Although the quality of his work varied widely, its average level did not drop off in his last years.

In his large output he relied on a small number of formats. Typically, his marinescapes are painted from sea level and show a parabolic stretch of beach or coastline with a view to the open sea balanced by masses of rocks or a large promontory. Seaweed, driftwood, ship spars, and beached rowboats are frequent accents. Strongly horizontal (the width is usually twice the height), they most often are calm, sun-drenched views spelling out the effects of light and weather at different times of day. He often paints the same locale with slight variations and sometimes combines two or more views of it.

Sunsets are unusual in Bricher's marine paintings, where daytime is the rule and the sun is usually shining.[7] In the present example, however, color and contrast are muted in a late sunset view of Bailey Island in Casco Bay, Maine. The seaweed-strewn beach is in shadow and only the sloping tops of a series of large rocks at the left catch the last rays of the setting sun. Beyond them, across the water in the background, sits a bluish promontory festooned with low-lying clouds and crowned by a garland of golden light. A broad curving band of gray-, blue-, yellow-, and pink-hued clouds counterbalances the rocks and land mass. On the right, the placid bluish water faintly tinged with pink extends back through the reflections of three boats hovering on the surface, whose sails also catch the dwindling light. Like the gulls hovering around the promontory, they are invariable staples of Bricher's marine paintings. Executed with painterly brushwork, the rich but subdued colors of this simple horizontal composition invoke the light and shade effects of the waning sunset, freezing time in a characteristically Luminist fashion. In the summers of 1904 to 1906, Bricher sketched in the Casco Bay area and painted at least eight views of Bailey Island, which he exhibited at the 1907 American Watercolor Society and National Academy of Design annuals and at Gill's in 1907 and 1908.[8] There is at least one close variant of the present work.[9]

1. See Brown and Lee.

2. National Academy of Design, the Brooklyn Art Association, the American Society of Painters in Water Color.

3. Chicago, 1875-83; Cincinnati, 1879-86; Philadelphia Centennial Exposition, 1876; Paris Exposition Universelle, 1878 and 1889; Chicago Columbian Exposition, 1893.

4. Concerning Smith as a collector of American painting and of Bricher in particular, see Baekeland and Dean Flower and Francis Murphy, *A Catalogue of American Paintings, Water Colors and Drawings (to 1923) in the George Walter Vincent Smith Art Museum Springfield, Massachusetts* (Springfield, MA: George Walter Vincent Smith Art

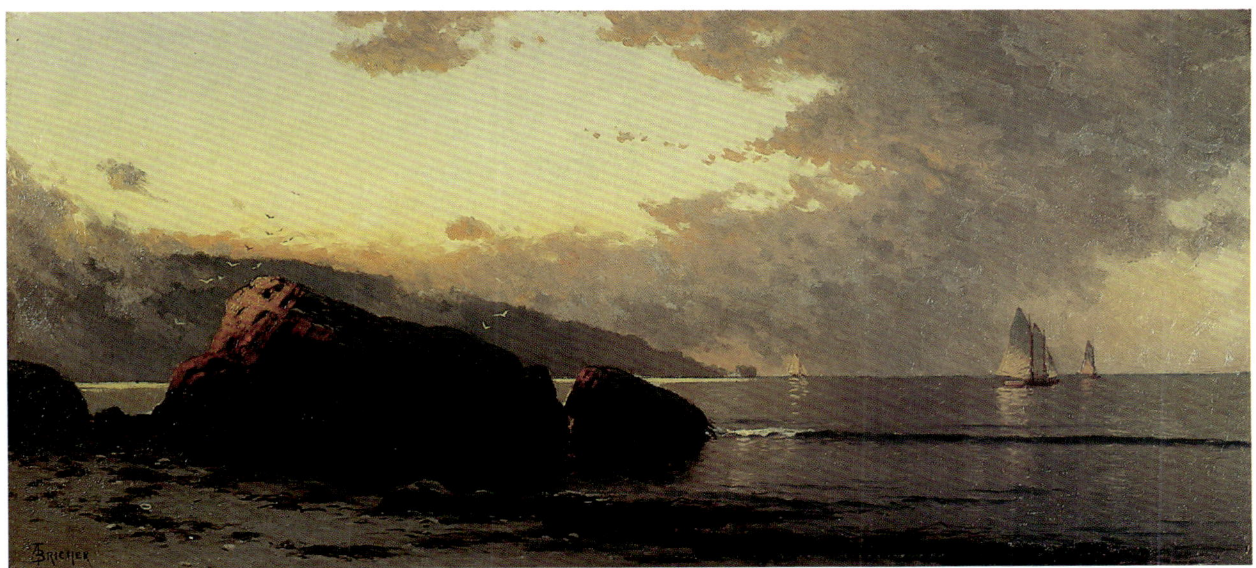

Alfred Thompson Bricher, *Sunset, Bailey Island*, ca. 1907. Oil on canvas, 15" x 32".

Museum, 1976), 9-13, 21. Smith probably owed his interest in Bricher to his friendship with James D. Gill (1849-1934), a Springfield art dealer who exhibited seventy-five of his works in his annual exhibitions from 1878 until the artist's death and five more in 1913, 1916, 1919, and 1921. Gill, the first art dealer to specialize in American paintings, and Seth M. Vose in Providence, Rhode Island were largely responsible for Bricher's following in New England. See Brown and Lee, 86-88.

5. His first Grand Manan painting was exhibited in 1976, and Grand Manan figured in other exhibitions at least seventeen of the next thirty years. See Brown and Lee, 20-21.

6. Out of a sample of two hundred fifteen published Bricher paintings, fifty-eight (27%) are landscapes and one hundred fifty-seven (73%) are marine views. Of his landscapes, twenty-eight (48.3%) are twenty inches or less in each dimension, forty (69%) are dated, seventy-five (34.9%) are of known sites, and fifteen (25.9%) are autumn scenes. Of his marine paintings only forty-six (29.3%) are dated, seventy-five (47.8%) are of known sites, and one hundred forty-eight (94.3%) of them are daytime views.

7. Only ten (6.4%) are of dawn, dusk, or night (seven being sunsets).

8. See Brown and Lee, 36-37, 101. See also *Bailey's (sic) Island, Maine*, no. 22, ill. p. 29 of Franklin Riehlman and Glenn C. Peck, *The American Spirit: Paintings, Watercolors and Sculpture from 1817 to 1987* (New York: H.V. Allison Galleries, 1988) and *The Landing, Bailey Island, Maine*, ill. p. 23 of *Selections from the Permanent Collection: The Butler Institute of American Art* (Youngstown, OH: The Butler Institute of American Art, 1979).

9. *Sundown, Bailey's (sic) Island, Casco Bay, Maine*, Sotheby-Parke Bernet, 6/23/79, no. 178. The Montclair Art Museum, Montclair, New Jersey, also has a related work, *Bailey Island*, 79.26, gift of Mrs. John M. Davidson.

Bibliography

Brown, Jeffrey R., and Ellen W. Lee. *Alfred Thompson Bricher 1873-1908*. Indianapolis: Indianapolis Museum of Art, 1973.

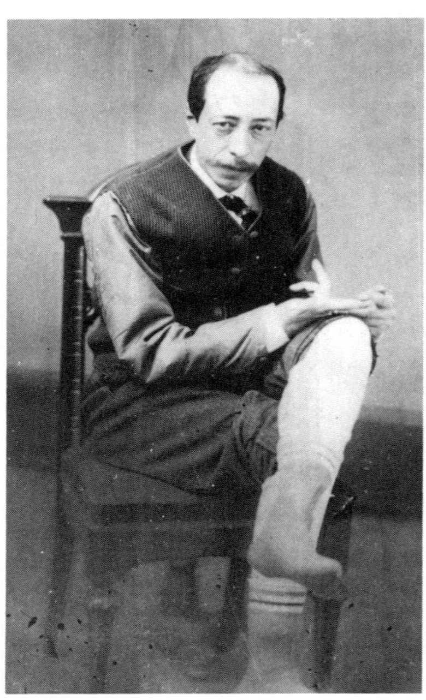

Moritz Statfeld, *Portrait of John La Farge*, ca. 1877. Yale University Art Gallery, gift of Henry A. La Farge.

37. John La Farge

(born 1835, New York; died 1910, Providence, Rhode Island)
Moonlight, ca. 1870
Watercolor on paper board
9 1/4" x 15 1/2"
Unsigned

Even after most nineteenth-century American painting fell into disrepute, the art of John La Farge continued to have a definite if limited cachet because of its great variety and innovative features. Starting in 1966, a number of exhibitions and extensive scholarly studies began to give a new impetus to his popularity among museums and collectors, who now vie to pay high prices for his work.

The son of cultivated, wealthy, and strongly Catholic French émigrés from Santo Domingo, he was born in New York City in 1835. Despite an early interest and training in art, he received a classical education at Mt. St. Mary's College in Emmetsburg, Maryland, earning his bachelor's degree in 1853 and his Master's two years later. In 1856 he interrupted two years of law study in New York for the sake of a year in Europe, where he traveled widely. While in Paris he studied briefly with Thomas Couture (1815-1879) and extensively copied old master paintings in the Louvre. After his return in 1858, he began to practice law, but also rented a studio in the Tenth Street Studio Building which he kept for the rest of his life. When he received a substantial inheritance from his father the following year, La Farge gave up his law practice and, on the advice of architect Richard Morris Hunt (1829-1879), began to study painting in Newport, Rhode Island, under Hunt's brother, William Morris Hunt (1824-1879), a former student of Couture and Jean-François Millet (1814-1875). By 1865 Newport had become his permanent residence. In the late 1860s, La Farge was already painting the atmospheric floral still lifes and landscapes which made his reputation as an oil and watercolor painter. Elected to the American Society of Painters in Water Color in 1868, he became an Academician at the National Academy of Design the next year and in 1874 exhibited at the Paris Salon.

After 1875, La Farge's main interests lay outside of easel oil painting. He became deeply involved in the design of stained glass windows and mural painting for which he did preparatory studies in watercolor. In the sterile field of stained glass, he made the important innovation of opalescent glass, which allowed modulations in color, three dimensional effects by shading, and the elimination of painted detail. Starting with Trinity Church in Boston in 1877, over the next decade he also did extensive murals for three neo-Gothic Episcopal churches in New York City.

An interest in Japanese art dating back to 1863 led him to travel in Japan in 1886 with the writer Henry Adams (1838-1918), returning to tour the South Seas together in 1890-1891. Both trips resulted in many watercolors. From 1893 until his death in 1910 La Farge, a highly cultivated man and a brilliant conversationalist, was also active as a teacher, lecturer, and writer on art history and aesthetics.

Because of the many media in which he worked and the multiple influences to which this cosmopolitan artist was subject (Venetian old master and Barbizon painting, Impressionism, Pre-Raphaelitism, and Japanese art), it is hard to summarize his painting. In any case, starting under Barbizon influence, he eventually formed his own kind of decorative Impressionism where color, light, and tonal variation rather than outline were important.

Moonlight, a subdued, poetic watercolor which was probably done around Newport, suggests the loneliness and immensity of the sea. Its elements are simple: a dark gray headland, a few distant sails, and a cloudy gray sky with the moon breaking through to animate

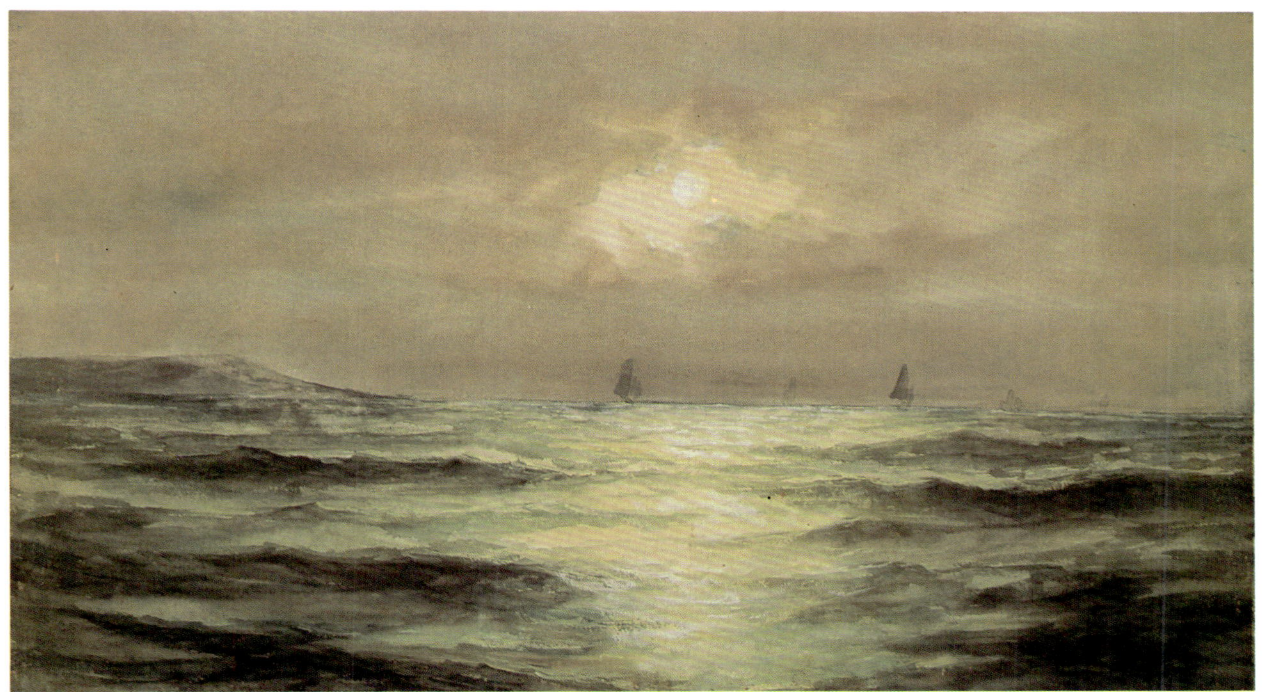

John La Farge, *Moonlight*, ca. 1870. Watercolor on paper board, 9 1/4" x 15 1/2".

the heavy swells of the bluish green sea with its light. With overlaid wet washes that let the paper show through in places, the artist makes the most of tonal variations and the intermixing of colors within a narrow range. Exposed as a child to watercolor, it became his favorite medium. He summarized his attraction in this way, "The painter of watercolor exercises far more skill, must be far more resourceful, and, in the end, with his simple means, often suggests more than the oil painter is able to represent."[1]

1. Quoted by Kathleen A. Foster, "John La Farge and the American Watercolor Movement: Art for the 'Decorative Age,'" in Adams et al., 125.

Bibliography

Adams, Henry, et al. *John La Farge*. Washington, D.C.: National Museum of American Art, Smithsonian Institution, 1987.

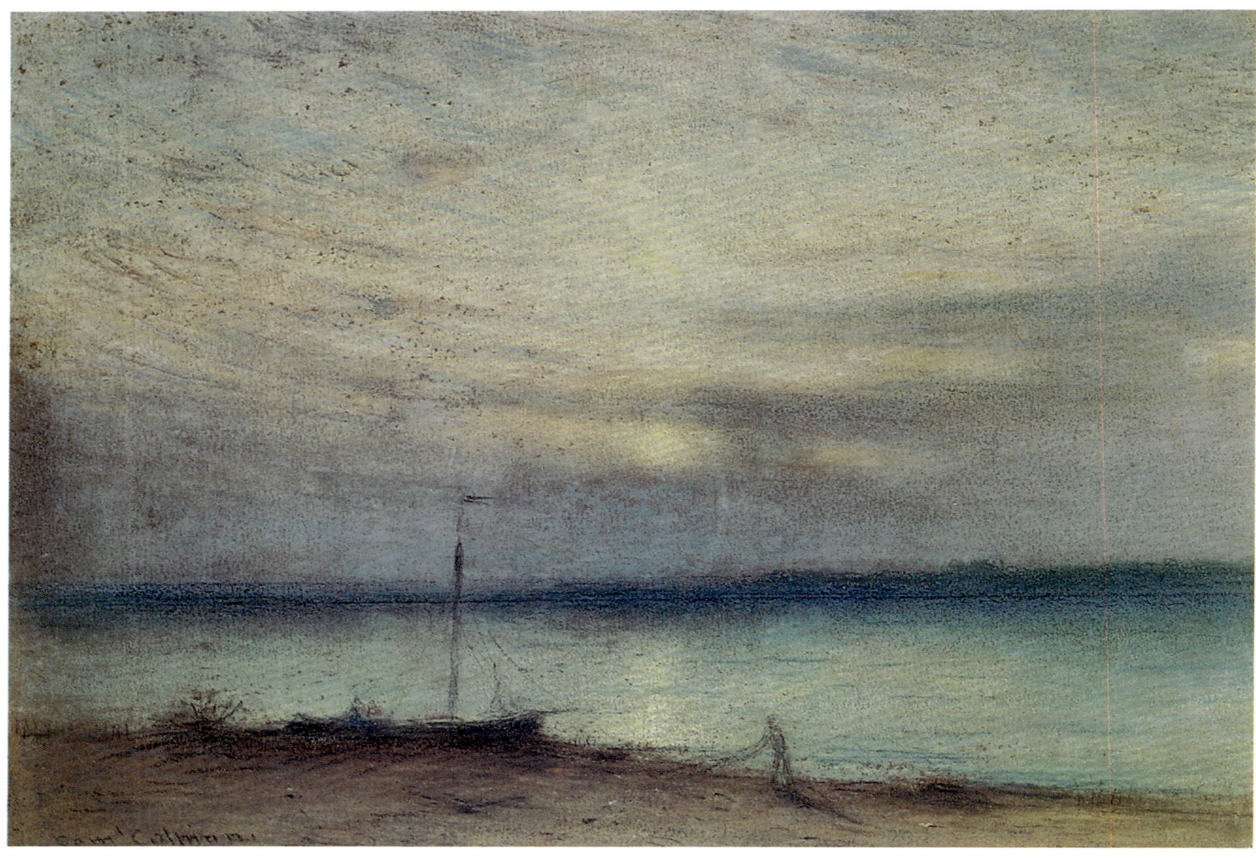

Samuel Colman, *Barnegat Bay at Sunset, Mantaloking, New Jersey*, ca. 1914. Pastel on paper, 7 1/4" x 10 3/8".

38. Samuel Colman

(born 1832, Portland, Maine; died 1920, New York)
Barnegat Bay at Sunset, Mantaloking, New Jersey, ca. 1914
Pastel on paper
7 1/4" x 10 3/8"
Signed lower left: 'Sam' Colman

(See cat. 22 for a discussion of Colman's life and oeuvre.)

Like most essays in Tonalism, this moody beach scene suppresses detail and reduces its subject matter to a few elements. On the narrow strip of beach one can barely make out the dark, shadowy form of a small sailboat, framed by the post to which it is moored and a little bush. Across the blue water tinged with reddish purple, a darker strip suggests the far shore and trees. Just above the horizon, a band of pale, dull lavender clouds almost obscures the setting sun, which makes a track in the water. Throughout this lonely, poetic scene the artist uses a typically narrow range of rich, muted, and subtly mixed colors. For all the vagueness of its forms, it is solidly composed; the boat, post, and sun, emphasized by its reflection, make a triangle that anchors the eye and gives a sense of space.

Pastels became a dominant late interest of Colman and he seems to have done many of them not far from New York. They all share simple compositions and abstraction of form. This is one of several known views of Barnegat Bay.[1]

1. See Sotheby's, 9/23/81, no. 83 for several other examples dated 1914. Mantaloking is an oceanside resort community south of Bay Head. It faces inland toward Barnegat Bay.

Genre Painting

When nineteenth-century American painting was banished to outer darkness, genre was summarily dismissed as "anecdotal." Typical, commonplace, everyday activities contemporary to the artist are indeed its stock in trade. Because it elicits the pleasure of recognition, it has always been one of the most popular forms of painting, although relegated near the bottom in traditional rankings. Since its flowering in seventeenth-century Holland, it has fallen between two extremes. One is objective, humorous, or satirical and often favors plebian subject matter. The other, more straightfaced, glosses over the mores of the middle and upper classes. In the eighteenth and early nineteenth centuries, European genre painting became increasingly sentimental and moralistic despite the sallies of occasional satirists such as William Hogarth (1697-1764). Both poles clearly reflect the cultural ideals and social myths of their time by choosing to depict certain aspects of contemporary social life and ignoring others.

America's first genre painter, the immigrant artist John Lewis Krimmel (1789-1821), reflected a sentimental European tradition. Later, William Sidney Mount (1807-1869) and George Caleb Bingham (1811-1879) typified pre-Civil War genre's emphasis on farmers and pioneers through their objective and humorous portrayals of rural life and frontier society. By the 1850s, however, the pendulum began to swing back toward sentimentality, as the growing urban middle class preferred the widely exhibited narrative genre painting of Düsseldorf artists and their American counterparts to such objective realism. Above all, they did not want to be reminded of their rural origins. As a result, most American genre painting now strove to edify and uplift in keeping with the moralism and idealism of John Ruskin (1819-1900), whose more bourgeois philosophy became popular at mid-century, replacing Ralph Waldo Emerson's (1803-1882) earlier espousal of the mundane.[1]

Although some artists continued to depict rural themes as a protest against the industrial revolution, most turned to urban life. Paintings of children were especially favored. Starting in the 1840s, they became one of the most popular and sentimental categories of genre as the innocence of childhood was increasingly glorified. Before the 1850s this may have been a response to high death rates among children. In any case, it certainly did not correspond to everyday thinking which, for all practical purposes, treated those who survived simply as small adults.[2] Nor did art reflect the realities of child poverty and child labor which persisted even after the Civil War.[3] Rather, artists such as J.G. Brown (1831-1913) idealized and sentimentalized street urchins and waifs in the guise of bootblacks and newsboys, presumably as the first stage of the rags-to-riches myth popularized by the Horatio Alger stories.

Children engaged in adult tasks form an important subcategory throughout much of the nineteenth century. John O'Brien Inman's early adolescent farm boy dressed in his Sunday best and reading a newspaper as he waits to stir the pot (cat. 39) may be substituting for his mother, but in an age that hardly recognized adolescence as such in the modern sense he probably put in a full day's work. Other popular subcategories were children playing and learning, as in James Wells Champney's *Puss-in-Boots*, 1875 (cat. 40), where a young girl tries to show her little brother how to read.

Another area of disagreeable social reality was black poverty, which persisted hardly unchanged even after emancipation. Painters usually focused on poor blacks in demeaning stereotypes of picturesque poverty. On the other hand, some depictions of blacks were sympathetic and objective character studies, such as Thomas Waterman Wood's *Shining Shoes*, ca. 1865 (cat. 41) and Harry Roseland's *The Snooze*, 1904 (cat. 42).

Yet another popular category of genre painting showed upper-class women of leisure. According to Thorstein Veblen, leisure-class women proclaimed their status by doing little but consuming conspicuously.[4] Starting in the 1890s and into the 1920s they were compellingly depicted by Boston school artists such as William McGregor Paxton and Frederick A. Bosley. Typically they were shown in chiaroscuro, fashionably dressed and in elegantly decorated interiors. In *The Telegram,* 1918 (cat. 43), Paxton has, however, chosen to illustrate a sadly common event during the First World War, while Bosley instead portrays adolescents in a school pageant rehearsal (cat. 44). On the other hand, Gertrude Fiske, an upper class Bostonian, shows herself at work as an artist, a career successfully pursued by a number of Boston area women (cat. 45).

Although social realism and satire did exist in post-Civil War genre, it was rare and hardly popular. How unwelcome it was is suggested by William Holbrook Beard's successful career. In his work, social satire is safely conveyed through the use of animal substitutes, as in his *The Gossips*, 1890 (cat. 46).

1. In his address to the Harvard Class of 1837 he said, "The literature of the poor, the feelings of the child, the philosophy of the street, the meaning of household life are the topics of the time." (Ralph Waldo Emerson, "The American Scholar," in *The Works of Ralph Waldo Emerson*, ed. J.E. Cabot, vol. 1 [Boston and New York: n.p., 1883], 110-11). He often repeated such ideas in lectures given under the auspices of the American Art-Union.

2. Daniel J. Boorstin, *The Americans: The Democratic Experience* (New York: Vintage Books, 1974), 227.

3. Philanthropists concentrated on pauperism rather than poverty and it was believed that only an especially unlucky individual could not rise out of it. Boorstin, 214.

4. According to Veblen, "She is petted, and is permitted, or even required, to consume largely and conspicuously — vicariously for her husband or other natural guardian. She is exempted, or debarred, from vulgarly useful employment — in order to perform leisure vicariously for the good repute of her natural (pecuniary) guardian." Thorstein Veblen, *The Theory of the Leisure Class* (1899; New York: The New American Library, 1985), 232.

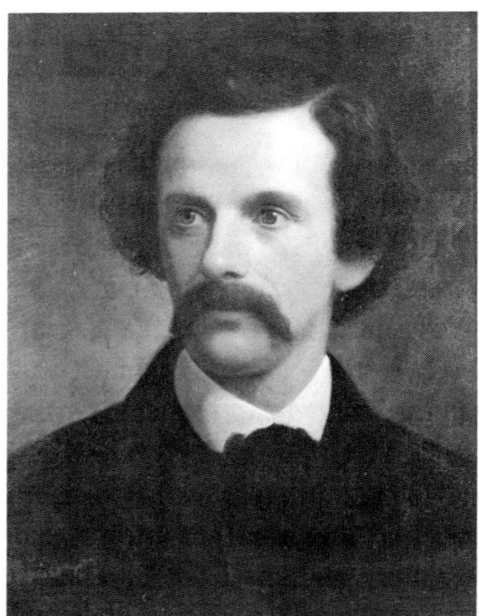

John O'Brien Inman, *Self-portrait #1*, 1865. Collection of the National Academy of Design, New York; photo courtesy of the Frick Art Reference Library.

39. John O'Brien Inman

(born 1828, New York; died 1896, New York)
Catching Up on the News, 1863
Oil on board
10" x 12 1/4"
Signed lower right: J. O'B. Inman '63

John O'Brien Inman was an excellent still life and genre painter who has been overshadowed by his father, the portrait, miniature, genre, and landscape painter Henry Inman (1801-1846). He was born in New York City and trained with his father. By 1853 he had started exhibiting at the National Academy, where he continued to submit genre paintings during the next three decades.[1] After working as a portrait painter in the South and West during the late 1850s, he returned to New York City to open a studio and specialize in small flower and genre paintings. In 1865 he became an Associate of the National Academy of Design. Like so many other artists, he was drawn after the Civil War to Europe, working in Rome and Paris from 1866 to 1878. He then returned to New York, where he painted until his death in 1896.

Inman favored young women and children in his typically small genre paintings. This example shows a well-dressed adolescent boy stretched out on the floor intently reading a newspaper. He has his back to a fireplace with an iron pot suspended over a smoking fire. The hat by his feet tells us that he has just come in, while a wooden spoon by his left hand suggests that he has been set to the task of stirring the pot from time

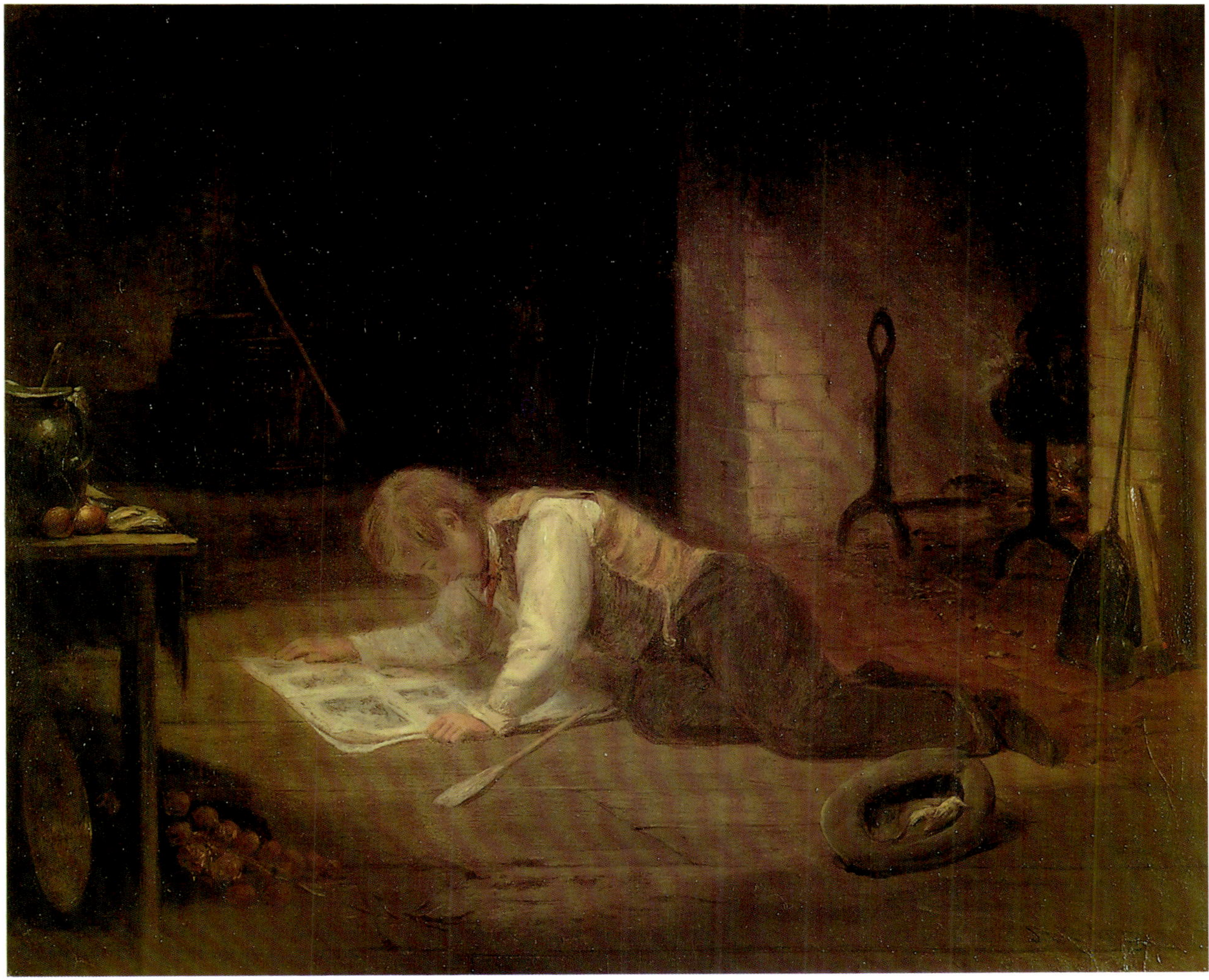

John O'Brien Inman, *Catching Up on the News*, 1863. Oil on board, 10" x 12 1/4".

to time. This little picture exemplifies two of the artist's strengths, sound composition and carefully rendered detail. Along with many other diligently observed objects, the boy takes on the quality of yet another, larger still life element. Both the quiet, restrained mood and subdued colors are reminiscent of Eastman Johnson (1824-1906), who had already established himself as a successful genre painter by 1863, when Inman painted this picture.[2] Later, during and after his sojourn in Europe, the artist lightened his palette under the influence of French Salon painting.

1. See Naylor, 480-81.
2. See Patricia Hills, *Eastman Johnson* (New York: Whitney Museum of American Art, 1972) for relevant examples.

Bibliography

Gerdts and Burke. 69.

Groce and Wallace. 340.

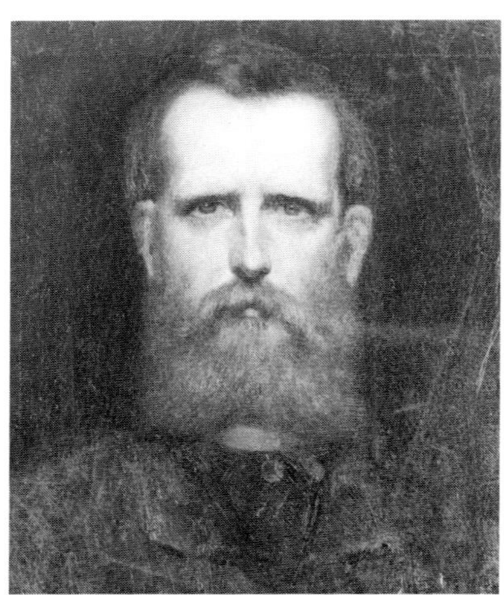

James Wells Champney, *Self-portrait*, 1892. Collection of the National Academy of Design, New York; photo courtesy of the Frick Art Reference Library.

40. James Wells Champney

(born 1843, Boston; died 1903, New York)
Puss-in-Boots, 1875
Oil on panel
10" x 7 1/4"
Signed lower left: Champ '75

James Wells Champney is one of many excellent but currently unfashionable secondary artists who, Cinderella-like, await reevaluation. A distant cousin of Benjamin Champney (cat. 58) he was born in Boston in 1843, but after his mother's death in 1850 was brought up by two aunts in Roxbury. An early interest in art led him to study drawing at the Lowell Institute and apprentice to a Boston engraver at the age of sixteen. He served for a short time in the Union forces during the Civil War, but was discharged because of malaria. From 1864 to 1866, he taught drawing at Dr. Dio Lewis's Young Ladies Seminary in Lexington, Massachusetts, where he met his future wife, Elizabeth Williams. Except for 1870, when he had a studio in Boston, he traveled and studied in London, France, Belgium, Italy, and Germany from 1866 to 1872. He first trained with the genre painter Pierre-Edouard Frère (1819-1886) at Ecouen near Paris and then with Joseph-Henri-François van Lerius (1823-1876) at the Royal Academy in Antwerp.

In search of subject matter for magazine illustrations, Champney went to Leavenworth, Kansas, in 1873, and there met Elizabeth Williams again. Rather than face the prospect of an arranged marriage with a prosperous local farmer, she eloped with Champney. She subsequently became a popular, prolific, and successful author of children's books, which were often illustrated by her husband.

Over an eight-year period, Champney made a number of trips far afield to do illustrations on commission for special feature articles in domestic and foreign publications.[1] In 1874 he visited France and Spain and exhibited at the Paris Salon, where he began signing his paintings "Champ" to distinguish himself from other artists with the same last name. In 1876 his participation in the Philadelphia Centennial Exposition highlighted a successful exhibition career. In the same year, he established a studio in his in-laws' original homestead in Deerfield, Massachusetts. After 1879, when he opened a studio in New York City, the Deerfield house became his summer home and a base for his domestic landscape painting. He also kept a studio in Paris and made frequent trips to Europe. From 1877 to 1884 he was professor of art at Smith College, where he was one of the founders of its art gallery, and in 1882 was made an Associate of the National Academy of Design.

In 1883 he started doing pastels, which soon became his favorite medium. He was the highest paid pastelist of his time. Working in subtle, refined colors and soft, smooth textures, he did portraits and copies of old master paintings, both of which were in great demand. In 1903, at the height of his powers and success, he was leaving the Camera Club in New York when his elevator became stuck between the fourth and fifth floors. When he tried to jump to the fourth floor, he fell down the shaft to his death.

Champney was an extremely versatile artist whose oeuvre spanned landscape, portraiture, genre, and illustration, and who worked with equal facility in oil, watercolor, and pastel. Moreover, he also had a serious interest in photography, which he used to work out the details of some of his compositions. Since about a third of his work is dated, it is possible to trace its development. Eventually, his landscapes and watercolors underwent Barbizon and Impressionist influences respectively. However, his less numerous genre paintings, most of which were executed in the 1870s and early 1880s, did not. Instead, they retained his teacher Frère's concern for clarity and precision. Often they juxtapose children and old people, portray craftsmen at work, or show children playing.[2]

The charming, small painting reproduced here shows a little girl holding and looking at an open book,

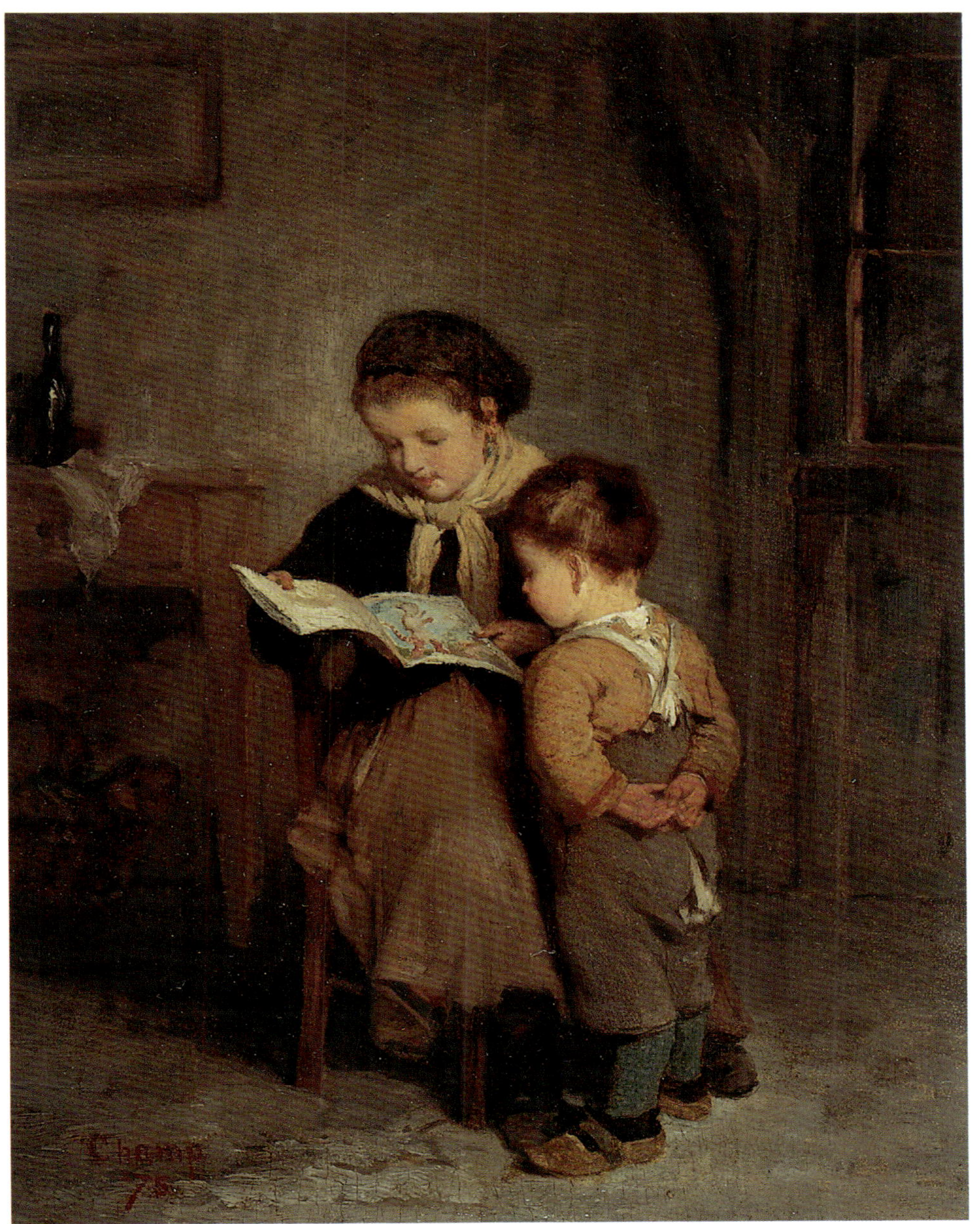

James Wells Champney, *Puss-in-Boots*, 1875. Oil on panel, 10" x 7 1/4".

one page of which illustrates Puss-in-Boots. With his hands clasped behind his back, her younger brother looks on intently, oblivious to the tear in the seat of his pants. The prime elements of the scene, their faces and the book, stand out in a low-keyed color scheme otherwise restricted to grays and browns. He has painted their highlighted figures with great precision, while less distinctly indicating the background details. All elements, even the children, function as still life objects in a well-organized composition that carefully balances verticals and horizontals. A wine bottle and glass and the children's costumes suggest that they are not American but French. This is borne out both by the date, 1875, when the artist was still in France, and an old label of a Leeds, England art gallery that until recently was attached to the back of the frame. Champney's teacher, Frère, exhibited at the Royal Academy in London from 1868 to 1885 and was popular among English collectors.[3] Presumably, his pupil's stylistically similar works also had a following there.

1. He did illustrations for four such articles: 1873, on the Reconstruction South for *Scribner's Monthly*; 1874, on American life for *L'Illustration* in Paris; 1878, on Brazil for *Scribner's*; 1880, with his wife, on Africa, Spain, and Portugal for *Harper's* and *Scribner's*.

2. In the sample of one hundred seventy-one works located in museum, dealers', and auction catalogues and a 1984 National Museum of American Art Inventory of American Paintings list, forty-seven (27.4%) are dated, thirty-five (20.5%) are genre paintings, forty-eight (28.1%) are portraits or self-portraits, and sixty-three (36.8%) are landscapes. Seventy-three (42.7%) are oils, sixty-two (36.2%) are pastels, and thirty-six (21%) are watercolors.

3. See Weisberg, 290.

Bibliography

James Wells Champney: 1843-1903. Deerfield, MA: Hilson Art Gallery, Deerfield Academy, 1965.

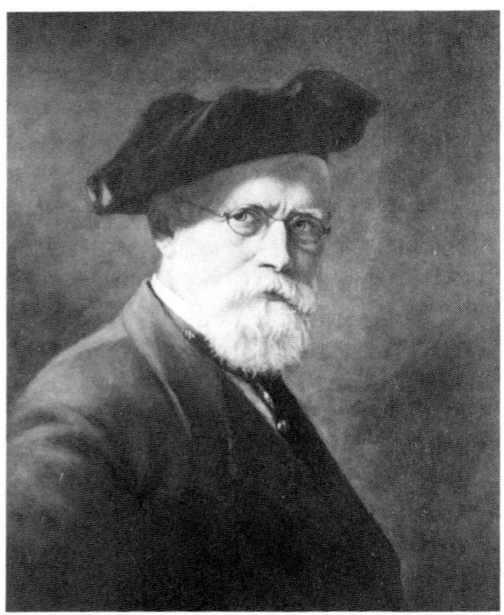

Thomas Waterman Wood, *Self-portrait*, 1895. Collection of the National Academy of Design, New York; photo courtesy of the Frick Art Reference Library.

41. Thomas Waterman Wood

(born 1823, Montpelier, Vermont; died 1903, New York)
Shining Shoes, ca. 1865
Oil on canvas
13" x 10"
Signed lower left: T.W. Wood

In his time Thomas Waterman Wood was a famous genre and portrait painter. Today, however, his depictions of small-town life have been eclipsed by those of currently much better known artists, such as William Sidney Mount (1807-1868), George Caleb Bingham (1911-1879), Eastman Johnson (1824-1906), and Winslow Homer (1836-1910).

Born in 1823 in Montpelier, Vermont, Wood worked in his father's cabinet shop until 1846. He became interested in art through an itinerant portrait painter. Although he learned to draw by copying instruction books, it is unclear whether or not he owed his ultimately excellent technique only to self-study.[1] In any event, by 1850, when he married and built a summer home and studio in Montpelier, he was already a successful portraitist. Portraiture took him to Canada and Washington, D.C. in 1855 and to Baltimore in 1856, where he lived for two years and started painting genre subjects. In 1858, he went on a tour of London and Europe to study old master and contemporary artists and execute commissions for American patrons. Returning to the United States the following year, he did portraits and genre paintings in Nashville, Tennessee, until 1862, lived in Louisville,

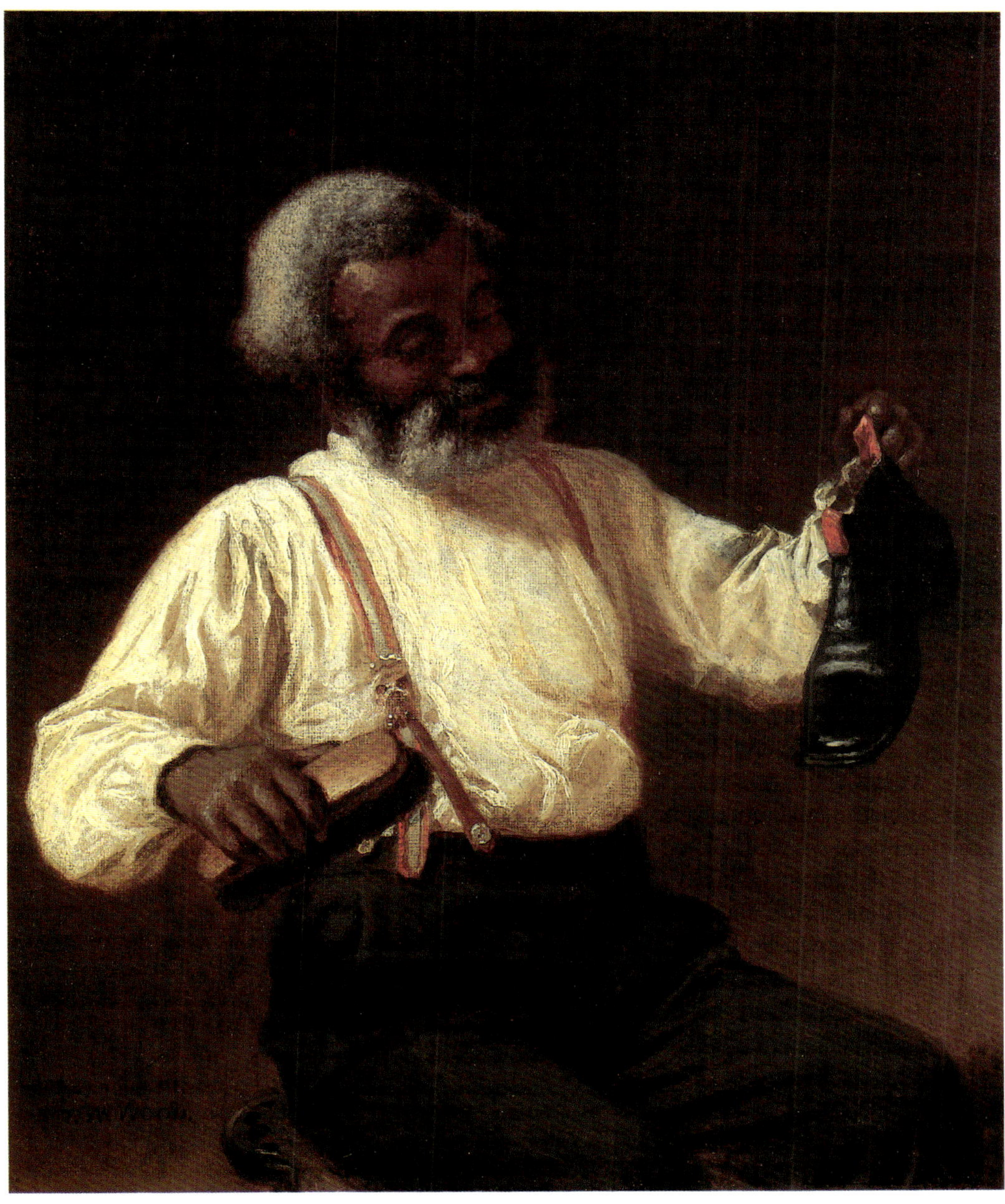

Thomas Waterman Wood, *Shining Shoes*, ca. 1865. Oil on canvas, 13" x 10".

Kentucky, until 1866, and then established a studio in New York City. Except for trips abroad, he typically spent three-quarters of the year working there and summered in Montpelier until his death in 1903.

The rest of his life was a continuous success story. It included an active career in the National Academy of Design, where he was a lifelong exhibitor. Elected as an Associate in 1869 and made an Academician two years later, he also served as an instructor, vice-president, and later president of the Academy. Wood was also affiliated with other organizations, serving as president of the American Water Color Society and vice-president of the American Art-Union during the 1880s. During the 1890s, he largely confined himself to painting his lucrative and sought-after portraits. The money made from them helped him realize his goal of establishing a permanent art gallery in Montpelier which opened in 1895. He donated copies of old master paintings made on special trips to Europe as well as many of his own paintings and examples of the work of some of his leading American contemporaries.

Considering the extent of his official duties and his careful, painstaking technique, Wood was an extraordinarily productive artist. He turned out over 1500 paintings, at least two-thirds of which were neither copies of old master paintings nor alternative versions of his own work. Most of them are currently unlocated, but as his oeuvre is reassessed and better appreciated, many will doubtlessly appear on the art market to enter public and private collections.

Wood's genre paintings champion hard work and egalitarianism. They reflect the middle class values of the small-town rural society in which he grew up and reimmersed himself each summer. His forte both as a genre and portrait painter is his ability to suggest a sitter's individuality through accurate observation of gesture and facial expression. Indeed, the protagonists of his genre pieces were often friends and associates, a procedure that could not help but enhance their air of authenticity. His explicit, straightforward realism depends on the kind of detailed, meticulous technique advocated by the Düsseldorf Royal Academy and popular in the United States after mid-century. His genre works are usually dated and are of two kinds. Most elaborate are his carefully composed multifigure portrayals of small-town life. Typically set in a barn or in a blacksmith's shop, they illustrate a political discussion or the tender interaction of an old man or woman with a little girl. He often repeated his most successful works in this category. Simpler and more appealing to modern taste are his single-figure genre paintings, which run the gamut from children to the elderly and from pure character studies to occupational genre.

Most interesting, perhaps, are his portrayals of blacks. Starting in 1858 and extending over a span of thirty-five years, they are based on figure studies he did in the South and are mostly occupational genre. The earlier examples, which depict free Southern blacks, are the best. Later, Wood fell into the faithful black servant stereotype. Nonetheless, early or late, they are always marked by a sympathetic and objective specificity. Unlike Harry Roseland's (cat. 42) black genre pieces, no individual becomes a type or is ever repeated. With some exceptions, Wood's best genre paintings were done by 1880, after which many are marred by the sentimentality popular at the time.[2]

The work illustrated here stands near the end of a long tradition of distinguished portrayals of older men which started in the Renaissance and proceeded through the Baroque, most notably in the hands of Rembrandt van Rijn (1606-1669), down through the eighteenth and nineteenth centuries. By Wood's time, however, the primary context had shifted from a religious to a secular one. Penetrating observation of facial expression, strong, dramatic color contrasts and chiaroscuro, and convincing depiction of surfaces mark Wood's best character studies. Here they are seen to advantage in his portrayal of a late-middle-aged black man shining shoes. Cocking his head, he inspects a black shoe with red elastics to see if it needs more polishing with the brush held in his other hand. The expression on his handsome face is a complex blend of the quizzical and satisfied. His shirt and trouser folds are rendered with great skill as is the modeling of his body which, within the confines of a shallow picture space, is totally convincing in its three dimensionality. Even more compelling is his deep inner dignity.

1. Although he is credited with an 1846-1847 period of study with the well-known Boston portrait painter Chester Harding (1792-1866) and another in 1858 with the Düsseldorf artist Hans Fredrik Gude (1825-1903), neither can be substantiated. However, his style is consistent with such training.

2. Out of a sample of fifty published works, forty-six (92%) are dated. Of the forty-five genre pieces, twenty-nine (64.4%) portray a single figure.

Bibliography

"American Painters — Thomas W. Wood, N.A." *The Art-Journal* n.s. 2 (1876): 114-15.

Catalogue of the Pictures in the Art Gallery in Montpelier. Montpelier, VT: Wood Gallery of Art, 1913.

Benjamin, n.p.

Blaugrund, Annette. "The Tenth Street Studio Building: a Roster, 1857-1895." *The American Art Journal* 14 (1962): 64-71.

Clement and Hutton, 2. 359-60.

Hasker, Leslie A., and J. Kevin Graffagnino. "Thomas Waterman Wood and the Image of Nineteenth-Century America." *Antiques* 118 (November 1980): 1032-042.

MacAgy, Jermayne. "Three Paintings by Thomas Waterman Wood (1823-1903): *Moses the Baltimore News Vendor, Negress, Cogitation.*" San Francisco, California, Palace of the Legion of Honor, *Bulletin* 2 (May 1944): 9-15.

Lipke, William C. *Thomas Waterman Wood, P.N.A., 1828-1903.* Montpelier, VT: Wood Gallery of Art, 1913.

N.C.A.B. vol. 3. 345.

Sheldon. 109-10.

Tuckerman. 488-89.

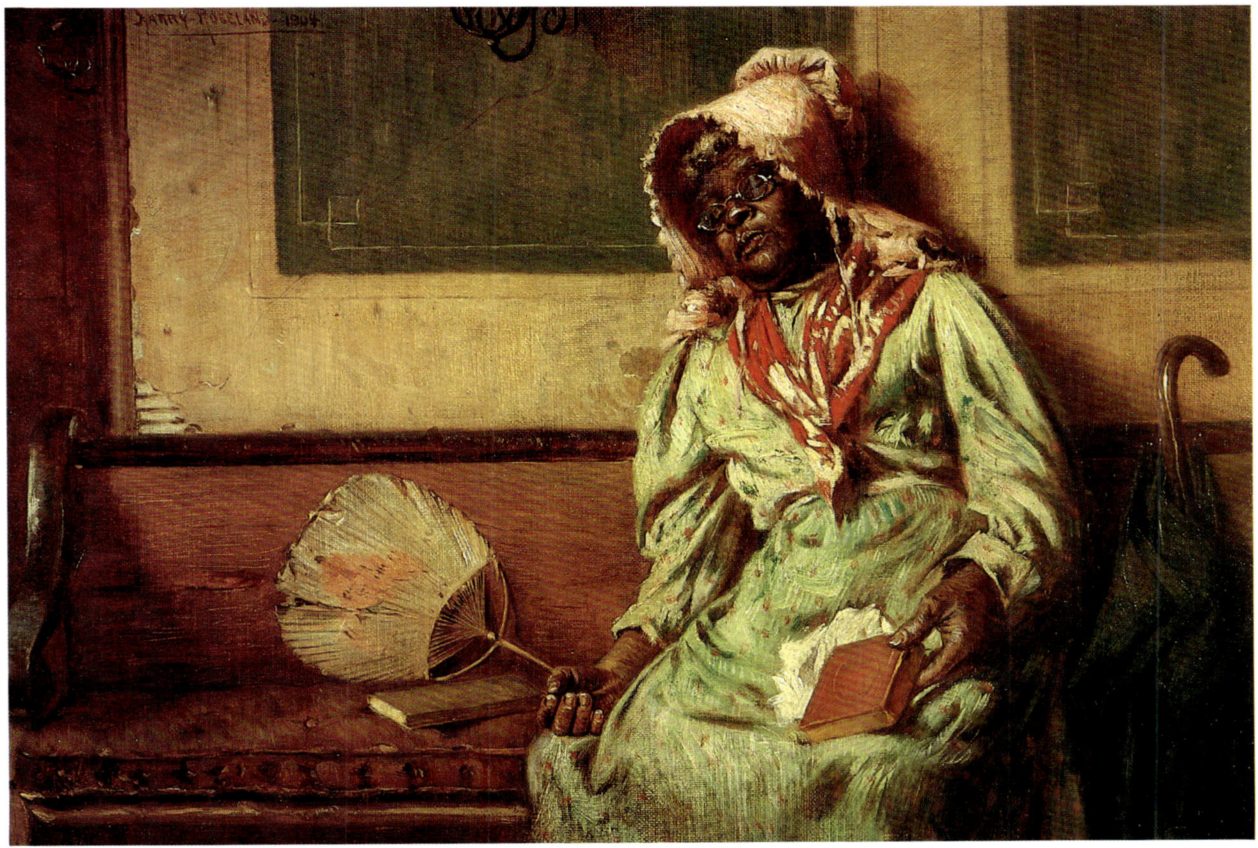

Harry Roseland, *The Snooze*, 1904. Oil on canvas, 14 1/4" x 20 1/4".

42. Harry Roseland

(born 1868, Brooklyn, New York; died 1950, Brooklyn, New York)
The Snooze, 1904
Oil on canvas
14 1/4" x 20 1/4"
Signed upper left: Harry Roseland 1904

Although they are widely sold, the paintings of the once popular figurative artist Harry Roseland are shunned by museums and larger collectors, and, with one exception, they have figured only in exhibitions sponsored by smaller institutions.[1]

Born in Brooklyn in 1866, he studied with the portrait painter John Bernard Whittaker (1836-1926) at the Adelphi Art Academy in Brooklyn and then with landscape, genre, and portrait painter James Carroll Beckwith (1852-1917). From 1884 on he often exhibited at the National Academy of Design and on occasion at the Brooklyn Art Association. Between 1887 and 1907 he won at least seven prizes and medals at various exhibitions. Thereafter, his career is poorly recorded.

What has limited interest in this able artist more than anything else is the niche he made for himself as an interpreter of the life of poor blacks. At first his depictions of them were varied, fresh, and convincing. However, they settled into a narrow range of subject matter that became a personal cliché many current viewers find distasteful.

Fortunately, much of Roseland's published work is dated. Although he did at least one landscape, several still lifes and figure studies, and a handful of portraits, he was basically a genre painter. His earliest known work is a surprisingly competent female nude done in 1881 at the age of thirteen.[2] From 1888 to 1898 he concentrated on occupational genre, especially agricultural scenes done in Queens, Brooklyn, and Long Island. Some of them are large, complex, and well composed multifigure works.[3] In them he was able to draw on the work of American artists such as Eastman Johnson (1824-1906) and Winslow Homer (1836-1910), as well as currently popular French painters such as Jean-François Millet (1814-1875), Jules Breton (1827-1906), Julien Dupré (1851-1910), and Léon Lhermitte (1844-1925), who made their names through renditions of peasant life.[4] The market for Roseland's less exotic agricultural genre, however, was probably limited.

In any event, although he seems never to have visited the South, starting in 1895 he began to examine the subject of the poor black in his paintings. His depictions of them, usually set in humble, poorly furnished, and slightly dilapidated houses, are of two kinds. The first draws on a limited cast of three characters, an elderly black man and woman and a little girl, presumably their grandchild. Confining himself to only a few models, he illustrates scenes of everyday life such as meal time, cooking, spinning thread, playing checkers, studying, courting, attending church, a doctor's visit, getting together money for the rent, and a creditor's visit. They prove him to be not only an excellent draftsman with a good eye for effective color harmonies and contrasts and a strong sense of composition but also a precise, accurate observer of homely still life details and personality. Although at times sentimental, they are more often than not effective character studies. Yet, the vision of black life that they present is a sanitized one of contented poverty. Moreover, their restriction to elderly blacks and little girls implies an underlying stereotype of weakness and ineffectuality.

Roseland's second type of black genre painting shows the visit of one or two young, attractive, and elegantly dressed upper-class white women (usually blonde) to an elderly black woman. Except for an initial 1895 image in which the white woman receives a knitting lesson, she is typically depicted having her fortune told by the black woman who reads cards or tea leaves. This kind of painting has damaged Roseland's reputation both because it demeans blacks by casting them in the role of servants and because of its archness. Dated examples of the first kind range from 1896 to 1905, and of the second from 1895 to 1909. Thereafter, the quality of Roseland's work dropped off as he seems to have given up depictions of black life in favor of sentimental mother-child paintings, still lifes, and even an equestrian portrait of George Washington.[5]

The Snooze shows the artist at his best as an accurate, sympathetic observer of everyday life. A study of the effects of sleep on facial expression and body posture, it shows an elderly black woman sitting in the back pew of a church. Asleep, she slumps back as her relaxed left hand barely retains its hold on a prayer book nestled in her lap on top of her handkerchief. Her right hand has lost its grip on the fan, which has fallen against the back of the pew to rest on top of a book. This unusual and effective composition relies on the figure's asymmetrical placement balanced by the expanse of wall and pew, and a carefully thought-out interplay of verticals and horizontals. The harmonious color scheme is a judicious counterpoint of greens, pink, and red. Roseland used several elements of this painting (pew, fan, prayer book, umbrella, and the theme of sleep) in an earlier more insistently anecdotal work also set in a church in which the elderly wife nudges her dozing husband to wake him up.[6]

1. See William H. Gerdts, *The Art of Healing: Medicine and Science in American Art* (Birmingham, AL: Birmingham Museum of Art, 1981), ill. p. 53; David M. Sokol, *Life in 19th Century America: An Exhibition of American Genre Paintings* (Evanston, IL: Terra Museum of American Art, 1981), no. 56, ill. p. 29; Chambers, ill. p. 48; Edwards et al., no. 92, ill. p. 64; and McElroy et al., ill. p. 103.

2. See Christie's East, 6/24/87, no. 147.

3. His most ambitious multifigure work, however, is an 1891 Coney Island beach scene. See Christie's, 12/5/86, no. 133A.

4. See Weisberg, fig. 49, 50, 302, 194, 195.

5. In a sample of seventy-three published works, thirty-three (45.2%) are dated. Twenty-two (30.1%) show blacks only, while twenty-three (31.5%) are devoted to black-white interactions. All but two of these have the fortunetelling theme.

6. See McElroy et al., 103.

Bibliography

Chambers, Bruce W. *Art and Artists of the South: The Robert P. Coggins Collection*. Columbia, SC: Columbia Museum of Art, 1984. 48.

"Harry Roseland." *Truth* (May 1899): 1-3.

N.C.A.B., vol. 11. 186-87.

Speed, Jonathan Gilmore. "Story-telling as a Motive in Painting." *Monthly Illustrator* 3 (1895): 234-42.

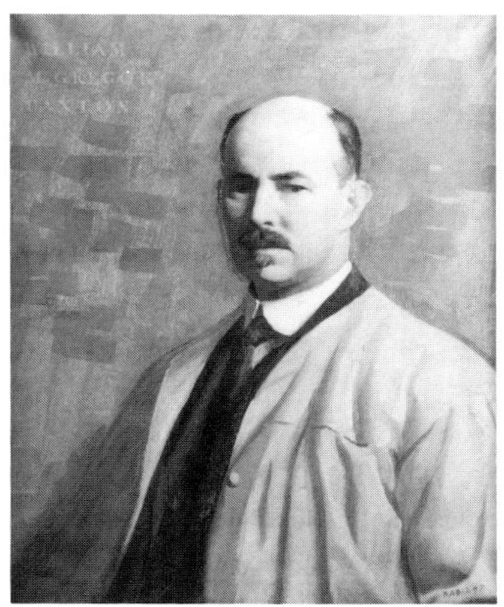

William McGregor Paxton, *Self-portrait*, 1917. Collection of the National Academy of Design, New York.

43. **William McGregor Paxton**

(born 1869, Baltimore; died 1941, Newton Center, Massachusetts)
The Telegram, 1918
Oil on board
18" x 15"
Signed upper right: Paxton

Like many other figurative realists trained around the turn of the century, William McGregor Paxton first enjoyed great success only later to slip into the critical limbo awaiting practitioners of out-of-fashion styles. From his death in 1941 until 1979, the date of a major retrospective exhibition of his work, references to him and his paintings were rare. Now that realism has been readmitted into the official fold, however, they are once more popular.

Born in Baltimore in 1869 but raised in Newton outside of Boston, Paxton was the son of a caterer. His father encouraged his early interest in art. While in high school he attended night classes at the Cowles School of Art and in 1887 was awarded a scholarship to study there under Dennis Miller Bunker (1861-1890), a gifted pupil of Jean-Léon Gérôme (1824-1904). In 1889 he left for Paris, where he studied at the Académie Julian with Jules-Joseph Lefebvre (1831-1911) and Jean-Joseph-Benjamin Constant (1845-1902) and, from 1890 until his return to the United States in 1893, with Gérôme himself, a very exacting teacher who was never entirely satisfied with his pupil's work. Returning to the Cowles Art School, he became friends with Joseph Rodefer De Camp (1858-1923), whose paintings of elegant interiors and attractive young women may have helped influence him to concentrate on such subject matter. In 1897 he made a trip to Madrid to study the paintings of Diego Velázquez (1599-1660), an important influence on his work. The following year he joined the Boston Art Club and exhibited at the Pennsylvania Academy of the Fine Arts for the first of many times. In 1899, after an acquaintance of six years, he was finally able to marry the artist Elizabeth Okie (1882-1972), who became an established still life painter herself and frequently modeled for him.

Paxton was given his first one-man show in 1900. From 1901 to 1935 he won eleven prizes and awards at a variety of expositions, Corcoran Biennials, and the Pennsylvania Academy of the Fine Arts for his depictions of interiors with female figures. However, it was mainly by his lucrative portraits that he supported himself. He was elected an Associate of the National Academy of Design in 1917 and made an Academician in 1928. When he won the Popular Prize at the Corcoran Biennial for the fourth time in 1935, his work was already considered passé, although his technical prowess remained undiminished up to his death in 1941.

Paxton did occasional landscapes and still lifes, but he is best remembered for his figurative painting. Like Edmund C. Tarbell (1862-1938), De Camp, and Frank W. Benson (1862-1951), he was known for his portrayals of appealing young women in luxurious interior settings. Such themes followed the lead of continental artists such as Alfred Stevens (1828-1906), James Tissot (1836-1902), and Paul Helleu (1859-1927), who were also interested in portraying everyday upper-class life. Like Gérôme, who was a pupil of Jean-August-Dominique Ingres (1780-1867), Paxton was a superb draftsman and excelled at depicting both the clothed figure and the female nude.[1] He recalled: "I spent endless days when I was a kid in Paris in the Louvre copying Ingres drawings. I think Ingres came nearer than any man who ever lived in achieving what he set out to do."[2]

Paxton's works, which frequently juxtapose different decorative patterns and excel in the meticulous rendering of textures, create an atmosphere of luxury and refinement. His attention to texture and pattern in incidental objects, concern with the rendering of reflections on metal, porcelain, and wood, and preoccupation with the passage of light and the way it falls on objects recall Jan Vermeer (1632-1675), as do the frequency with which letter writing, pictures within pictures, and objects in the immediate foreground occur in his paintings.[3]

Unlike his figurative studio compositions, his portraits rarely transcend prosaic accuracy to reveal the sitter's personality. However, when he succeeds it is in his portraits of women rather than men. Although he made a few early experiments with Impressionism,[4] Paxton preferred to follow the academic approach in which he had been trained, and his development as an artist was complete by 1908.

The Telegram, which typifies Paxton's best work, shows a young woman clasping a telegram tightly in her hand and looking away with a complex mixture of anxiety and introspection. The modeling of the figure and props, texture of each surface, and play of light and shadow are all deftly executed with invisible brush strokes. The color scheme, in keeping with the theme, is unusually subdued even for Paxton, who ordinarily prefers cool but lighter colors. Typical, too, are the way the figure is contrasted with a monochromatic background, the truncation of objects at the edge of the picture space, and the careful balance and juxtaposition of horizontals and verticals.[5] Characteristic of Paxton and his contemporaries, who were trying to assimilate the influences of recent Western contacts with China and Japan, is his use of oriental objects such as the Japanese screen at the left and the blue-and-white Chinese ginger jar on the table at the right, which recur in many of his other works. The attractive young model is one of the small number he used. The date of the painting, 1918,[6] its title, and the fact that she does not wear a wedding ring, suggests that she has just received notification of her fiancé's injury or death in the First World War. However, many other Paxton paintings with less informative titles seem to tell a story but turn out to be ambiguous and pseudoanecdotal.[7]

1. At times they verge on pinups. Their realism almost always stops short of showing pubic hair. Two exceptions are *Study for Gold Drapery*, Sotheby's, 12/6/84, no. 168 and *Nude*, 1911, Sotheby's, 10/26/84, no. 185.

2. H. Barbara Weinberg, *The American Pupils of Jean-Léon Gérôme* (Fort Worth: Amon Carter Museum, 1984), 95. Paxton also admired Leonardo da Vinci and Degas as draftsmen.

3. Vermeer was introduced to Boston through Philip Leslie Hale's (1865-1931) monograph on Vermeer in the 1904 *Master of Art* series no. 6, later expanded into *Jan Vermeer of Delft* (Boston: Small, Maynard and Co., 1913). Paxton helped Hale develop some of his ideas. See Lee, Krause, and Gammel, 53, no. 1 and Bernice Kremer Leader, "The Boston School and Vermeer," *Arts Magazine* 55 (November 1980): 172-76.

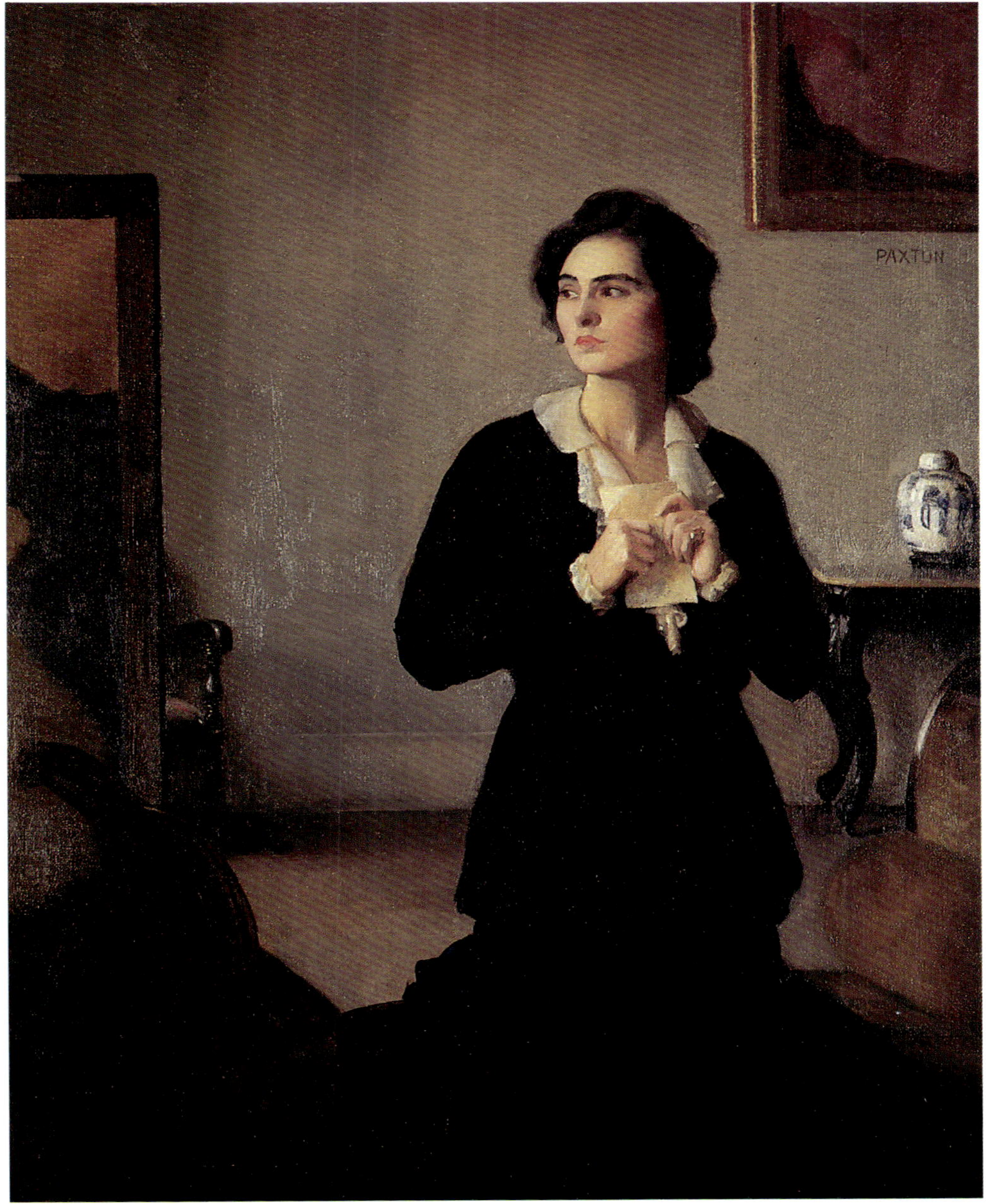

William McGregor Paxton, *The Telegram*, 1918. Oil on board, 18" x 15".

4. See, for example, *The Croquet Players*, c. 1898 and *The White Veranda*, 1904, in Lee, Krause, and Gammel, cats. 3, 6, ill. pp. 7, 11.

5. Pentimenti show that the table was originally positioned differently.

6. A mention of this painting in *American Art News* XVII. 4 (2 November 1918): 2 states that it was "fresh from the artist's easel."

7. For example, *The Other Door*, 1917 (Lee, Krause, and Gammel, no. 45, ill. p. 129), which shows a young woman listening at a door that is ajar, has elicited as many different interpretations as a Thematic Apperception Test.

Bibliography

Gammel. 109-21.

Lee, Ellen Wardwell, Martin F. Krause, Jr., and R.H. Ives Gammel. *William McGregor Paxton 1869-1941*. Indianapolis: Indianapolis Museum of Art, 1979.

Weinberg, H. Barbara. *The American Pupils of Jean-Léon Gérôme*. Fort Worth: Amon Carter Museum, 1984. 93-96.

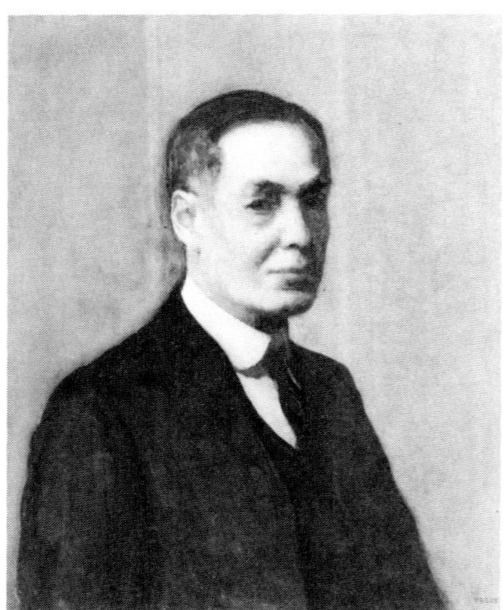

Frederick Bosley, *Self-portrait*, 1931. Collection of the National Academy of Design, New York.

44. Frederick Andrew Bosley

(born 1881, Lebanon, New Hampshire; died 1942, Boston)
The Pageant, 1925
Oil on canvas
38" x 45 1/4"
Signed lower right: F.A. Bosley 1925

At his best, the Boston School portrait, figure, and landscape artist Frederick Andrew Bosley is the equal of his much better known teachers, Frank W. Benson (1862-1951) and Edmund C. Tarbell (1862-1938). Born in Lebanon, New Hampshire, to an old New England family, he grew up in Winchenden, Massachusetts, where his father owned a foundry at which he worked Saturdays and vacations as a molder. His real interest, however, lay in art. Encouraged by a high school teacher, he finally overcame his father's opposition and entered the Boston Museum School in 1900. Despite having to work part-time in the family foundry, he was one of relatively few students to finish the full course of study, which he accomplished in six years rather than the usual seven. The favorite pupil of Benson and Tarbell, he won the school's Sears Prize and in 1906 was awarded the Paige Traveling Scholarship, which enabled him to study in European museums for the next two years.

After his return to the United States in 1908, he married his classmate Emily Sohier and taught art at several upper-echelon New England private boys' schools before succeeding Tarbell as director of the Department of Painting and Drawing and instructor of advanced painting at the Museum School in 1913. From 1909 to 1924, he had studios in Boston but worked afterwards in Concord. In 1926 he bought a farm in Piermont, where he tried unsuccessfully to start a summer art school. To Bosley, like so many other Museum School graduates, modern art was anathema and in 1931 he resigned in opposition to its introduction into the curriculum. His previously successful work gradually fell out of fashion and he began to suffer from depression and duodenal ulcers, from which he died. During his career he won a number of prizes and medals, most notably a bronze medal at the 1915 San Francisco Panama-Pacific Exposition, and was made an Associate of the National Academy of Design in 1931.

Bosley's impressionist technique is closest to Tarbell's, but it also recalls that of Benson and Abbott Handerson Thayer (1849-1921). Currently, as before, collectors favor his striking interiors with young women, alone or in pairs. Blurred outlines and the interplay of light and shadow give them an atmosphere of reflection, solitude, and mystery. His colors tend to be rich, muted, and subtly intermixed.

Although the painting illustrated here is typical of Bosley's mature style, its subject matter is unusual. Rather than one or two elegant young women, it shows three early adolescent girls preparing for a school pageant. He fleshes out the tableau with a number of still life details that provide additional color accents and contrasting horizontal forms. Free brushwork, richly intermingled colors, and extensive chiaroscuro make this an especially rich image. Dominated by the highlighted central figure, it establishes an overall mood of calm reflection. Each girl, isolated from the others in the cocoon of her own thoughts, is so effectively fixed in a moment of adolescent time that one realizes with a start that she must now be in her late seventies.

Bibliography

Bosley, E.S. *Frederick A. Bosley, A.N.A.* Boston: Vose Galleries, 1981 and 1984.

Gammel. 173, 184.

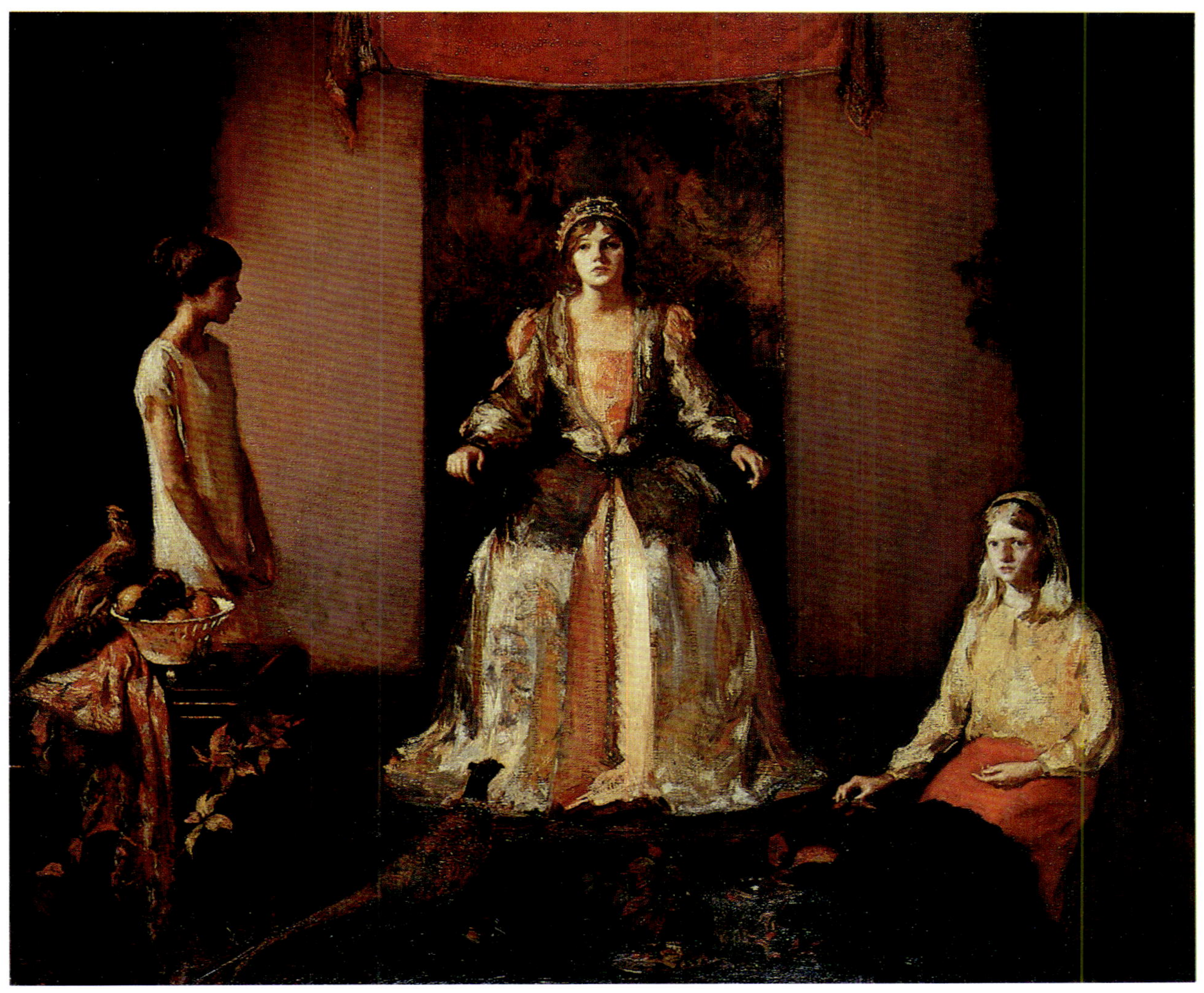

Frederick Andrew Bosley, *The Pageant*, 1925. Oil on canvas, 38" x 45 1/4".

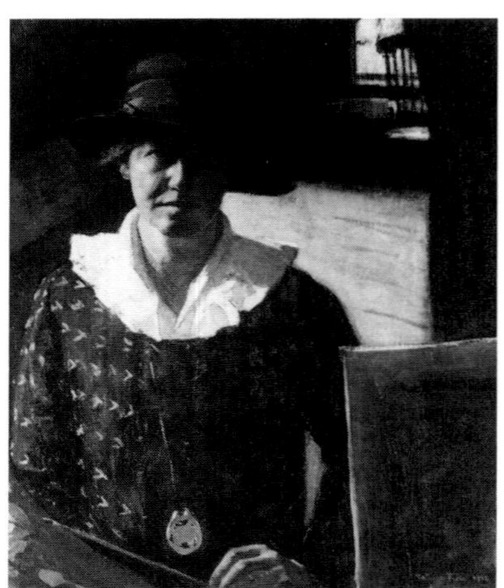

Gertrude Fiske, *Self-portrait*, 1922. Collection of the National Academy of Design, New York.

45. Gertrude Horsford Fiske

(born 1878, Boston; died 1961, Weston, Massachusetts)
The Artist in Her Studio, ca. 1925
Oil on canvas
30 1/2" x 36 1/4"
Signed upper right: Gertrude Fiske

From the 1890s to 1920 Boston had more fine women artists than any other art center in the country and among them were some of its best painters.[1] The most original and the least conservative of them was Gertrude Horsford Fiske. Of all the artists in this exhibition she had the most privileged background. Born in Boston in 1878, she was the eldest of six children. Her father, Andrew Fiske, a successful Boston lawyer, had a fall and spring estate in Weston, Massachusetts, a winter house in Back Bay in Boston, and a summer house in Cataumet, Massachusetts. Her mother, Gertrude Horsford, came from an old New England family and was a direct descendent of Governor William Bradford (1589-1657).

She led an active social life and was a championship golfer until 1904, when she began her training at the Boston Museum School with Edmund C. Tarbell (1862-1938), Frank W. Benson (1862-1951), and Philip Leslie Hale (1865-1931). One of the few to finish the full seven year course of training, she graduated in 1912. She had a studio in Boston, another in Weston, and summered near Ogunquit, Maine, where she attended the classes of the landscape painter Charles H. Woodbury (1864-1940).

A strong-willed but shy woman who never married, Fiske had a distinguished career. She became an Associate of the National Academy of Design in 1922 and an Academician in 1930. She was a founding member of the Guild of Boston Artists, a cofounder of the Concord and Ogunquit Art Associations, and a member of seven other art organizations. From 1929 to 1930 she served on the Massachusetts State Art Commission. By 1935 she had had ten one-woman exhibitions, and from 1915 to 1935 she won seventeen prizes for her work.

Although she painted landscapes from 1915 to 1935, her most prolific period, the bulk of her work consists of portraits and figure studies. She often portrayed young women in her figure studies, but unlike other Boston school artists she also often depicted tradesmen and old people. Her Museum School teachers' influence, greatest in her early portraits and interior figure paintings, is apparent in her attention to detail and her use of chiaroscuro. Later her brushwork became much looser in striking compositions with bright color accents and solidly modeled figures shown in a flickering light against decorative backgrounds. Ultimately, under the influence of Woodbury, she arrived at a semi-decorative kind of post-impressionism in her landscapes.

The impressionist work reproduced here (fig. 45) is characteristic of Fiske's mature figurative painting. With very free brushwork it shows a black smocked woman painter, probably the artist herself,[2] in her studio with another woman, either a visitor or her model. This strongly composed painting depends on careful repetition and contrast of verticals and diagonals and light and dark for its effectiveness. The partially obscured, expressionless faces, especially that of the artist, lend a note of ambiguity to the scene.

1. Thus, of ninety-seven painters whose biographies are given in Trevor J. Fairbrother et al.'s *The Bostonians: Painters of an Elegant Age, 1870-1930* (Boston: Museum of Fine Arts, 1986), 198-230, twenty (20.6%) are women and of the forty-four painters represented in this major exhibition catalogue, nine (20.4%) are women. Similarly, of the thirty-three artists discussed in Gammell, eight (24.2%) are women. An analysis of thirty artists in the same time frame covered in Eleanor Tufts et al., *American Women Artists 1830-1930* (Washington, D.C.: The National Museum of Women in the Arts, 1987) shows that Boston, with seven, leads Philadelphia and New York with five and four respectively.

2. Compare her 1922 self-portrait, illustrated on p. 140 of Michael Quick et al.'s *Artists by Themselves: Artists' Portraits from the National Academy of Design* (New York, National Academy of Design, 1983) and a photograph of the artist reproduced on p. 187 of Gammell.

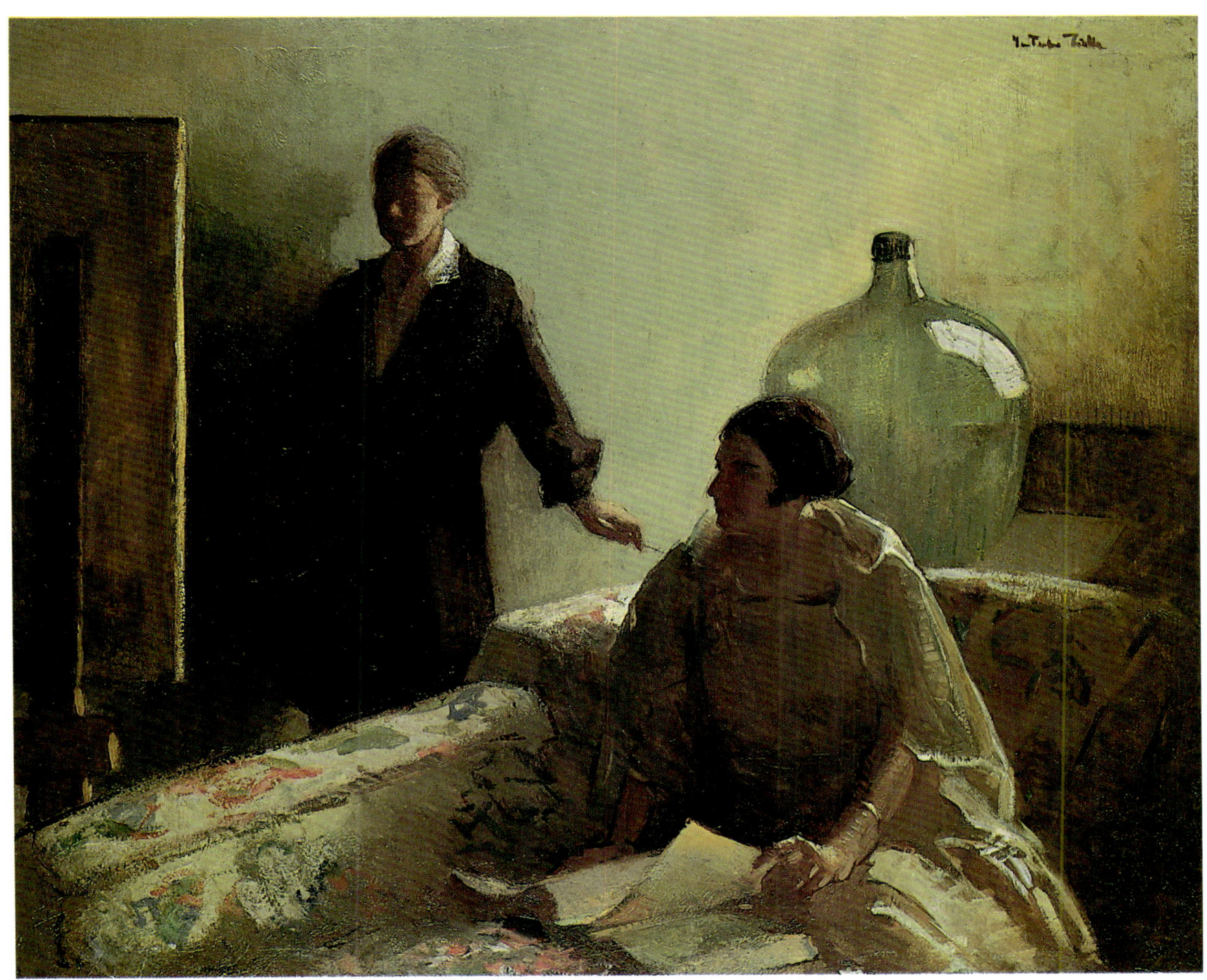

Gertrude Horsford Fiske, *The Artist in Her Studio*, ca. 1925. Oil on canvas, 30 1/2" x 36 1/4".

Bibliography

Gammel. 173-74.

Walker, Carol Aten. *Gertrude Fiske (1878-1961)*. Boston: Vose Galleries of Boston, 1987.

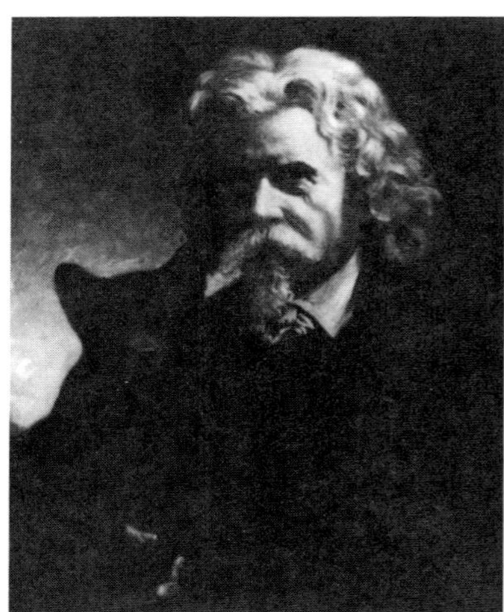

Thomas Waterman Wood (1823-1903), *W. H. Beard,* ca. 1885. Photo courtesy of T. W. Wood Art Gallery, Vermont College.

46. William Holbrook Beard

(born 1824, Painesville, Ohio; died 1900, New York)
The Gossips, 1890
Oil on canvas
18" x 24"
Signed lower left: W.H. Beard 1890

During his lifetime, William Holbrook Beard was a popular and respected animal painter. In recent years, he has regained some of his former popularity with private collectors, but he is much less well represented in museums.

Born in Painesville, Ohio, in 1824, he was a practicing artist in New York City by 1846, where he got some instruction from his older brother, the portrait and animal painter James Henry Beard (1812-1893). In 1850, after a three-year stint in Cincinnati, he settled in Buffalo where he had family ties. Because of his unwillingness to flatter his sitters, he fared poorly as a portraitist and turned to genre. From 1856 to 1858 he visited Italy, Switzerland, and Düsseldorf, where he may possibly have received some formal instruction. After his return home he started showing his work at the exhibitions of the National Academy of Design, where he remained a regular contributor throughout his career. In 1869 he moved to New York City and rented space in the Tenth Street Studio Building. He lived in New York the rest of his life. Besides painting he also wrote several art books (*Humor in Animals*, 1885 and *Action in Art*, 1895). By the time of his death in 1900, his formerly successful paintings were already passing out of fashion.

Because of his versatility, imagination, humor, and involvement with social issues, Beard's work is unlike that of most other nineteenth-century American painters. Over half of it consists of animal paintings, followed by landscapes, fantasies, and genre pieces. His landscapes are mostly restricted to the 1850s. Favorite themes in his genre pieces are hunting, an animal outwitting boy hunters, and deer in a woodland setting. His inventive, allegorical fantasy paintings tend to be large and elaborate. Often eerie and usually quite dramatic, they personify subjects such as death, storm, and the seasons. His currently little published but equally imaginative and fanciful illustrations of nursery rhymes and fairy tales were also popular.

It is his animal satires, however, that made his name. Before Beard and his brother, animal paintings satirizing human behavior had only depicted monkeys. Beard painted his *singeries* in outdoor as well as their traditional indoor settings,[1] often using other common animals, especially bears. His satires range from sallies against pride, greed, jealousy, drunkenness, and gluttony to lampoons of the doctrine of evolution, scholars, scientists, politicians, and businessmen. Otherwise, his animals are involved in simple, everyday activities to which their presence lends a mildly humorous flavor.[2]

Some of his animal satires offended contemporary critics. A case in point is his *Jealousy*, shown at the National Academy of Design in 1863. Following Tuckerman's description, "two rabbits are making love, and a third stands on his hind legs and peers over a cabbage leaf, with an expression of jealous surprise in his fierce and fixed eyes that is inimitable."[3] *Mutatis mutandis*, the same kinds of censorship issues still make news in this country.[4]

Beard worked from sketches and memory. Unlike some other animal painters, he did not keep animals at home nor did he work directly from photographs. At times, however, he used sculptured models. Not infrequently he made multiple versions of his more popular works.

The charming painting reproduced here has all the features that once made Beard's animal genre so popular and sustains its appeal to the modern viewer: humor, sound composition, accurate observation of animals, and a good sense of color harmonies. A gray squirrel and a brown rabbit confront each other. The

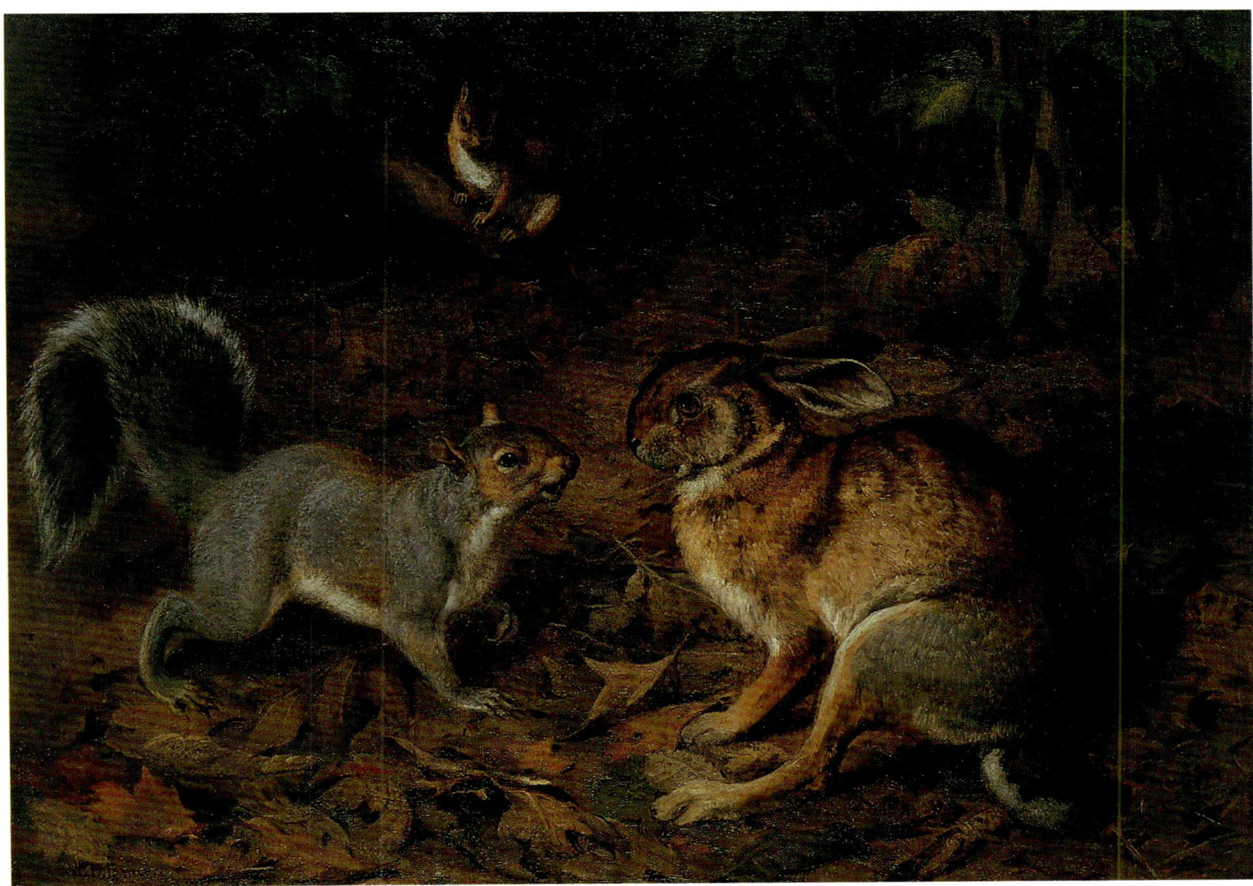

William Holbrook Beard, *The Gossips*, 1890. Oil on canvas, 18" x 24".

squirrel looks intently and expectantly at the rabbit, which appears shocked at what it has just heard. A red squirrel eavesdrops in the background. Their postures and facial expressions easily translate into human emotions and their anatomy and coats are very skillfully rendered. The title, *The Gossips*, strikes us as entirely apt. Beard must have enjoyed the challenge of painting squirrels and rabbits because they figure in a number of his other works, none of which is so openly satirical.[5]

1. *Singeries* have a long history in European painting starting with Jacopo del Zucchi (1541-1604) in the sixteenth century and extending to such nineteenth-century artists as Alexandre-Gabriel de Camps (1803-1868), Charles-Michael-Marie Verlat (1824-1890), and Sigmund Lachenwitz (1820-1868), any of whom could have influenced Beard to try this kind of painting.

2. In a sample of sixty-nine works illustrated in museum, dealers', and auction catalogues, forty-six (66.7%) are dated, thirteen (8.8%) are landscapes, eleven (15.9%) are fantasies, nine (13%) are genre works, and thirty-six (47.8%) are animal paintings. Of these, monkeys occur alone or in combination with other animals eleven times (30.6%) and bears thirteen times (36.1%)

3. Tuckerman, 498.

4. For a detailed account, see Gerdts (1981A), 17-19.

5. See *The Disputed Way*, 1884, Gerdts (1981A), 31, no. 8, *Forest Friends*, 1882, Christie's, 12/3/82, no. 5, *Squirrel and Mice*, 1859, Gerdts, (1981A), 26, no. 5, and *Squirrels (The White Squirrel)*, 1860 or earlier, Gerdts (1981A), 27, no. 6.

Bibliography

Benjamin, Samuel G.W. "An American Humorist in Paint, William H. Beard, N.A." *Magazine of Art* 5 (1882): 14-19.

Gerdts, William H. *William Holbrook Beard: Animals in Fantasy*. New York: Alexander Gallery, 1981. [Gerdts, 1981A]

Sheldon. 56-60.

Still Life Painting

Still lifes can be enjoyed simply for the color, charm, or beauty of their fruit and flowers, which, because of their perishability, are symbols of the transience of living things. Alternatively they can be appreciated on purely formal grounds. According to modern ideas of abstraction and art for art's sake, a painting, like a poem, should not mean but be. Consequently, like the lilies of the field, still lifes, which so often arbitrarily assemble objects, ought to have an inherent advantage over other kinds of painting. Yet, from the seventeenth century well into the twentieth century, art critics relegated them, however beautiful, to the bottom of an aesthetic hierarchy ruled by meaning, morality, and instructional value. Still life was not regularly taught in any American art institution until the 1890s, and only in 1921 did a history of the genre appear. The first American collection specializing in still lifes was not formed until the early 1950s.

Nevertheless, throughout the nineteenth century it was the John's other wife of art buyers, who purchased enough of it to support many still life specialists, beginning with Raphaelle Peale (1774-1825) in Philadelphia. In works such as *Basket of Apples*, ca. 1865 (cat. 47), John F. Francis amplified Peale's chaste approach to tabletop still lifes in a richer, more painterly vein. In other, more cluttered works, however, he was part of a growing mid-century trend toward profuseness of subject matter. Such still lifes of abundance mirrored the increasing prosperity and materialism of the post-Civil War era, when they were widely used to decorate dining rooms and bars.

Like other branches of painting, still life fell into two general stylistic types. One, precise and highly finished, relied on invisible brush strokes. The other took a softer, more painterly tack. Some artists of the first group in this exhibition came to America fully trained from Germany or France. Others studied abroad while a few learned to paint in the United States. Wherever they were trained, all of them shared a preoccupation with the play of light and shadow on carefully and sensuously described surfaces. Some of the earlier fruit pieces show the imprint of Düsseldorf and Johann Wilhelm Preyer (1803-1889) but by the turn of the century artists such as Paul de Longpré reflect the influence of Art Nouveau, as in the asymmetrically composed *Flowers and Insects*, ca. 1900 (cat. 55).

Among the more painterly group of still life artists, at least three repudiated an earlier, more precise manner. The outdoor format advocated by John Ruskin (1819-1900) was popular with a number of American artists from the late 1850s into the 1870s. Although Benjamin Champney uses it in his *Pansies*, ca. 1880 (cat. 58), he eschews both his former detailed approach and the slavishly precise illusionism of the American Pre-Raphaelites. It is not surprising that all but one of the still lifes in this second, more painterly group are depictions of flowers. A looser, freer approach may have seemed more appropriate to their softness and irregularity. In any event, it is interesting that three are by little-known women painters. In this respect, they are typical of the later nineteenth century when exhibition records list many obscure women still life artists, most of whom were flower painters.

In the last third of the century, a new kind of illusionistic still life conceived by William M. Harnett (1848-1892) emphasized man-made objects rather than fruit and flowers. Often trompe l'oeil in technique, they are frequently crammed with objects, which range from the mundane to the costly and exotic. The poorly recorded provincial artist Kate E. Bissell's *Lemons and Lace*, 1894 (cat. 54), tempers this approach with a simplicity indebted to seventeenth-century Dutch and Spanish painting. Before long, such beguiling hyperrealism would be considered hopelessly out-of-date for several generations, until abstract painting gave still life a new and vital impetus.

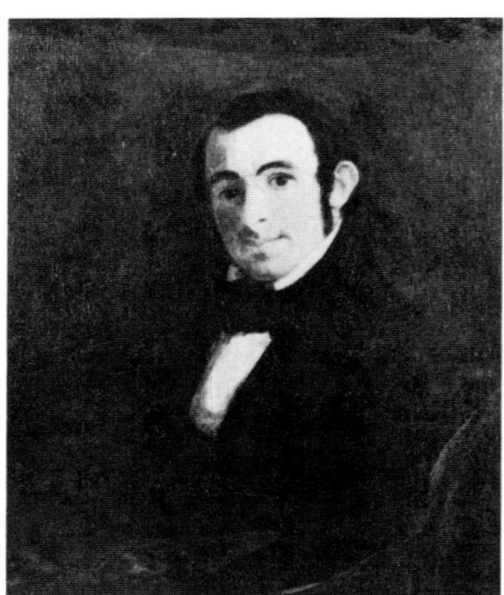

John F. Francis, *Self-portrait.*

47. John F. Francis

(born 1808, Philadelphia; died 1886, Jeffersonville, Pennsylvania)
Basket of Apples, ca. 1865
Oil on canvas
15" x 19"
Unsigned

Although nineteenth century critics preferred the more highly finished still lifes of Martin Johnson Heade (1819-1904), William Michael Harnett (1848-1892), and George Henry Hall (1825-1913) (cat. 52), modern taste finds those of John F. Francis equally appealing. Unlike Heade, a landscapist who also did studies of hummingbirds and flowers, and Harnett, a specialist in trompe-l'oeil depictions of everyday objects, but like Hall, a figurative artist who was also a specialist in fruit and flower painting, Francis turned from a successful career as a portraitist to concentrate on the more mundane and unglamorous specialty of table-top still lifes of fruit, alone, or with crackers, cheese, cakes, and table utensils.

Born in Philadelphia to parents of French Catholic extraction who died when he was young, Francis was brought up by relatives. It is not known how he got his training, but by 1832 he was already painting portraits in central Pennsylvania. Regularly returning to Philadelphia, he exhibited there from 1840 to 1858 at the Artists Fund Society and the Pennsylvania Academy of the Fine Arts. His first known still lifes were painted in 1849. Just as everything seemed to be going his way he suffered double hammer blows of personal loss: in 1856 his two children died in the last major United States cholera epidemic and in 1858 he lost his wife. He soon left Philadelphia to lead the life of a recluse until his death in 1886. By 1860 his now-chronic depression led him to abandon portrait painting with all its interpersonal demands. His last known dated work was executed in 1880.

Francis still lifes fall into three categories. Most popular and elaborate are his dessert and luncheon pictures. At best, they are profuse, at worst, cluttered. Both capitalize on the contrast between round and vertical objects arranged in zigzag linear arrays. The dessert pictures feature food (cakes, fruit), elaborate ceramic, glass, or metal containers, and often a colorful, patterned napkin. The lunch images are even more intricate arrangements of fruit, nuts, cheeses, oyster crackers (one of his trademarks), and partly filled wine glasses and bottles of various sizes. Pictures of fruit (apples, cherries, pears), most often in baskets, form the simplest, smallest, and least popular kind of Francis still life.[1] However, their clear, vivid contrasts and more compact compositions make them particularly appealing to the collector who feels that more is less and less is more.

His still lifes owe an obvious debt to those of his Philadelphia predecessor Raphaelle Peale (1775-1825). However, Francis is more painterly, using tablecloths rather than bare table surfaces, sturdier utensils, and fruit that is often imperfect. Whereas Peale imbues his usually sparser compositions with a chaste, more abstract quality,[2] Francis's arrangements of objects are less planar, and he individualizes them more with strong color and textures.

In the colorful, striking fruit piece illustrated here, the artist has imposed complex balance and repose on the apparent disorder of an overturned wicker market basket of apples strewn on a tabletop. Ranging from all russet to yellowish red with a variety of mixtures of the two colors, the apples are also marked by imperfections and blemishes. Despite its simple components, the roughly pyramidal composition is a complicated one that balances and contrasts the round, solid forms of the carefully counterpoised groups of apples, the hollowness of the basket, and the linearity of its handle, rim, and parallel bands of wicker.

The mundane has become monumental in a work with many typical features. The white tablecloth, wicker basket, and ribbon, for example, are almost trademarks. Like many other Francis still lifes this one is unsigned and undated.[3] However, it is stylistically

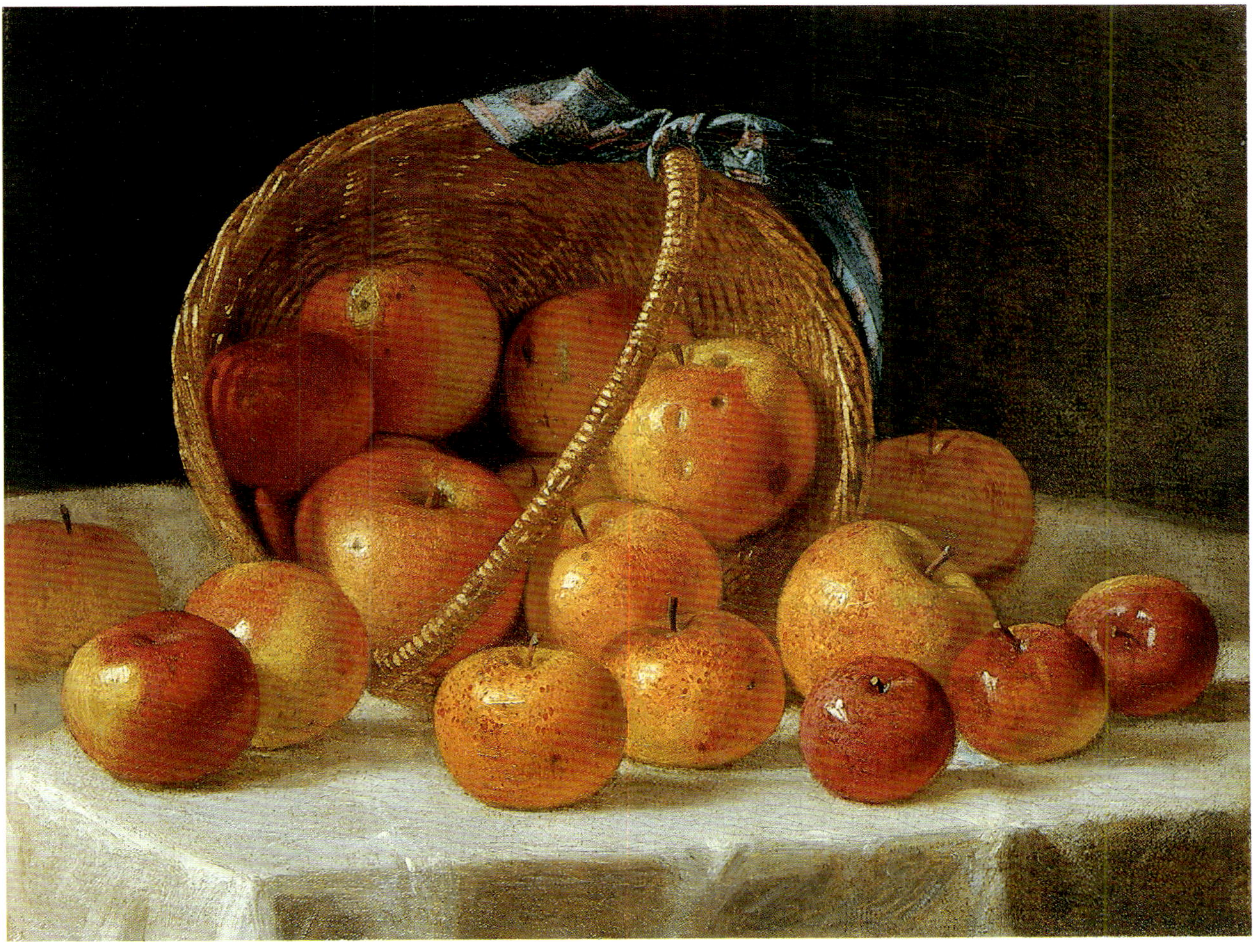

John F. Francis, *Basket of Apples*, ca. 1865. Oil on canvas, 15" x 19".

consistent with many of his signed works, including at least three other closely related paintings of apples spilling out of wicker baskets.[4] Unfortunately for the art historian, he often replicated his subject matter with variations at wide intervals. In this instance the dated works range from 1855 to 1867. Although his later works tend to have freer brushwork, it is hard to establish an exact stylistic chronology. In any case, this still life's appeal lies in its sound composition and its typically adroit use of color accents, chiaroscuro, and clear, simple color contrasts.

1. Ten of fifty-four or 18.5% of those surveyed fall into this category.

2. See Nicolai Cikovsky, Jr., Linda Bantel, and John Wilmerding, *Raphaelle Peale Still Lifes* (Washington, D.C.: National Gallery of Art, 1989).

3. Twenty-two out of a sample of fifty-four, or 40.7% are unsigned, while twenty-six of the sample or 48.2% are undated.

4. See *Still Life: Yellow Apples and Chestnuts Spilling from a Basket*, 1856, fig. 78 in John Wilmerding, et. al.; *Basket of Apples Overturned*, 1855, ill. p. 5 of *For the Collector: Selected American Paintings of the 19th and 20th Centuries* (New York: Wunderlich and Co., 1986); and *Still Life with Apples and a Basket*, 1867, Sotheby's, 6/2/88, no. 39. The last is an especially close variant.

Bibliography

Dunn, David W. *A Suitable Likeness: The Paintings of John F. Francis 1832-1879.* Lewisburg, PA: The Packwood House Museum, 1986.

Frankenstein, Alfred V. "J.F. Francis." *Antiques* 59 (May 1951): 374-77, 390.

Gerdts (1981). 89-93.

Gerdts and Burke. 60-61.

Hersey, George L. *A Catalogue of Paintings by John F. Francis.* Lewisburg, PA: Bucknell University, 1958.

Weber, Bruce. *"Who Was John F. Francis?" John F. Francis: Not Just Desserts.* New York: Berry Hill-Galleries, 1990. 2-4.

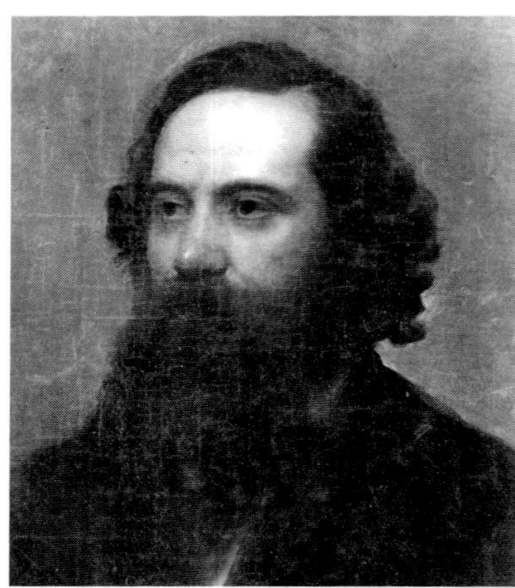

John Williamson, *Self-portrait*, 1861. Collection of the National Academy of Design, New York; photo courtesy of the Frick Art Reference Library.

48. John Williamson

(born 1826, Toll Cross, Scotland; died 1885, Glenwood-on-the-Hudson, New York)
Vase of Flowers, 1861
Oil on board
9" x 7 1/2"
Signed lower left: JW 1861
Inscribed lower right: Brooklyn New York
Exhibition: Brooklyn's Bounty: Natural Splendor and Domestic Opulence, Museum of the Borough of Brooklyn at Brooklyn College, April 16-May 21, 1985.

On the basis of what turns up in the art market, Williamson is thought of primarily as a landscapist who recorded views of New England, Pennsylvania, and New York, especially the Hudson River and Lake George,[1] and also painted a few still lifes. Yet, even though he concentrated almost exclusively on landscapes during the last fifteen years of his life, National Academy of Design and Brooklyn Art Association records show that until 1870, he painted many still lifes.[2] His abandonment of still lifes after that suggests their fall in the esteem of post-Civil War collectors.

He was born in Scotland in 1826, but five years later came to the United States and spent all but the last few years of his life in Brooklyn. It is not known with whom he studied, but he was represented in the 1852 American Art-Union sale and from 1850 to 1885 often exhibited at the National Academy of Design, where he was made an Associate in 1861. He was also active in the Brooklyn Art Association, where he held several offices and regularly showed his work until 1882. After a long career he died at Glenwood-on-the-Hudson in 1885.

The charming flower painting illustrated here successfully flouts the standard art school admonition not to divide a composition symmetrically down the middle. A small light tan vase, set on a gleaming polished tabletop against a dark background is subordinated to a much larger mass of flowers above it. The contrasting colors of a red-and-white carnation, a purple-and-yellow pansy, dark red gladioli, and a pink-and-carmine fuchsia make this little still life a sumptuous, concentrated image.

1. Of a sample of sixty-six paintings culled from exhibition and auction catalogues and a 1984 National Museum of American Art Inventory of American Paintings list, sixty (90.9%) are landscapes, fifteen (25%) and seven (11.7%) of these Hudson River and Lake George views respectively, while only five (7.6%) are still lifes.

2. From 1861 to 1870, they amounted to sixty of 131 (45.8%) and from 1861 to 1885 sixty of 190 (31.6%). Of these, twenty-six of sixty (43.3%) are flower pieces. See Naylor, 1041-043 and Marlor, 380-81.

Bibliography

Groce and Wallace. 691.

Marlor. 5, 7, 14, 21, 39.

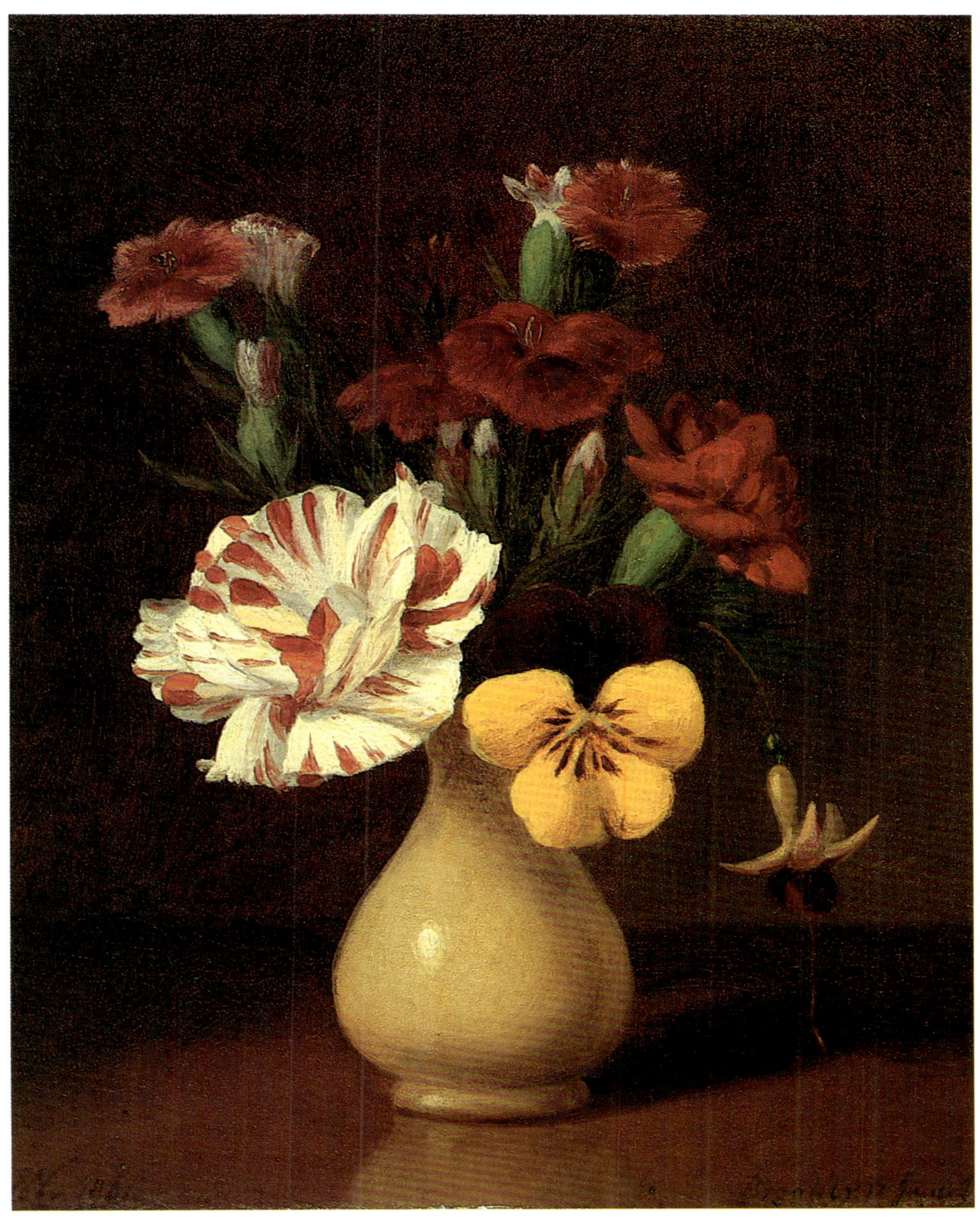

John Williamson, *Vase of Flowers*, 1861. Oil on board, 9" x 7 1/2".

49. George Forster

(active 1844-1890)
Still Life with Fruit, Bird's Nest and Broken Egg, 1876
Oil on canvas
14" x 17 1/4"
Signed lower right: G. Forster 1876

The productive fruit painter George Forster is familiar to collectors of still lifes. He has nevertheless been neglected by museums, perhaps because art historians know so little about him. Yet, there are a few clues. His compact, centralized pyramidal arrangements of fruit with their precisely drawn, clearly defined forms are reminiscent of those of the influential Düsseldorf still life painter and teacher Johann Wilhelm Preyer (1803-1889). Both his name and a dedication in German on the back of one of his paintings[1] suggest that he was born in Germany. If so, his activity dates, 1844-1890, would be consistent with those of an artist who came to the United States just before the political turmoil at home in 1848 and decided to stay on after it.

His usually small paintings of fruit are often dated. Although some are more softly rendered than others, they show no stylistic progression. The number of kinds of fruit shown tends to be a function of size. Most often they are grapes or peaches and plums, one of which is often split open, but many other types of fruit also figure in Forster's oeuvre. A third of his paintings are set outdoors, usually a rock ledge, and half of these have landscape backgrounds. His tabletop pieces usually have simple accessories like wine glasses or glass bowls, but the bird's nest is a virtual trademark. Sometimes it is supplemented with or replaced by broken eggs, and insects and even more unusual additions like a white mouse or a lizard also provide contrasts of scale.[2] Such details, which are also a pretext for the artist to give additional proof of his technical prowess, are derived ultimately from the vocabulary of seventeenth-century Dutch and Flemish still life.

The painting reproduced here is typical of Forster's best work. Under the flag of realism an arbitrary array of objects has been made to share the dramatically lit stage of an irregularly shaped, tan rock ledge. These include a bunch of greenish yellow grapes with their branch and leaves, a bird's nest with four white eggs, four plums, and a broken egg. Although the overwhelming emphasis is on precision of detail this is not hard-edge realism. Rather, softly blurred outlines and subtle gradations of tone and color give the translucent grapes with their bluish white bloom and the other objects a gentle, slightly romantic quality. Forster developed the formula he so successfully uses here early in his career and never felt the need to change it. However, by 1890 it must have seemed quite out-of-date.

1. See *Still Life with Grapes, Bird's Nest and White Mouse*, 1858, no. 62, ill. p. 49 of Nancy Allyn Jarzombek and Nancy E. Green, *Cornell Collects* (Ithaca, NY: Herbert F. Johnson Museum of Art, Cornell University, 1990). On the back of this work on panel a neat hand has inscribed in flowing script, "Samuel Seidels seinem Doctor Schwarzschild 4 Februar 1860."

2. Of nineteen paintings located in books and dealers', auction, and museum catalogues and fourteen others listed in a 1981 National Museum of American Art Inventory of American Paintings list, twenty-one (63.6%) are dated. In twenty-two (66.7%) one dimension is less than or equal to twelve inches, while in nine (27.3%) it is greater than or equal to twenty inches. Eight of nineteen (42.1%) have outdoor settings. Nine of eleven table top pieces (81.8%) have accessories and the bird's nest with eggs figures in seven (36.8%) of them. Insects occur in six (31.6%). Two paintings also depict flowers, but only one is a pure flower piece.

Bibliography

Gerdts and Burke. 67.

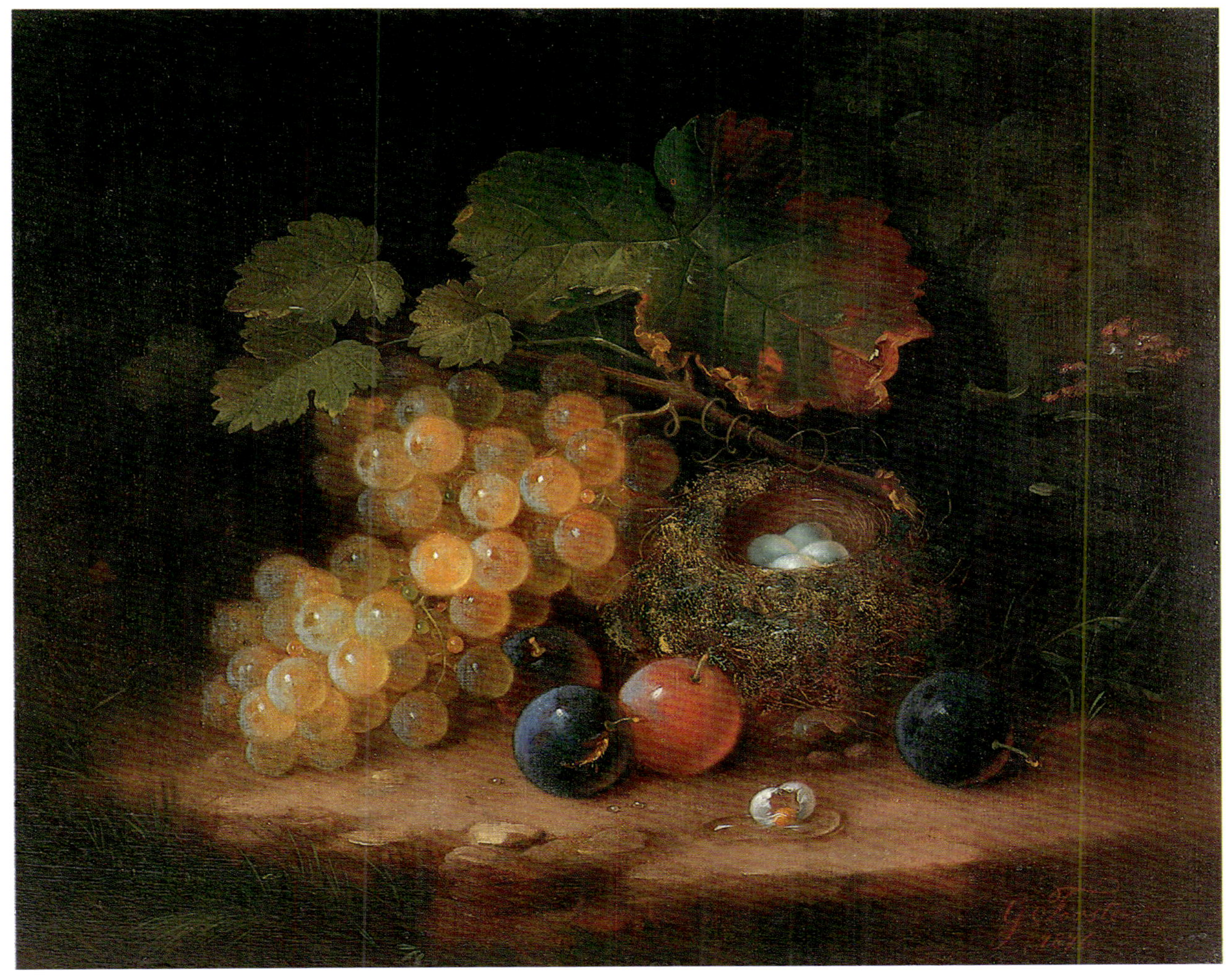

George Forster, *Still Life with Fruit, Bird's Nest and Broken Egg*, 1876. Oil on canvas, 14" x 17 1/4".

50. Paul Lacroix

(active 1858-1869, died 1869, New York)
Vase of Flowers and a Shell, 1867
Oil on artists' board
14" x 10"
Signed lower left: P. Lacroix. N.Y. 67.

Despite his skill and the number of his extant paintings, details of still life specialist Paul Lacroix's life remain relatively obscure. Judging by his name and a few works illustrating scenes in French and Swiss cities, he may have been born in France or Switzerland. In any event, he is known to have lived in New York City from 1859 to 1866 and in Hoboken, New Jersey, from 1867 until his death in 1869.

His submissions to the National Academy of Design from 1863 to 1869 and to the 1867 exhibition of the Brooklyn Art Association as well as various published works suggest that, except for a few landscapes, he painted only still lifes. They usually depict fruit on a stone step or ledge or on a stone or marble tabletop. Although most often set indoors without any accessories, his arrangements include several outdoor pieces with landscape backgrounds. Rare examples portray vegetables or flowers. His well thought-out compositions favor pyramidal or vertical arrangements and are usually dramatically lit at the center. His still lifes are of two kinds. One, smaller and more sensitive, is typically dated. The other, larger and usually undated, overflows with an artificial profusion of many kinds of fruit reminiscent of Severin Roesen (active 1848-1871). Since Lacroix did not appear in New York City until Roesen had left for Pennsylvania, this second type has led Gerdts to speculate that he worked in Roesen's studio.[1]

In the present still life, Lacroix forgoes his usual subject matter, fruit, for the sake of a stunning portrayal of flowers spilling out of a tall, slender wine glass set in the center of a narrow ledge. The bouquet's center of gravity on the left and an elaborately marked shimmering seashell at the right of the glass save the composition from static symmetry. The large central orchid, its petals glistening with drops of water, the snapdragon and fuchsia to either side, and the shell all stand out dramatically against smaller flowers and a dark background. The precise but soft technique, subtle tonal variations, and centralized composition recall the work of Martin Johnson Heade (1819-1904), but the profuse imagery and drama are Lacroix's own.

1. Gerdts (1981), 103-04. Out of a sample of twenty-two Lacroix still lifes, thirteen (59.1%) are dated, twenty (90.9%) depict fruit, one vegetables, and another flowers. Nineteen (86.4%) are set indoors and only three (13.6%) have accessories. Seven (31.8%), all but one undated, are Roesenesque. Of the rest, twelve of fifteen (80%) are dated.

Bibliography

Gerdts, William H. "Paul Lacroix." *Antiques* 102 (November 1972): 855-61.

Gerdts (1981). 103-04.

Gerdts and Burke. 67.

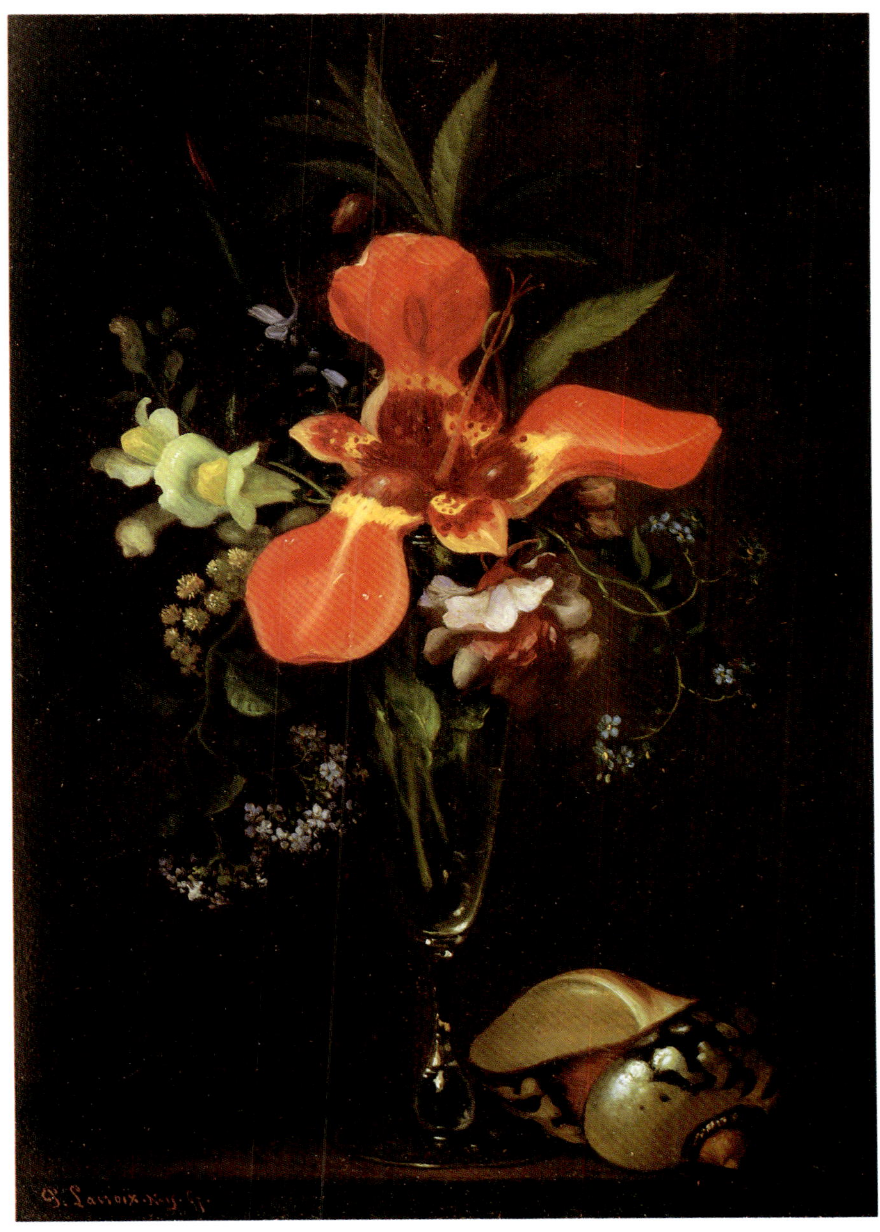

Paul Lacroix, *Vase of Flowers and a Shell*, 1867. Oil on artists' board, 14" x 10".

51. Lemuel Everett Wilmarth

(born 1835, Attleboro, Massachusetts; died 1918, Brooklyn)
Peaches and Grapes, 1885
Oil on canvas
15" x 9 1/2"
Signed lower left: L.E. Wilmarth 1885

Like a number of artists in this exhibition, Lemuel Everett Wilmarth divided his efforts between still life and the more prestigious and lucrative area of genre, for which he was better known. He underwent one of the longest periods of formal academic training of any artist in this exhibition and also had an important teaching career.

Born in Attleboro, Massachusetts in 1835, he initially chose a career as a watchmaker. As a young man pursuing his trade in Philadelphia in 1857, he began attending night drawing classes at the Pennsylvania Academy of the Fine Arts. In 1859, he abandoned the watchmaking business to go to Munich to study for three-and-a-half years at the Royal Academy of the Fine Arts with its director, the figure painter Wilhelm von Kaulbach (1805-1874). During this period, he supported himself by teaching drawing to local families to whom von Kaulbach had introduced him. Starting in 1862, he attended the Ecole des Beaux-Arts in Paris for two-and-a-half years, where he was the first American pupil of the prestigous teacher and figurative painter Jean-Léon Gérôme (1824-1904). He returned in 1865 to the United States to make his name as a genre painter and teacher.

He exhibited extensively at the National Academy of Design (1866-1893) and the Brooklyn Art Association (1866-1884). After first organizing and teaching classes at the Brooklyn Academy of Fine Arts, he became director of the Academy Schools at the National Academy of Design in 1870, where he was appointed its first professor of art. He resigned in 1887, when his eyesight began to fail, and did little painting after 1893. In his later years he lived in Brooklyn, where he devoted himself to writing articles on the religious teachings of Emmanuel Swedenborg and other religious and social subjects. He died in 1918.

Although Wilmarth is thought of as a genre painter, a third of the works he exhibited at the National Academy of Design and the Brooklyn Art Association were still lifes.[1] They must have been similar to the painting reproduced here, which has the same basic features as his genre paintings. Notable are the high finish of its soft velvety surfaces, its accurate draftsmanship, the subtlety and finesse with which the interplay of light and shadow is handled, its careful opposition of shapes and patterns, and its compelling illusion of depth within a shallow picture space.

It shows peaches and grapes[2] piled on a tabletop in front of a plaited basket. Although the artist renders the foreground peach leaves with photographic sharpness, the other objects become progressively less well defined as they recede from the viewer, just as they would if one were actually seeing them while focusing on the leaves in the immediate foreground. This kind of realism was unusual for its time, when all elements of a still life were usually accorded equal detail. Unusual, too, is the shallow composition, which provides an intimate snapshot rather than the usual more expansive view.

1. Allowing for multiple submissions of the same work, ten out of thirty were still lifes. See Naylor, 1044-045 and Marlor, 381-82.

2. With one exception (*Fruit*, 1890, NAD, no. 166) all of Wilmarth's still lifes listed in National Academy and Brooklyn Art Association records depict only one kind of common fruit, either peaches, grapes, or apples.

Bibliography

Clement and Hutton, vol. 2. 355-56.

D.A.B., vol. 20. 312-13.

N.C.A.B., vol. 8. 424-25.

Sheldon. 110-11.

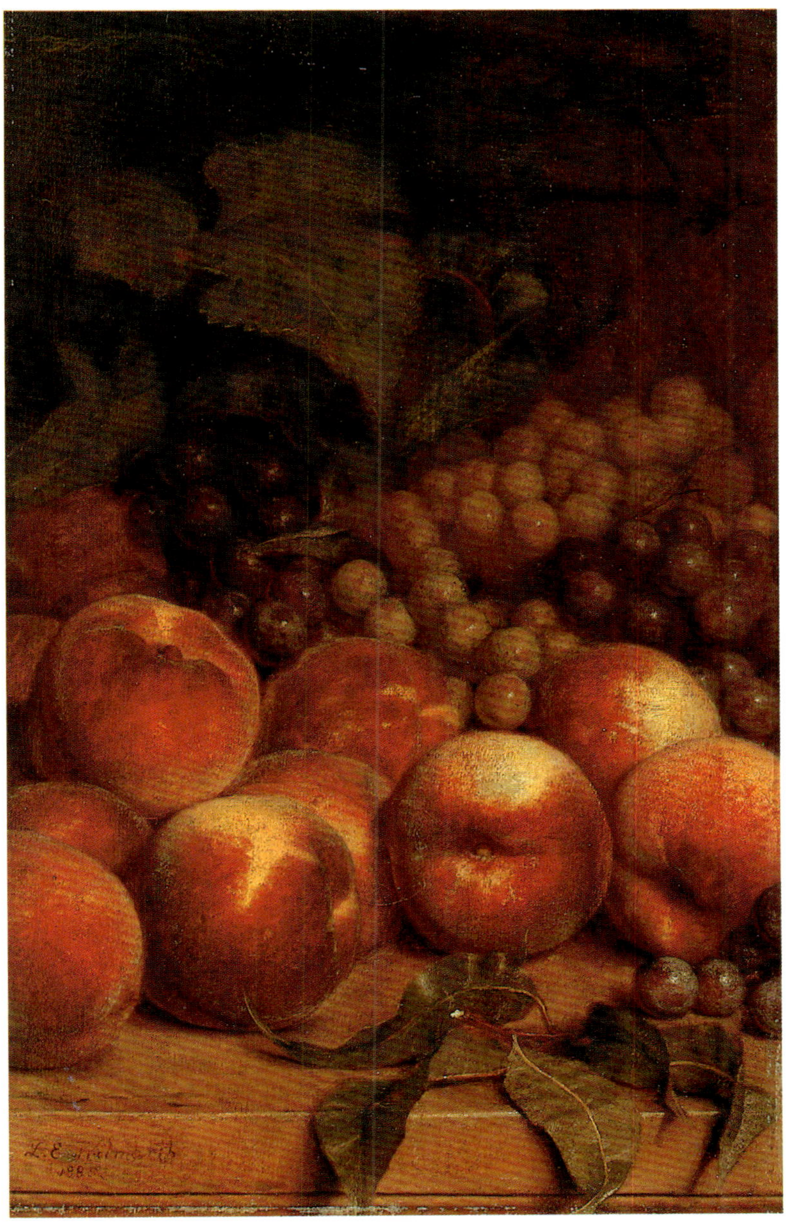

Lemuel Everett Wilmarth, *Peaches and Grapes*, 1885. Oil on canvas, 15" x 9 1/2".

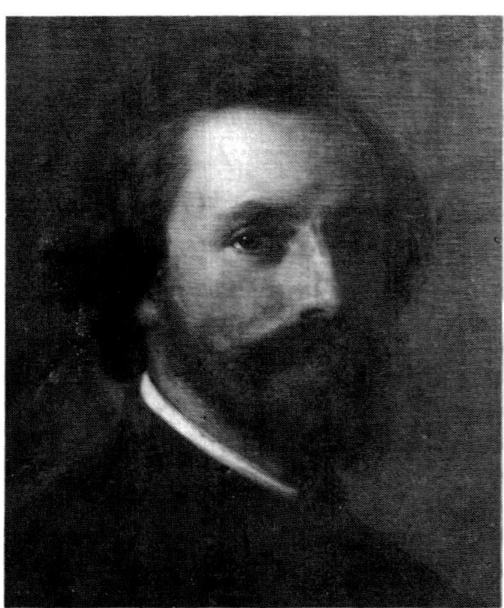

George Henry Hall, *Self-portrait*, 1853. Collection of the National Academy of Design, New York; photo courtesy of the Frick Reference Library.

52. George Henry Hall

(born 1825, Manchester, New Hampshire; died 1913, New York)
The Twins, Chianti Grapes, 1885
Oil on canvas
18 1/8" x 14 1/4"
Signed lower right: Geo Henry Hall Siena, 1885

It is the fate of many painters to go out of fashion with art critics and their equally fickle public. George Henry Hall, however, currently ranks just as high on the lists of both as he did in his own time. Between the Civil War and 1900 this fruit and flower artist vied for ascendancy with the trompe-l'oeil bric-a-brac specialist William Michael Harnett (1848-1892). Indeed, in 1867 Hall was the only still life painter the critic Henry Tuckerman saw fit to discuss. Noting Hall's popularity, he seemed bemused that seventy-five of the painter's small works, sold in 1865 to raise money for a trip to Europe, fetched the "large sum" of $12,000.[1]

Hall was born in Manchester, New Hampshire, in 1825 but after his father's death in 1829 was brought up in Boston. By the time he was seventeen, he was already active as a self-taught figurative painter. In 1846, he began to exhibit at the Boston Athenaeum where he continued to show his work sporadically for the next twenty years, and in 1848 also exhibited at the American Art-Union. Despite his success, he apparently felt the need for formal training. Accordingly, in 1849 he went with Eastman Johnson (1824-1906) to study at the Royal Academy in Düsseldorf. Unlike Johnson and most other Americans there, he found the instruction so unbearably dry and dull that he fled the following year first to Rome, then Paris where he opened a studio. In 1852 he returned home, established himself, and over the years became a frequent and popular exhibitor at a number of important venues.[2]

Already an Associate of the National Academy of Design by 1855, it was during this period that he began painting the still lifes for which he rapidly became so well known. In the 1860s his production of them increased to the point that they largely supplanted his figurative work and earned him election as Academician in 1868. Despite his popular and official success, the influential critics James Jackson Jarves (1818-1888) and Clarence Cook (1828-1900) branded his still lifes as unpoetic and barren of art. Cook, moreover, deemed them inferior to those of the English Pre-Raphaelites and their American followers. Probably stung by their criticism, Hall painted almost no still lifes from 1869 to 1880. His abandonment of the genre may have also been a response to the revival of interest in figure painting emphasized at the time in Paris, which had become a mecca for American art students.[3]

At the National Academy in 1881, however, he exhibited his unusually large and complex *Bric-a-Brac Still Life of Damascus, Seville, and Rome*, 1880, which showed a variety of objects related to his travels in Spain (1860, 1867-1868), Italy (1872), and Egypt (1874).[4] It was a great success and still lifes again predominated in his work of the 1880s, only to be once again superseded by genre paintings in the 1890s.[5] A relic of another era, he died in New York City in 1913, the year of the Armory Show.

About a third of his still lifes depict flowers. They range from smaller works showing one kind only to larger ones with several types. A few portray flowers and fruit, but his favorite subject was fruit, usually focusing on a single type in each representation. Their variety is wide, but raspberries, peaches, grapes, and strawberries are most common. Most of Hall's still lifes are dated tabletop pieces but in the 1860s a number have outdoor settings. In rare examples, the subject is grapes hanging against a wall.[6]

Like a standing nude without props, this simple theme presents a difficult challenge that quickly reveals an artist's technical limitations. In most hands it is translated into mechanical repetition of forms and hard surface effects. Here, however, Hall's simply

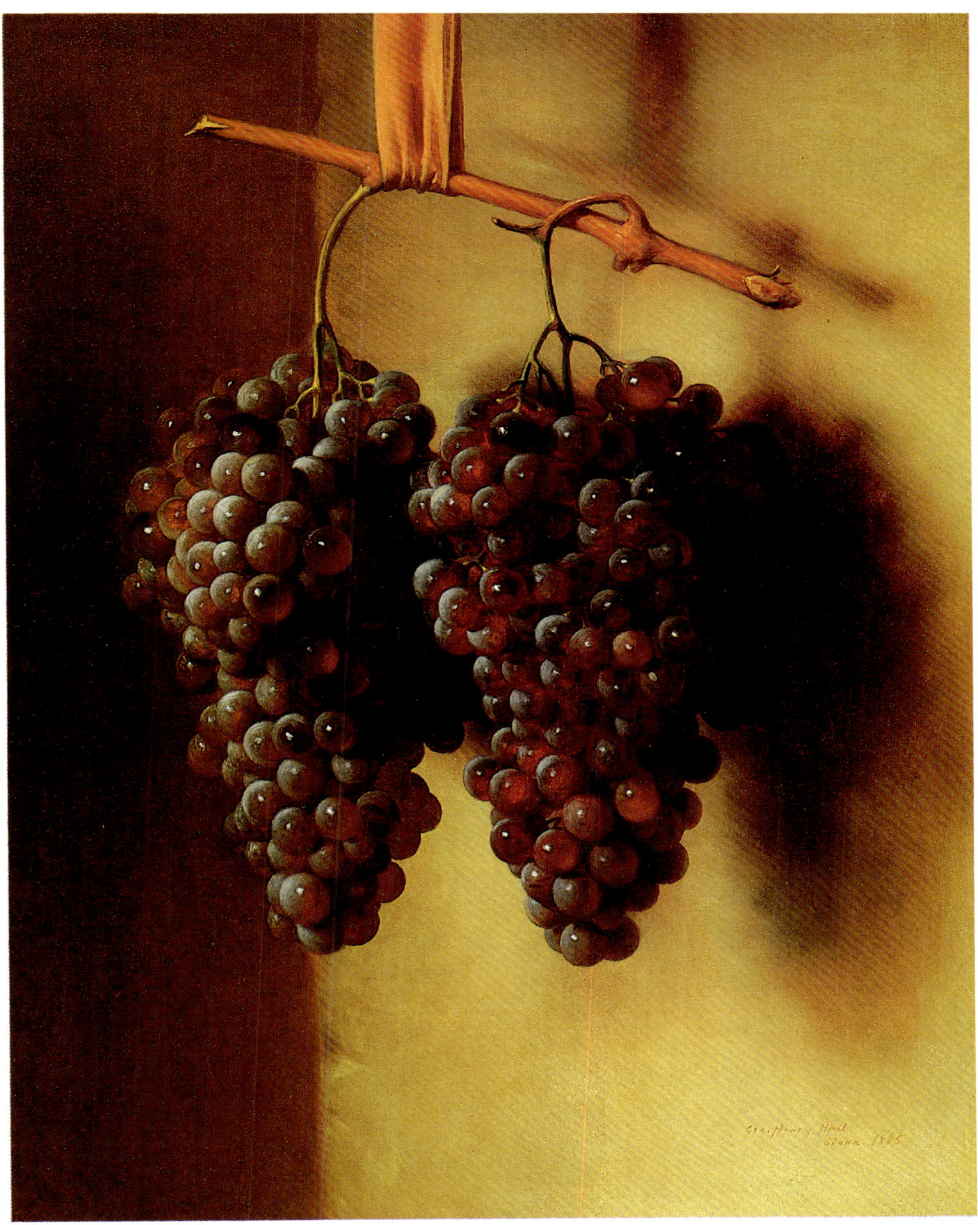

George Henry Hall, *The Twins, Chianti Grapes*, 1885. Oil on canvas, 18 1/8" x 14 1/4".

composed but sumptuous study accomplishes with an almost surreal precision, textbook instruction about the play of light and projection of shadows on curved and plane surfaces. Its elements are few: two pyramidal bunches of red grapes hanging side-by-side against a grayish tan wall. The artist's meticulous, seamless technique effortlessly captures the translucency and sparkling highlights of the ripe grapes, their bluish white bloom, and subtle variations in color. Their convincing palpability contrasts dramatically with the soft dark shadows that repeat their outlines on the wall. Here, breathtaking three dimensionality verges on trompe-l'oeil. Hall, an inveterate traveler who spent more than twenty years abroad in Spain, Italy, Egypt, and France in search of exotic genre subjects, painted this still life in Siena in 1885, ten years before he made his last trip abroad at the age of seventy.

1. Tuckerman, 482-83.

2. The Pennsylvania Academy of the Fine Arts (1850s and 1860s), the Brooklyn Art Association (1861-1881), and the National Academy of Design (1862-1908).

3. See Gerdts (1981), 93. Out of a sample of twenty-seven dated still lifes from 1856 to 1885, sixteen (59.2%) belong to the 1860s. On the other hand, from 1869 to 1880 only one out of twenty-nine entries at the National Academy was a still life. See Naylor, 384-85.

4. See Gerdts (1981), 94, fig. 5.8.

5. They were 80% of his production in the 1880s but only 3.6% of it in the 1890s. See Naylor, 385-86.

6. Out of a sample of thirty-three, twenty-seven (81.8%) are dated, ten (30.3%) show flowers, nineteen (57.6%) are fruit pieces, and eight (24.2%) are set out-of-doors.

Bibliography

Gerdts (1981). 93-97.

Gerdts and Burke. 66-67.

53. Carducius Plantagenet Ream

(born 1837, Lancaster, Ohio; died 1917, Chicago)
Apples, ca. 1890
Oil on board
13 1/2" x 18 1/2"
Signed lower right: C. P. Ream

Relatively little is known about this prolific fruit specialist whose brother, Morston Constantine Ream (1840-1898), was also a still life painter. He was born in Lancaster, Ohio, in 1837, may have studied abroad, and exhibited at the Royal Academy in London. He started specializing in still lifes early in his career and Lewis Prang and Company chromolithographed some of his work for mass consumption. He worked in New York City in the mid-1870s but settled in Chicago in 1878. His *Just Gathered* was the first painting by a Chicago artist that the Art Institute of Chicago included in its permanent collection. He died in Chicago in 1917.

Because Ream rarely dated his work it is virtually impossible to trace his stylistic development. About half of his paintings have outdoor settings. These usually show one kind of common fruit (plums, peaches, grapes, raspberries, or apples) arranged in the grass in a close-up view with dramatic lighting, but a few examples depict grapes on the vine hanging against a wall. The rest have indoor settings. Some of these feature white marble tabletops but most are set on polished wood surfaces. Unlike his outdoor pieces, about half of his interior arrangements show mixtures of fruit, a feature unrelated to the size of the painting. In most of them accessories such as knives, wine glasses, and glass or silver bowls supplement the fruit. Ream's works vary widely in size and quality. At their best, they skillfully render the surface textures and variations in color of various kinds of fruit, their reflections on polished surfaces, and the interplay of light and shadow on the objects. His compositions are often linear.[1]

Typically, the elements of this still life are simple. Set against a green wall, five red and yellow apples lying among their leaves on a polished tabletop form a compact, roughly oval group that recedes from left to right. A strong light makes them stand out vividly against their dark surroundings, and their slightly painterly, solid modeling gives them a monumental quality that belies their humble nature.

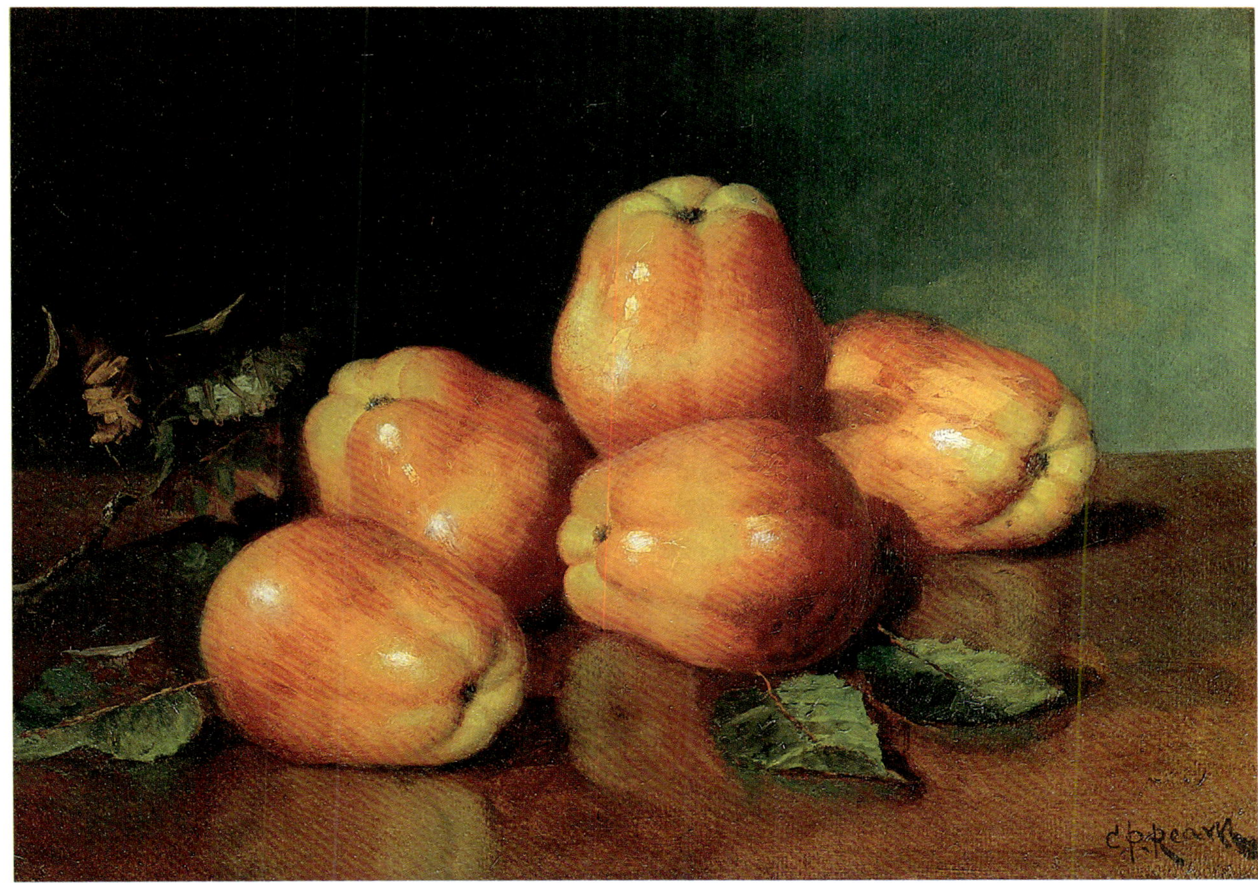

Carducius Plantagenet Ream, *Apples*, ca. 1890. Oil on board, 13 1/2" x 18 1/2".

1. In a sample of forty-five works illustrated in various books and dealers', auction, and museum catalogues, only two are dated and twenty-two (48.9%) have outdoor settings. Of these, sixteen (72.7%) depict only one kind of fruit. Twenty-three (51.1%) are tabletop pieces. Among them, five (21.7%) have marble tabletops, while twelve (52.1%) feature mixtures of fruit.

Bibliography

Gerdts (1981). 113.

Gerdts and Burke. 73.

54. Kate E. Bissell

(active Jackson, Michigan, 1877-1894)
Lemons and Lace, 1894
Oil on canvas
18" x 22"
Signed lower right: Kate E. Bissell 1894

Besides *Lemons and Lace*, only one other work by Kate E. (Mrs. Alonzo) Bissell has been located.[1] She is also known to have painted landscapes, flowers, and animals. Otherwise, nothing is known about this Jackson, Michigan, artist who worked toward the end of the century.

Lemons and Lace is unusual in the context of American still lifes. Although Bissell depicts contemporary objects — a colorful and elaborately decorated nineteenth-century red Kutani ware cylinder vase and sugarer and an intricately worked lace tablecloth — her selections of exotic imports from Japan and Belgium, respectively, are unusual. Only the pile of lemons and a spectral glass of water with a lemon slice floating in it are mundane. Her sedulously thought-out composition makes the most of all these objects through the juxtaposition of two groups whose shapes and formal relationships echo each other. The ceramics, lemons, and white tablecloth take on a surreal intensity against the dark background. An impressively precise, illusionistic technique reveals every surface detail. The play of light and shadow on the vertical folds of the tablecloth, reflecting ceramics, glass, and spoon, gives them a monumentality that belies their size and suggests the artist's study of seventeenth- and eighteenth-century Dutch, Spanish, or French still lifes.

1. *Studio Interior with Woman Painter*, 1885, in a private collection, is possibly a self-portrait of the artist. *The Studio*, 1885, a different work, was owned by the Memorial Art Gallery, University of Rochester before it was deaccessioned.

Bibliography

Gibson, Arthur H. *Artists of Early Michigan*. Detroit: Wayne State University Press, 1975. 53.

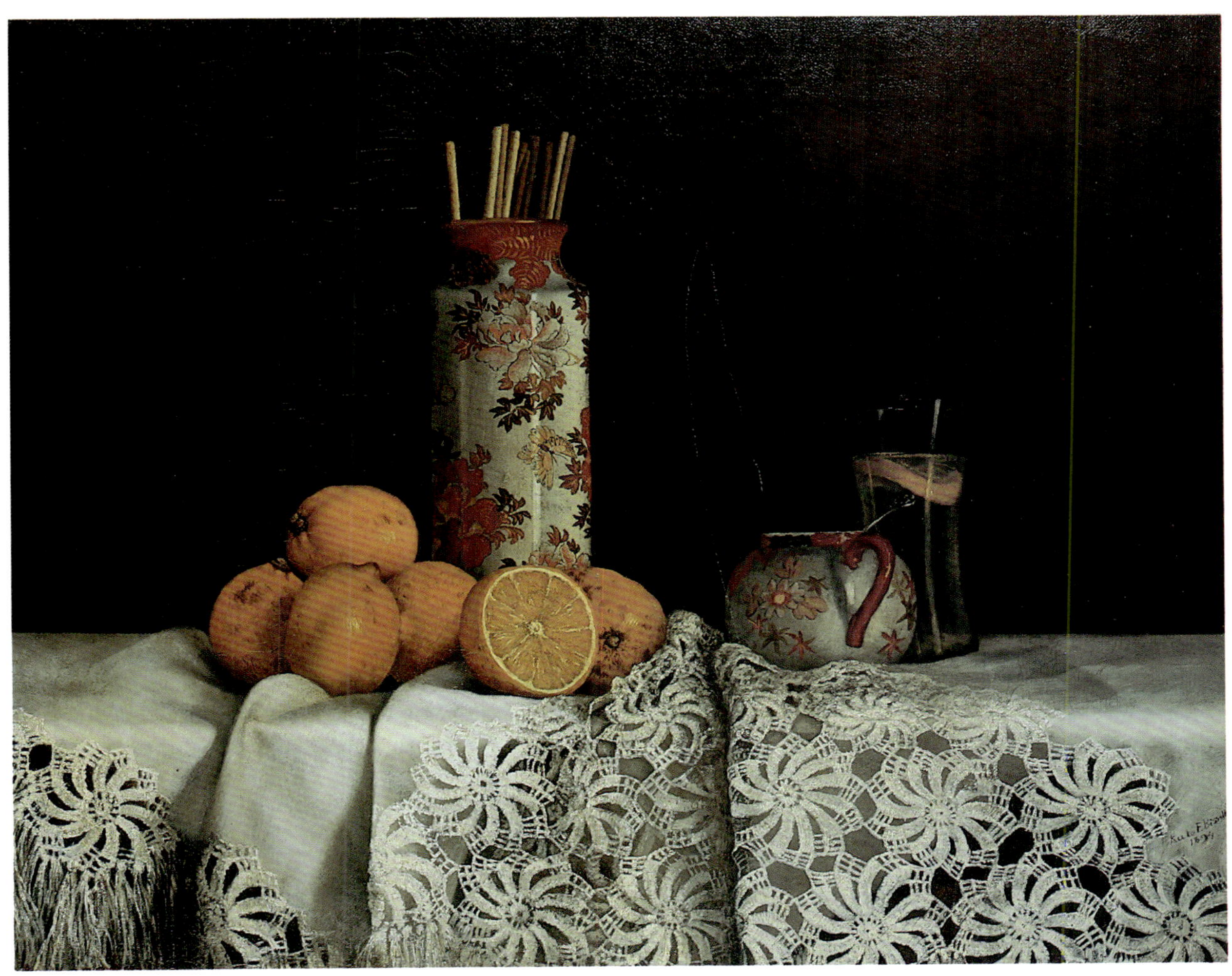

Kate E. Bissell, *Lemons and Lace*, 1894. Oil on canvas, 18" x 22".

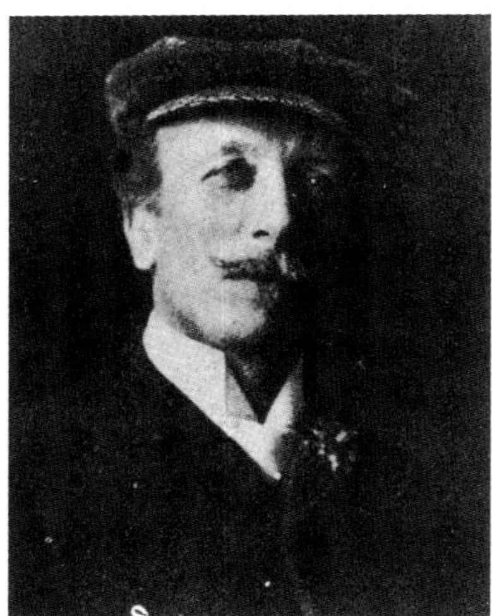

Paul de Longpré. Photo courtesy of the UCLA Library.

55. Paul de Longpré

(born 1855, Lyon, France; died 1911, Hollywood, California)
Flowers and Insects, ca. 1900
Watercolor on paper
22" x 16"
Signed upper right: Paul de Longpré

The flower painter Paul de Longpré is one of a handful of California artists who are well known in the East. Much of his oeuvre lies in the no man's land between fine art and botanical illustration. Born in Lyon, France, in 1855, he came by his specialty naturally as his father and uncles all painted flowers on silk and ivory fans sold in expensive Paris shops. Besides learning from them he obtained an extensive knowledge of flowers during the course of thirteen years spent at the conservatory of the famous horticulturalist M. Paillet at Chanteney near Paris. He married in 1873 and exhibited a flower painting at the Paris Salon of 1876. In 1890, after a bank where he kept his money failed, he moved to New York City. His floral watercolors proved very popular there, but in 1898 he moved to Hollywood, California. His Moorish style house with its three-acre garden of flowers, to which sightseers were welcome, attracted as many as 25,000 visitors a year. His son Raoul and his daughters also became flower painters. De Longpré died in Hollywood in 1911 after a successful career.

Although he painted an occasional pastel or oil he was known for his large, highly accomplished watercolors of flowers. Their fetching color harmonies, sound compositions, and skillfully modulated washes, often combined with crisply outlined forms, have made them perenially popular. He painted a wide variety of flowers ranging from poinsettias to California poppies, but roses were his favorite subject. The majority of his paintings are dated. About half are tabletop pieces. In many of them the flower stems are truncated in the manner of botanical studies.[1]

This still life of flowers and insects is unusual both in its backdrop, a wall dappled with sun and shadow, and in the softness with which the lavender clematis, white arbutus, and green leaves are outlined. Traditionally insects in still lifes were usually depicted at rest (see Forster, cat. 49). Here, however, two bumblebees[2] hover above a clematis bloom at the upper left while at the lower right two monarch butterflies approach the viewer almost head on like dive bombers. The convincing three dimensionality of the flowers and leaves and interplay of light and shadow among them demonstrate a high order of technique. The asymmetrical placement of the flowers and vines in a triangle at the upper left balanced by bare wall at the lower right is an example of the so-called "occult balance" often seen in Chinese and Japanese painting. Here it probably represents an influence of Art Nouveau, which started in France and took much of its inspiration from Japanese art imported there in the nineteenth century after Japan was opened to the West.

1. Out of a sample of thirty-one, twenty-eight (90.3%) are watercolors, twenty (64.5%), ranging from 1889 to 1908, are dated; out of a smaller sample where the subject matter is clearly identified, ten out of twenty-four (41.7%) are roses. Thirteen different kinds of flowers are represented among the rest. Of eleven illustrated works located, six (54.5%) are of the truncated, botanical type.

2. The only insect besides butterflies in his paintings, they occur in five of twenty-four (20.8%) examples.

Bibliography

Gerdts (1990), vol. 3. 302, 304-05.

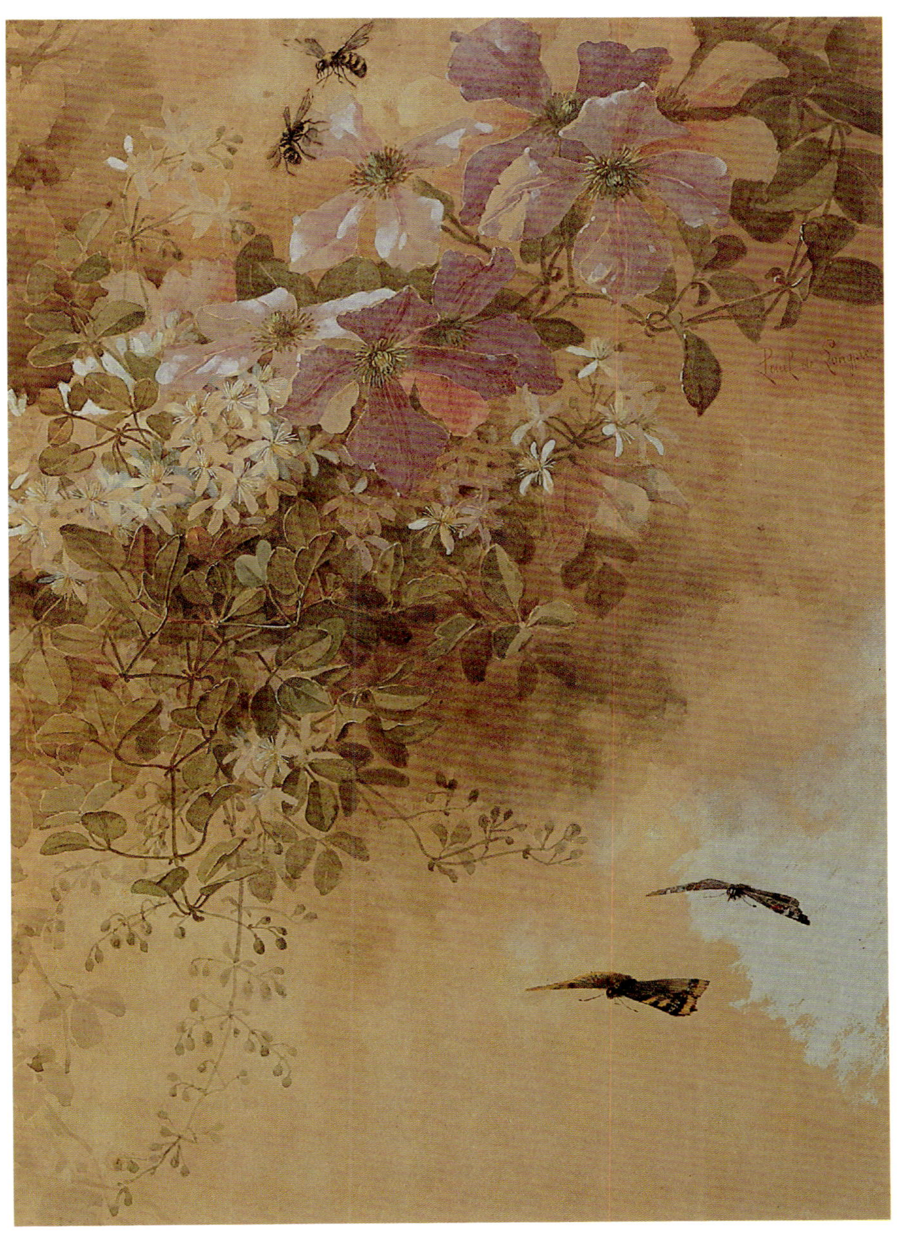

Paul de Longpré, *Flowers and Insects*, ca. 1900. Watercolor on paper, 22" x 16".

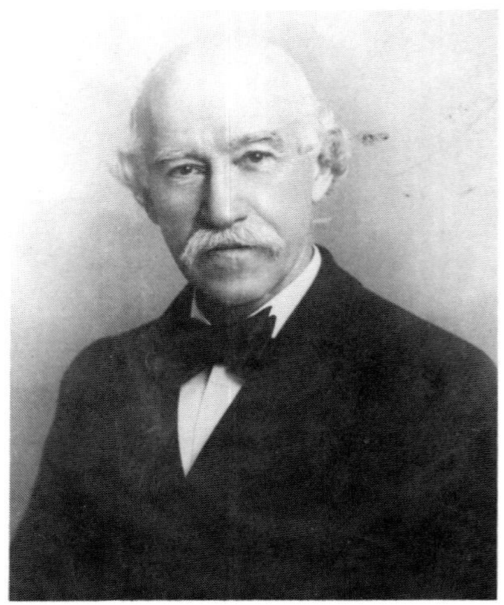

Robert Spear Dunning, ca. 1905. Collection of the Fall River Historical Society.

56. Robert Spear Dunning

(born 1829, Brunswick, Maine; died 1905, Westport Harbor, Massachusetts)
Still Life of Fruit, 1900
Oil on canvas
9 1/4" x 11 1/8"
Signed lower right: R. S. Dunning

Until recently Robert Spear Dunning suffered the obscurity of the provincial artist. Now, however, collectors and museums vie for his still lifes. Born in Brunswick, Maine, in 1829, he moved at age five to Fall River, which had become a major industrial town because of its textile mills and for which his father built its first marine railway. Before first studying art with James Roberts in Tiverton, Rhode Island, from 1844 to 1847, he worked in a textile mill and for three years on coastal vessels. Then, from 1849 to 1852 he trained in New York City with the well-known portrait, figurative, and landscape artist Daniel Huntington (1816-1906). After exhibiting genre paintings and portraits at the American Art-Union and the National Academy of Design, in 1852 he chose to isolate himself from the New York art scene by returning to Fall River, where he spent the rest of his life. Exhibiting and selling there as well as in Providence and Boston, he became the central figure in its artistic life. He taught both privately and at the Fall River Evening Drawing School, which he helped to found in 1870. According to one of his students he was a demanding instructor who insisted that they use only the finest materials, become meticulous craftsmen, and develop their own individuality. After a long, productive career he died at his summer home in Westport Harbor, Massachusetts, in 1905.

After 1865, when he painted his first documented still lifes, Dunning for unknown reasons gave up genre painting. Although he did occasional landscapes and continued to execute portraits of prominent Fall River gentry, he concentrated on the still lifes for which he became best known. Typically highly finished, they lavish attention on variations in the surface textures of luscious, perfect fruit, one piece of which is often opened up. They are usually dated and range from occasional works showing one kind of fruit in an outdoor setting to tabletop pieces with many different kinds. The latter always feature a highly polished, reflecting tabletop parallel to the picture plane. In larger, more complex examples an elaborately carved table edge is often visible. They typically include a large, ornate silver, crystal, or ceramic container and, at times, a patterned cloth or napkin. Sometimes the fruit is supplemented by flowers. In several of his most interesting still lifes Dunning transcends his usual luxuriously literal description of objects to suggest the nearby presence of people by details like their straw hats or hands. His earlier paintings tend to be darker, richer, and more highly detailed and those he did later softer and lighter.[1]

However, highly illusionistic treatment of surfaces is still apparent in late works like the one illustrated here. As in his other small still lifes, size restriction dictates a simple, compact composition, here a squat pyramid organized into three planes in a narrow but totally convincing picture space. One piece each of four common kinds of fruit is arranged so that neither repeats another's position and each counterbalances the other. Their glistening surfaces, minutely described with compelling precision, stand out against a neutral but modulated grayish brown wall and their much softer colored reflections on a highly polished tabletop. Enhanced by the interplay of light and shadow, they take on a monumental, almost surreal quality.

1. Out of a sample of twenty-nine still lifes, twenty-two (75.9%) are dated, twenty (69%) are larger than twelve inches square, and twenty-four (82.8%) are tabletop pieces, of which three (12.5%) also include flowers. Fifteen of sixteen (93.8%) of the larger tabletop pieces also feature accessories.

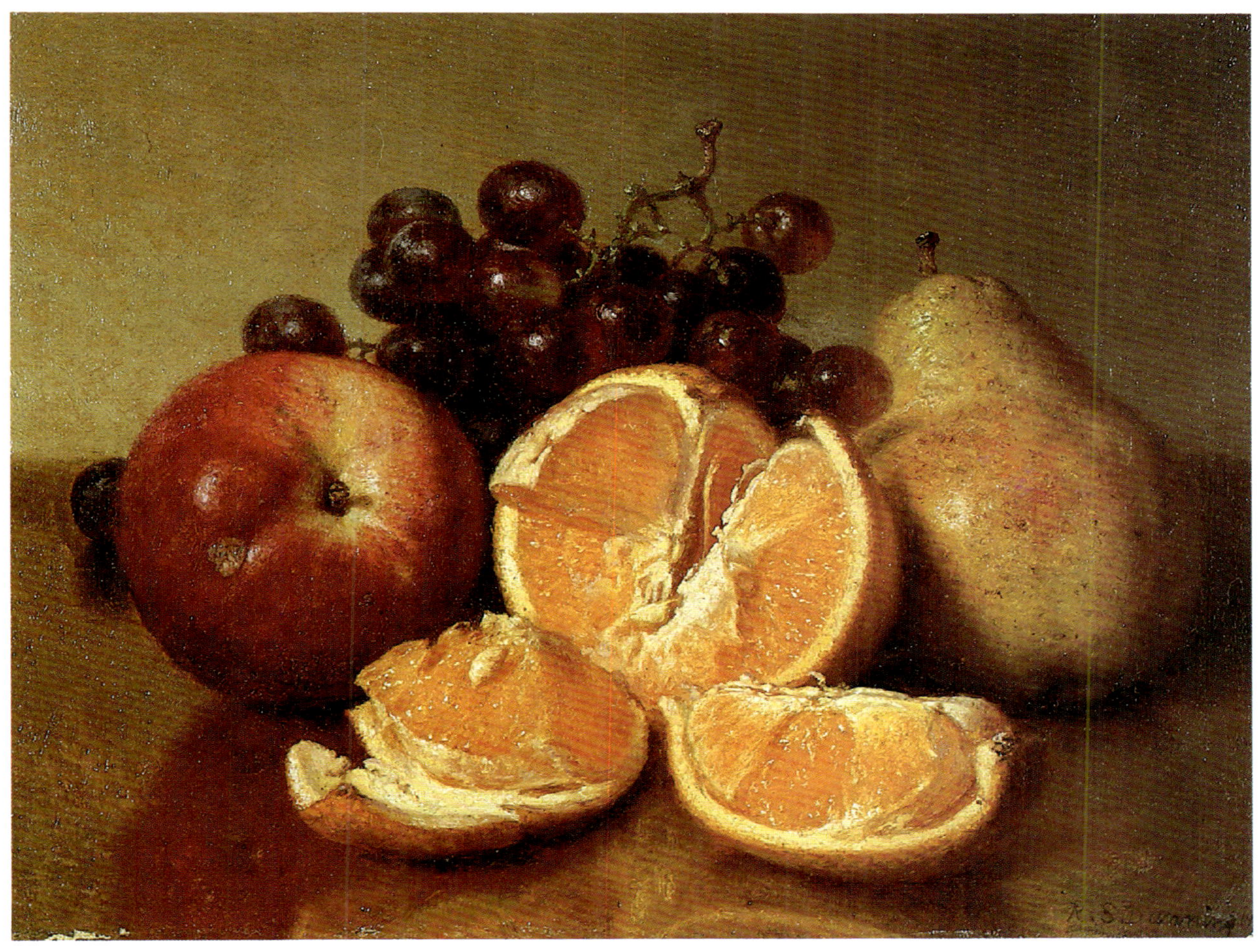

Robert Spear Dunning, *Still Life of Fruit*, 1900. Oil on canvas, 9 1/4" x 11 1/8".

Bibliography

Blaugrund, Annette. "Robert Spear Dunning." In Ferber and Gerdts. 252.

Gerdts (1981). 116-17.

Gerdts and Burke, 169, 174-75.

57. Bryant Chapin

(born 1859, Fall River, Massachusetts; died 1927, Fall River, Massachusetts)
Still Life with Fruit, ca. 1900
Oil on canvas
14 1/4" x 18"
Signed lower right: Bryant Chapin

It is easy to mistake some of Bryant Chapin's still lifes for those of his teacher Robert Spear Dunning (1829-1905) (cat. 56), who considered him his best pupil. A lifelong resident of Fall River, like Dunning he taught at the Fall River Evening Drawing School. He was a prolific artist who did portraits and landscapes which took him to Europe several times, but his primary interest lay in still lifes.

They fall into two groups. One, very reminiscent of Dunning, depicts the luscious, softly lit, and slightly hazy forms of perfect fruit displayed on highly polished tabletops in which they are prominently reflected. The other relies on a much more painterly, atmospheric, and suggestive style to show close-ups of fruit on the bare ground outdoors against a generalized green background. A variant depicts peaches or strawberries spilling onto the ground out of brown paper bags or wooden boxes.[1] According to Gerdts and Burke, the table top pieces tend to be earlier than the outdoor ones,[2] although there is much overlap between them.[3] They also point out that the latter are the revival of a form popular in the 1860s.[4]

The sumptuous still life illustrated here displays an inviting oval group of choice, ripe examples of common types of fruit. Set on a highly polished tabletop in which they are clearly mirrored, they stand out against a richly modulated tan wall. Light falling from above makes the smooth-skinned pieces of fruit glisten with highlights. The artist accurately but softly renders their surface textures in an inviting array of warm colors. This carefully thought-out, well balanced composition based on crossed diagonals is closely related to two others dated 1897 and 1909.[5]

1. The theme of strawberries spilling out of a basket may have been suggested by the striking examples that Chapin's contemporary, Joseph Decker (1853-1924), painted in the 1890s and early 1900s. See Helen A. Cooper, "The Rediscovery of Joseph Decker," *The American Art Journal* 10 (May 1978): 55-71 and William H. Gerdts and Evdokia Savidou, *Joseph Decker (1853-1924): Still Lifes, Landscapes and Images of Youth* (New York: Coe Kerr Gallery, 1988).

2. Gerdts and Burke, 175

3. Thus, six dated outdoor still lifes located by the writer range from 1898 to 1922 while three dated tabletop pieces were painted between 1897 and 1909.

4. Gerdts and Burke, 175. Dunning's example may have directly inspired Chapin to paint so many out-of-door still lifes. Five dated Dunnings with outdoor settings located by the author range from 1866 to 1895.

5. See *Tabletop Still Life,* 1897, Sotheby's Arcade, 10/24/86, no. 45 and *Fruit on a Polished Table,* 1909, Christie's, 9/21/84, no. 53B.

Bibliography

Gerdts and Burke. 175.

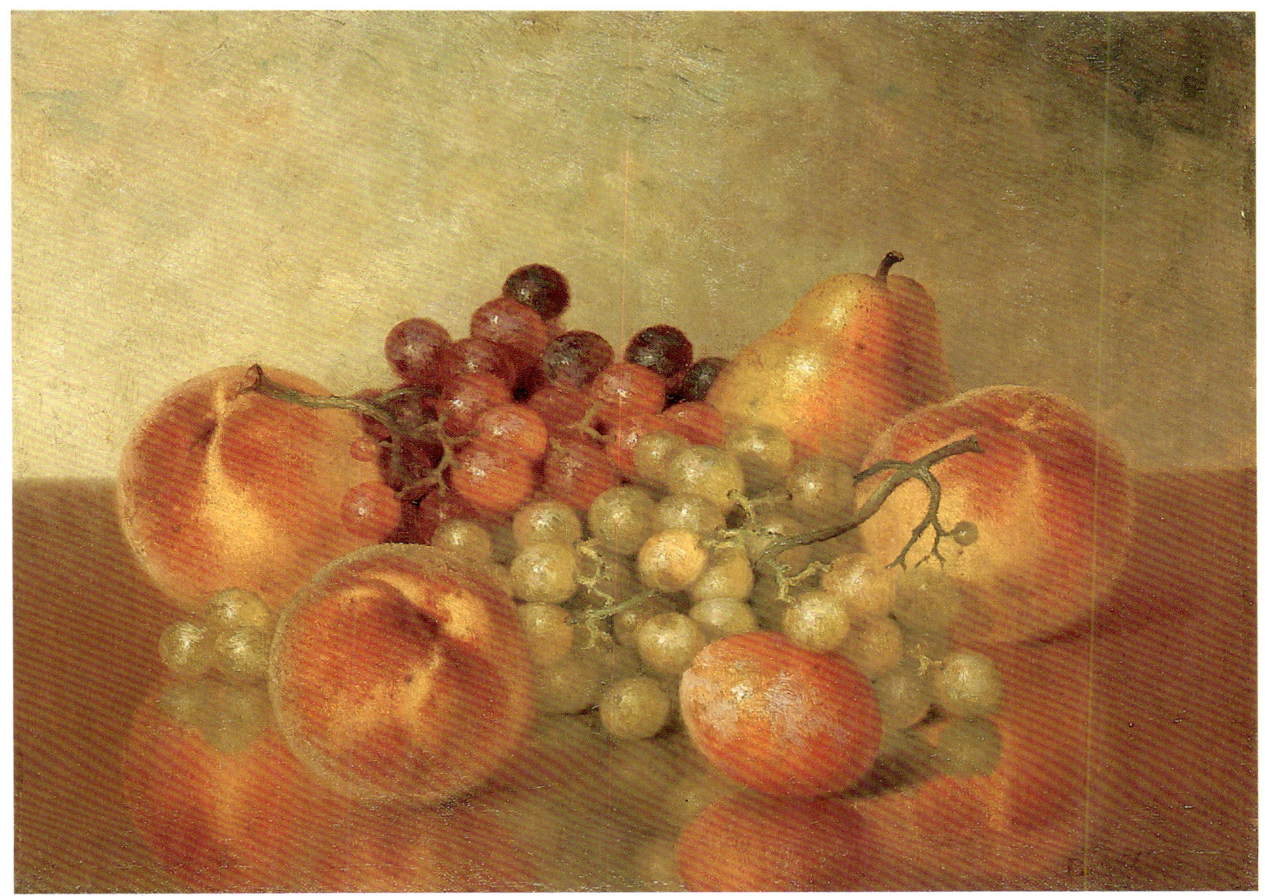

Bryant Chapin, *Still Life with Fruit*, ca. 1900. Oil on canvas, 14 1/4" x 18".

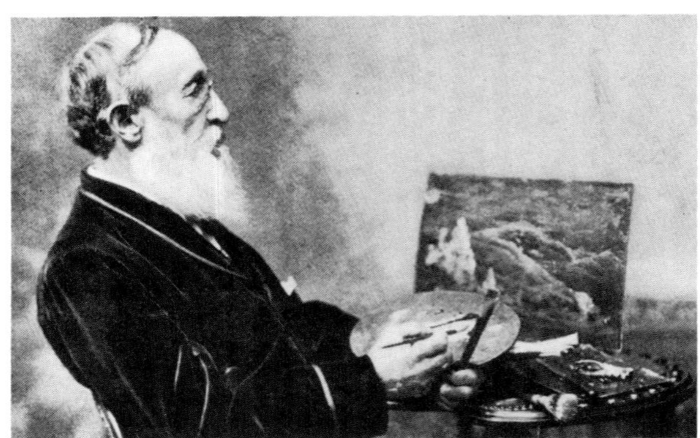

Benjamin Champney, ca. 1900.

58. Benjamin Champney

(born 1817, New Ipswich, New Hampshire; died 1907, Woburn, Massachusetts)
Pansies, ca. 1880
Oil on canvas
12 1/2" x 17 1/2"
Signed lower right: B. Champney

During the course of his long life, the landscape and flower painter Benjamin Champney witnessed major changes in nineteenth-century American painting. In 1900 he discussed them and his life in an autobiography to which we owe most of our information about him as well as many interesting and perceptive comments about his contemporaries.

His early years are typical of those of American painters who grew up before 1850, both in having to go to work at a tender age and his difficulty in obtaining formal artistic training. One of seven siblings, he was born into a family of New Hampshire lawyers in 1817. After his father's death, the ten-year-old Champney went to live with an aunt in Lebanon, New Hampshire, where he worked in his uncle's cotton factory until he returned home in 1831, when he became interested in drawing. Two years later he went to work for a shoe dealer in Boston. He had the good luck to meet Robert Cooke, a draftsman in a lithography firm who taught him the rudiments of art and encouraged him to take up the same line of work. He and Cooke subsequently took a studio together to paint portraits. Although he became a successful portraitist Champney wanted above all to become a landscapist. After some initial efforts, he showed a painting to Boston's most famous artist, Washington Allston (1779-1843), who encouraged him to study abroad. Accordingly, in 1841 he went to Paris, where he worked in Eugène Boudin's (1824-1898) atelier and spent much time in the Louvre sketching. The gregarious Champney made many friends, including the American artists Casilear (cat. 11) and Durand (cat. 3), and shared rooms with John F. Kensett (1816-1872). Together, via the Rhine and Switzerland, they made a trip to Italy, much of it on foot because of lack of funds. Though Champney returned to Boston in 1845, he made a second trip to Europe the following year in order to paint a panorama of the Rhine. After sketching along the river and visiting Düsseldorf, he took a studio in Paris, where he hired assistants to help him execute this huge work. It was exhibited in Boston in 1848 and three years later at the Crystal Palace in London, where it was destroyed when the Palace burned down in 1853. In an age without photography, such panoramas of exotic, spectacular, or picturesque scenery were a popular form of entertainment which, like movies today, charged an admission fee. If successful, they could be quite profitable for an artist. Moreover, their scale was a challenge.

In 1849, Champney began to summer in the White Mountains of New Hampshire. One of the first of many artists to appreciate their scenery, especially the land around North Conway on the Saco River, he introduced many others to the region and eventually became its artistic grand old man. He married in 1853 (a son, Kensett, was born in 1854) and bought a house there. During the rest of the year he lived in Woburn, Massachusetts, while maintaining a studio in Boston. In 1856 he became president of the Boston Art Club, mainly exhibiting there and at the Boston Athenaeum.

Champney became known as a specialist in views of New Hampshire, in particular the North Conway region. However, many now prefer his smaller, less pretentious oil sketches painted directly from nature to his tightly controlled panoramas with their slightly flat, topographic flavor. In his later years he turned more and more to flower paintings.[1] Increasingly painterly, they came to reflect post-Civil War trends away from tight, academic realism.

In the colorful but muted work illustrated here, he successfully realizes his stated aim in painting flowers, "to find the juste milieu between slouchiness and too much exactness of form, — to make a suggestive picture rather than a positively realistic one."[2] A spindle-shaped array of pansies extends across a low, grassy bank bordering a narrow strip of water which reflects the nearest blooms. Vaguely indicated trees and

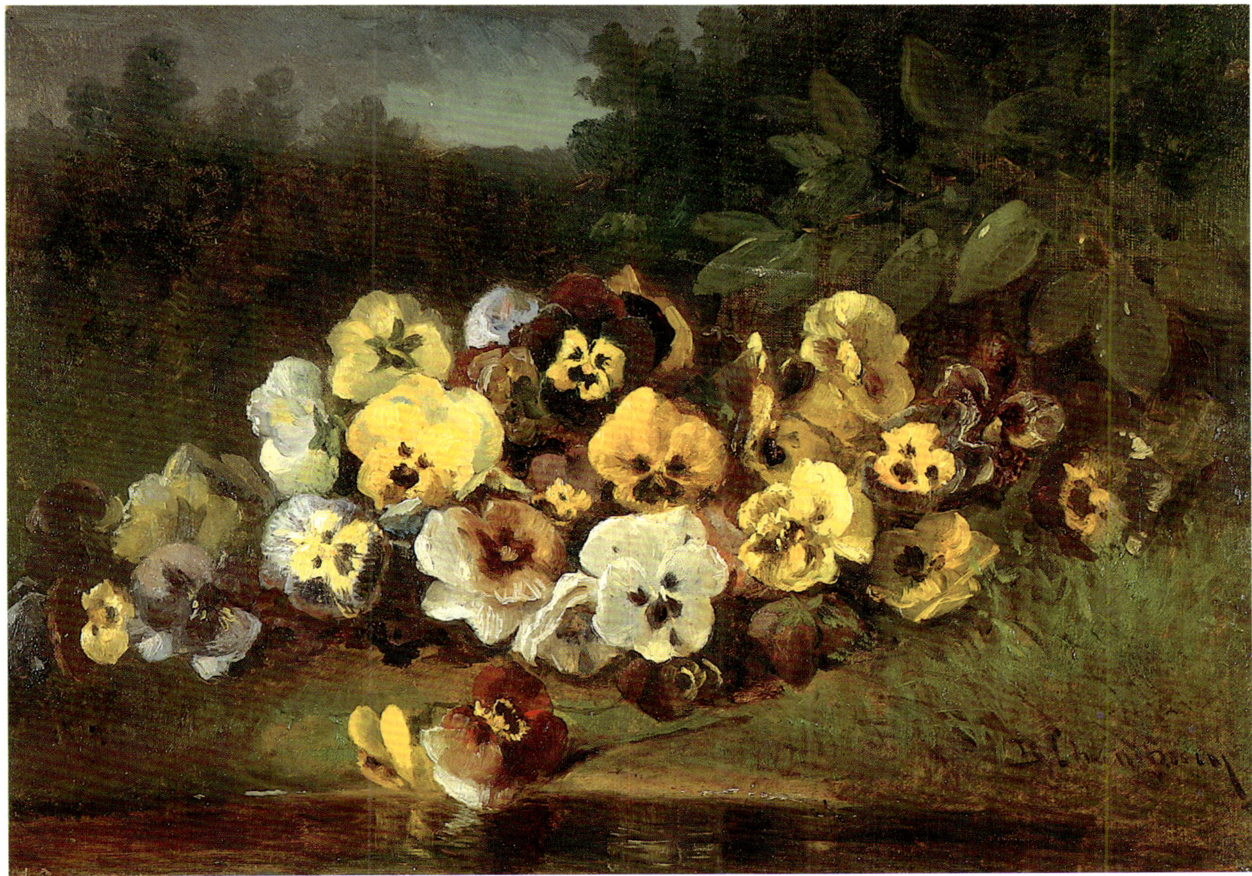

Benjamin Champney, *Pansies*, ca. 1880. Oil on canvas, 12 1/2" x 17 1/2".

a cloudy sky serve as a backdrop. Lying on the ground rather than growing from it, the pansies constitute an arbitrary outdoor arrangement that violates strict Ruskinian precepts of truth to nature. Yet, their rich, contrasting colors and the way they preempt their outdoor stage like a group portrait translated into flowers make these luxuriant, freely brushed pansies seem convincingly at home where they are.

1. A small sample of twenty-five published works, however, includes only three flower paintings (12%).

2. Champney, 154

Bibliography

Champney.

Gerdts and Burke. 108.

Groce and Wallace. 118.

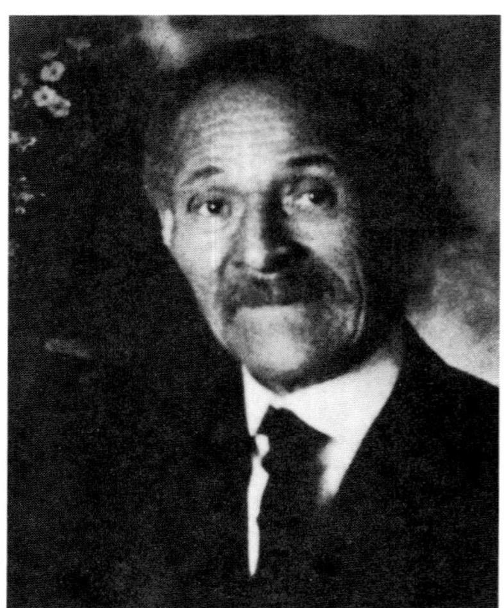

Charles Ethan Porter, ca. 1911.

59. Charles Ethan Porter

(born 1847, Hartford, Connecticut; died 1923, Rockville, Connecticut)
Pink Hollyhocks, 1884
Oil on canvas
20 1/4" x 12 1/8"
Signed lower right: C.E. Porter
Publication: Helen K. Fusscas, et al. *Charles Ethan Porter 1847-1923*, (Marlborough, CT: The Connecticut Gallery, 1987), 33, pl. X.

Before 1885 or 1890 artistically talented and ambitious blacks were rarely able to surmount the barriers of racial discrimination. However, a few such as Robert Scott Duncanson (1817-1872), Edward Mitchell Bannister (1828-1901), and Henry Ossawa Tanner (1859-1937) enjoyed varying degrees of success. Their paintings are reasonably well known, but until recently the work of Charles Ethan Porter was obscure even to specialists in American painting.

He was born in Hartford, Connecticut, in 1847 to an illiterate father who worked as a farmer and laborer and a literate mother who was a servant. Charles was the sixth of their seven children who survived infancy. After 1857, his family moved to the nearby manufacturing town of Rockville, an almost exclusively white community with only two other black families. He received his first drawing lessons in high school, although he had to stop them before graduating in 1865 because of lack of funds. Little is known about his life after that until 1869 when he moved to New York City. Until 1873 he taught art while studying both at the National Academy of Design and privately for a year with Joseph Oriel Eaton (1829-1875), a successful portrait and genre painter. After exhibiting at the National Academy in 1871 and 1876 and at the American Water Color Society in 1873 and 1875, he moved back to Hartford in 1878.

His work, largely fruit and flower paintings, was well received. They show the successive influences of Raphaelle (1774-1825) and James Peale (1749-1831), the Düsseldorf artist Johann Wilhelm Preyer (1803-1889), and the American Pre-Raphaelites. After a visit in 1879 by Frederic E. Church (1826-1900), who praised him as a colorist, he also began painting landscapes.

In 1881 in order to raise money to study in Paris, he auctioned off the contents of his studio for $1,800. He went abroad with a letter of introduction from Mark Twain, who opposed racial injustice and was interested in sponsoring him as a black artist. In an 1883 letter to Twain, Porter writes about how many of his Hartford friends and others were "anxious to see how the colored artist will make out," but that "there is something of more importance, the colored people — my people — as a race I am interested in, and my success will only add to others who have already shown wherein they are capable the same as other men."[1] He seems to have been influenced by Henri Fantin-Latour (1836-1904) still lifes since many of his works from 1881 to 1890 resemble them both in subject matter and composition.

In 1884 Porter returned to Hartford because of lack of funds. He now had so much trouble selling his work that he had to auction it off several times. It is likely that racial discrimination was a problem. Finally he moved back to his parents' house in Rockville, exhibiting there and in Springfield and Hartford. From 1890 on his work gradually deteriorated, especially after 1900. Between 1900 and 1915, when he stopped painting, he would carry his canvases from door-to-door, bartering them for food or flowers to paint. He was forced to do odd jobs to support himself, but he had a number of devoted pupils. He died in poverty in 1923.

The painting illustrated here is probably the one described in the *Hartford Times* of July 15, 1884, executed after Porter's return from Paris. Like most of his later work, it is rather freely brushed. This depiction of pink and white hollyhocks set against a subtly varied lighter green wall compares favorably with renditions of the same subject by John La Farge (cat. 37).[2] Despite its shallow picture space, the two flowering plants in this strongly organized composition are remarkably three-dimensional, their deep green

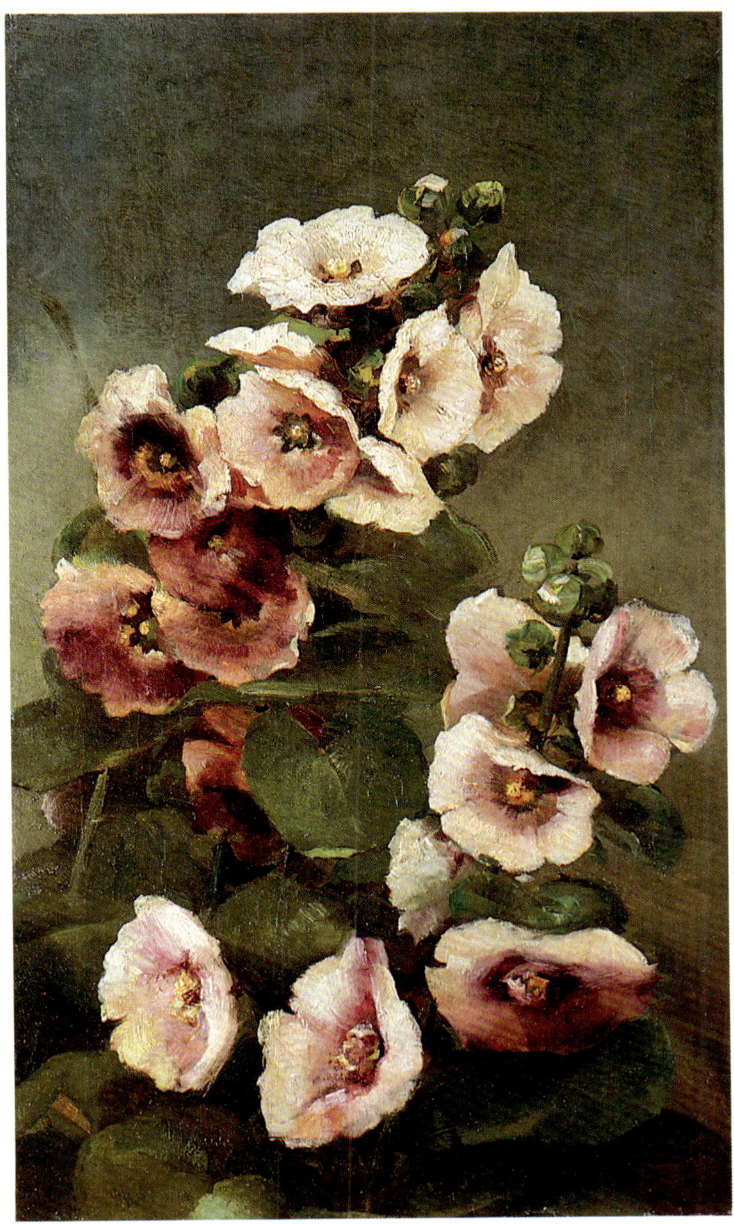

Charles Ethan Porter, *Pink Hollyhocks*, 1884. Oil on canvas, 20 1/4" x 12 1/8".

leaves and richly varied, colorful flowers appearing to jut out at the viewer.

1. See Thomas P. Riggio, "Charles Ethan Porter and Mark Twain," in Fusscas, et al., 76-87.

2. See, for example, *White Hollyhocks* and *Red Hollyhocks*, ca. 1863 in Henry Adams, et al., *John La Farge* (Pittsburgh: The Carnegie Museum of Art, 1987), 22, figs. 7, 8 and *Hollyhocks*, Sotheby's, 11/30/89, no. 65.

Bibliography

Fusscas, Helen K., et al. *Charles Ethan Porter 1847-1923.* Marlborough, CT: The Connecticut Gallery, 1987.

60. George W. Platt

(born 1839, Rochester, New York; died 1899, Denver)
Two Pears on a Dish, 1880s
Oil on board
10" x 14"
Signed lower left: G.W. Platt.

Only a handful of paintings by this rare and interesting still life, portrait, and landscape painter have been located. Since 1969, when Alfred Frankenstein exhumed him from obscurity, no new information has come to light.

He was the son of a Rochester, New York, picture framer, and one of his sisters, Helen, was a landscape artist who taught art in Boston for many years. It is not known where and when he got his first training in art, but after graduating from the University of Rochester he studied at the Pennsylvania Academy of the Fine Arts, probably from 1871 to 1876, and then in Munich and Italy in the late 1870s. In the 1880s he lived and exhibited in Chicago, but in the 1890s worked in Denver, where he taught at the University of Denver and painted until his death in 1899.

Vanishing Glories, Platt's trompe-l'oeil depiction of a buffalo head, Winchester rifle, Colt revolver, and other Wild West accoutrements mounted on a barn door, created a sensation at the 1888 St. Louis Exposition. While Frankenstein focuses on such works, the painting reproduced here belies his judgment that the artist "painted many fruit and flower still lifes of dubious merit." Unlike most tabletop fruit pieces of the period, it opts for monumental simplicity rather than intricate abundance. The subject matter is the simplest: two pears and a knife on a plate resting on a tablecloth set against a wall. Within this limited theatre, the artist plays with the viewer's expectations of order and symmetry. A subtle but forceful tension is forged through the placement of one pear almost but not quite parallel to the picture plane and at the same time almost, but not quite, at right angles to the second pear. In a similar manner, the knife handle protruding diagonally at the left stretches the arrangement into a taut but precarious equilibrium, creating a dynamic asymmetrical balance. Otherwise, this composition depends on contrasts between curved and linear elements and among bright, dark, and neutral colors. A strong, dramatic light falling from above creates highlights and shadows that help to forge a compelling illusion of three-dimensional form. As Frankenstein noted in connection with Platt's trompe-l'oeil door paintings, the artist achieves a remarkable combination of realistic illusionism and free brushwork.

An old label on the back of the canvas indicates that it was painted in Chicago which dates it to the 1880s.

Bibliography

Frankenstein, 128-31.

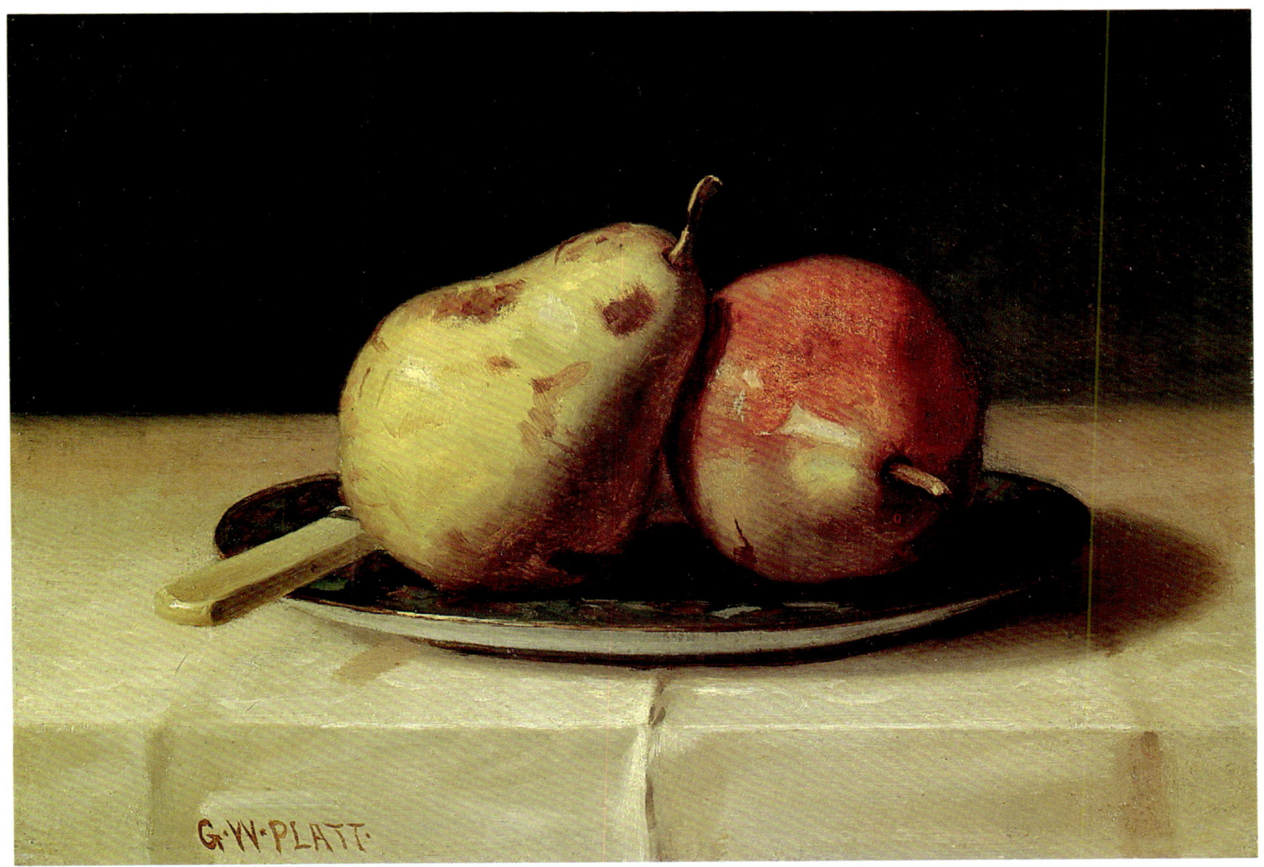

George W. Platt, *Two Pears on a Dish*, 1880s. Oil on board, 10" x 14".

61. Harriet Cheney

(born 1838, Middletown, Connecticut; died 1913)
White Roses, ca. 1890-1900
Oil on canvas
10" x 16"
Signed lower left: H.M.C.

On the basis of this example of her work, it is surprising that the Connecticut painter Harriet Elizabeth Cheney is almost unrecorded. She may have moved in artistic circles because she married her cousin, James Woodbridge Cheney (1838-?), who was the nephew of the South Manchester engravers and portraitists John (1801-1885) and Seth Wells Cheney (1810-1856). She exhibited figurative works at the Boston Athenaeum in 1860 and three times at the National Academy of Design from 1861 to 1866. Beyond this and her birth and death dates nothing is known about her, not even her maiden name which, on the evidence of the inscription on this painting, must begin with the letter M.

White Roses[1] is one of several Cheney still lifes that have surfaced in Connecticut in recent years. Its asymmetrical, truncated composition indicating the influence of Japanese art suggests that it was painted not long before the turn of the century. It shows the flat, open blooms of a tilted, low, pyramidal mass of white roses set in a shiny, muted green celadon vase. With painterly brushwork, Cheney makes the most of its simple composition and restricted palette by opposing the vertical of the vase and the diagonal of the roses and setting off their white blooms with yellow centers against the lighter greens of the vase and leaves and the dark, reddish brown background.

1. The roses are a hybrid variety, possibly either of the Alba or hardy Rugosa family.

Bibliography

Groce and Wallace. 122-23.

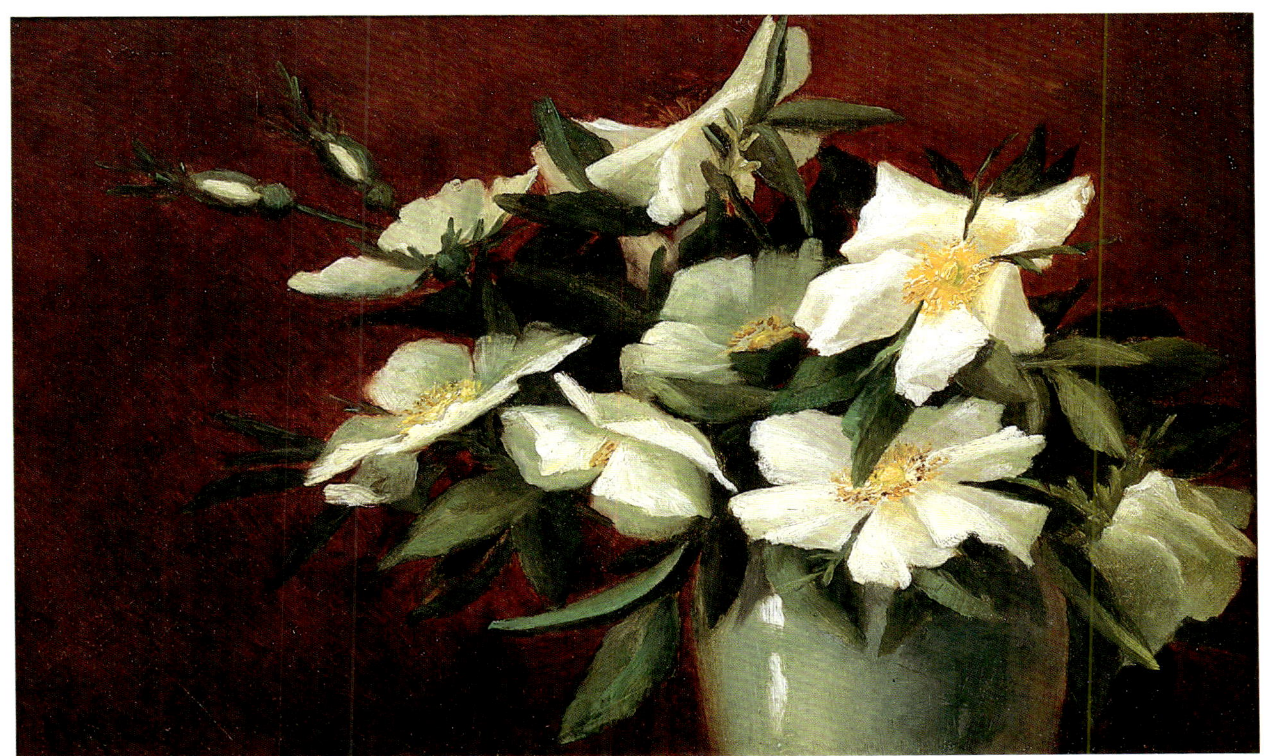

Harriet Cheney, *White Roses*, ca. 1890-1900. Oil on canvas, 10" x 16".

62. Anna Eliza Hardy

(born 1839, Bangor, Maine; died 1934, South Orrington, Maine)
Roses, ca. 1900
Oil on canvas
11 1/2" x 16"
Signed lower left: A.E. Hardy

More is known about the flower painter Anna Eliza Hardy than Kate Bissell (cat. 54) and Harriet Cheney (cat. 61) but, like most other provincial artists, her work has been little studied. Born in Bangor, Maine in 1839, Hardy was first taught art by her father, Jeremiah Pearson Hardy (1800-1887), an itinerant portrait, landscape, genre, animal, and still life artist. Later she studied briefly in Paris with Georges Jeannin (1841-1915), a prize-winning Salon, flower, and still life specialist, and figurative and landscape artist Abbot Handerson Thayer (1843-1921). She was described as "a beautiful woman with red-gold hair, delicate fair skin, and a bird-like manner, living a frugal but high-minded life with her fascinating family."[1] She was active as a teacher and at least seven Bangor women painters were students of hers. Except for a portrait of her eighty-year-old father, she apparently concentrated on still lifes of fruit and flowers. While the fruit studies are simple and precisely rendered, her flower paintings, which she exhibited at the National Academy of Design in 1876 and 1877, are typically of roses executed in a painterly style with increasingly soft pastel colors.

This painting shows cabbagelike pink and red roses[2] strewn on a gray stone slab set against a grayish tan wall. At first glance they seem casually arranged, but they are carefully laid out in a compact zigzag in which the different orientation of each flower is balanced against its neighbor's. Their size and rich colors, pink massed against red, contrast with those of the much smaller light green leaves among which they nestle, and the vividness of the ensemble is enhanced by the neutral setting. Their colors, slightly loose brushwork, and blurred, irregular outlines give a soft, sweet effect.

1. Rubinstein, 65.

2. These roses have the flat centers characteristic of nineteenth-century hybrid varieties, unlike modern hybrids which have high centers and a more pronounced swirl to their petals.

Bibliography

Gerdts, William H. *150 Years of American Still-Life Painting*. New York: Coe Kerr Gallery, 1970. 19.

Gerdts (1990), vol 1. 21-22.

Gerdts and Burke. 98. Groce and Wallace. 291.

Rubinstein, Charlotte Streifer. *American Women Artists.* New York: Avon Books, 1982. 65.

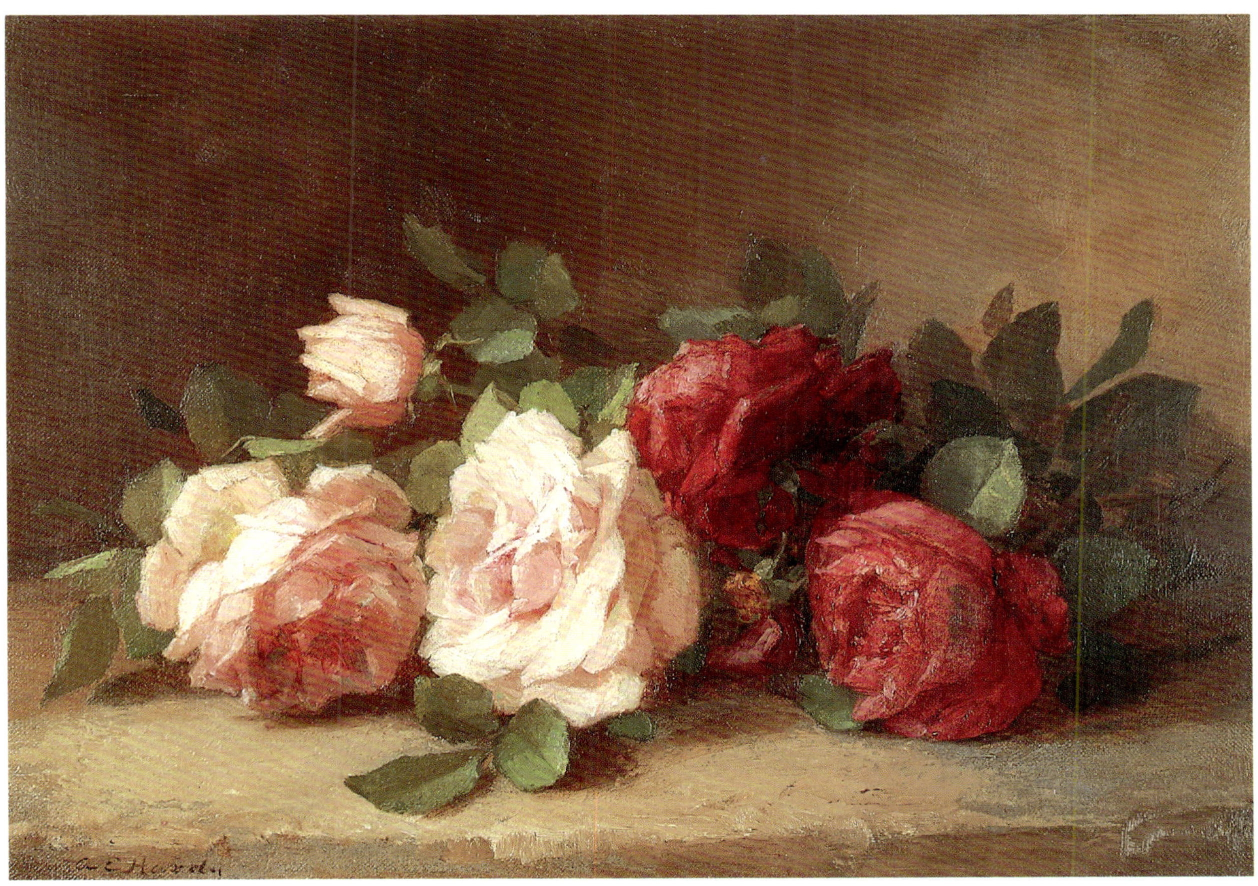

Anna Eliza Hardy, *Roses*, ca. 1900. Oil on canvas, 11 1/2" x 16".

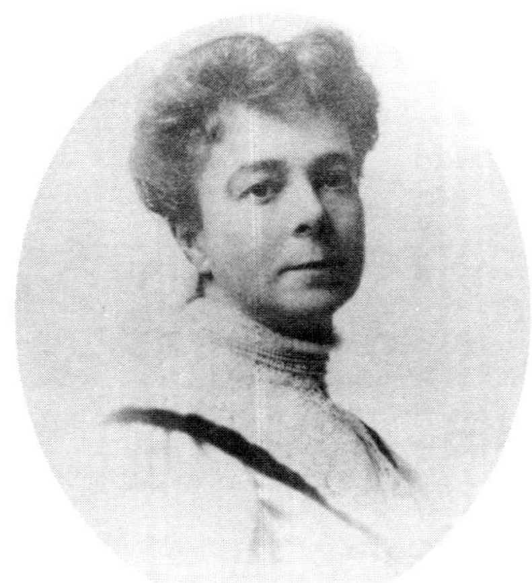

Alice B. Chittenden, ca. 1890. Photo courtesy of Virginia Larribeau.

63. Alice Brown Chittenden

(born 1859, Brockport, New York; died 1944, San Francisco)
Still Life with Roses in a Vase, 1909
Oil on canvas
21 3/4" x 18 1/4"
Signed lower right: Alice B. Chittenden 1909

Like many excellent and successful California artists, Alice Brown Chittenden's name is obscure in the East. Although a competent portraitist, she is best known as a flower painter.

Born in Brockport, New York, she moved to San Francisco as an infant. Her carpenter father encouraged her interest in art. Starting in 1877 she studied at the California School of Fine Arts with its director, Virgil Macey Williams (1830-1886). She married briefly in 1886 and remained single thereafter. Subsequently she made trips to New York, France, and Italy to exhibit and study, winning a medal at the Société des Artistes Français in Paris in 1908. From 1880 to 1940 she exhibited widely on the West Coast and won a number of medals at expositions. The 1939-40 Golden Gate International Exposition devoted a building to her paintings of the flowers of California.

Chittenden made her name in the West with sumptuous, sensitive depictions of flowers like the one reproduced here, which shows an ovoid bronze vase filled to overflowing with roses[1] and set against an indistinct background. The carefully thought-out, solidly balanced composition can be read as a set of right to left or left to right diagonals, or else as a zigzag. The large, soft, irregular, and freely brushed forms of the light yellow and white blooms contrast vividly with those of the small, crisp, and regular outlines of the darker red buds and green leaves that weave their way among them. The overall effect is that of a rich tapestry of color and form.

1. The yellow roses in this painting probably belong to the Noisette family, named after Philippe Noisette, who introduced it around 1814 in Charleston, South Carolina. The cream colored roses may be the variety *Souvenir de la Malmaison*, a Bourbon rose introduced in 1842 and particularly popular in America.

Bibliography

Gerdts (1990), vol. 3. 266, 269.
Hughes. 101-02.

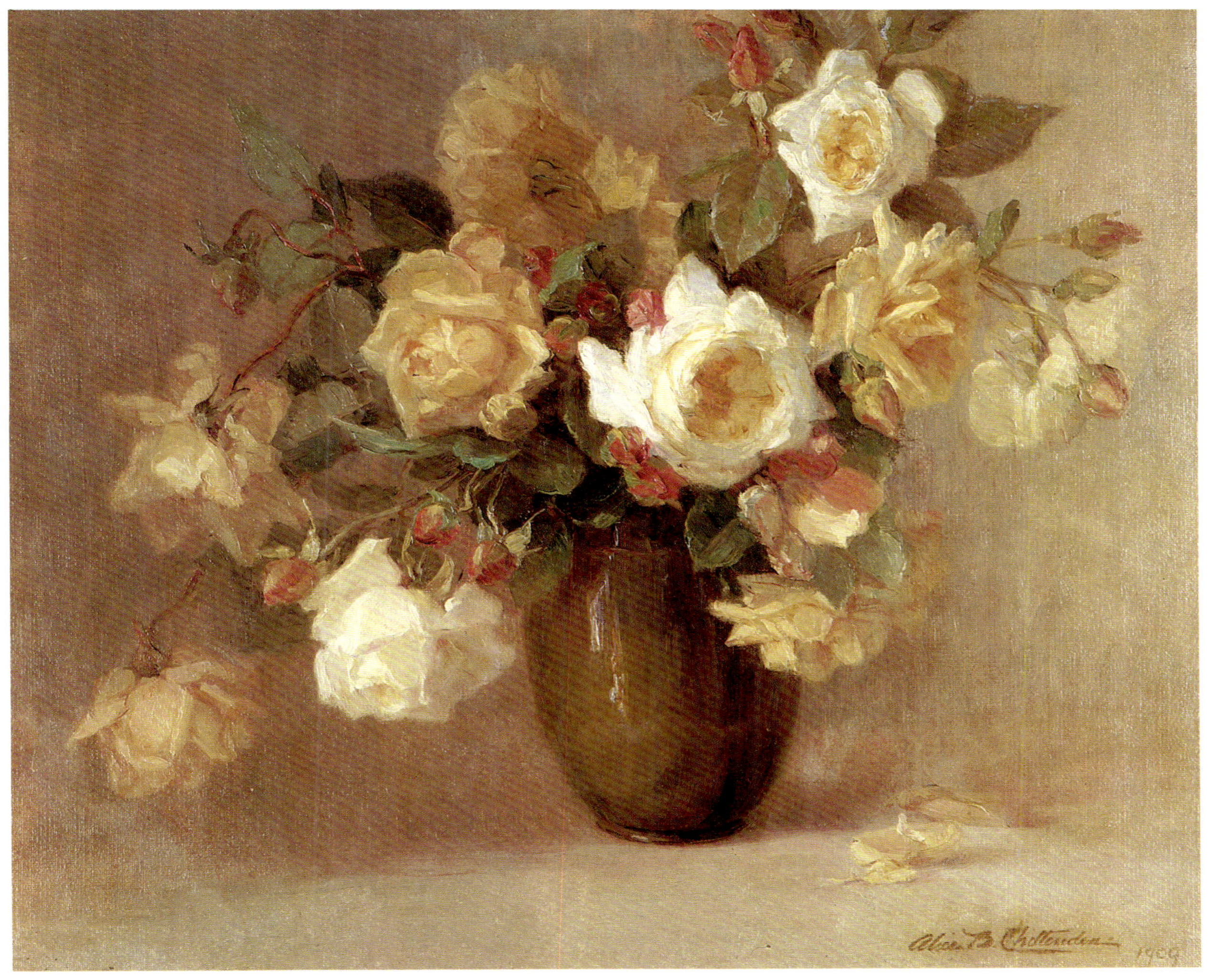

Alice Brown Chittenden, *Still Life with Roses in a Vase*, 1909. Oil on canvas, 21 3/4" x 18 1/4".

Selected General Bibliography

Anderson, Jeffrey W., and Barbara J. MacAdam. *Old Lyme: The American Barbizon.* Old Lyme, CT: The Lyme Historical Society, Florence Griswold Museum, 1982.

Avery, Kevin J., et al. *American Paradise: The World of the Hudson River School.* New York: The Metropolitan Museum of Art, 1987.

Baekeland, Frederick. "Collectors of American Painting, 1813-1913." *American Art Review* 3.6 (1976): 120-66.

Benjamin, Samuel B.G. *Our American Artists.* Boston: D. Lothrop & Co., 1879.

Bermingham, Peter. *American Art in the Barbizon Mood.* Washington, D.C.: Smithsonian Institution Press, 1975.

Boime, Albert. *The Art of Exclusion: Representing Blacks in the Nineteenth Century.* Washington, D.C.: Smithsonian Institution Press, 1990.

Bouret, Jean. *The Barbizon School and 19th Century French Landscape Painting.* Greenwich, CT: New York Graphic Society, 1973.

Brandt, Frederick R., and John Wilmerding. *American Marine Painting.* Richmond: Virginia Museum of Fine Arts, 1976.

Burke, Doreen Bolger. *American Paintings in the Metropolitan Museum of Art.* Vol. III. New York: The Metropolitan Museum of Art, 1980.

Campbell, Catherine H., and Marcia Schmidt Blaine. *New Hampshire Scenery: A Dictionary of Nineteenth-century Artists of New Hampshire Mountain Landscapes.* Canaan, NH: Phoenix Publishing, 1985.

Champney, Benjamin. *Sixty Years' Memories of Art and Artists.* Woburn, MA: Wallace and Andrews, 1900.

Clement, Clara Erskine, and Laurence Hutton. *Artists of the Nineteenth Century and Their Works.* 2 vols. Boston: Houghton Mifflin and Co., 1880.

Cowdrey, Mary Bartlett, et al. *American Academy of Fine Arts and American Art-Union.* 2 vols. New York: The New York Historical Society, 1953.

Edwards, Lee M., Jan Seidler Ramirez, and Timothy Anglin Burgard. *Domestic Bliss: Family Life in American Painting 1840-1910.* Yonkers, NY: The Hudson River Museum, 1986.

Fairbrother, Trevor J., et al. *The Bostonians: Painters of an Elegant Age, 1870-1930.* Boston: Museum of Fine Arts, 1986.

Falk, Peter Hasting, ed. *Who Was Who in American Art.* Madison, CT: Sound View Press, 1985.

______. *The Annual Exhibition Record of the Pennsylvania Academy of the Fine Art*s. 2 vols. Madison, CT: Sound View Press, 1988.

Ferber, Linda S., and William H. Gerdts. *The New Path: Ruskin and the American Pre-Raphaelites.* Brooklyn: The Brooklyn Museum, 1985.

Finch, Christopher. *American Watercolors.* New York: Abbeville Press, 1986.

Flexner, James Thomas. *That Wilder Image: The Painting of America's Native School from Thomas Cole to Winslow Homer*. Boston and Toronto: Little, Brown & Co., 1962.

Frankenstein, Alfred. *After the Hunt: William Harnett and Other American Still Life Painters 1870-1900.* Rev. ed. Berkeley: University of California Press, 1969.

Gammel, R.H. Ives. *The Boston Painters 1900-1930.* Orleans, MA: Parnassus Imprints, 1986.

Gerdts, William H. *Painters of the Humble Truth: Masterpieces of American Still-Life 1801-1939.* Columbia: University of Missouri Press, 1981.

______. *American Impressionism.* New York: Abbeville Press, 1984.

______. *Art Across America: Two Centuries of Regional Painting 1710-1920.* 3 vols. New York: Abbeville Press, 1990.

Gerdts, William H., and Russell Burke. *American Still-Life Painting.* New York: Praeger, 1971.

Gerdts, William H., Diana Dimodica Sweet, and Robert R. Preato. *Tonalism: An American Experience.* New York: Grand Central Art Galleries Art Education Association, 1982.

Groce, George C. and David H. Wallace. *The New York Historical Society's Dictionary of Artists in America 1564-1860.* New Haven: Yale University Press, 1957.

Hills, Patricia. *The Painters' America: Rural and Urban Life, 1810-1910.* New York: Praeger, 1974.

Hoopes, Donelson F. *American Watercolor Painting.* New York: Galahad Books, 1981.

Hoopes, Donelson F., and Nancy Wall Moure. *American Narrative Painting.* Los Angeles: Los Angeles County Museum of Art, 1974.

Hughes, Edan Milton. *Artists in California 1786-1940.* 2nd ed. San Francisco: Hughes Publishing Co., 1989.

Johnson, Allen, et al., eds. *Dictionary of American Biography.* 31 vols. New York: Scribner's, 1928-1958. [D.A.B.]

Ketner, Joseph D., II, and Michael J. Tammenga. *The Beautiful, The Sublime, and The Picturesque: British Influences on American Landscape Painting.* St. Louis: Washington University Gallery of Art, 1984.

Keyes, Donald D., et al. *The White Mountains: Place and Perceptions.* Hanover, NH: University Press of New England, 1980.

Leader, Bernice Kramer. "Antifeminism in the Paintings of the Boston School." *Arts Magazine* 56 (January 1982): 112-19.

McElroy, Guy C., et al. *Facing History: The Black Image in American Art 1710-1942.* Washington, D.C.: The Corcoran Gallery of Art, 1990.

McGrath, Robert L., and Barbara J. MacAdam. *"A Sweet Foretaste of Heaven:" Artists in the White Mountains 1830-1930.* Hanover, NH: Hood Museum of Art, 1980.

Marlor, Clark S. *A History of the Brooklyn Art Association with an Index of Exhibitions.* New York: James F. Carr, 1970.

Myers, Kenneth. *The Catskills: Painters, Writers and Tourists in the Mountains, 1820-1895.* Yonkers, NY: The Hudson River Museum of Westchester, 1988.

The National Cyclopedia of American Biography. 63 vols. New York: James T. White and Co., 1892-1984. [N.C.A.B.]

Naylor, Maria K. *The National Academy of Design Exhibition Record 1861-1900.* 2 vols. New York: Kennedy Galleries, 1973.

Novak, Barbara. *American Painting of the Nineteenth Century: Realism, Idealism, and the American Experience.* 2nd ed. New York: Harper & Row, 1979.

______. *Nature and Culture: American Landscape and Painting 1825-1875.* New York: Oxford University Press, 1980.

Nygren, Edward J., et al. *Views and Visions: American Landscape before 1830.* Washington, D.C.: The Corcoran Gallery of Art, 1986.

Opitz, Glenn B., ed. *Mantle Fielding's Dictionary of American Painters, Sculptors and Engravers.* Rev. ed. Poughkeepsie, NY: Apollo Book, 1983.

Rosenfeld, Daniel, and Robert G. Workman. *The Spirit of Barbizon: France and America.* San Francisco: The Art Museum Association of America, 1986.

Sellin, David. *Americans in Brittany and Normandy.* Phoenix: Phoenix Art Museum, 1982.

Sheldon, G. W. *American Painters.* New York: D. Appleton & Co., 1879.

Spassky, Natalie, et al. *American Paintings in the Metropolitan Museum of Art.* Vol. II. New York: The Metropolitan Museum of Art, 1985.

Stebbins, Theodore E., Jr. *American Master Drawings and Watercolors: A History of Works on Paper from Colonial Times to the Present.* New York: Harper & Row, 1976.

Stein, Roger B. *Seascape and the American Imagination.* New York: Clarkson N. Potter, 1975.

Sterling, Charles. *Still Life Painting from Antiquity to the Present Time.* New York: Universe Books, 1959.

Strickler, Susan E., et al. *American Traditions in Watercolors: The Worcester Art Museum Collection.* New York: Abbeville Press, 1987.

Tuckerman, Henry T. *Book of the Artists.* 1867. New York: James F. Carr, 1966.

Williams, Hermann Warner, Jr. *Mirror to the American Past: A Survey of American Genre Painting: 1750-1900.* Greenwich, CT: New York Graphic Society, 1973.

Wilmerding, John. *American Marine Painting.* 2nd ed. New York: Harry N. Abrams, 1987.

Wilmerding, John, et al. *American Light: The Luminist Movement, 1850-1875.* Washington, D.C.: National Gallery of Art, 1980.

Wilmerding, John, et al. *An American Perspective: Nineteenth-Century Art from the Collection of JoAnn and Julian Ganz, Jr.* Washington, D.C.: National Gallery of Art, 1981.

Index